The Married Widows of Cornwall

The story of the wives 'left behind' by emigration

Lesley Trotter

Humble History Press

www.humblehistory.com

First published 2018

Humble History Press
www.humblehistory.com

© Lesley Trotter, 2018

The right of Lesley Trotter to be identified as the Author of this work has been asserted in accordance with the Copyright, Design and Patents Act 1988.

All rights reserved. No part of this book may be reprinted or reproduced or utilised in any form or by any electronic, mechanical or other means, now known or hereafter invented, including photocopying and recording, or in any information storage or retrieval system, without the permission in writing from the publisher and copyright holder.

ISBN: 978 1 9996104 0 1

Front cover image:
By kind permission of Falmouth Art Gallery.
Henry Scott Tuke, RA RWS (1858-1929): Study for the Message - Mrs Fouracre, signed and dated 1890, oil on panel, 28 x 20 cms. Falmouth Art Gallery Collection. Purchased in 1997 with grant-aid from the NACF, V & A Purchase Grant Fund, Cornwall Heritage Fund and a donation from George Bednar.
FAMAG: 1997.1

Contents

Foreword by Philip Payton i
Preface and Acknowledgements v

Introduction 1

1
Considerable Numbers? - Taking a count of the wives 15

2
Money from Abroad - Remittances and home-pay 34

3
Making Ends Meet - Work and credit 52

4
'If You Can Accord' - Support from family and community 72

5
Deserted, Desperate & Destitute? - The wives and the Poor Law 94

6
'Unworthy' Wives and 'Forgetful' Husbands - Deceit and collusion 114

7
Lodgers and Lovers - Facing the consequences 141

8
Double Standards and Five-Dollar Divorces - Ending the marriage 162

9
Meeting Again on Earth or in Heaven - Hope for a happy reunion 177

10
Under Sailing Orders
"I will endeavour to give you all the instructions I can" 192

11
Two Lives Compared - Sophia Paynter and Mary Ann Dower 207

12
Choice and Power - Perceptions and emotions 219

13
The Worst Kind of Widowhood? - Conclusions 235

Notes and References 251
Index 275

Foreword

Very occasionally a new book appears which at a stroke alters the landscape of Cornish history. This is one of those moments, and this is the book. Based on her ground-breaking PhD thesis, expertly re-written here for the general as well as scholarly reader, Lesley Trotter's epic tale of *The Married Widows of Cornwall: The story of the wives 'left behind' by emigration* adds a new and hitherto almost entirely unexplored dimension to the ever unfolding saga of Cornwall's 'great emigration'. Instead of contributing yet more to our increasingly detailed knowledge of the Cornish in distant parts, she focusses on those at home. More especially, she draws back the veil on that elusive, almost mysterious, subject of the wives 'left behind' in Cornwall as their husbands ventured overseas.

Until now, the elucidation of the Cornish emigration in the 'long nineteenth-century', roughly from 1815 until 1914, from the end of the Napoleonic wars to the eve of the Great War, has sought to identify Cornish destinations – Moonta in South Australia, Grass Valley in California, the Rand in South Africa, and so on – as well as to chart the Cornish cultural and technological impacts in those lands and to describe the emergence of a Cornish transnational identity, based around the 'myth of Cousin Jack'. This myth, perpetrated by the Cornish themselves, and for a time highly persuasive on the international mining frontier, insisted that the Cornish were innately qualified as superior hard-rock miners, especially when compared to competing ethnic groups.

This myth, of course, was overwhelmingly a masculine construction, and such was its enduring (even subversive) power that it influenced (should we say, seduced?) almost everyone who sought to write about Cornwall's 'great emigration'. A.C. Todd's *The Cornish Miner in America*, first published in 1967, established this heroic masculine genre, its subtitle 'the men called Cousin Jacks' explicitly indicating the book's male-oriented narrative. This was followed in 1969 by A.L. Rowse's *The Cornish in America*, a seemingly gender-neutral title, although its American edition, with its prefix *The Cousin Jacks*, betrayed the book's orientation. So too with John Rowe's *The Hard-Rock Men: Cornish Immigrants and the North*

The Married Widows of Cornwall

American Mining Frontier, first published in 1974. Later, in 1984 my own book *The Cornish Miner in Australia: Cousin Jack Down Under* compounded the error – even the Eurocentric phrase 'down under' serves to raise eyebrows today in this determinedly post-colonial era. More recently, Sharron Schwartz, who has added much to our increasingly nuanced understanding of the Cornish transnational identity and is a leading advocate of women's history in Cornwall, has nonetheless entitled her new book, published in 2016, *The Cornish in Latin America: Cousin Jack and the New World* (the term 'New World' can also raise those same post-colonial eyebrows).

Slowly, perhaps even painfully, those who wrote about Cornish men overseas recognised that there was a female dimension to Cornwall's emigration. Gradually, and sometimes self-consciously, even awkwardly, women were woven into the story (I contrived to include a chapter 'Women, Methodists and the Triumph over Adversity' in my *Making Moonta* in 2007), as the predominantly male chroniclers of the 'great emigration' woke up to the significance of this female dimension. Indeed, before long a parallel 'myth of Cousin Jenny' was at last identified, one which asserted the particular qualities of Cornish women on the international mining frontier, where Cousin Jenny would rise to the challenge of establishing order and domesticity in a harsh environment, succeeding where lesser women might fail.

Yet it is only very recently that historians have realised that the experience of those wives who stayed at home in Cornwall when their husbands emigrated (temporarily and occasionally permanently) is an integral and essential part of the emigration story, as vital to our understanding of this vast panorama as the exploits of Cornish men – and women – overseas. Lesley Trotter, with her rare gift for combining quantitative and qualitative research, of manipulating and blending numbers and percentages with the real-life stories, often poignant and always illuminating, of the women who remained, provides us with a thrilling account of those *Married Widows*. It is a clever, paradoxical, title, which, as Lesley Trotter explains, had its origins in nineteenth-century Cornwall, where the phenomenon was commonplace and widely recognised, especially in the mining areas – from St Just-in-Penwith in the west to St Cleer and beyond in the east. But the subtitle *Wives 'left*

Foreword

behind' is equally insightful, with its play on words suggesting more than the obvious fact that these women stayed at home. In what sense were these wives 'left behind'? Lesley Trotter invites us to consider. Were they disadvantaged, as the term might suggest, socially constrained and financially embarrassed, sometimes driven to desperate measures, or were they able to take advantage of their possibly new-found freedom and the sense of agency that it lent?

As Lesley Trotter shows, stereotypical depictions of 'left behind' wives as abandoned and often destitute are, at best, just a small part of the story. There were those who managed households successfully on the remittances sent home from abroad by absent husbands, and others who took on paid and sometimes unpaid work to make end meet. Sometimes help was accepted from family, friend and neighbours, and the financially astute made the best use of whatever credit was available and rationalised or minimalised their accommodation costs, often by taking in lodgers. Only occasionally did such women turn to the poor law guardians for relief. There were, inevitably, cases where remittances dried up, and there were instances where husbands overseas, tired of maintaining the links with home, built new lives and new families. Wives 'left behind' could also make similar decisions, although much more difficult when living in close-knit communities, and there were cases of bigamy, adultery and illegitimacy, and even divorce.

More often than not, the decision that the husband should emigrate and the wife remain in Cornwall was a collective one, agreed by the two spouses and no doubt approved by members of the wider family. At root it was an economic decision, taking advantage of the multiplicity of opportunities that existed for Cornish skills on the international stage, and building on the conduits of emigration that had been steadily constructed since 1815. Often a husband would absent himself for an agreed period, sending remittances home as best he could, before returning to Cornwall and then perhaps venturing abroad again. Sometimes a wife might eventually join her husband in Mexico, Brazil, New Zealand or wherever; sometimes a husband might come home to Cornwall for good. But in all this the wives were not passive victims of emigration. More often than not, they had been active partners in devising an advantageous economic strategy, and in doing so, as Lesley Trotter demonstrates in this remarkable and highly readable account, helped establish "the transnational nuclear family [as] a major feature of emigration from Cornwall throughout the 19th century".

This is a distinguished work which should sit on the shelves of all those interested in Cornwall's 'great emigration'. It will also be warmly welcomed as an important comparative study by all students of emigration from the British Isles and Europe in the 19th century.

Philip Payton

Emeritus Professor of Cornish & Australian Studies,
University of Exeter.
Professor of History, Flinders University,
Adelaide, Australia.
24 June 2018.

Preface and Acknowledgements

I first became aware of the wives 'left behind' when I noticed references in the 19th century census returns for Cornwall to married women who had husbands 'abroad', 'in America', 'in Chile' or some other distant country. From the experiences of friends and relatives I was aware of the challenges that arose when modern-day husbands spent long periods working overseas, in the armed forces, oil or engineering industries. How much more difficult must it have been for wives in the past who couldn't easily contact their husbands by phone, text or email; for women living in a society where their options and actions were restricted by a lack of legal rights, little education and limited work opportunities? How did they manage on a day-to-day basis when life for women was very different from today? With so much having been published on emigration from Cornwall, I searched for the book that would surely answer all these questions... but found none.

At the same time I was casting about for a dissertation topic for my MA at the Institute of Cornish Studies, and this seemed like fascinating new territory to explore. Soon I was hooked, and carried on the research beyond the MA, completing my PhD on the experiences of the wives 'left behind' in Cornwall at the University of Exeter in 2015.

Although this book is based on that research, and hopefully offers new insights useful to academic historians, it as much a book for the general reader. It fills in the gaps for the family historian who has heard stories of a great grandmother remaining in Cornwall when her husband went abroad, and wants to understand what she went through. It is the book that I had hoped to find when I just wanted to read more about the women I had encountered in the census back at the beginning of this journey.

For those readers who want to delve deeper, supporting material from my thesis, such as detailed distribution maps and an explanation of my research methods can be found on my website: www.humblehistory.com, along with a growing database of the wives 'left behind'.

The research on which this book is based would not have been possible without the enthusiasm and help of numerous family historians who have preserved, recorded and transcribed the material evidence of Cornish wives 'left behind'. In particular, I would like to thank Michael McCormick for permission to copy and manipulate the Cornwall Online Census Project data.

I am grateful to representatives of Cornish associations around the world for help in publicizing my appeal for documents and stories, especially: Wendy Ashenden (New Zealand Society of Genealogists); Nick Bartle (New Zealand Cornish Association); Tony Berry (Cornwall Family History Society); Carolyn Bray (Pennsylvania Cornwall Association); Liz Broekmann (London Cornish Association); Liz Cool (Cornish Association of South Australia); Myra Cordrey (Online Parish Clerks (Genealogy) Coordinator, Cornwall); Gage McKinney (California Cornish Cousins); Tommi O'Hagan (Cornish American Heritage Society), and well as all those unknown to me who forwarded the appeal to their contacts.

It is impossible to acknowledge all those that responded, but special mention goes to those who shared the family stories mentioned in this book: Elizabeth Cameron, Liz Coole, David Coppin, Francis Dunstan, Teresa Farris, Carolyn Haines, Elaine Hamby, Charlotte Hearle, Jane Hollow, Allan Lance, Lorna Leadbetter, Linda Lowrey, Kitty Quayle, Courtenay V. Smale, Margaret Stevens, Shirley Westaway and William & Patricia Woolcock. Thanks also to Bernadette Fallon, Mark Johnson and Pam Weeks for passing on leads.

Special thanks goes to Moira Tangye for generously sharing her transcriptions of emigrant correspondence, much of which was collected as part of the Cornish Global Migration Project. Thank you to the staff at the Barr Smith Library, University of Adelaide for enabling access to the Dower correspondence. Acknowledgement is also due to the work of the late John Tregenza in preserving these copies of Cornish emigrant letters, especially those by John Dower and William Paynter. I am indebted to the descendents of the letter writers featured in this book for permission to quote from their ancestor's correspondence. The Dower letters were made available to Dr Tregenza by the late Kathleen Embree and material from John Dower's letters is reproduced by kind permission of his descendant Emily Jane Oldenburg. Material from William Arundell Paynter's letters is reproduced by kind permission of his descendant, Marleen Carver, whose book, *The Paynter Family from Cornwall to Moonta*, tells more of the family's story. Material from Ann Goldsworthy's letter is reproduced

Preface and Acknowledgements

by kind permission of her descendant Amanda Drake, and I am indebted to a descendant of Joel Eade for allowing his words to be used. Attempts to identify and contact descendants of the remaining individuals whose letters are briefly mentioned in this book have sadly proved unsuccessful.

I would like to thank Garry Tregidga, Bernard Deacon and Briony Oncuil for their helpful guidance and comments on my research and thesis, and especially Philip Payton for his welcome endorsement of my work. To Anthea Colgate, Miranda Lawrance-Owen and Rebecca Ryder, my team of hawkeye proofreaders, thank you for your dedication, stamina and patience in discussions on the finer points of grammar!

I am also grateful to Falmouth Art Gallery for granting permission and supplying the digital file for Henry Scott Tuke's wonderful study of Mrs Fouracre to be used on the cover of this book.

And finally, a special thank you to all those who have heard about my research along the way, through talks and social media, and whose interest, support and enthusiasm for this project have helped keep me going through the years spent in bringing this book to completion.

Lesley Trotter
Cornwall,
30 July 2018.

The Married Widows of Cornwall

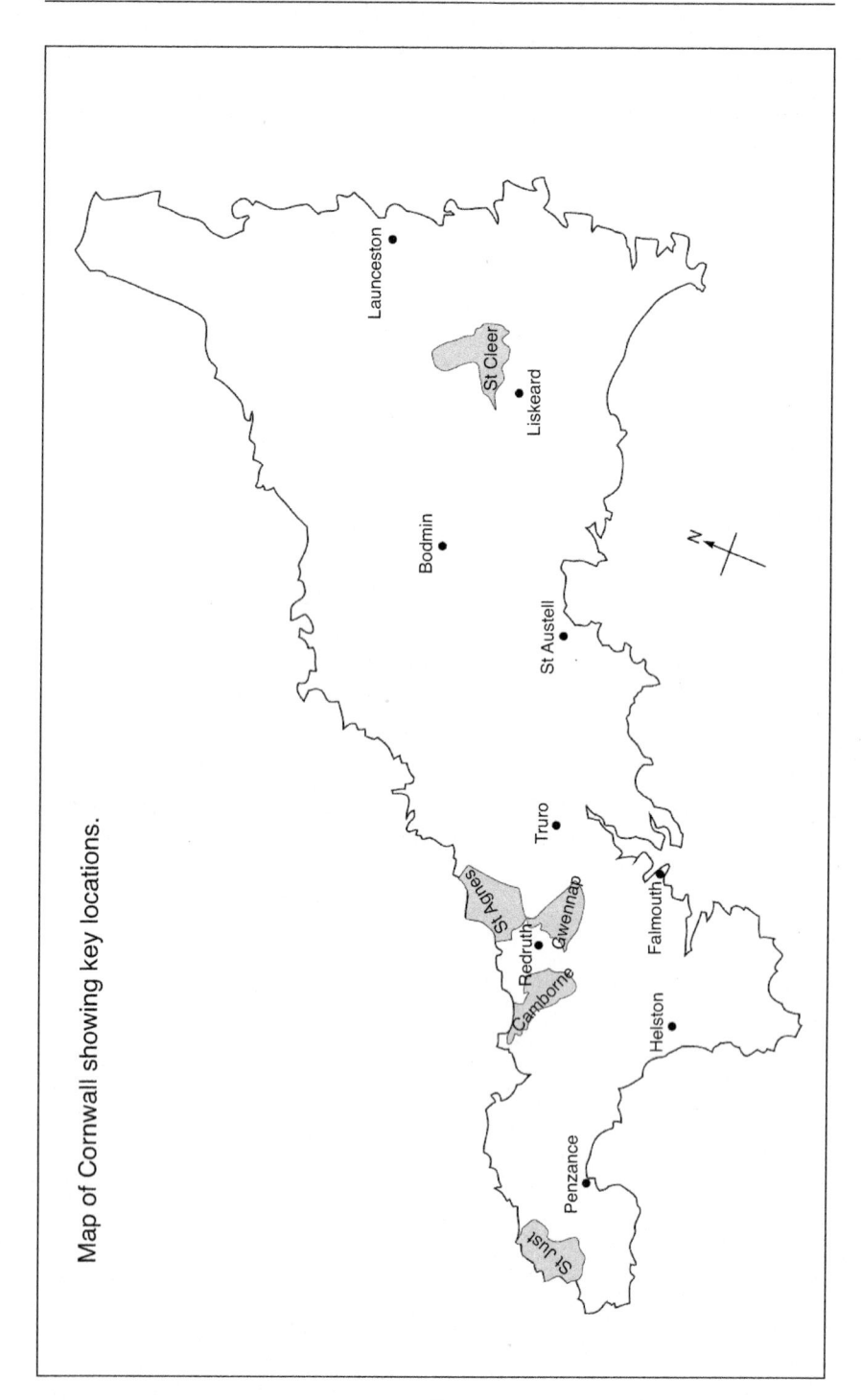

Map of Cornwall showing key locations.

Introduction

> *"These poor creatures are known here as 'married widows',
> to me the worst kind of widowhood. There are, however,
> a few happy exceptions, where the absent husbands
> send home good round sums to their wives."*[1]

In the summer of 1876 an anonymous correspondent from Liskeard wrote to the *Royal Cornwall Gazette* commenting on the "considerable" numbers of women in the area whose husbands had "deserted or half-deserted them". These 'married widows', as he called them, were the wives who remained in Cornwall when their husbands went abroad, and they are an overlooked aspect of what is known to Cornish historians as the 'Great Emigration'.

In the 19th century Cornwall, situated in the far south west of the British Isles, experienced an exodus that saw its people and culture spread to the far-flung corners of the world. The scale and duration of this emigration, with its large waves of movement to the Americas (North, South and Central) from the 1830s, to Australia from the 1850s and to South Africa from the 1880s, puts Cornwall on a par with many of the major European emigration centres.[2] Writing in 1967 A.C. Todd estimated that a third of the population left Cornwall in the 19th century.[3] More recently Bernard Deacon put the emigration figure at over 240,000 in the period 1840-1900, with almost as many again migrating to other parts of the United Kingdom.[4]

Written histories of emigration from Cornwall have overwhelmingly concentrated on those who migrated, recording the experiences of the Cornish… 'Overseas', 'in America', 'in Australia', or 'in South Africa'.[5] This emphasis on those who went abroad reflects what has been defined by academics as the 'traditional emigration-immigration dichotomy', suggesting in the words of migration historians Harzig and Hoerder: "a mono-directional one-way move from a 'home' in one state to a foreign 'new world'".[6] The volume of these sometimes romanticised accounts of the achievements of the Cornish abroad has distracted from detailed exploration of the impact of migration on the Cornish 'in Cornwall'. While so much has been written about the migrants themselves, the people they left behind have received very little attention.

One of the reasons why the wives who remained in Cornwall while their husbands worked overseas have gone unnoticed is that they form part of this wider neglected group of people remaining in sending communities. This neglect is partly due to the way in which historians have approached migration in the past. Traditionally, research has focused on the causes of migration, its streams and processes from the point of view of the migrants. It is only in more recent times that we have begun to think outside notions of simple one-way 'flows' of people or 'waves' of migration from sending to receiving communities. We now think in terms of 'multiple options' of migration, with it being potentially, as Harzig and Hoerder note, "many-directional and multiple, temporary or long-term, voluntary or forced".

It is clear that in order to understand migration we need to explore a much more complex, varied phenomenon involving a dynamic, nuanced interplay between individuals, families and communities in two or more places. As Harzig and Hoerder suggest, we must study "the agency of men and women who, within their capabilities, negotiate societal options and constraints in pursuit of life plans". From a narrow focus on the examination of the Cornish abroad, research on migration from Cornwall is gradually adopting a more holistic consideration of transnational families and communities with members living oceans apart.[7] There is now a wider appreciation that decisions concerning migration were not taken by individual migrants in isolation, and a greater emphasis on the active role in the migration process played by those in the sending community: as links in international information networks, facilitators of migration, and most importantly as participants in the decision to migrate from Cornwall.[8]

The political and social implications of present day migrations have stimulated a wealth of research, which includes a growing body of work on modern sending communities. This has contributed to a wider understanding of transnationalism and the impact of migration on these communities, particularly from the point of view of those 'left behind'.[9]

Introduction

These studies encompass migration of both sexes, but as more often than not it is the men who move, the majority focus on the women who do not. There is now a considerable body of literature created by sociologists and anthropologists on husbands and wives living in different countries amongst modern emigrant communities.[10] But it is an aspect of emigration little examined by historians, despite the need to explore the lives of these women being highlighted as long ago as 1991 by Silvia Pedraza when she suggested: "Flows of migration that are dominated by men require that we consider "the woman's side" when the women themselves are left behind in the communities".[11]

Men certainly dominated the migration flows from Cornwall. It has been calculated that, between 1861 and 1900, 10.5% of Cornish men went abroad compared with only 5.3% of the female population.[12] The need to move around to optimise work and life opportunities is a common human experience, and emigration has obvious attractions for single young men eager to make their own way in the world. Nearly 45% of the male population of Cornwall aged between 15 and 24 are believed to have gone abroad in the last 40 years of the 19th century. Although many Cornish emigrated as family units, the decision was often made, for a variety of reasons, that only the main family bread winner (almost always the husband and father) should make the move, at least in the first instance, leaving the rest of the family, including his wife, in their settled location in Cornwall.

This gendered migration had its roots in the nature of the Cornish economy. The main industries in 19th century Cornwall were mining, agriculture and fishing. Migration associated with the fishing industry has a distinct character, normally being both seasonal and temporary. The experiences of the wives of fishermen and other mariners have been partly explored elsewhere,[13] so the focus of this book will be on the women married to men with land-based occupations – mining and agriculture. Although some miners may have participated in fishing activities, they were usually separate occupations. There is generally less distinction between mining and agriculture in Cornwall with many miners having some connection with the land, frequently operating smallholdings or retiring as farmers.[14] In addition, a number of occupations, such as blacksmith and carpenter, relate both to mining and agriculture. Although farmers and agricultural labourers also emigrated,[15] gender-biased migration from Cornwall in the 19th century has traditionally been associated with the mining industry and its related trades.

Mining has always been a mobile occupation with workers moving around to exploit different mineral deposits as they were discovered and eventually worked out. This led to the growth and decline of mining centres in different parts of Cornwall, resulting in localised periods of boom and bust within the industry, with associated population movements.[16]

With its geography as a peninsula with an extensive coastline fostering a sea-faring tradition and its mineral-rich geology a mobile mining one, Cornwall had a long-established 'culture of mobility' that was to come to maturity during the mass emigrations of the 19th century, a culture that was fully embraced by the 'rambling' Cornish miner.[17] As the mining industry became increasingly globalised in the 19th century, the skills and reputation of mine workers and engineering equipment from Cornwall found a ready market, and the ramblings of Cornish miners extended around the world.

Social and family historians have long been aware that the migration of miners resulted in unusually large numbers of married women in Cornwall managing families and households single-handedly while their husbands were abroad. They are the quiet folklore heroines remembered in many Cornish families. Anecdotal references to the wives appear in local histories. For example, Schwartz and Parker give some examples of the difficulties faced by women in the mining village of Lanner, highlighting the potential family problems and complications that ensued when the men returned, while similar anecdotal material features in descriptions of other mining settlements such as St Day.[18]

However, the role and experiences of these women although they are usually mentioned, albeit fleetingly, in most narratives of Cornish emigration, have been generally neglected by historians. The wives 'left behind' make only limited appearances in some of the literature looking at various aspects of Cornish life. The women are discussed briefly by Philip Payton in his major work on *The Cornish Overseas*,[19] by Mark Brayshay in relation to mid-19th century Cornish demographics and household structures,[20] by Sharron Schwartz, Gill Burke and Lynne

Introduction

Mayers in the context of female employment in the Cornish mining industry,[21] by Magee and Thompson in their examination of the remittance economy,[22] and by Lyn Bryant and Bernard Deacon in their accounts of what Deacon describes as the 'dispersed Cornish family'.[23] These works rarely consider the wives specifically; they are almost always submerged in a wider grouping of 'family' in Cornwall. This lack of distinction creates unjustifiable generalisations. Whereas the parents of young men might, albeit reluctantly, accept their sons' emigration as an extreme form of the natural process of leaving home and gaining their independence, the wife's situation in what can be termed a 'transnational nuclear family' was somewhat different. A wife would have had every expectation that she would share a home with her husband for life. Therefore, it is important that their experiences should not be simply amalgamated into a general consideration of the families 'left behind' as is so often the case.

Overlooked by historians, the wives 'left behind' are completely left out of the story presented to the Cornish public and visitors exploring Cornwall's heritage. The invisibility of women in this material, other than as bal maidens (surface mine workers), pasty makers and prostitutes, is well illustrated by the following quote found on the Cornish Mining World Heritage Site website: "a miner's home was usually clean, his children as well fed as possible and their clothes, although old, laundered and neatly patched".[24] This totally omits any mention of the wife who presumably shared both the home and the children, and almost certainly did the cleaning, cooking, washing and patching!

An understanding of what happened to these wives is important, not just because of their perceived numerical dominance at times with some mining villages being described as "half-denuded of men",[25] but because of the potential implications of this phenomenon for society in Cornwall. Their experiences impacted on the local economy at the time, as controlling conduits for the vast sums of money earned by their menfolk abroad or as recipients of poor relief, but must also have affected the evolution of Cornish society through formative influences on subsequent generations. Writing in 1993, Deacon and Payton maintained that women "must have had a strategic, though so far unexplored, role in reproducing the Cornish culture of the crucial last quarter of the 19th century".[26] The contribution of the wives 'left behind' has begun to be recognised; these are the women who, according to Payton, kept "the otherwise disintegrating fabric of Cornish society together – at least in the depressed working class mining districts".[27] However, until now it has remained undocumented and the lack of a detailed study of these women left a significant female-shaped hole in our understanding of 19th century Cornwall and its Great Emigration.

Given their probable large numbers and the suspected social implications, why is it then, that these 'married widows' have always been at the periphery of the Cornish emigration story? One explanation, suggested by Payton, is the gendered perception of the mining-based Cornish diaspora, with women "all too often overlooked in the male-oriented narrative of the Great Emigration, with its emphasis on masculine occupations and masculine culture (everything from hard-rock mining to male-voice choirs)". This mining-centric (and thus male-centric) tone was set by the authors acknowledged as the founding fathers of Cornish emigration history: A.C. Todd, John Rowe and A.L. Rowse, whose major works were published in the mid-20th century.[28] Predating the establishment of the women's history movement, these works reflected the gender bias of their time. It is telling that the subtitle of Todd's book *The Cornish Miner in America*, although making anecdotal references to wives both in Cornwall and overseas, refers simply to the contribution made by "the men called Cousin Jacks".[29] It is only in more recent years, coinciding with the emergence of female voices, namely Sharron Schwartz,[30] Lyn Bryant,[31] Lynne Mayers[32] and Gill Burke,[33] that women have begun to feature in works on 19th century Cornwall and the diaspora.

That the role of women in Cornish migration has always been overshadowed by that played by their husbands, fathers and sons was highlighted by Philip Payton in *The Cornish Overseas*. He recognised that: "Cornish women – the 'Cousin Jennies' – were a vital part of the story at home and abroad".[34] Whereas the pioneering exploits of the Cornish women abroad have received some attention, those who remained at home have been largely ignored. If the women who 'went' can be seen as only just stepping out from the shadows of history, those who 'stayed' can be described as practically invisible. With their obscurity as females

Introduction

compounded by their exclusion from the more historically noticeable migrant group, one should not be surprised that the women who remained in Cornwall have received so little attention.

This academic neglect of 19th century wives 'left behind' in the British Isles is not confined to Cornwall. *Emigrant Homecomings*, a collection of papers on return migration by a range of eminent migration scholars, makes no mention of any wives waiting at home for the returning migrants.[35] One of the authors, Eric Richards, does discuss emigration from Cornwall along with that from the rest of the British Isles in his own work, *Britannia's Children*. However, he only mentions wives not emigrating with their husbands in the context of emigration being a means of desertion by the men.[36] William Jones in his book on Welsh miners in the United States makes only a fleeting mention of "marriage ties stretched across the Atlantic" resulting in bigamy, desertion and adultery.[37] Similarly, in *Emigrants and Exiles*, Kerby Miller goes no further than a brief acknowledgement that many wives were left behind in Ireland by emigrating men.[38] Likewise, in his major work on the Scottish diaspora, T.M. Divine discusses the "dynamic interaction between homeland and host-land" but makes no reference to any wives in Scotland beyond noting that missionary wives were the first to accompany their husbands due to concerns that sending men abroad alone carried considerable risks that they would develop liaisons with native women.[39] The exception here is Marjory Harper's work, which in discussing the temporary emigration of artisans from Scotland notes that these men were more likely than other migrants to leave their wives behind, and briefly touches upon the hardship caused if the men failed to send money home.[40] Mention should also be made of Lynn Abrams' work on the 'woman's world' of 19th century Shetland, although emigration was only one of a complex combination of factors contributing to the demographic imbalance there.[41]

One explanation for this lack of detailed discussion is the paucity of source material. Most of the evidence that exists concerning wives 'left behind' is both fragmentary and scattered. There is no clearly defined term for the women as a group; their only commonality is that they are all female, married, and at some point non-migrants, none of which provide particularly helpful index or search terms to aid location of relevant material. No inviting diary or other obvious major 'go-to' source beckons the historian.[42] Although comprising one end of the volley of letters passing between emigrants and their places of origin, those from relatives 'at home' are significantly under represented in the archive collections of emigrant correspondence that constitute a major source for historians of migration.[43] Hence, the wives 'left behind' are largely absent voices in published collections, such as David Fitzpatrick's *Oceans of Consolation* or David Gerber's *Authors of Their Lives*.[44] As a result the reader is left with little more than tantalising glimpses of these women; their existence in emigrant sending communities in England, Wales, Scotland and Ireland, as well as Cornwall, implied but not elaborated upon.

Despite the lack of a substantial body of evidence, the large numbers of absent husbands in 19th century Cornwall is often interpreted as posing a major social problem.[45] Much of the literature in this vein draws on the classic 1950s work *Cornwall in the Age of the Industrial Revolution* by John Rowe, in which the wives are mentioned in the context of the distress in Cornwall at the 'End of the Copper Kingdom'. Citing newspaper reports of the period Rowe notes, for example, that in 1867 hundreds of men migrated from the St Austell, Helston and Penzance Poor Law Union districts over the preceding two years, each leaving on average a wife and three children who received "meagre and irregular remittances".[46]

However, this refers to a very limited period (the late 1860s), and twenty years later contemporary reports present a somewhat different picture, with it being observed "Our miners go abroad and send home plenty of money to the wives and families and we seldom hear of a case of neglect".[47] One report suggested that it was common for husbands to stay away for 20 years,[48] while another commentator stressed the propensity of emigrant miners to return to take out their wives and families. It was "one of the most pleasing traits in the miner's character", he observed, although adding: "It must, however, be said that cases also occur where the poor law guardians discover that the emigrants have found it convenient to forget their families".[49]

Such conflicting accounts present a confused picture. Some reports imply that the 'married widows' were 'poor creatures' to be pitied.[50] On the other hand, other wives were thought of as benefiting from their husbands' absence through greater financial support, to the extent of being criticised for 'mad' and frivolous spending.[51]

Introduction

Although these ambiguities also suggest a variety of experiences and outcomes among the wives affected, they betray a generally negative perception of these women's lives. As Sharron Schwartz reflects in her 2002 critique of Cornish migration studies: "one gains the impression that these women were somehow deeply impoverished by the departure of their men-folk".[52]

There appears to have been an over reliance on a limited amount of source material. Perceptions of the women have been based on individual examples drawn from a small number of more accessible contemporary newspaper reports, journals and letters. It is questionable as to how representative these are, both in terms of production and survival. For example, it is logical to assume that newspaper reports would tend to focus on the more interesting, unusual or dramatic cases. Letters that reveal more traumatic episodes in the family history are more likely to have been preserved within the family, or come to the attention of and been quoted by historians, than those containing more mundane material. In addition, the repetition in the literature of particular eye-catching stories is likely to have helped produce a distorted picture of universal distress amongst the Cornish wives 'left behind' that takes no account of potential variation across place or time.

What is already a vague and confused image of the wives' experiences is clouded by this limited palette of sources frequently being viewed through a lens coloured by negative perceptions of these wives as the passive victims of migration. This has been the traditional role assigned to women in similar situations in other parts of the world, for the 'married widows' of Cornwall, were not alone in their predicament. They had contemporaries in the 'vedove bianche' (widows in white) of Sicily, and the 'viuvas dos vivos' (widows of the living) of northern Portugal.[53] These were communities from which there was mass emigration of men, but individual cases of wives 'left behind' by men working abroad were probably widespread in the 19th century.

Although a more nuanced understanding of migration means that research has paid greater attention to the non-migrants by looking at 'both ends of mobility', it does not address the deep-seated model of migration as progress. The approach suggested by Harzig and Hoerder that migration history should ask what it means for families, communities and whole societies to lose members, or for the societies of destination to receive 'human capital' in the form of new members, does indeed place the migrant in the context of a wider social grouping. However, it retains the idea that migration is positive for the receiving community and negative for the sending one; migrants still move "from a limited old world to unlimited new opportunities".[54] This model of migration carries with it the implication that the 'brightest and best' move, resulting in a sending community that is depleted both in quantity and quality. Hence the concerns about 'deterioration' of the people of Cornwall that emerged in the early 1900s evolved into the dominant view by the end of the 20th century that the consequences of the Great Emigration on Cornish society were, within Cornwall, 'almost wholly bad'. As Deacon notes "Emigration was seen as fostering a culture of loss, fatalism and poverty, with a passive, inert and undynamic population pitifully dependent on the remittances sent back from overseas".[55] Although dominant, this view has not gone unchallenged, with Schwartz stressing the "need to transcend the polarized positions offered in much conventional literature where migration is deemed a triumph in overseas communities but a tragedy for those at home".[56]

The triumph/tragedy paradigm is entwined with another that casts migrants and those remaining in sending communities in gendered roles independent of sex.[57] In her study of Sicilian 'widows in white', Linda Reeder points out that "gendered descriptions of transoceanic migration that equated migration with masculinity and modernity, and identified those who remained at home with femininity and rural backwardness, while often conflicting with lived experience, have profoundly shaped our understanding of mass migration at the beginning of the 20th century".[58]

The result is an ingrained and gendered concept of those in sending communities that permeates how the evidence relating to the wives who remained in Cornwall has been interpreted. This has coloured how they are perceived by academia and represented to the general public. As both females and members of a sending community, the 'married widows' of Cornwall have been portrayed, if they have been portrayed at all, as passive and, in the absence of any detailed research, this has resulted in a popular notion of wives 'left behind' as 'victims' in the migration narrative. Mark Brayshay, for example, in his 1977 study of changes in household structure

Introduction

in the three mining parishes of Camborne, Redruth and St Just in Penwith, consistently refers to the wives whose husbands were absent as having been 'deserted'. He assumes that few of them were being supported by their husbands, and privileges poverty as the only motivation for wives working or moving in with relatives while their husbands were away.[59] Despite the confusing picture given by contemporary reports, it is the image of the women as deserted, and therefore destitute, that often persists in the academic and popular imagination.

The passive victim role traditionally assigned to those in sending communities tends to be preserved in the language used, even amongst anthropologists studying modern communities, with authors struggling to find alternatives to referring to these women as 'stayers' or 'left behind'. Archambault has pointed out that the very concept of 'left behind' is based on two outdated theoretical paradigms: 'left' implying that the individuals in question had no say in the decision, and 'behind' equating with the static and backward compared with the progression of the migrant.[60] In the absence of more appropriate terms, authors signal their discomfort by the use of inverted commas.

Hence the very words used to describe these women reinforce perceptions of them. In labelling the wives as 'deserted', Brayshay, for example, may simply have been using a shorthand term for these women. Nonetheless, the use of this language creates, and perpetuates, an overall impression that the women were victims with little control over their fate, thereby influencing later interpretations. However, it is difficult to avoid subjective terminology when writing about these wives (e.g. 'left behind' implies passive victim whilst 'stayed behind' implies active choice). A more objective and appropriate academic description of the wives' situation might be 'spatial spousal separation associated with migration' - a somewhat inelegant and unwieldy term! For the sake of simplicity, and because it is commonly used in comparable studies, I will refer to the wives as 'left behind' (with emphasis on the inverted commas) or as 'married widows'.

The dilemma over a workable terminology illustrates how difficult it is to dislodge the habit of assigning to those who did not migrate a passive role; affected by the migration process but not actively participating in it. This is particularly true of the women remaining in the sending communities who, as Schwartz notes, are "cast as the passive participant in the migration decision; it is the men who migrate and the women who wait".[61]

However, whether examining present-day communities in the Third World or past communities elsewhere in Europe, some research on non-migrants in emigration centres has questioned negative perceptions of those, especially women, who remain at home while others migrate. Studies of the 'widows in white' of Sicily, the 'widows of the living' in Portugal and comparable women in Italy, France, Spain and Russia by Linda Reeder, Donna Gabaccia and Caroline Brettell and others all highlight the impact of male emigration on the women 'left behind' using a considerable variety of approaches and methodologies.[62] Brettell looks at the demography of a single Portuguese parish, while Reeder examines the way male emigration transformed the cultural identity and role of Sicilian women. Both authors combine historical and anthropological perspectives, extending their studies into the 20th century enabling access to living subjects for interview. Gabaccia, primarily a migration historian, complements Reeder's work by looking at the economics of the transnational Italian family in the 19th century.

Although concerned more with internal migration rather than emigration, to these we can add Peavy and Smith's work on wives whose husbands went on ahead of them in the 19th century westward movement in America, and Christina Twomey's research on the welfare of Australian women deserted by their husbands during 19th century gold rushes.[63] This limited, but diverse, group of studies has undermined negative perceptions of migration, and particularly of the women 'left behind' in sending communities.

They have convincingly challenged the portrayal of the women as merely 'waiting', demonstrating their active role in their families' migration strategies. From her study of the effects of male labour migration on rural Sicilian women, Reeder concludes: "far from being abandoned or forgotten in a world populated only by women and weak men, the women who stayed in Sicily actively participated in the migration process". Managing households and acting as 'kinship keepers', these women were often directly involved in arranging and financing their husbands' voyages. As Reeder eloquently put it: "These women did not cross the Atlantic;

Introduction

instead they invested their dreams in the decision to send a family member overseas".[64] Looking at wider Italian emigration, Gabaccia has analysed the financial benefits of transnational family economies and concluded that the strategy of the husband migrating alone provided a surer foundation for family security than the migration of the complete family unit.[65] Caroline Brettell's study of the Portuguese parish of Lanheses also highlighted women's active involvement in this form of migration (whilst not actually leaving their home community). She maintains that the seasonal and temporary migrations of the men were only "made possible by the work that women and children engaged in to maintain small family plots while their husbands and fathers were absent".[66]

In light of these findings, there was clearly a need to question representations of migrant miners' wives in Cornwall. In the absence of any in-depth research, the real experiences of the Cornish 'married widows' had only been guessed at, creating a speculative and frequently negative mythology. Sharron Schwartz has drawn attention to the lack of any basis for many of the assumptions about the women who remained in Cornwall.[67] Nevertheless, such negative representations are often repeated in literature on Cornish women and families, tempered by recognition of the need for more research. Gill Burke speculated in her 1981 thesis on the Cornish mining industry that the "life of a woman alone, bringing up a family on remittances from abroad, must have been grim indeed", but concluded that "much more needs to be discovered about their lives".[68] In his 2004 book *The Cornish Family* (written with Sharron Schwartz and David Holman), Bernard Deacon suggested that while some of the consequences of long-distance husband and wife relationships logically might be forecast, any conclusions require more detailed study.[69] These authors have all recognised the paucity of evidence on which these perceptions are founded and have called for more research into these women's lives, seeing it as long overdue.

This book is based on research that was the first to answer this call and explore in depth the subject of the 'married widows' of Cornwall, the wives 'left behind'.[70] It aims to reassess the myths, assumptions and generalisations about their experiences in order to better understand this period in Cornwall's history. Much of what has been found about their experiences is likely to apply to wives 'left behind' in other parts of the

UK, but there are aspects that are probably distinctive of the scale and concentration of Cornish emigration. The words of the anonymous newspaper correspondent from Liskeard at the start of this introduction encapsulate many of the issues raised by this phenomenon, and pose a suite of questions that this book seeks to answer. The report, especially when read in conjunction with similar references, implies that these women posed a social concern, if not problem, not least because of the apparent numbers involved. If the numbers were "considerable" in the Liskeard area alone, what was the scale of the phenomenon and its associated social problems across Cornwall as a whole, and over what timescale did they occur?

The choice of words used by the report's author illustrates some uncertainty over the wives' situation. The position of a 'deserted' wife is clear enough; her husband has, in violation of his marital duty, promise and obligations, abandoned her with no intention to return.[71] She has lost both his financial and emotional support. But what does 'half-deserted' mean? Whereas 'deserted' suggests finality and certainty regarding their status, 'half-deserted', like 'married widow' is a seeming oxymoron, implying an indeterminate and uncertain state. It suggests the emergence of a potentially large number of women in Cornwall whose practical experience did not conform with 19th century expectations of married life. How did these women manage under these circumstances: financially, practically and emotionally?

What has been written to date about the wives 'left behind' is full of ambiguities. It hints at a variety of experiences and outcomes among the wives affected, presenting an ambivalent but generally negative perception of these women's lives. Does the evidence support this? What did it really mean be a 'married widow' in 19th century Cornwall?

1

Considerable Numbers?
Taking a count of the wives

We can only fully understand the lives and experiences of the wives 'left behind' in the context of the overall scale of the phenomenon. So let's start by trying to establish just how many women we are talking about, and explore how their distribution across Cornwall changed over time.

Cornishmen have taken their mining skills to different parts of Cornwall and beyond for centuries. There is evidence of Cornish miners being recruited to work abroad in 1769,[1] and at other times during the 18th century they are recorded as working in Devon, Derbyshire and Wales.[2] It is impossible to determine how many of these pre-19th century Cornish miners moved with their families and how many left wives and children behind in Cornwall. It is relatively straightforward to find evidence of Cornish families who migrated as a unit. For example, birth and baptismal records demonstrate the presence of wives and children in the receiving community. However, a married man travelling without his wife is largely indistinguishable from a single man. As few historical records before the mid-19th century censuses indicate the marital status of men; the existence of a wife, let alone her whereabouts, often remains unknown.

Although individual Cornish husbands inevitably travelled abroad for work earlier, the seeds of a culture of married Cornish miners migrating for work overseas in large numbers can be traced back to mining developments in Latin America in the early decades of the 19th century.[3] Increasing British investment in these mines created a labour market that became focussed on recruiting experienced miners from Cornwall through personal recommendation, direct recruiting and newspaper advertising. The opportunities created by this well paid contract work attracted married as well as single men.

The Married Widows of Cornwall

Among them was mining engineer Richard Trevithick who was commissioned in 1814 to provide machinery and men to restore the abandoned mines at Cerro de Pasco in Peru. When Richard himself followed them to Peru two years later to resolve technical problems, his wife Jane (whose experience is described later) became one of the first among generations of women who remained in Cornwall while their husbands pursued careers abroad.

We know of other wives 'left behind' in Cornwall in the first half of the 19th century by men working in Latin America and elsewhere from what has been passed down in family histories and a limited number of documentary sources. A surviving trust deed created in 1834 by John Chynoweth of St Agnes reveals that his wife remained in Cornwall when he left to work in South America.[4] Mentions can also be found in the Cornish newspapers; the *West Briton* of 2 February 1849 carried the brief announcement that the wife of William Collins of Cuba had given birth to a son in St Day in Cornwall.[5]

Although we encounter individual women in documents and family stories, trying to establish how many wives were 'left behind' has proved far from easy. Various sources hint that as the 19th century progressed significant numbers of wives remained in Cornwall while their husbands worked abroad. It has been suggested that by 1871 up to 35% of young married women in Redruth, and 26% in St Just, were living apart from their husbands.[6] However, no accurate records were kept documenting the numbers of people who left Cornwall, let alone official statistics on the dependants they 'left behind'.

The records of national censuses carried out every decade since 1801 provide historians with the best source of data concerning the population of England and Wales.[7] Marital status and information on relationships, both of which are needed to identify wives and whether their husbands were living in the same house, were not recorded routinely until the 1851 census onwards. However, the 1841 census does provide some clues on the numbers of wives 'left behind', as well as nuggets of information concerning individual women.

Although there was no requirement in 1841 to record who was married, those responsible for taking the census (the enumerators) did identify women as wives in some districts in Cornwall, recording a married woman whose husband was listed on the line above as "his wife". More importantly for our purposes, some enumerators chose to record the married women they encountered living in households that did not include their husbands (at least on census night) as the wife of a named individual or by reference to their husband's occupation, e.g. 'miner's wife'. A comprehensive search of the 1841 census for Cornwall found that there were 501 women identified as wives enumerated in households that did not include their husbands; of these 47 were recorded as the wives of miners, tin dressers or engineers. Most were listed as the first name on the schedule suggesting that they were acting as head of household in their husband's absence. The remainder, listed in the households of others, could have simply been away from their own homes as visitors on census night, but these would be indistinguishable from those staying with relatives or in lodgings while their husbands were away.

I am not suggesting that this gives a true estimate of the numbers of wives 'left behind' by miners in 1841; there is no way of knowing what proportion of the other women listed as the first name in each household were married, widowed or single. The identification of some heads of household as wives is, in all probability, exceptional, and may say more about the enumerator's personal approach to his role than the scale of the phenomenon. However, the distribution of these wives across Cornwall does not seem to be as random as might be expected if their recording was only an artefact of enumerator preference. The overwhelming majority of women noted as 'wife' in 1841 were recorded in the census as the wives of sailors, mariners or others in maritime occupations, and these are not surprisingly found in the ports and coastal parishes of Cornwall. Of the 47 miners' wives, 20 were in the Camborne/ Redruth/ Illogan/ Crowan area, ten in the Tywardreath/ St Blazey/ St Austell area and six in St Hilary/ Perranuthnoe area. This is a pattern of distribution that becomes very familiar as we look at later censuses (see below) suggesting that the identification of these heads of household as wives is not simply coincidental.

There is another way in which the 1841 census can shed some light on the practice of men emigrating leaving their families behind. The enumerators in 1841 had instructions to gather information both on the numbers from each district who were temporarily absent and those who had emigrated. They were to record the details in tables at the front of each Census Enumerator's Book (CEB) if such absences would have caused "a considerable increase or decrease of the Population of the District at the time of the Enumeration". The vagueness of this instruction left room for interpretation as to what constituted 'temporary' or 'considerable' allowing wide variation as to how consistently this information might have been recorded. Nonetheless, the tables do provide some useful clues, as in the enumerator's note for Carharrack (a mining settlement in the parish of Gwennap) that: "Six miners, whose families reside in the district are labouring in America or the West Indies".[8] Although there is no direct indication of these being married men, the reference to families does suggest that they were heads of household. Examination of the census returns for the corresponding enumeration district reveals several households consisting of an adult woman and children, one of whom, Anne Blamey, is listed as having "Husb - a miner", making her a strong candidate for a wife 'left behind'.

There is good reason to believe that there were many wives 'left behind' whose names are listed in the 1841 census but who cannot be identified as such from among the many female heads of household. For example, it is known that many men were recruited from the Gwennap area to work in the mines of Latin America in the 1830s,[9] and that absent husbands from that parish have been found working there in 1851. However, other than Anne Blamey, none of the 47 women with absent husbands recorded as miners' wives were in Gwennap. The only similar reference in the 1841 census for Gwennap is that Eliza Trebilcock's husband had "Gone off". It seems likely that the numerous female heads of household of unknown marital status listed in Gwennap include wives of miners who were working abroad. The 1841 census returns provide tantalising hints of wives 'left behind', but it is only when the census returns from 1851 onwards start to include more consistent recording of marital status does it become possible to attempt an estimate of the numbers of wives involved.

Although the census enumerators were instructed to record whether a woman was married from 1851, there was never any requirement to record if her husband, if absent, had gone abroad without her. Nevertheless, in the 1851 census returns for Cornwall there are 60 entries for women whose husbands were specifically recorded as being 'abroad'

Considerable Numbers?

or in a named overseas location. In 1861 there were 503 such references to husbands 'explicitly abroad', as I shall call them. Fewer appear in subsequent censuses with 348 in 1871, 299 in 1881 and 178 in 1891. These figures exclude husbands identified as having maritime, military or other occupations that would commonly require work away from home (eg. commercial travellers, carriers or preachers). Most of the absent husbands are described as miners (for copper, tin, iron, lead, coal, silver, gold and diamonds) or engaged in related trades, but not all. Butchers, quarrymen, farmers, cabinet makers, plasterers, boot makers, accountants even pensioners and retired publicans also went abroad leaving wives behind in Cornwall. In 1861 Elizabeth Chipman's husband was a cattle dealer in Australia, while in 1881 Ellen Phillipson's farmed ostriches in South Africa, no doubt profiting from demand for feathers in the European hat trade. In total there are 1388 references in the Cornish censuses between 1851 and 1891 to husbands being abroad, in locations ranging from the familiar (North and South America, Australasia and South Africa) to the less expected, such as Turkey and Russia.

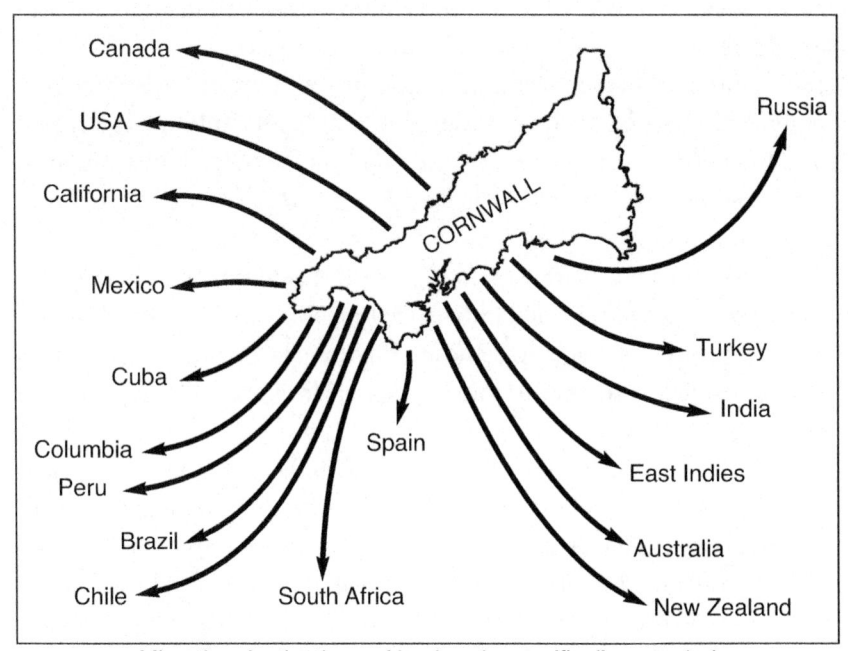

Migration destinations of husbands specifically recorded in the censuses taken in Cornwall from 1851 to 1891.

Although these references are unequivocal cases of wives 'left behind', their low numbers do not appear compatible with contemporary reports that suggested it was a common phenomenon. Neither do they include wives whose husbands were overseas but not recorded as such in the census. Therefore those with husbands 'explicitly abroad' cannot account for all the wives who remained in Cornwall while their husbands were abroad but can only be seen as the minimum number of wives involved.

In the absence of accurate census recording of husbands abroad, we have to look to other demographic observations to estimate the numbers of wives 'left behind'. The mining communities of 19th century Cornwall are perceived as becoming dominated by women. For example, one terrace of houses in Lanner was remembered as being inhabited entirely by women for much of the late 19th century.[10] Nearby St Day was described in these years as being 'half-denuded of men'.[11] Women have been shown to be increasingly outnumbering the men in Cornwall at this time and by 1901 there were only 85 men to every 100 women compared with 96 per 100 in 1861.[12]

This gender imbalance in the population is reflected in an increase in the number of households headed by women. In 1851 between 16-19% of heads of household in St Just were female; the proportions were higher in both Camborne and St Agnes at 21-23%, and higher still in Gwennap at 29%. In all these parishes more and more households had women in charge and by 1881 and 1891 they account for 36-43% of all households in these parishes.[13]

These figures put Cornwall on a par with Shetland, described as one of the most demographically imbalanced places in 19th century Europe where 24% of households were headed by females, rising to 41% in the town of Lerwick.[14] To put this into context, the average figure for England was 10%.[15]

High numbers of female-headed households have commonly been associated with the large-scale migration of men, and the biggest rise in the proportion of female-headed households in mining areas of Cornwall has been attributed to an increase in the number where the head was a married woman with no husband present.[16] From this one might think that figures for female heads of household could be used as a proxy for the number of wives 'left behind'. However, there is a problem with this –

none of the figures above make any distinction as to whether the women in question are married or not.

On closer examination of the census, widows have been found to account, by far, for the largest proportion of female heads of household. In Gwennap over 20% of all households were headed by widows between 1851-1891, peaking at over 27% in 1881.[17] Similar numbers have been found in Lanner, Camborne, Redruth and St Just.[18] In addition, a small proportion of female heads of household were single; in Camborne, Redruth and St Just between 1851 and 1871 this has been calculated at around 1.4-2.2%,[19] and in Gwennap as high as 5% in 1891.[20] An increase in unmarried-mother households has also been found and partly attributed to migration disrupting the traditional Cornish practice of engaged couples waiting until pregnancy before getting married.[21]

While widows accounted for 20-27% of heads of household in Gwennap, only around 4-11% were headed by married women, a figure in line with findings from other mining parishes.[22] It is clear that widows, and to a much lesser extent spinsters, made a significant contribution to the observed high numbers of female heads of household in the mining districts of Cornwall.[23] One caveat is that, there is the possibility that some wives who had lost contact with their husbands chose to describe themselves as widows because they assumed (or preferred to assume) that they were dead.[24] In their defence one should perhaps consider that a wife whose husband had disappeared through deliberate desertion or accident would find it difficult to know whether she was a widow or not, and there is also the distinct possibility of transcription and other errors in the census returns.

By contrast, wives whose husbands were absent comprised only a small percentage of female heads of household. Despite this, they and the migration that created their situation appears to have been credited with a disproportionate effect on the demographic imbalance in late 19th century Cornwall. It seems far more likely that the shortage of men within some Cornish communities was as much, if not more, down to high death rates amongst miners rather than large-scale male emigration. This sits uncomfortably with a Cornish identity that views mining heritage with pride while casting emigration as the cause of Cornwall's woes.

This commonly held idea of mining being 'good' and emigration 'bad' for Cornwall has deflected attention from the numerous widows (a group who frequently become less 'visible' in society) and onto the wives 'left behind'. The notion of married women taking charge of the household fell outside social norms for the period, and the novelty of the situation would have attracted greater attention than the more familiar one of widows running their own households. The result is the mistaken impression that the increasing numbers of women in charge of Cornish households in the late 19th century was mainly the result of husbands migrating leaving their wives in charge.

The inclusion of large numbers of widows and some spinsters means that any estimate of the number of married women 'left behind' based on the figures for female heads of household alone would be greatly inflated. Instead we must consider only married female heads of household. Analysis of the entire population in the Cornish censuses has revealed that there were considerably more of them in Cornwall than the explicit references to husbands being abroad would suggest with nearly 1600 in 1851, rising to over 3000 in 1871 and 1881, and continuing upwards to just under 4000 in 1891.[25]

However, counting the number of married women heading households would underestimate the number of 'married widows' because not all

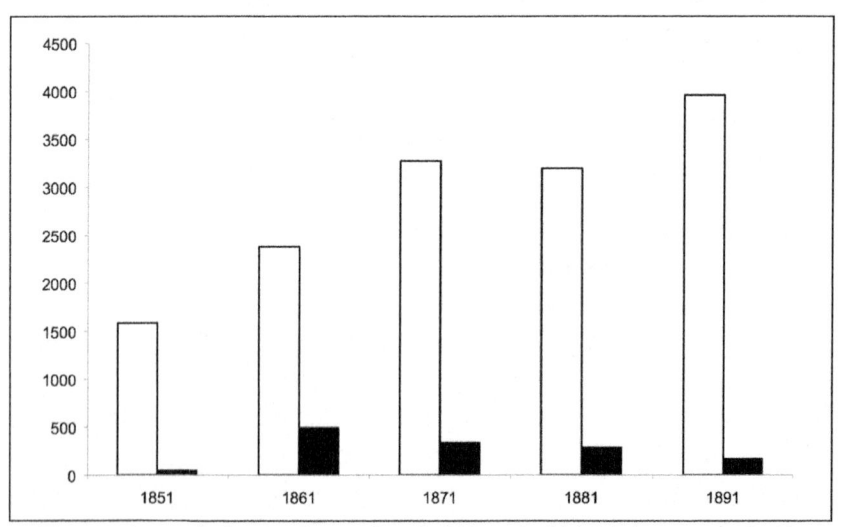

The numbers of wives acting as head of household (white) compared with those whose husbands are stated as being abroad (black) in each census year.

wives 'left behind' were heads of household in their husbands' absence. Many are recorded in the census as living in the households of relatives or as lodgers while their husbands were abroad.

Finding the number of wives 'left behind' who were not living in their own households is far more difficult. Female heads of household can be extracted from the census by simple data analysis but wives living in other households can only be identified by manual examination of the individual household schedules to confirm that the husband is not present, a labourious and time consuming process that was not practical to do for the entire Cornish population. However, it has been possible for a few selected parishes to count all the married women whose husbands were not present in the same household in the census, regardless of whether the wives were in charge of their own household or living in someone else's.

In Camborne, Gwennap, St Agnes, St Cleer and St Just in Penwith there is a steady, or some cases rapid, increase in numbers of wives with absent husbands from 1851 to 1871. There is little change in numbers between 1871 and 1881 in all of the parishes except Gwennap, which shows a sharp decrease before numbers stabilise in 1891. Of these parishes only Camborne and St Just show numbers increasing after 1881. However, when we consider these figures as a percentage of the total number of married women in these respective parishes, it is evident that some of this variation simply reflects population changes over the period. In four out of these five parishes between 3% and 6% of husbands are absent in 1851, and in most cases numbers rise steadily to between 14% and 21% by 1891.

Only Gwennap exhibits a different trend with a higher initial figure of over 9% in 1851 and a much more rapid increase and earlier peak of over 25% in 1871 before falling to similar levels as the other parishes. At times up to a quarter of all husbands from the parish were away leaving their wives to manage on their own. The mostly likely explanation is that mining activity peaked and declined in Gwennap earlier than in the other parishes. Mining in Gwennap was at its strongest in the early years of the 19th century at a time when it gained the reputation as the greatest copper producing area in the world. This resulted in a concentration of mining expertise and personal connections in the parish that made it an obvious target for those recruiting skilled men to develop the mines of South

America. This may explain the higher numbers and proportion of husbands away in 1851. However, the boom was not sustainable and the parish declined rapidly from the 1860s, its population and skilled workforce dispersed to other mining centres in Cornwall and abroad.

The differences between these mining parishes reflect the local ups and downs of the mining industry in Cornwall. The widely accepted narrative of mining in Cornwall describes the 18th century rise of copper mining in the western parishes centred on Redruth, a shift in production to the east, followed by decline from the 1870s. This was accompanied by a more dispersed exploitation of tin deposits, ranging from St Just in the far west to the eastern border with Devon, which by the late 19th century had became concentrated on the central mining district of Camborne and Illogan. Transient mid-19th century production of lead in discrete areas in west and south-east Cornwall, together with opportunistic exploitation of other minerals add to the complex story of Cornish mining. Supporting the industry with expertise and equipment were the engineering companies, such as Holman Brothers of Camborne, and the foundries at Hayle and Perranarworthal.[26] The localised nature of the mining industry and its diversity in nature and over time mean that we should be wary of Cornwall-wide generalisations.[27]

The fluctuations in the local economies within Cornwall[28] and in specific mining centres abroad, as well as the personalised nature of mining recruitment networks, mean that there was significant variation in migration patterns across Cornwall. As Sharron Schwartz's research on migration to Latin America has shown, mines in Cuba recruited mainly from Redruth in the early to mid-19th century because that is where their recruiting agents lived. The Williams family of Scorrier drew on their local miners from Gwennap and Redruth for mines in Brazil, while miners from Camborne in the early 1890s were more likely to take up work in Mexico.[29] As different localities in Cornwall experienced very different migration flows, it is logical that the numbers of absent husbands could vary between different (even neighbouring) communities, and also with time.

We can see this in the distribution within Cornwall of wives with husbands recorded as 'explicitly abroad' in the census, and of wives acting as heads of household. Both show a clear pattern with numbers concentrated in the mining districts, especially in West Cornwall, and detectable trends over time that reflect the rise and fall of these districts as the mining economy of Cornwall changed throughout the period. Significantly more references to 'husbands abroad' were found in the censuses for the St Agnes/ Kenwyn, Wendron/ Helston, and especially the Redruth/ Camborne/ Gwennap areas.[30] Other clusters were found in the mining or clay areas around Liskeard and St Austell. There is a clear increase in most mining parishes from 1851 through to 1871 after which numbers generally plateau or gently fall off, with the exception of Camborne and St Just in Penwith where numbers continued to rise.

A very similar pattern is found in the distribution of wives acting as heads of household.[31] Married female heads of household were not found in all parishes in Cornwall in any census, and many parishes had only one or two cases. Again, the focus of the phenomenon was clearly in West Cornwall, and although there was an overall increase in the 'background' numbers across Cornwall with time, the growth was concentrated primarily in the Central Mining District centred around Redruth, with additional concentrations in St Just in the far west and St Austell on the south coast. Smaller increases were detectable in the Liskeard area. Larger than average numbers were found in St Austell, both a port and a population centre for the china clay industry district, and the increase there could be associated with the emigration of china clay workers or maritime activities, although it is noticeable that there was no equivalent increase in the surrounding parishes of the 'Clay Country'.

Numbers also increased in some population centres with significant maritime activity, such as Falmouth, Penzance, and St Ives. The wives in these parishes may include those with husbands involved with maritime activities but not identified as such in the census (and therefore not excluded), as well as the wives of migrants. Overall there is considerable variation in the numbers of married women acting as heads of household across Cornwall with a good correlation with the presence of mining and clay working.

Although the numbers of wives 'left behind' varied significantly between parishes and over time, there is one apparent constant that has emerged from the close study of parishes where they could all be counted. Among the wives 'left behind' the ratio of wives who were living in their own households compared to those who were staying with relatives or lodging seems remarkably consistent. In each of Camborne, Gwennap, St Agnes and St Just, across all census years, the proportion of wives with absent husbands acting as heads of household sits within the range of 59-76%, with an average of 66-71%. If this can be extrapolated to other parishes, the figures for the married female heads of household for all of Cornwall may represent only around two thirds of the total number of wives with absent husbands. The other third were lodging or living with relatives.

As we know the number of married women heading households throughout Cornwall in each census year, and it is likely there was another third of wives who were living in the households or others, we can combine this information to estimate the maximum number of wives 'left behind', assuming this approximate ratio of 2:1 (heads of household:living with others) holds true for Cornwall as a whole. (For example, in 1851 there were 1587 married women acting as heads of household, and probably half as many again living in the households of other people. That would amount to up to around 2381 wives 'left behind' at the time of that census.) Although it can only be considered a very rough calculation, this

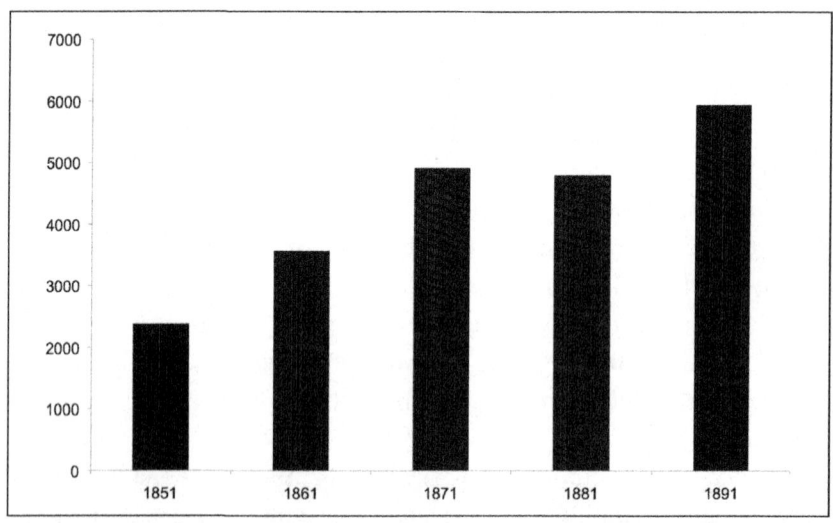

Estimated number of wives in Cornwall with absent husbands in each census year. Calculation based on the ratio of 2:1 (wives heading households:wives living with others) suggested by detailed analysis of sample parishes.

Considerable Numbers?

suggests that in 1851 alone over 2000 married women in Cornwall had been 'left behind', with the numbers increasing to around 3500 in 1861, still further to nearly 5000 in 1871 and 1881 respectively, and reaching nearly 6000 in 1891.

These figures can only be maximum numbers for those census years because there are numerous reasons, other than emigration, why husbands may have been away from home at the time of a census. Although the wives of men whose occupations would normally have involved absence from home, such as those in the maritime, military, professional, transport and service occupations were excluded from the analysis, some husbands may have had other reasons to be away from home on census night. For example, in the 1871 census the absent husband of Ann Sparnon of Camborne was enumerated in the West Cornwall Convalescent Hospital, along with a number of other married men, whose wives presumably would also have appeared in the census as having absent husbands. Examples were also found of husbands who were enumerated apart from their wives but were living very close nearby; Thomasine Eddy's husband, Gilbert, was found to be a miller enumerated at his mill, rather than the family home.

Even if the majority were the wives of men who had migrated, other than those cases where the census records the husband as being abroad, it is not known how far they migrated. Ann Jenking's husband, a mine agent called William, who was absent from the family home in Camborne in 1851, for example, was lodging in Menheniot. However, the absence of any significant surpluses of married male lodgers in any mining parish makes it unlikely that many of the absent husbands had remained in Cornwall. It is known, however, that a proportion of the missing men had migrated to other parts of the UK for work. The migration of the Cornish to Wales and the north of England is a subject that needs further research but they can to be found in census returns for iron ore or coal mining centres such as Glamorgan, Durham, Barrow-in-Furness in Lancashire, Millom in Cumberland, Brampton in Derbyshire, Penkridge in Staffordshire, Brotton and Farndale in Yorkshire, as well as the appropriately named Liscard in Cheshire.

Although this has some impact on our understanding of the number of wives whose husbands were abroad, it perhaps is debatable whether it made much difference to the day-to-day experience of a wife 'left behind' whether her husband was in Scotland or Nova Scotia – what mattered was the length of absence and the level of contact and support that the husband maintained.

The figures given above of between two and six thousand wives 'left behind' in any one census year, however, still underestimates the true number of women affected. The census only gives us a ten-yearly snapshot of the population. It doesn't tell us what was happening during the years in between. There would have wives whose husbands were only away for periods that fell between the census dates and therefore cannot be identified from the census returns.

We also have to consider turnover; if a large number of husbands were abroad in each census year, what proportion were the same husbands? Clearly if a different set of husbands were away far more wives were being affected by this experience than if many of the same husbands were away in consecutive census years.

Of the wives whose husbands were 'explicitly abroad' very few appear in more than one census suggesting a small accumulation of wives 'left behind'. A similar picture is found in the parishes where all the wives with absent husbands were counted. In Camborne, Gwennap, St Agnes and St Just the proportion of wives whose husbands were also absent in the previous census increases from 1861 to 1871. For Camborne, Gwennap and St Agnes this increase continues to 1881, after which Camborne continues to increase while Gwennap and St Agnes fall off.

Despite the increases in carryover of wives from one census to the next, the figures do show that the majority of wives identified in each census (at least three quarters and usually far more) were new recruits to the ranks of 'married widows'. Some may have moved into the parishes from elsewhere but an analysis of the ages of the wives in each census shows a very high proportion were too young to have been married at the time of the previous census and must represent new waves of wives whose husbands were absent.

This high turnover among the wives 'left behind' throughout the second half of the 19th century means that even more wives were affected than the numbers in any one census year would suggest. For example, in Gwennap alone more than a thousand different wives have been identified

Considerable Numbers?

from the census as living separately from their husbands at some point.

The steady increase in the proportion of absent husbands implied by the figures above may well mask fluctuations in the years between censuses due to local and international events. In 1862 it was reported that many people had returned from abroad, especially from America after the outbreak of the Civil War and the associated fall in the value of the dollar.[32] It seems likely that this would have triggered the return of some husbands, although some, like Christopher Candy Ellis married to Eliza from St Just, stayed and fought in the war.[33] Migration out of Cornwall overseas to America and Australia as well as to northern England and Wales picked up again in the Cornish mining crisis of the mid- to late 1860s and on into the 1870s. However, even at the height of the depression it was reported that as men were leaving Cornwall for various destinations, many of the miners who had gone to Scotland were returning disappointed with the work opportunities there.[34]

Contemporary concerns about poverty caused by the 1867 depression in Cornish mining led to the collection of statistics helpful in assessing the numbers of wives 'left behind'. In the summer of that year Cornwall's High Sheriff and county magistrates met as a committee to look into the level of economic distress amongst the population. One of the first things they did was to appoint local sub-committees drawn from the poor law unions to gather information and report back on the specific economic and employment situation in their districts, including the number of wives and families of men who had left their homes to seek employment elsewhere.[35] Their reports, published in detail by the local press, provide a reasonably comprehensive survey made by local poor law officers of the numbers of wives whose husbands had migrated in search of work at that time.

Officials from the Penzance Union found that the heads of 400 families in the union had gone abroad. Within this union it was reported that in the St Just district there were 360 wives whose husbands were in the North of England, America, Australia, and California.[36] A report given a week later said there were upwards of 300 families in the St Just district whose heads had left home in search of employment. The heads of 64 families had left the parish of Ludgvan since 1865, and only about a quarter had taken their families with them, suggesting that around 48 wives had been 'left behind'. From Lelant and St Erth, the sub-committee heard that 460 men had either gone to the north of England or abroad, some leaving families behind. They later reported to the main committee that there were around 200 unemployed miners from their district, of which: "A few (it may be twenty, it is at least 14) of these miners have gone abroad, taking the families with them; nearly one hundred have gone leaving their families at home; the rest are unaccounted for." It was also noted that two men had gone from St Ives leaving their families behind, while 30 miners had emigrated from Marazion, some of whom had left their families behind.[37]

The Helston Union sub-committee reported that: "The numbers of wives and families of men who have left their homes to seek employment, etc, exclusive of Crowan parish (reported in Camborne), were women 143; children under 14 years of age, 258." Reporting at the same meeting the superintendent of police gave a figure of 304 for the number of married miners who had left the union for employment reasons.[38]

From the Truro Union 30 to 40 heads of family were said to have gone from Chacewater and about 250 adult males had left St Agnes during the previous 12 months for California, many of whom had left wives behind. The St Columb sub-committee reported that in Newlyn there were 11 wives and families of men who had left their homes in search of employment. St Austell Union did not provide a full report but mentioned the existence of wives and families left behind in St Blazey and Tywardreath.

Significantly, no figures were provided by the Redruth Union (which included Camborne and Gwennap),[39] because its board of guardians had come to the conclusion "that there was no distress in the Redruth Union which warranted their seeking for public assistance". However, they did acknowledge that there was distress among the wives of migrant miners who had been left with no means of support. Similarly the sub-committees from the remaining unions (Falmouth, Bodmin, Launceston, Camelford, Liskeard, St Germans and Stratton) only provided brief reports without figures as they had no significant amount of mining or distress.[40]

The lack of standardisation in the way the figures were reported makes precise analysis difficult, and it is clear that there is under-reporting of the numbers of wives who had been 'left behind' in areas where the authorities

Considerable Numbers?

did not feel that there was any particular cause for concern. There was also little distinction made as to whether the men had gone abroad or elsewhere in the UK. Nonetheless the official summary of reports presented to the Central Committee revealed in August 1867 that about 600 men had emigrated from the St Austell, Helston and Penzance Union districts, each leaving behind, on average, a wife and three children.[41]

Comparing this figure of 600 with the numbers of husbands 'explicitly abroad' from the parishes in these same unions in the census years (1861 and 1871) either side of these events (St Austell: 35 and 28; Helston: 16 and 52; Penzance: 51 and 47; Total: 102 and 127), suggests either that there was a very dramatic increase and then fall in the number of husbands abroad in this period, or that, as proposed above, there were many more husbands abroad than were specifically recorded as such in the census. The latter seems more likely, as in the same unions 679 women in 1861 and 1091 in 1871 were recorded as acting as heads of household, figures far closer to those produced by the local officials. Indeed, the figure of 304 given by the superintendent of police for the Helston Union in the summer of 1867 is very close to the number of wives there (325) acting as heads of household just under four years later when the 1871 census was taken. Similarly the patchy figures given for the Truro Union appear consistent with the census findings, and there are few census references to husbands being abroad in the eastern Cornish unions that did not provide any figures.

The most interesting response is that of the officials from Redruth Union who did not think the numbers of married men who had left families behind worth estimating, especially as this was the union that had the highest number of husbands specifically recorded as being abroad in the censuses of 1861 (327) and 1871 (152), and the highest concentration of wives acting as heads of household. One piece of evidence from Redruth suggests a local acceptance of wives managing households in their husband's absence as being nothing out of the ordinary. *A Directory of Redruth and its Neighbourhood* printed and published by John S. Doidge in 1866 unusually indicates the marital status of female householders, giving the unlisted husband's occupation for married women. The directory includes 119 householders listed as 'miner's wife', plus a further 22 described variously as the wives of tin dressers, mine agents, engineers or engine fitters and other mining related trades.[42] Of this total of 142 likely 'married widows' in Redruth in 1866, at least 48 are known to have had husbands specifically noted as being abroad in either the 1861 or 1871 census.

Although the Redruth authorities recognised that there was some distress among the wives who were not receiving financial support from their husbands, they do not seem to have perceived it as a crisis. Their response seems similar to other unions where there appear to be far fewer absent husbands and no perceived problem. It is possible that significant numbers of absent husbands went un-noticed by the authorities if their wives managed well without any need to call on the parish for assistance.

The idea that the authorities only took note of the numbers of wives 'left behind' when it caused a problem is reflected in later reporting of the phenomenon where numbers are only referred to in the context of wives who are not receiving adequate support from their husbands abroad. An example of this is the report of there being 'considerable' numbers of women in and around Liskeard in 1875, deserted or half deserted by their husbands.[43]

To summarize, although there are no comprehensive contemporary statistics on the numbers of wives 'left behind' by men migrating from Cornwall, by combining a range of analytical techniques it has been possible to arrive at minimum and maximum figures, at least for the census years. From explicit references in the censuses, we know that there were at least 1359 wives in Cornwall whose husbands were abroad between 1851 and 1891. However the limited statistics produced by contemporary poor law officials show that this underestimates the true figure, which is better reflected in the number of married women heading households (approx. 1600 in 1851 rising to nearly 4000 in 1891). It has also been shown that in the absence of their husbands half as many wives again were living in the households of others. Together these findings suggest that at times during the 19th century as many as two to six thousand married women were 'left behind' in Cornwall by migrant husbands. Although these are very broad ranges they do provide some insight into the numbers involved at any one time.

However, it must be re-emphasised that the census only provides ten-yearly snapshots of the population and it has been demonstrated that there

Considerable Numbers?

was considerable turnover among the wives 'left behind', so the overall numbers of women involved are likely to be much higher. When all these factors are considered, it is not unreasonable to suggest that the phenomenon affected a number of wives in the order of the low tens of thousands. The impact of these large numbers would have been intensified by the fact that they were not evenly distributed across Cornwall but primarily concentrated in areas associated with mining, especially the Central Mining District around Redruth. In these mining parishes it is clear that the practice of wives being 'left behind' by husbands migrating for work was a significant phenomenon and one that became increasingly common throughout the 19th century.

2

Money from Abroad

Remittances and home-pay

Central to any understanding of what life was like for the wives 'left behind' in Cornwall is how they managed financially in their husbands' absence. It is well documented that remittances, the money sent home from family members working abroad, make an important contribution to the economies of sending communities. Historical remittances have usually been considered primarily in terms of money being sent back to enable other family members to migrate or to pay back loans that enabled the migrant to leave, ideas embedded in the one-way emigration paradigm, rather than the concept of the transnational family split between two or more places. In recent years the work of Gary Magee and Andrew Thompson has addressed this "vital but neglected dimension of the migrant experience", and it is now understood that the remittances sent back to Cornwall were more than an act of gratitude on the part of the migrant to those who had helped improve his circumstances or a means to enable further emigration.[1] As Magee and Thompson point out, the migrant men "conceived their move as a strategy to maximise the income and material well-being not just of themselves but of the family as a whole" and so they "continued to feel responsible for the wives, children, parents and other dependent relatives that they had left behind". They refer to this as an 'implicit contract', but in terms of husband and wife it was more than that. Not only was it a moral responsibility, it was a legal one.

Throughout the 19th century husbands were under a moral and legal obligation to support their wives; an obligation that was blind as to whether the couple were living in the same house, country or continent. In failing to support his wife a husband was breaking the social contract integral to the marriage and he risked public reprobation, not to mention prosecution and imprisonment.[2] Of course one would hope that the majority of husbands supported their wives out of love and respect, but the social pressures in the background reinforced the notion to all concerned that this was the norm.

It is in the light of this expectation that a wife would be supported by her husband, regardless of where he was, that we should view the evidence of how the wives whose husbands were abroad managed financially. Therefore a description of a woman in the census, for example, as a miner's wife, carries with it the implicit understanding that the husband's occupation will provide at least some income to the wife. It is important that this factor should not be left out of the equation when considering how the wives coping on their own managed to make ends meet.

This is counter to an assumption made in the past that only those wives who are recorded as 'annuitants' in the census were receiving money from their husbands. Several studies have used the number of women recorded in this way, or as having 'independent means', as a measure of the scale of migration dependency among the female population.[3] In the mining village of Carharrack numbers ranged from 21% in 1841, down to 8% in 1871 and up again to 24% in the 1880s/90s. In neighbouring Lanner Schwartz puts the figure for women with independent means at 6% in 1851 and 26% in 1891. However, these figures make no distinction regarding marital status and are likely to include many widows, and therefore are of little help in assessing the level of financial support the wives received. It is also questionable to assume, as Brayshay does, that only wives described as annuitants or similar were being supported by their husbands abroad.

A fresh analysis of the census suggests a much more complex story. Of the 60 wives whose husbands were stated as being abroad in the 1851 census 20 were described as annuitants, with one, Jane Bray from Redruth, explicitly stated as having "income an annuity from husband" in Peru. A further three were noted as being 'supported by husband': Mary Praed also of Redruth, whose husband was in Cuba, and Susan Faul of Crowan and Mary Rapson of Gwinear, both with husbands in America.

Likewise, of over three hundred similar wives in the 1871 census only five are described as receiving an "annuity from husband abroad". All of these (Elizabeth A. Cardew, Susan Dobb, Matilda Miles, Grace Miles and Caroline Pearce) are in the parish of Breage, suggesting that the use of this wording was the choice of a particular census enumerator. A further 25 wives are indicated as receiving some form of financial support from their husbands, described variously as allowances, income, maintenance, support and, in the case of Mary Ann Eva of St Clement near Truro, "husband sends from California".

By contrast none of the hundreds of wives with husbands 'explicitly abroad' in the 1861, 1881 or 1891 censuses were described as annuitants. (In 1891 this is because enumerators were required to use the standard phrase 'living on their own means' to encompass all those who are receiving an income from investments rather than employment.)[4] A similar picture emerges when we look at all the wives with absent husbands in the parishes studied in detail, with none or only one or two wives being described as annuitants in any census, with the exception of Gwennap in 1881 where 22 were recorded. As in the other census years, only a small proportion of cases show any indication of support coming from the husband.

If, and the manner in which, wives' income from abroad was recorded in the census appears to have been at the discretion of the census enumerator involved. In 1861, for example, all 23 such records occur in only a handful of parishes. The enumerator for one particular district of St Austell was particularly meticulous, not only recording that certain wives were being 'supported' by their husbands abroad but also stating where the husbands had gone. The husbands of Elizabeth Bate, Mary Ann Ripper, Elizabeth Williams, Maria Tregonning and Caroline Long were in Australia, while those of Sarah Hicks, Mary Job and Ann Ninnis were in America. The only cases in Marazion, Elizabeth Rowse and Eliza Simons, were similarly recorded as being 'supported' by husbands in Australia. In Redruth the same term was applied to Mary H. Bray and Elizabeth A. Trengove. Gwennap census enumerators Richard Skinner and Mark Morcom also chose to record wives (Elizabeth Blamey, Caroline Lang, Susan Mills, Mary Trebilcock and Martha A. Youren) as 'supported by' their husbands (although they don't give their location), while their colleagues Joseph and Henry Michell described Elizabeth Bray, Loveday Kinsman and Martha Lance as receiving 'income from' their husbands abroad. The only other records in the 1861 census of wives being in receipt of anything from their husbands abroad were Margaret Tyack in Crowan

Money from Abroad

("income") Frances Wills in St Minver Lowlands ("maintenance"), and Jane Williams in Mullion getting "pay" from her husband in America.

Likewise, in the five cases of support from husbands abroad specifically noted in the 1881 census, different enumerators used different terms: 'income' was received by Mary Martin in St Gluvias, Penryn; 'maintenance' by Elizabeth Jane Nicholls and Bessie Rowe both from St Blazey, and 'support' by Jane Warren in St Just and Mary A. Bartle in St Erth. The 1891 census shows a similar pattern with the very small percentage of wives recorded as have some form of support, and all being found in a very limited number of parishes.

It is clear that only in a very small proportion of cases is there any specific record in the census of the wives receiving an annuity or indeed any financial support from her husband, and these appear simply down to enumerator preference. This raises questions as to the significance of some wives being described as 'being in receipt of an annuity'; was it just another way of referring to remittances (a term that incidentally never appears in the census returns), does it imply some more formal arrangement that would have given those wives a more regular and secure income, or were these women receiving their annuities from sources other than their husbands?

Some women obviously were not receiving any or enough financial support from their husbands, as illustrated by the handful of census entries where the husband was noted as having deserted his wife (described as a pauper), or was 'somewhere abroad' and clearly was not in regular contact, like the husband of Mary Ann Berryman from Penzance who in 1881 was "at Cape, but out of touch". Mary Jenkin from Gwennap was noted as only receiving "some income" from her husband abroad. In a couple of cases contributions from other family members were recorded. In 1861 Elizabeth Blamey from Gwennap was being supported by her husband and son, who were both abroad, while in the same parish and year Jane Reed's father made it clear that he was supporting his 36-year-old married daughter in the absence of her husband.

However, in the overwhelming majority of cases, whether the husband was known to be abroad or was simply recorded as absent, there is no indication in the census of what financial support the wife may or may not have been receiving from her husband. It is counter-intuitive in the light of what is known about the large amount of money from abroad being received by families in Cornwall at the time,[5] combined with an understanding of the husbands' moral and legal obligations, to suppose that those wives for whom there is a census record of support from their husbands were the only ones. With this in mind, the idea that wives were only receiving money from their husbands if they were described as 'annuitants' in the census is flawed as it takes no account of the notion that neither the wives nor the enumerators would have thought it necessary to record what to them would have been obvious; that the wife was being supported by her husband, regardless of whether the money arrived from abroad or was handed to her personally by a husband in residence. The fact that references to husbands being abroad were noted in the wives' occupation column perhaps infers that it was viewed as a source of income like any other occupation.

Discussion of remittances resulting from Cornish emigration is usually framed in the context of the migrant experience or monetary flows between receiving and sending communities.[6] By contrast, little has been written about the practicalities of remittances and how those in receipt of them in Cornwall, some of whom would have been illiterate, negotiated the conversion of what arrived into the means to buy everyday necessities.

The methods by which wives received funds from their husbands abroad varied and became more sophisticated throughout the 19th century as new systems for international money transfer developed, often as a result of the pressures of mass emigration. Men abroad in the early part of the century would normally have sent money home in the form of cash, either via trusted individuals ('pocket' remittances) or enclosed in letters or packets ('envelope' remittances).[7] Bank notes might be enclosed with letters, or coins hidden in the wax used to seal letters or packages.[8] Mary Hodge of Mullion, writing to her children in America in 1851 referred to a gold dollar having arrived in a neighbour's letter.[9] Some coins it seems were sent more as novelty gifts rather than for their monetary value. In 1864 Joel Eade enclosed four "three cents peces [sic]", one for each of his children, in a letter to his wife.[10]

Sending cash in the post required an act of faith that the letter would safely arrive at its destination, and that, even without any consideration of theft, was not a certainty. Lack of co-operation between nascent, unintegrated and sometimes unreliable national postal services, bad weather and shipwreck could all result in letters going astray or being severely delayed. Not surprisingly many senders preferred to rely on personal couriers among friends or relations making the journey back home.[11] Mine captain Henry Richards frequently used this method to get money from America to family members back in Cornwall, entrusting at various times: $20 to a family associate, $40 and $10 to one of his miners, and £8 to a man that had been boarding with him.[12] Networks could also be used in quite complex ways. On one occasion, Richards arranged for one of his blacksmiths in America to get his own father in Camborne to pay £10 to Richards' family in Cornwall, which Richards would then reimburse to the blacksmith in America.[13]

Some remittances might arrive in a more unusual form; in 1877 a work colleague of a Mr Hosking from Lanner called on his wife and delivered a gold nugget weighing 123 ounces found by her husband in South Africa.[14] Mrs Hosking was reported to have quickly deposited the nugget in a bank in Redruth. A clue as to how she might convert it into goods is given by a court case in 1862 where it was recorded that Elizabeth Rundle from St Blazey had exchanged two small gold nuggets and a gold American dollar given to her by her husband, for goods with John Trewin, a silversmith who also kept a general shop in the parish.[15] Whether local traders would have been willing to accept foreign bank notes is uncertain, but the women must have learnt to negotiate some formal or informal methods of currency exchange.

Another option was to use the banking system, but the costs involved meant that this was only suitable for larger amounts. One way around this problem was for men to combine their remittances into one banker's draft, which the wives could cash and divide among themselves, or other family members. For example, in August 1867 Harriet Sheers from Tywardreath received a draft for £40 from her husband in America, of which half was for the wife of another miner in the village, and the two women went to the bank together to cash the order.[16] Similarly in 1864 John Gundry wrote from Houghton, Michigan to his young wife to let her know: "A few days since, Thomas and me gave an order to have 500 each sent home to you, of course half the money is for Gertrude".[17] Gertrude was the wife of John's brother, the Thomas mentioned in his letter.

John went on to write "How much it will be I cannot tell, for we have not received the receipt yet, it will depend on the percentage when the order gets to Boston…". This highlights the complicated costs involved in currency transfer and exchange. Joel Eade writing in 1864 explained to his wife: "I ham allowed for to send home fifty dollars once in three months at fifteen per centage and if I minto send any more I must pay the ful per centage [sic]."[18]

The problems of using the banks to send remittances home were quickly recognised. Caroline Chisholm, who became known as 'The Emigrant's Friend' for her work assisting those in Australia, noted in a letter to *The Times* in August 1852 that until recently there had been no way for emigrants in Australia to safely and cheaply remit small sums to England. When she tried to help emigrants in Sydney send money home she found that "the banks charged as much for £15 as for £50 and that they altogether declined to take the trouble of remitting small amounts". With the intercession of the Colonial Secretary she persuaded the banks to agree to accept small remittances… but only if Caroline personally accompanied the depositor. Not surprisingly she found it impossible to devote enough time "to introducing shepherds and stockmen with their £5 or £10 to the cashiers of banks" and wrote that many men when they found they could not send their remittance as planned ended up spending the money in a drunken spree. On her return to England Caroline and her husband set up a system, in conjunction with the bankers Messrs Coutts and Co, to facilitate the transfer of small remittances through the Family Colonisation Loan Society that they had formed, but this still required personal involvement at the Australian end and the decision was made for her husband to return to Australia without her. This was not the first time that Caroline had experienced a lengthy separation from her husband, and it goes a long way to explain the empathy with families separated by emigration demonstrated by her work on their behalf.[19]

The system set up by the Chisholms was only one of a number that emerged to meet the pressing need for a reliable and affordable means of sending money home from migration destinations. Some emigrant groups, such as the Irish Emigrant Society in New York, set up their own banks, while shipping firms, exchange agencies and press agencies also offered remittance services.[20]

Money from Abroad

The Post Office also recognised the growing need for simple, affordable international money transfer. It had been possible to send small amounts of money within the UK by money order since the late 1830s, and this had been extended to offer a limited overseas service in 1856 to allow soldiers serving in the Crimean War to send money home. The service was gradually expanded to other parts of the British Empire. In 1858 a reciprocal money-order system was set up between Britain and Canada that enabled remittance of any sum of shillings and pence under £5, something not possible by banker's draft. A similar agreement was reached with the United States Post Office in 1871, and by the end of 1873 it was possible to send remittances by money order from any British colony.[21]

Some official records of money being posted back to Cornwall have survived, and these offer a window into the amounts sent and their regularity. Of the 44 money letters registered at Bruce Mines Post Office in Northern Ontario, Canada between 11 Dec 1857 and 29 July 1861, 18 were to married women.[22] By comparing the names and addresses with the closest census (1861), five of these could confidently be identified as wives (Anne Fox, St Neot; Elizabeth Martin and Mrs Josiah (Elizabeth) Martin both of St Day; Phillippa Martin, Devoran; and Catherine Treloar, Liskeard). A further two were probably wives, while five were positively identified as widows, and the remainder not found. In the two and half year period covered by this source most women were sent only one or two remittances from this office.

Another surviving record of postal remittances is the 'Register of British International Money Orders' issued in the 1870s by the office in Central City, Colorado.[23] Among the 87 women with addresses in the parishes of Camborne, Gwennap, and St Just who were sent orders between 6 November 1871 and 28 June 1875 by men of the same surname, 21 could be positively identified as wives with absent husbands identified either in the 1871 or 1881 census. Of these only one (Jane Angwin in the 1881 St Just census) had a specific reference to her husband being abroad, supporting the argument made earlier that many of the Cornish husbands absent from the census return had emigrated. The register records a single money order of $50 sent to Jane by her husband William in February 1875, and a number of the other known wives were sent only one or two orders during this period, possibly because their husbands moved on. For others however, there is a record of regular remittances, either sent monthly (sometimes combining two months pay into a single remittance) or quarterly. This snapshot of the records from one office over a short three and a half year period can only give a flavour of the pattern of remittances to the wives in Cornwall. It is unknown, for example, why payments started and stopped when they did, but neglect of the wives should not be automatically assumed. Research has found that some of these named wives had been widowed, and some reunited with their husbands either in Cornwall or Colorado. In other cases the men may have moved to a new area, been out of work, ill, either party may have died or the couple may have been reunited elsewhere.

Dealing with such international money transfers would have been a totally new experience for those used to conducting their financial exchanges in cash. For some, dealing with paper money was unfamiliar, as witnessed by Joel Eade writing home to his wife in 1864: "…the mines paid all in paper but wee can have any thing for it the same as for gold or selver and if I minto change the paper money I must pay a very high per centage [sic]."[24] The wives too must have been negotiating new financial territory as the process of cashing orders and banker's drafts was not something that they would necessarily have been familiar with and so they would have needed to acquire the knowledge of what to do.

When a draft was arranged abroad the bank there would issue the husband with an order to be posted to his wife, and would also send a matching notification to the corresponding bank in the UK. Drafts were made out to a named individual and had to be presented at a bank, which would then send it to London in order to obtain the money. This quite complicated process would require the wife to travel to a bank,[25] which may have involved a long walk or arranging transport, as well as possibly taking time off work and organising child care. Money orders also had to be presented at the named Post Office. William Dawe was careful in writing to the recipient of a money order sent in 1885 to mention that: "they have made out the Order for Pool instead of Carn Brea".[26]

Recipients of both drafts and money orders had to sign their name to cash them, therefore it was important that it was made out in the correct name. As Mary Trescowthick instructed her relatives in 1876: "You will also find an order for ten pounds it is entered in the Post Office Elizabeth

Martha Henwood so you will know how to sign when you recive [sic] this."[27] Being informed as to exactly how she was named on the draft was probably important because, as demonstrated by the census schedules, the same woman might over time use a wide range of variations of her given name, sometimes exchanging first and middle names, or becoming widely known by a diminutive. Naming patterns were repeated within families and a relatively small selection of female first names were in use, so it was not unusual for a woman to alter her name to differentiate herself from others living locally with the same name. Senders also had to take care to put the order in the name of someone they were confident would be able to go to cash it. "I am sending an order payable to you, in case Auntie wld [sic] not be able to go out", wrote John J. King in 1900.[28]

Some drafts (also known as bills of exchange) were negotiable and so could be endorsed to be paid to another party and this provided a more informal way of cashing foreign drafts. In a civil court case for unpaid debt reported in 1884 evidence was given that a Mrs Tregonning in receipt of foreign drafts from her husband in America "occasionally paid" those drafts to a local shopkeeper, Mr Carter, for groceries.[29]

It is not clear how a wife who received a draft or order made payable to her alone, and who could not go in person to present it, or was illiterate and could not sign her name to either cash or endorse it, would have managed. To put the degree to which signing for the draft may have presented problems in context, according to the Registrar General's report of 1865 just over half of brides married in the Redruth registration district, shown above to have particularly large numbers of wives with husbands abroad, were unable to sign their name in the marriage register.[30] This report should, however, be treated with some caution as a superintendent registrar in Cornwall noted that subsequent inquiries about couples who both made their mark in the register rather than signing revealed that often one of the couple actually could write, but would "feign ignorance to spare the ignorant one's feeling – a little disturbing for statistical purposes, but showing real kindness".[31] One suspects that brides may have been more likely to 'feign ignorance' than grooms in order to preserve their new husband's pride.

Although remittances sent as drafts or money orders were more secure than cash they were not immune to theft or fraud. A name alone would not have reliably identified the individual for whom the remittance was intended, especially given the extent of name duplication amongst the female population. When Elizabeth Datson wrote to relatives in 1886 she instructed them to address their reply using her daughter Katey's name, explaining "the reason we adress in kateys name is thir is another Eliz Datson and she do open my letters [sic]".[32]

The means by which remittances were delivered also left them vulnerable to going astray, or worse. In a court case in 1869 Belinda Morcom described how she collected remittance letters from Helston Post Office and, not being able to read, marked them with pins to identify the recipients (after the woman she lived with, Mary Ann Perry, had sorted them for her).[33] After storing the letters under her pillow wrapped in her apron overnight, she delivered them, in one case giving the letter to a little boy to give to the addressee. In spite of Belinda's good intentions and ingenuity in working around her illiteracy, when the letter arrived the £10 draft that had been enclosed was missing, and was believed to have been stolen by a shoemaker, James Barry, who lodged in the same house as Belinda.

Having acquired the draft, Barry's attempts to get it cashed demonstrate in part how the system worked if the recipient wanted the cash immediately. First he tried a bank in Camborne without success, but the cashier at the West Cornwall Bank in Redruth was more obliging, and explained that he could obtain the cash right away (that is, without the draft having to be sent to London) if he could get a responsible person known to the bank to endorse the draft. Barry duly returned with someone the cashier knew, forged the intended recipient's signature and left with the cash. Apart from illustrating the potential for letters to go astray as a result of an ad hoc delivery system, this case also shows how a wife with respectable contacts willing to vouch for her at the bank might be able to circumnavigate the delays involved in awaiting confirmation from London and thereby obtain the cash sooner.

Concern over remittance letters not reaching their destination was a constant worry. In 1854 an article from the *Melbourne Argus* was reprinted in the *Royal Cornwall Gazette* warning readers of "the dangers they incur in sending home remittances to the friends in England" after a £20 draft addressed to someone in Cornwall was found in a dust-yard having been

Money from Abroad

lost or stolen, and a further case where a £40 remittance had failed to reach its intended destination.[34] The remittance letters one husband sent home from the Australian gold fields never reached his wife but were found at Dead Letter Office in London. They were only discovered there when one letter from him finally did arrive expressing surprise that he had not heard from his wife or family for several years. This letter came as a shock to the wife, who after such a long silence had made enquiries, been misinformed that he had died, and had remarried![35]

Requests for confirmation that drafts and orders had arrived safely were a regular theme in letters sent home. If a draft failed to arrive, for whatever reason, the sender could arrange for a replacement duplicate, and a 'second' order would have to be sent. Sadly, this was no help to Harriet Sheers when she and her friend presented the £40 draft intended for them to share at a bank in St Austell in 1867. The draft was a 'second' order replacing one that had never arrived. However, when it was sent to London it was found that the original order had already been cashed by someone who had forged Harriet's signature. The two wives had been robbed of the money that they so urgently needed. Such cases were probably not common, but did raise local concerns, the newspaper report noting that: "The affair had created some sensation in the neighbourhood, as miners abroad often write home to say they have written letter after letter, and had no reply".[36]

Fraud was not the only reason why the safe arrival of a remittance letter did not guarantee cash in hand. Bank failures were also an issue. When her son, John, died in Cuba in 1840 Elizabeth Ennor in St Blazey received a letter from Alfred Jenkin, local agent for the Cobre Mining Association, telling her that the $200 in American Bank notes held by her son no longer had any value. Fortunately for Elizabeth, the captain of an American ship was subsequently persuaded to exchange the notes for £35.[37] In 1852 a report from the *New York Tribune* carried by the English press referred to "repeated failures of houses engaged in drawing bills on Great Britain and Ireland for such small sums as the immigrant population wish to send home". It reported that in the previous two years the failure of 'bill-drawing houses' had amounted to a loss of $50,000 in remittances to Ireland alone.[38] Several years later, writing from Michigan, Henry Richards complained: "Most all the banks in the cuntry is broke & tis hard work to git anay money & what you do git you cannot tell if it is good or not [sic]".[39] In the autumn of 1875 the problem hit closer to home when word reached Cornwall that the Bank of California had suspended business creating "something akin to panic in the neighbourhood of Redruth". Entire life savings had been lost, local traders were in trouble having cashed credit notes, and "a great number of families are well nigh ruined, being dependent upon remittances from California through this channel", reported the *West Briton*.[40]

This uncertainly over when, or if, remittances would come focussed the wives' attention on the arrival of the overseas mail. Mrs White, the postmistress in Pendeen, St Just, recalled how difficult she found doing the delivery rounds on streets where wives and families would be waiting at doors or windows for her, and she felt embarrassed for those she had to disappoint when there was no remittance letter for them.[41]

In the 1890s people would gather at the Post Office in Redruth when the train bringing the Cape Mail bearing remittances from the miners in Africa was due. In nearby St Day, the school's headmaster, Richard Blewett, noted that Monday was "the great day in the week, for the Africa mail comes in".[42] It was estimated that £8,000 to £10,000 a week was then coming into Cornwall's mining district from abroad.[43] At that time the South Africa mail was landed at Southampton, and in 1898 authorities in Cornwall were campaigning to get the mail landed much closer to speed up delivery of the remittances. The Falmouth Chamber of Commerce favoured Falmouth, while the Redruth Board of Guardians petitioned the government for the mail to be landed at Plymouth.[44] These campaigns clearly met with some success as later the mail is described as being offloaded from the ship anchored in Mounts Bay, and taken without delay to the Post Office in Penzance. There all the staff would be assembled, day or night, in order to get the mail sorted and out to the waiting families as quickly as possible.[45] The Redruth Guardians' interest in the matter stemmed from problems caused by delayed remittances, as they often had to deal with the consequences, as we shall see later.

Even if men regularly mailed banker's drafts or money orders home, there was always the risk of their letters being delayed or lost en route. However, there was another, more secure, way in which wives could receive financial support from their husbands' earnings abroad. This was for them to be paid via a trust set up before the husbands departed, or directly by the men's employers. Evidence that some husbands set up arrangements to ensure that their wives received a regular income in their absence is provided by the case of John Chynoweth from St Agnes. Just before he left to work in South America in 1834 John had a document drawn up appointing two of his male neighbours as trustees to pay his wife £2 a month out of the money that he would be sending back to Cornwall.[46] In what may have been a similar arrangement, Jane Ching was allocated a weekly allowance when her husband Richard left as a labourer on the Wakefield expedition to New Zealand in 1841.[47]

Such arrangements were probably quite common, and many companies recruiting men in to work in their mines overseas had formalised systems of home-pay, whereby a proportion of the men's wages was paid directly to their dependents back home. An example of a contractual arrangement whereby the employee's pay was paid partly to him abroad and partly to another party in Cornwall is the agreement signed in 1842 by William Nicholls of Illogan when he took up a three year contract as a miner in Cuba. In an additional clause William requested "that there may be retained in England, out of my salary, the sum of forty-eight pounds annually to be paid in quarterly payments to Messrs M. Williams Jr and Brothers reserving seventy two pounds to be paid to me in Cuba".[48]

It is not known what proportion of wives whose husbands were abroad would have received regular pay via employers' agents within the UK as opposed to that coming in directly from abroad. Home-pay has been largely excluded from discussion about the amount of remittance income coming into Cornwall, primarily due to the paucity of the surviving evidence, which limits any quantitative analysis.[49] Nonetheless, rare surviving documents list some wives who were paid directly this way.

The Real del Monte Mining Company, which employed many Cornishmen in Mexico, operated a compulsory home-pay system for over 20 years until 1847, with payments being made to families in Cornwall from the company's London office.[50] Ledgers detailing these remittances have survived and have been studied by Sharron Schwartz who gives examples in her book on *The Cornish in Latin America*. Many of the men are sons sending money home to help support their parents and siblings, but some can be identified as married men. In June 1883 the *Cornubian* reported that around a hundred Cornish mine workers from Camborne and Pool recruited for mines in Ecuador had contracts that would pay 12 guineas a month, of which a quarter would go to relatives in Cornwall.[51] A further example emerges from a dispute in 1893 between Stephen Jeffery and the Cape Copper Company about a sum he believed to be outstanding from his employment with them in South Africa, during which time his wife in Cornwall was to receive half his pay directly from the company.[52]

Home-pay wasn't confined to employees at mines in Latin America and Africa. Fragmentary records of the monthly remittances made in 1876 for Cornish miners in the northern peninsula of Michigan by the manager of the Central Mine through the UK-based Manchester and County Bank can be found at the Royal Institute of Cornwall.[53] In a list of 27 recipients, mostly female, of the October 1876 remittances, nine can be positively identified from their addresses and the census records as being the wives of the miners sending the money. Of these, four are from St Cleer (Emma Husband and her two sisters-in-law, Cordelia and Mary Short, and Sara Hicks), four from Camborne (Elizabeth J. Bawden, Phillipa Bawden, Elizabeth Ann Carter and Amelia Sincock) and one, Mrs Francis (Eliza) Praed from Marazion. The November list, and the surviving part of the December one, do not give the recipients' addresses, preventing further identifications, but six of the nine wives from the October list appear in all three consecutive months.

There is a degree of consistency in the amounts that the wives are receiving. In October they are listed in pounds sterling and five of the wives were each sent £3 14s 1d, with the remaining wives receiving variable amounts between £2 15s 7d and £4 12s 7d. These 'odd' amounts of pence suggest that this is what the wives actually received after currency conversion from a more 'rounded' amount in dollars. The November and December lists appear to confirm this as the amounts here are given in dollars ranging from $15 to $23, with $20 being the most common remittance; $20 being closely equivalent to £3 14s at the 1876 exchange rate.[54] There is every indication that while these men were working at the Central Mine in Michigan, their wives back in Cornwall were receiving a reliable monthly income.

Money from Abroad

This was certainly what William Arundel Paynter had in mind when he accepted a contract with the Wheal Ellen Mining Company to go to Australia. However, writing to his wife Sophia in Gwennap while he was preparing to set sail in 1859, William was concerned whether the system would work smoothly: "I think I shall feel more comfortable about you when you begin to receive your pay…perhaps you may get a months pay before I leave England whether or not I will see that right or I will not leave". Two weeks later he was able to reassure her: "you will get your money at the end of every month by post office order for Truro post office beginning on the end of March". There are hints that Sophia might have been getting her money more reliably than William as he later complained of not receiving his full pay but reassuringly wrote her: "you need not despair for that they must pay you your money".[55]

The wives who received a proportion of their husband's pay directly from their employers were better insulated against the uncertainties of money supply at the mines abroad and the unreliability of the international postal services. This put them in a much more secure position than those wives who had to rely on remittances posted home by their husbands. Contrast Sophia Paynter's situation described above with that of her contemporary, also from Gwennap, Mary Ann Dower. Mary Ann's husband John left Cornwall in 1865, also to work in Australia, but worked under the tribute system where small groups of miners would contract to work a section of the mine, which was more akin to being self employed and earnings would be reliant on the mineral wealth of the section and the men's skill. As a result, John's remittances to Mary Ann were much more irregular. Having left Cornwall in July, John's first chance to write to her came when he arrived in mid-October but he does not appear to have sent any remittance home until mid-December, five months after he left. Even then he apologises that it was not as much as he had intended, as work was slack. John posted an order for £12 the following March and another for £20 in June, but was disturbed to hear from Mary Ann that neither had arrived. He sent a replacement 'second' order in July but wrote that he did not intend to send any more until he was sure that his remittances were reaching Mary Ann. We have to assume that his letters must have arrived eventually as they were preserved by the family, and in June of that year he sent £60, part of which was intended to repay the family loan that funded his emigration. After that John's remittances appear to become smaller and even more irregular, and his letters refer to being too busy to get to the bank and a run of bad luck.[56] Mary Ann was clearly in a far less secure position than Sophia as John's work abroad was more speculative than William's.

Wives receiving home-pay also had direct contact with their husbands' employers giving them someone to go to if there were problems. It was local agents, like Alfred Jenkin, who dealt directly with the wives and families in Cornwall, liaising with the employer's London offices on how much to pay and to whom. Alfred was very conscious of how dependent the families were on home-pay. In June 1836 he wrote reminding the William Leckie, secretary of the Cobre Mining Company in London: "As the present quarter is nearly ended I shall hope to receive instructions as to the payment of wages in time to prevent the disappointment which has sometimes arisen." It was Alfred who had to deal with any problems:

> *"I have again been applied to by Alice Andrewartha for wages due to her husband respecting which I have heretofore written. Her husband she says, by his letters supposes that she is in regular rect of a portion of his wages. I believe that the poor woman is quite unconvienced [sic] by the delay and I shall be glad to receive authority to relieve her. I suppose that thou canst ascertain speedily what proportion of his wages Andrewartha has been receiving in Cuba."*

One of the issues that worried Alfred was that the advance of wages paid to the men before they left was normally deducted from their first quarter's pay, leaving their families short.

> *"I have in the cases of Jos Thomas, Zacharias Johns, Josuah Gribble, Wm Eden, Jn Pearce, Josiah James & Jos Roberts availed myself of the permission to deduct ½ only of the £10 advanced them out of their first quarters salary, they having left families behind them who I had reason to believe would be distressed had the whole of the advance been deducted and they will not be entitled to receive any more money until after midsummer next".*[57]

Money from Abroad

It is clear from these individual personal histories that wives' experiences of remittances varied widely. Some were sent regular amounts over periods of months or years while their husband appeared relatively settled. For others the money was irregular in both timing and amount, or came from different places as their husbands moved around, all of which would have resulted in financial, and emotional, insecurity. Bernard Deacon's assessment of the situation, that "those women who received regular remittance cheques had never had it so good, while others who did not receive such money had probably never been so miserable",[58] is undoubtedly correct to some extent, but does not fully accommodate the fact that individual circumstances could, and did, change very rapidly if anything affected the husband's ability or willingness to send money home. It is perhaps more apt to say that many wives had never had it so good while the remittances kept coming, but misery might only be a missed or delayed payment away.

3

Making Ends Meet
Work and credit

A society where wives and families in Cornwall were fully maintained by the wages their husbands earned abroad fitted well with the domestic ideal of separate spheres that became increasingly powerful during the 19th century; the wife managing affairs in the home supported by her husband's labour in the world of work outside.[1] However, for working class couples, it was an ideal rather than a true portrait of reality, and most wives would have expected to contribute to the family income.[2] Nevertheless, it was an ideal that families aspired to. One of the motivations for men to leave their wives at home to take up work overseas, and what made it more culturally acceptable, was the Methodist tenet of self-improvement dominant in the mining communities in Cornwall.[3] With self-improvement came upward social mobility, and a wife who didn't need to work but could devote her time to home and family was a badge of success.

This created something of a dilemma for a wife 'left behind'. How was she to contribute to a family strategy that called for accumulating money in order to achieve success whilst adopting a more leisured lifestyle and display of status that demonstrated the family was on its way to that success, all the time being mindful that her income from abroad could be irregular and unreliable? It was a balance that had to be reached by the wives as they strove to make ends meet.

Some opted for, or were forced to find, paid employment. The details in the occupation column of the census returns provide some indication of the types of work the wives did while their husbands were abroad. However, it is accepted that women's employment, especially that of married women, is under-recorded in the census.[4] Being a wife was viewed as the woman's main occupation; hence the entry in the occupation column for the majority of wives with absent husbands is given in terms of their husbands' occupations, e.g. miner's wife. There is rarely a record of any additional work in which she was engaged in order to support herself and her children or to supplement the existing family income. There is no way of knowing how many of the wives with no given occupation had no paid work and were totally reliant on funds from their husbands, and how many were doing paid work outside the home that has gone unrecorded.

Of the wives whose husbands are specifically stated as being abroad in 1851 to 1881 only 6-13% had named employment. Just one of the 178 similarly described wives in 1891 census gave an occupation; Constantine Harry in Breage was recorded as a grocer. A higher proportion of the wives with absent husbands had specified employment between 1851 and 1891: Camborne 15-30%, Gwennap 13-21%, St Agnes 9-18% and St Just 9-24%. This difference may simply be that for the wives whose husbands are stated as being abroad the enumerator has used the space in the occupation column to record that in preference to any note of the wife's work.

Whereas in other industrialised parts of Britain these wives might have found work in mills, there were few opportunities in Cornwall for female factory workers. Nevertheless, a couple of the wives, Priscilla Bartle from Camborne in 1871 and Dorothy Wellington from Camborne in 1881 and 1891, were described as safety fuse or wire workers employed in factories associated with the mining industry.

Although living in predominantly mining areas, and many probably having worked as bal maidens (female surface workers at mines) prior to marriage,[5] very few of the wives are described as having returned to that work. Examples among the wives whose husbands were stated to be abroad in 1861 include Ann Bennetts from Camborne and Tammy Oats from St Just in Penwith, both employed as copper ore dressers, while Elizabeth Mathews from Redruth and Nanny Pooley from Camborne did unspecified mine labour. Work in mines would have been available for much of the period; Elizabeth A. Smith was employed at a tin mine in Redruth in 1881, although is what capacity isn't recorded. However, opportunities lessened as the mining industry became more mechanised, and it was increasingly seen as unsuitable employment for women. This was not due primarily to the hard physical nature of the labour; without modern labour-saving devices, washing and cleaning as laundress or charwoman would also have been physically arduous. The 'rough' and sometimes rowdy work environment was viewed as inappropriate for females, and certainly for wives and mothers whose husbands were engaged in a project to 'better' their families. The same might be said of those wives who worked as agricultural labourers, such as Mary Ann May and Elizabeth Robarts from St Allen in 1861; Mary Ann Trenbath from Marazion in 1871; and Elizabeth Matthews, Mary Stevens and Grace J. Williams who did field work in Ludgvan in 1881.

The majority of occupations recorded among the wives are 'feminine' ones; paid extensions of the normal domestic activities involved with running a home, feeding, clothing and nurturing the family, that were the focus of female education and training.[6] Although a handful had positions as teachers (in 1861 Anna Goldsworthy, Margretta Reynolds and Mary Jane Terrill were all schoolmistresses in Redruth) few women had any formal or extensive education. Those recorded as nurses (eg. Jane Ann Congdon from Liskeard in 1871) would not have been the qualified professionals we know today. For most wives the only skills they had were what they had been taught within the family with the expectation that they would be wives and mothers. For these women there were very limited employment opportunities.

Those with some ability with a needle might find employment making clothing or hats. This was one of the two most common occupation groups among the wives 'left behind'. In 1861 these included dressmakers Mary Dingle, Mary Ann Edwards, Grace Gribble, Mary Harris, Jane Kernick, Eliza Michell, Elizabeth Penrose, Elizabeth Peters, Ann Polkinghorne, Mary Powell, Lovday Rabey, Catherine Stephens, Rebecca Trestrail and Nancy Williams in Redruth alone, with many others listed in other parishes throughout the period. Grace Temby of Redruth was described as a seamstress, while possibly more skilled were tailoresses Eliza Davey and Mary A. Francis (Redruth), Mary Pollard, (Kenwyn), Hannah Rogers (Gwinear) and Louisa Dunstan (Gwennap). Mary Payne did related work in Redruth as a dyer in 1861. At the same time, Elizabeth Benny from Illogan, whose husband was in California, was working as a milliner, as was Susan Job of Redruth. With her husband in Cuba in 1851, Elizabeth Williams specialised in making straw bonnets in Redruth.

The other main occupations among the wives 'left behind' were charring and laundry work. For older women, whose eyesight wasn't as good as it was, needlework may not have been an option, and the only respectable marketable skills that most women had were those connected with housework. Among the charwomen in 1861 were Mary Angove, Grace Chappell, Elizabeth Francis, Patience Hocking, Mary Ann Hocking, Elizabeth Jackson, Eliza Thomas and Rosamond Tippett in Redruth, Mary Gwennap (St Buryan), Philippa Webber (Feock) and Margaret Coakes (Illogan). In 1871 Elizabeth Quiller could be found cleaning in Liskeard and Catherine Williams in Crowan. Jane Richards (Madron), Lavinia Semmens (Ludgvan), Louisa Tinney (St Columb Minor) and Eliza Jane Trinniman (Gwennap) were likewise employed in 1881.

Redruth wives 'left behind' working as laundresses in 1861 included Louisa Carvolth, Elizabeth Clark, Emma Gibson and Elizabeth Stephens, while Eliza Lakeman found similar labour in Madron. In 1871 Mary Kneebone (Marazion) and Sarah Parkyn (Liskeard) were also described as laundresses. That Mary Midling, whose husband had 'gone foreign' (Kenwyn, 1851), Elizabeth Tonkin, (Redruth, 1861) and Elizabeth Penglaze (Redruth, 1871) were recorded as washerwomen may imply a slightly different role or status. Elizabeth Thomas was listed in the Redruth directory of 1866 as a "miner's wife and mangle keeper".

The occupations of charwoman or laundress are usually thought of as being low status and therefore only undertaken as a last resort, hence an association with poverty and distress, but perhaps we should question whether this is viewing the past through modern (and gendered) eyes. Today washing and cleaning (i.e. housework) are seen as necessary chores because there are so many more interesting activities open to us both in employment and in our spare time. The only economic value put on these tasks is how much we would have to pay someone else to do them. As traditionally the vast majority of housework has been done by women as wives and mothers at no monetary cost to the men in society it is not surprising that historians, predominately male, fail to see any value in these activities as occupations. Hence they are viewed as low status, especially as they have connotations of being in service and subserviency.

If, however, we look at these occupations from the viewpoint of the married woman in the 19th century a possibly different picture emerges. We should not forget that before the days of vacuum cleaners and washing machines, washing and cleaning was a lot more complicated, requiring knowledge and use of a wide range of materials and techniques. As this was one of the few areas in which a woman could demonstrate excellence it is not surprising that even in the most humble cottages wives would take pride in their housekeeping. In this context, being paid to do something, albeit hard physical labour, that you know you can do well, and which you do all the time without pay, can be viewed in a more positive light. There may even have been perks in terms of being given cast off clothing, food leftovers, and unwanted or damaged but useable household items, as well as the possible pleasure of being able to see and handle household objects of a quality that you could only aspire to. If today, when there are so many alternatives, there are women who choose to clean other people's houses and do ironing as a way of earning money, for 19th century women who chose to seek employment, working as a charwoman or laundress were obvious, and not necessarily unattractive options. Some could be considered entrepreneurs, and at least one saved a considerable amount of money by setting up as a laundress.[7] Therefore it is questionable whether it should be assumed that an occupation given as charwoman or laundress always equated to financial distress.

Some wives, like Thirzah Harris (Redruth, 1861) were also in various grades of domestic service, from maids to cooks. A job advert for "a steady, respectable woman servant" run in the *Cornishman* in May 1883 stated that a "married woman whose husband is abroad not objected to".[8] Although 'not objected to' in this case, the fact that it is mentioned at all suggests that there may have been some ambivalence within the servant-hiring class about the suitability of these wives for service. (Reservations about the respectability of the wives 'left behind' is a theme we will return to later.)

Domestic service is usually associated with unmarried people, because of the requirement to 'live-in'. This wasn't a problem for wives without

---

WANTED

A STEADY, respectable WOMAN SERVANT; she must be able to cook nicely; a widow or married woman whose husband is abroad not objected to. — Apply at 4 Morrab-terrace, Penzance.

Cornishman, 31 May 1883

young children. Once her son was grown up, Susie Bullock was employed as housekeeper to the same farming family near St Columb Major for at least 20 years while her husband, Richard, became a legend in the American West as 'Deadwood Dick'.[9]

However, even wives with younger children were employed in service if suitable child care could be arranged. Interviewed in 1976, Lillian Harry recalled how her grandmother, Mary Grenfell, a mother of three, worked as a cook in Penzance when her husband, Will, in America failed to send any money home: "She came home once a week to see the children on the Sunday afternoon, have tea with her mother. She would leave Penzance at four o'clock in the afternoon, walk home, and be back again at ten o'clock in the evening."[10] Other 'domestic' work opportunities were as count house women or cooks, like Charlotte Penaluna from St Just in 1861 or Fanny Francis from Camborne in 1891, who provided meals and housekeeping services to the management staff of the mines.[11]

In years of economic depression there were more limited opportunities even for charwomen, for example in 1878, when few could afford their services. "What can these poor women find to do in a place like St Just is now?", asked a guardian. "The times won't permit of people employing others. Each does his or her own work. Very few persons can afford anybody else to 'chur' for them - there are no 'churs' to be done".[12]

A limiting factor on the wives' ability to take up employment was the dispersed nature of Cornish settlements, making access difficult. One miner's wife who had been left by her husband abroad to support four children, had to walk six miles a day to work at a mine, where she earned six shillings a week.[13] However, for many of the wives the main stumbling block was the necessity to find work compatible with looking after children. In November 1898 Angelina Richards, a mother of six who was only receiving irregular small remittances from her husband in Africa, told the Penzance Board of Guardians that: "She could get her living by shop work, but she had her hands full to attend to her children".[14] Occupations, such as sewing, that could be done as piecework at home, or running a small retail business from the front room, were the most practical options.

For those who needed paid work, but could not find any that they could do at home, child care was a major issue. The lucky ones had relatives or neighbours who could help out but some had the stark choice of either not working and so not being able to feed their children, or leaving them alone for long periods. One wife whose husband had gone to South America was described in 1867 as having to leave five of her six young children alone all day in order to earn 5d to 7d a day.[15]

Older children might be kept at home to look after the younger ones, but after the 1870 Education Act there was greater pressure for these babysitters to be in school. One woman facing this problem was a Mrs Maddern who lived with her two children aged seven and five at Boswarthan near Madron.[16] She would give the children breakfast before she had to leave for work at 7am and then lock them in the house all day, leaving something for their dinner as she would not get home until 8pm. If the older child had to go to school the younger would be left alone. In winter the dilemma was made worse. Should she leave them with a fire to keep them warm and risk injury or worse (fatalities among young children unattended with open fires were all too common), or leave them in a freezing house?

There was a proposal in 1879 that a creche might be set up in rural parts of Cornwall to enable women like Mrs Maddern to go out to work,[17] but no record has been found to indicate that this happened. In Australia, where there was a similar issue of men (including Cornishmen) leaving their wives with little support in the cities while they were prospecting for gold in the bush, charitable bodies were wrestling with the same problem of balancing child care with the wives being able to support themselves. In response the Melbourne Ladies Benevolent Society set up a system whereby they would pay one wife with several children to take care of the child of another wife, thereby freeing her to go out to work or take up a post in service.[18] This ingenious approach enabled the charitable ladies to help two families with a single payment. In Cornwall, it appears similar, but informal, reciprocal networks of exchange operated amongst the wives and their extended families in Cornwall.

Within the structural restraints of limited education and child care responsibilities, there was the potential for the wives to exercise an entrepreneurial spirit that would not be apparent from a census entry. Someone described as a laundress might be an overworked skivvy or might be operating a profitable laundry business. Similarly there is wide variation among 'dressmakers', from simple plain sewing to highly skilled embroidery and tailoring. More obvious as businesswomen were those with retail outlets, one of the more common occupations among the wives. Most were grocers or greengrocers. Catherine Bailey brought her children born in New Grenada, South America home to Cornwall and ran a grocers in her birthplace of Towednack (1871) and later Ludgvan (1881) for many years while her husband was in New Zealand. From the census more examples include: in 1861 Grace Hooper (Illogan), Louisa Pearce, Eleanor Rickard and Mary Ann Youren (all in Redruth), Ann P. Pengelly (Phillack) and Elizabeth Tregonning (Gwennap); in 1871 Jane Faul in Liskeard and Olivia Treglown in Marazion; in 1881 Mary Ann Gill (Gwennap), Jane Martin (Ludgvan), Catherine Noall (St Ives), Anna A. Rodda (Gwithian), and in 1891 Mary Ann Berryman, a greengrocer in Penzance. Others like Ann Stevens (St Erth, 1861) found employment as grocers' assistants.

The census does not say what type of goods shopkeeper Jane G. Trethewey was selling in St Dennis in 1861, but as well as grocers, the wives 'left behind' included drapers, bakers and sellers of fancy goods. The attraction of this kind to business is that it could often be carried out from home, using a front room as the shop. Another source of income open to married women that didn't involve working outside the home was keeping a boarding house (e.g. Annie Nicholls, Redruth in 1861) or taking in lodgers (e.g. Elizabeth Eddy, St Just in 1871). During her husband's absence, Eliza Hancock of St Austell was described as a 'managing innkeeper' in 1881, while Mary Veal ran the *Queen's Arms* in Botallack Road in St Just.

Some of these businesses and trades may have been ones run by the husband before he went abroad. This might explain some of the more unlikely business occupations such as 'carpentress' Elizabeth Magor, and Louisa Collins, a cart driver delivering sand and a coal carrier, both in Gwennap. In that parish it is noticeable that the number of these businesses fall sharply between 1861 and 1871 probably because of the crash in the mining industry. It is thought that many local shopkeepers went bankrupt at this time due to miners leaving the country without settling their debts.[19]

In addition, some of the wives are described as fundholders or receiving income from properties and may have had an active role in managing these investments. Ellen Lean (née Gray) is said to have managed her own family's property, Gray's Terrace in Lanner, while her husband, William, worked in Australia and South America throughout the second half of the 19th century. Other wives who had independent incomes while their husbands were abroad include fundholder Mary Hodge (Redruth, 1861), landed proprietor Jemina Stephens (Redruth, 1861), land owner Frances Maria Lemon (Marazion, 1871) and Ann C. Tabb from St Clement in 1871 who was receiving income from residential property.

The census gives no indication of the business level at which these women were operating, although the enterprises of six wives in Camborne were doing well enough for them to be classified as employers in the 1891 census, including baker Louisa Orchard and grocer Jane Vincent. At the same time Jane Tregellas was also employing staff in her grocery business in Gwennap. It is reasonable to suppose that some of these occupations and enterprises could have generated significant incomes, while even small shops and businesses would have produced at least some level of additional support for the family.

Equally we should not lose sight of the notion that some of the wives may have chosen to work more than was financially necessary, that occupations supplied needs beyond simple survival, but could also provide the women with a sense of personal fulfilment, companionship, an escape from household duties, and additional financial independence.

Unfortunately, the details of women entrepreneurs are often only revealed if their businesses ran into difficulties that were reported in the press. One such businesswoman was Mary Vivian. She is listed, aged 37, without her husband in the 1881 census as a draper in Trelowarren Street, Camborne. At that time she had three children aged between three and six years old, and a servant to help out. Mary herself had been abroad, having lived in Norway in the mid-1870s, and her two eldest children had been born there. She had first started business in her husband's name but he went abroad again for four years, not returning until the summer of 1881. He stayed for two years and then departed for America in 1883, leaving her with a further two children. Since then she had been trading in her own name. By the spring of 1886 Mary's drapery business was in trouble; trade was poor and customers were not paying their bills. She could not collect debts owed to her, and she was having to support herself and the children on her own, having not received anything from her husband for the previous two years. Mary found herself fending off trade creditors and named in the press as insolvent.[20] Shortly afterwards she and the children sailed to America to join her husband there.[21]

Another businesswoman was Ethelinda Curnow, who in 1888 was running a beer house while her husband was abroad. A male friend of the husband had been asked to help her when the house was busy, tapping the beer barrels, and so on. However, when he and Mrs Curnow featured in a court case, the judge's immediate assumption was that it was the male friend that had been left in charge not only of the beer house but of Ethelinda as well. Despite this, it was Ethelinda who was charged with selling alcohol to a drunk customer.[22]

The discovery that some of the wives 'left behind' in Cornwall were trading in their own right accords with the findings of other researchers that married women were far more active as businesswomen in the 19th century than traditional interpretations of the way coverture worked would suggest.[23] Coverture defined the legal status of a married woman as being under the protection and authority of her husband to the extent that she had no separate legal identity, and was unable to enter into legal contracts or exercise control of real or personal property. In practice, coverture may have been less of a restraint than previously thought, as discussed by Joanne Bailey in her work on early modern marriage.[24] Nicola Phillips has drawn attention to the ways in which common law could be interpreted to circumnavigate the strictures of coverture, and thereby adapt to accommodate social change and, by implication, specific situations such as the physical absence of husbands.[25] The divergence between coverture in theory and in practice is also highlighted by Helen Doe's study of businesswomen in the 19th century shipping industry, which reveals married women routinely carrying out transactions that should have been illegal under the rules of coverture.[26]

The participation of married women in trade in Cornwall is surely worthy of further research, especially if male absence through emigration created different conditions there than elsewhere. In addition, these studies illustrate the divergence in the operation of coverture *de jure* and *de facto* (in theory as opposed to reality), suggesting that married women had more financial independence than previously assumed.

This appears true even for wives without business interests. Josephine Maltby has found evidence of working-class wives in the north of England operating their own savings bank accounts independently of their husbands before the 1870 Married Women's Property Act gave them ownership of their own money.[27] References have been found to wives 'left behind' in Cornwall opening savings accounts in their own names, but only after 1870. In 1882 legal advice was sought in the case of an unnamed but "obstinate wife" who had been saving money sent home by her husband in America and had accumulated £260 in an account at the West Cornwall Bank in her own name. Upon the husband's return she had refused to hand over the money, the deposit notes, or let him deal with it in any way, leaving the lawyers puzzling over whether the bank could pay the money to the husband without being sued by the wife.[28] Whether the wife was acting in the family's best interests or her own in this case is not known. By comparison, Rosalie Jane Wills, described as a "cunning and ungrateful wife" used the money sent home by her husband, Thomas, to buy a house as he had instructed, but did so in her own name, subsequently mortgaging it, separating from her husband and going abroad herself with the proceeds.[29]

Although unrepresentative, such stories circulated amongst the men abroad, stoking concerns as to what their wives were doing with the money they sent home. Joseph Tucker found out in 1898 that his wife Amelia had been putting some of the money he had sent home into a Co-op savings account in her own name. He likened her actions to that of a wife of another miner in South Africa who had done likewise, and on his return "refused to let him have a shilling".[30] As a result Joseph became increasingly mistrustful of Amelia, writing to the couple's son:

> "I will say right here that I am suspicious of every move your mother do make after doing what she did and after she tried so hard to get me to sell the house and buy a larger one while I was out here before. It was only to try to get the house in her name."

However, it is evident even from Joseph's grumbling letters that Amelia put aside the money for the family, not for herself; the only surviving fragment of a letter from Amelia is a detailed accounting of her expenditure on household bills and shoes for the children. Joseph's real issue was with Amelia's act of independence and lack of deference to him.

On the other hand wives would have been aware of cases that would have motivated an understandable desire to place at least some funds beyond their husband's control. Prior to the 1870 Married Women's Property Act wives had no protection against a husband who returned, took any savings or property she had accumulated through her own efforts during his absence, and left the country again. Even after that date the law did not offer complete security. The husband of innkeeper Elizabeth James of the *Tolcarne* in Newlyn, who had deserted her several years previously after selling her out and leaving with £29, returned only to order her out of the house, sell everything again and depart once more with the proceeds.[31] One wife, Mrs Hocking (née Redford) from St Ives, found herself in Madron workhouse in 1892 after her husband in America deserted her having spent the £300 she brought to the marriage.[32] The husband of another wife from Roseworthy in Camborne departed for Africa with his mine pay and one halfpenny that she had.[33]

Cases such as these in the newspapers, however, should not be seen as representative of widespread marital mistrust. Less visible in the historical record are the couples such as the Tregonnings who had a joint account at the Bolitho Consolidated Bank in Redruth and had a power of attorney drawn up in 1900 that enabled the wife Elizabeth to access the account while her husband William Thomas was working in South Africa.[34]

It has been argued that many of the wives 'left behind' would have been empowered by their role as decision makers and financial managers in their husband's absence.[35] However, regardless of whether their husbands were at home or abroad, it was normal for wives to manage the household budget, and 19th century Cornwall, it has been suggested, was probably less patriarchal than other places.[36] If the wives normally controlled the day-to-day housekeeping it is hard to see how control of how the money sent home was spent gave the wife any additional freedom.

What is more, there were constraints to any potential financial liberation. Kathryn Gleadle has pointed out the paradox in women's role as financial managers, as it was "at striking variance with their position (until 1882) under common law, which technically denied married women an economic role".[37] In addition, it was the men who controlled how much money was sent home. With face-to-face contact the wife could negotiate the amount she received, but that was far more difficult, if not impossible, with the husband abroad. Distance put control of how much money the wives had access to firmly in their husbands' hands meaning that the wives 'left behind' had less financial autonomy.[38]

The wives' productive work did not always involve waged transactions. There was an established tradition among the largely rural Cornish mining communities of supplementing the family food and fuel needs with the produce of smallholdings, allotments and customary rights to cut furze or turf.[39] This additional subsistence farming was an important element in the family economy and one for which the wives often took responsibility, especially in their husbands' absence.[40] Whereas no references have come to light regarding wives in paid employment in the emigrant letters examined, an example has been found of an exchange about the management of the family plot. John Dower writing in October 1865 from Australia to his wife Mary Ann in Gwennap hopes that she and her brother had bought a pig as they had discussed, and wonders how she is getting on with her potatoes.[41]

The importance of the family plot went beyond subsidising the family diet. In her study of home ownership and subsistence in West Cornwall, Damaris Rose argued that it was integral to the whole life enterprise, describing the smallholding miner's household as being "at least in part" a peasant one, with the food products derived from the plot contributing to nearly half the family's requirements.[42] Smallholdings gave mining families a form of independent support free from the uncertainties and fluctuations of mine earnings, and provided a cushion to 'fall back on' if the main breadwinner was unable to work through injury or ill health, and in retirement. However, to set themselves up with the security of a cottage and few acres of land required investment and, working in a dangerous occupation, miners found it difficult to raise funds through mortgages. This, Rose has suggested, "made miners particularly inclined to seek opportunities for fairly large lump-sum earnings over a short period"; exactly the type of opportunity offered by time spent working abroad either as a well-paid contractor or speculative gold digger. Therefore the smallholding tradition amongst the Cornish mining communities can be seen as both motivating and facilitating temporary labour migration of the men; husbands could leave Cornwall for high wages abroad in the knowledge that their wives and children would maintain, and be partially supported by, the family's 'investment' in a smallholding at home. In addition to the handful of the wives described as farm labourers and similar in the census mentioned earlier, some were running their own farms. Mary Nicholls had a modest four acres in Gulval in 1881, but Ann James was managing 50 acres in St Just in 1861. In 1891 Rebecca Tiddy and Martha Chynoweth ran farms in St Agnes substantial enough for them to be to be classified as employers.

There are direct similarities here with the wives 'left behind' in other parts of Europe. In northern Portugal the 'widows of the living' maintained similar family plots while their husbands worked overseas.[43] Whereas agriculture there was traditionally seen as women's work, in Auvergne, France emigration of the men resulted in changes in working practices with the wives becoming more involved in working the land.[44] By contrast, the wives in Sicily whose menfolk were abroad, the 'widows in white', avoided agricultural work as to be seen labouring in the fields brought dishonour to themselves and the family, and was at odds with the migration project's aim of raising the family's status.[45] Amongst Cornish transnational families there also is evidence of a tension between the needs of the family economy and the desire to display success by emulating the perceived status of the domestic ideal.[46] Although John Dower, as noted above, showed an interest in his wife's management of the family plot, he also wrote to her: "I would much rather you were at the Tea meeting than tilling potatoes".[47] Therefore, the under-reporting of married women's occupations in the census may also be explained by attempts to preserve family pride and unity, with the wife loyally presenting to the outside world, as represented by the enumerator, an ideal of her absent spouse as such a good provider and husband that she had no need to work.

The wide range of occupations, from menial jobs to running businesses, that are given for the wives in the census, together with the evidence for unpaid work in running smallholdings, suggest that many of them were determined to take a very active and visible role in making the best of their situation, using their skills and drive to help support themselves and their families. For most this involved making ends meet through various combinations of different income streams: remittances, employment (of herself and/or her children), rent from lodgers, and/or profits from businesses and investments, depending on individual circumstances. In cases where income failed to meet needs, some wives were said to have turned to prostitution.[48] Redruth, a parish that had particularly high numbers of wives 'left behind', is also said to have had the biggest prostitution problem in Cornwall in the 1860s and 1870s.[49] However, any direct association with the wives of emigrant miners is unproven and would require further research.

It is clear that many of the wives smoothed out their finances by obtaining goods on credit, which was often essential to tide them over between remittances. Without credit few wives would be able to make ends meet even if the husband was in work and earning a sufficient wage. This is illustrated by the case of an unnamed woman with four children from Park Bottom who had to turn to the Redruth Board of Guardians in March 1891. Her husband was only getting board where he worked in Colorado and she could not cash his pay cheques until July. He had told her to 'get trust' from a shop in the meanwhile, but she was having some difficulty in getting credit and had to be helped with a loan from the poor law guardians.[50] Discussing the case of another unnamed wife who had not received sufficient funds from her husband in Montana, the Redruth guardians debated whether she could get credit at the shop for a little longer but decided that it might be difficult "as, doubtless, there were nest-eggs at the various shops".[51] In the depression years of the late 1860s shopkeepers in St Just were reported to have trusted some families with £30 to £60 of credit in hope of remittances that had not arrived. This put the shopkeepers themselves in a precarious financial position.[52]

The principle of coverture that made a husband responsible for his wife's debts presented a dilemma for traders owed money; the person that they could hold to account for the debt, the husband, was out of the country and could not be brought to court, while the person they could get into court, the wife, could deny liability and frequently had no means to pay what was owed. This is illustrated by Samuel Drew's attempt to sue Ellen Rogers in Redruth County Court in July 1897. The case was dismissed without costs because she "pleaded 'no means' as her husband being abroad and earning nothing".[53] Similarly, when in March 1885

Making Ends Meet

William Turner & Sons, builders of Camborne, claimed possession of a cottage, garden and premises in Camborne occupied by Mary Ann Harvey, whose husband was abroad, the judge ruled that the claim should have been made against the husband not the wife.[54]

This was another reason why the wives' management of finances while their spouses were away became contentious, as husbands were sometimes met with nasty surprises upon their arrival in Cornwall. In 1855, five days after returning from working in Cuba and America for four years, Richard Trethewy from Tuckingmill near Camborne was arrested for debts his wife had run up in his absence when the remittances he had sent home were insufficient to maintain the family.[55] The wife of Gwennap miner Samuel Richards had accrued so much debt with the local grocer while her husband worked in Chile that he was bankrupted.[56]

In 1895 John Bawden found himself being sued for goods supplied to his wife while he was in Africa, despite the fact that he had sent regular remittances and instructed her not to go into debt. The judge told him that he should have announced that he would not be responsible for her debts if he did not want tradesmen to extend her credit.[57] The accepted way of doing this was to place an advert in the local press and such notices appeared regularly in the Cornish newspapers.[58]

Several examples appeared in the *West Briton* in 1856 alone. Benjamin Rule, a miner in Pachuca advertised that he "would not be answerable" for any debts that his wife Elisa in Camborne might contract after 10 July 1856. Richard Magor in South Australia placed a similar advert concerning his wife Jecoliah in Gwennap, as did James Martin employed in the Pentworth Gold Mine, Australia, cautioning the public against trusting his wife Elizabeth Martin of Lelant as he would not be answerable for any debt contracted by her after this notice. Likewise, James Vivian a mason working in Brazil refused to be responsible for any debts of his wife Martha back in Redruth, while William Henry Burrows residing in Chile took steps to protect himself debts incurred by his wife, Elizabeth Ann Burrows.[59] Similar notices continued to appear in the pages of the local press. In 1862 Jane Andrew of Wendron must have been humiliated to see the notice her husband James placed from the Cobre Mines in Cuba appear in the *West Briton*, sandwiched between an appeal for a lost beagle hound and a call for creditors to a deceased's estate.[60]

PUBLIC NOTICES
[Examples extracted from the *West Briton*]

I, BENJAMIN RULE, Miner, Pachuca, Mexico, Hereby Give Notice that I will not be answerable for any debts my wife ELISA RULE, of Camborne, may contract after this notice. (signed) Benjamin Rule.
(Witness) THOMAS BAWDEN. Dated Pachuca, Mexico, July 10th, 1856.

I, JAMES ANDREW, Cobre Mines, Cuba, hereby give Notice that I will not be answerable for any Debts my wife, Jane Andrew, of Wendron, many contract after this notice.   JAMES ANDREW.
February 7th, 1862

I HEREBY GIVE NOTICE that I will not be answerable for any Debt or Debts which my wife, MARIA HARRIS may contract after this date.
(signed)   RICHARD HARRIS.
Dated Checo Mines, Chili, March 6, 1862.

I Hereby give notice that I will not be answerable for any debt or debts that my wife, Ann Nicholls, may contract after this date.
(signed)   THOMAS NICHOLLS.
Dated Tocopilla Mines, Bolivia July 28th, 1862

I HEREBY GIVE NOTICE that I WILL NOT be ANSWERABLE for any DEBT or DEBTS my wife, EMILY JANE SIMS, of Carnon Downs, near Devoran, may contract after this date.
WILLIAM TAYLOR.
Witness - WILLIAM HENRY COLLINS.
Port Nolloth, Cape of Good Hope, February 20th, 1873.

THIS IS TO GIVE NOTICE, that I CHRISTOPHER BENNETT, late of Camborne, but now of Colorado, America, will NOT be ANSWERABLE for any DEBT or DEBTS that my wife, FRANCES MARY BENNETT, of Camborne, may contract after this notice.
March 11th, 1874.

I, the undersigned, will NOT be ANSWERABLE for any DEBTS my wife, FANNY BAWDEN, living in St. Day, may contract after this notice.
(signed)   JOHN BAWDEN, Chili.
[published 17 September 1874]

I, CHARLES H. ELLIS, will not be answerable for any DEBTs that my Wife, ELIZABETH ELLIS, may contract after this date, April 23rd, 1879.
Signed, CHARLES H. ELLIS,
Bald Mountain, Gilpin County, Colorado.

Notices like these were also placed as a result of marriage breakdown, but some were clearly attempts to control the wife's spending while the husband was abroad. For example, in 1858 James May advertised that he would not be answerable for any debts which his wife Elizabeth May in St Ewe might contract during his absence in Australia because, "A competent allowance is regularly paid to her".[61] As mine engineer James was back living with Elizabeth in St Ewe in 1861, there is no reason to believe that this was part of a formal settlement following a failed marriage.

However, such notices did not relieve the husbands of all liability. As a judge in Kent ruled in 1870: "With respect to the insertion of an advertisement, that only protected a husband from a wife pledging his credit for what were extravagancies, but it did not by any means relieve him from his liability in respect to what were necessaries".[62] Necessaries as defined by law included lodging, food, clothing, medicines, education for any children and comfort appropriate for the family's station in life.

In court tradesmen and their lawyers argued that the goods supplied were necessities to strengthen their cases against husbands. However, Judge Granger in the Bawden case above identified a problem: "a woman might waste her husband's money on dress or pleasure, and he would be saddled with the burden of paying bills for necessaries for his family".[63] Granger "admitted that in a county like Cornwall, from which so many people emigrate, the law may act harshly". He could only suggest that shopkeepers ought to make a prior arrangement. "At all events it would be monstrous for a man to send home a maintenance for his wife and then come home and find himself loaded with debt".

Judge Granger's belief that unscrupulous wives would spend remittances frivolously on non-essentials and then pledge their husband's credit for necessaries,[64] was reinforced by another case that came before him a few months after the Bawden hearing. Arthur Hodge, a mining engineer recently returned from America, was being sued over his wife Elizabeth's debt with a local butcher. It was revealed in court that Elizabeth had also spent £14 with a shoe dealer in just three months on many 'gaieties', including pink, yellow and white slippers and shoes from Paris.[65] Elizabeth was decried as a 'traitor' in her husband's house, and Granger again recommended that if husbands were going away, they should warn tradesmen against giving credit to their wives. Granger's view was that: "if the husband made proper provision for his wife's maintenance, and forbade her to pledge his credit, he was not liable for any debts she might contract".[66] However, rulings that such debts should be paid by the wife out of her own funds were of little consolation to traders owed money. As one lawyer retorted in frustration: "But she has none. These women with husbands abroad are dependent upon them for support."[67]

The publicity given to such cases fuelled husbands' suspicions of the wives' motives and competence in handling the money they sent home, and helped create or bolster a perception of the wives as wasteful spendaholics. St Day headmaster Richard Blewett described:

> "Wives, hitherto used to a domestic economy based upon a pound a week or less, suddenly blazing in the glory of £20-30 a month. A Bank Draft headed with the magic words 'Standard Bank of South Africa'... miserly saving or mad spending: new furniture, a piano and all the children learning music... Methodist Chapels a tournament of fashion... ostrich plumes floating from head and neck, gold mounted lions' claw broaches..."[68]

However, there may have been more to these conspicuous displays of wealth than mad frivolity. The standard to which his wife and children dressed and lived in Cornwall was an indicator of how well the husband was doing abroad, and no-one wanted to be judged a failure, especially compared with migrant neighbours who had returned with new wealth. This introduced an element of competitive consumerism in the mining communities that fuelled spending, and probably debt, with some wives and families having unrealistic expectations of what their menfolk abroad could supply.[69] As the 'necessities' that a wife could legitimately charge to her husband's account were expected to reflect the couple's station in life, she might feel justified in purchasing fine clothes and other goods as necessary to demonstrate her husband's success and the family's improving social status.

While husbands going away were advised to caution tradesmen against extending credit to their wives,[70] the press warned tradesmen not to trust wives who appeared to get ample money from husbands.[71] It was suggested that shopkeepers should check in advance with the post office whether the husbands of wives asking for credit were sending money home regularly.[72] Faced with difficulties in getting debts settled and warnings about their potential un-creditworthiness, tradesmen and shopkeepers were sometimes understandably reluctant to give the credit that for some wives was an essential component in making ends meet.

This highlights the practical problems caused by the tension between the principle of coverture and the realities of increasing numbers of couples in Cornwall united in marriage but separated by long-distance migration. Coverture, based on the 'legal fiction' that a married couple were a single unit,[73] assumed the couple would be in close proximity and to function relied on the presence of the legally responsible spouse. Integral to coverture was that, although the wife had few rights, she also was relieved of legal responsibility for maintaining herself. But without the husbands being available to take that responsibility, there was a risk that tradesmen and landlords would be reluctant to do business with the wives. This had the potential to interfere with the smooth functioning of society within Cornwall. Judge Granger appears to have recognised this in dealing with Elizabeth Treglown of Camborne's defence that it was her husband, abroad for seven years, who should be held liable for unpaid rent as she, as a wife, had no separate estate. Finding against Elizabeth, the judge explained: "If I were to hold a married woman irresponsible under such circumstances nobody would let a house to a married woman".[74]

Thus it can be argued that legal interpretations of coverture were influenced by the increase in the type of transnational marriage that became so common in 19th century Cornwall. A similar pragmatic approach is also shown in the responses of Cornish poor law officers when, for whatever reason, the wives could not make ends meet and turned to them for help, which is the focus of a later chapter. However, miners and their families are reputed to have been reluctant users of the poor laws, relying more on support from family and community.[75]

4
'If You Can Accord'
Support from family and community

Although some wives had access to independent forms of support such as their own employment, smallholdings or investments, it is doubtful that many would have been able to maintain themselves and their children completely without the remittances sent home by their husbands. When those remittances were insufficient, delayed, intermittent or ceased completely, for whatever reason, if they had not managed to put aside some savings to tide them over, the wives would have had to turn to others for help. However, the assistance needed by the wives 'left behind' was not only financial, and this chapter also explores the practical and emotional support available to them from relatives, friends and neighbours.

The first port of call for a wife needing help was usually family. Cornish families are often portrayed as being particularly close and supportive.[1] This has been ascribed to a combination of factors. The peninsular and rural nature of Cornwall provides the conditions for a separateness from neighbouring parts of England that fosters greater internal connectivity and a strong cultural identity, while the historical main occupations of mining, fishing and farming are all ones seen as not merely ways of earning a living but as 'ways of life' that were based on co-operation within the extended family. In addition, the high male death rates associated with both mining and fishing are recognised as drawing the women of the family and community into their own mutually supporting networks.[2]

Bernard Deacon has posed the question as to whether migration, including the phenomenon of spousal separation, led to a greater reliance on kin, inferring that it might logically have been expected to do so.[3] Certainly there are examples where help from family members proved crucial in enabling women to manage in the absence of their husbands. Jane, wife of the renowned mining engineer Richard Trevithick, was almost entirely supported by her brother Henry Harvey when her husband in Peru failed to provide her and their six children with any income for eleven years. As Trevithick's friend, Davis Gilbert, complained in a letter to him about his negligence, "their very support and maintenance has been owing to the kindness of Mr Harvey". Henry not only paid his brother-in-law's debts, he provided Jane with a degree of independence by giving her charge of the *White Hart Hotel*, which provided hospitality for important visitors to the family-run Harvey's foundry in Hayle. He also assisted the family by being an active father figure to the Trevithick children, treating his extended family "with love and responsibility".[4] Jane's case, however, is somewhat unusual, both in that this amount of detail (albeit still limited) is known about her life while her husband was away, and because Henry was a wealthy, and rather unconventional, man who could afford to be generous. As well as caring for the six Trevithick children and another six orphaned by the death of his sister, Henry was father to his own nine children by his mistress Grace Tonkin, in all supporting a total of 21 children.

It seems likely that neglected wives in other families received similar help but details are sparse. The census returns provide very little hard evidence of financial support from family members other than husbands. The 1861 census reveals that Elizabeth Blamey of Gwennap and her children were being supported by her son as well as her husband abroad, while Elizabeth Bennetts, Elizabeth Richards and Mary A. Phillips, also from Gwennap, were in receipt of income from unspecified relatives abroad. Jane Reed was being supported by her father, with whom she lived in the same parish. References to support from family members also appeared in the local press. Mary Ann Carlyon was sent money from her brother abroad when her husband failed to do so,[5] and from a court case in August 1895 it is known that Catherine May, whose husband, Elijah, had gone to America eight years previously, was dependent on her brother for support. Her father, John Honey of Germoe, was found liable for the money she owed a local shopkeeper.[6] In the close-knit mining communities of Cornwall, where many families were inter-related, it is often difficult to distinguish between family and community help. In 1892 Rev Harry Oxland, a Redruth guardian, pointed out that: "In Illogan there are people earning 15s a week who not only gladly pay the rates to help support these deserted families but also give them money out of their pocket in direct assistance".[7]

Much of the financial, practical and collateral help given by families to wives struggling to manage is unlikely to have left much trace in the historical record. An exception, however, is where families provided accommodation for the women. Co-residence of this nature, creating extended or multiple family households (i.e. containing more than one nuclear family), is a visible expression of family co-operation that can be quantified from the census returns. Described as the 'collapsing' or 'huddling' of households, this is recognised as a common response of families faced with economic problems.[8] The financial motive is illustrated by an 1867 report from St Just that: "Mothers and children have joined families, so that 8 to 11 people are found in a three-roomed house. This is to save the rent."[9]

The proportion of Cornish households containing extended families has been shown to have increased following crises in the mining industry. In the parish of Tywardreath, for example, the number of households containing three generations doubled between 1851 (7%) and 1881 (14%). Camborne saw a similar doubling in just the ten years from 1861 to 1871. Combining the figures from Camborne with those from Redruth and St Just, a little under 21% of households contained co-resident kin in 1871. By 1881 a quarter of all households in most registration districts in West Cornwall comprised extended families (compared with the national average for England of 18%).[10] Because it has been observed in some studies that most of the collapsed households contained wives with absent husbands, the increase in their number has been directly associated by some with an increasing number of wives co-residing with relatives. The tendency, it has been suggested by Mark Brayshay in his studies of household composition in West Cornwall, was for deserted wives and their families to move in with parents, grandparents or other close relatives.

However, as we will see, there are several problems with this assertion. One concerns the methods used to arrive at these figures, which rely on accurately identifying the relationships between individuals in a household. Another is the question of whether the households analysed are representative of all those in the parish. On the first point, experience from following the life stories of many hundreds of wives 'left behind' indicates that without detailed family reconstruction it is impossible to be sure that individuals recorded in the census as lodgers (and sometimes servants) were not actually relatives; it is noticeable that the smallest proportion of co-resident relatives coincides in 1861 with the highest proportion of lodgers. Married daughters, granddaughters, mothers, sisters and nieces with absent husbands can all to be found in the census living in the homes of relatives where they have no stated relationship to the head of household.

On the second point, it also seems likely that the households selected for some studies may not have reflected what was really going on in the parish. As analysing the census can be very labour intensive (even more so in the past when the figures above were produced) a common research practice is to take a 10% sample i.e. examine every tenth household schedule. This works fine as long as the different types of people you are interested in are evenly distributed across the parish. In reality, people tend to cluster in certain districts according to class or occupation; there are rich and poor streets. It has come to light that the wives 'left behind' were frequently clustered in certain streets or parts of a parish, and the impact of these clusters would have been missed by examining only every tenth schedule. An example is the dwellings in Redruth known in 1861 as the Old Work House where 11 out of 19 heads of household were wives with husbands abroad. This is an extreme case, probably due to the nature of the accommodation, but other clusters are found in streets without associations with charitable housing.

By contrast, more recent research has benefited from the availability of census returns covering a longer timespan, and in a form that can be analysed by more sophisticated computer software to examine a much larger proportion of the Cornish population as whole parishes or the entire population.[11] This has enabled the household composition to be analysed for all the wives in Cornwall whose husbands are recorded as having been abroad in the census, as well as all those wives with absent husbands in selected sample parishes, two of which (Camborne and St Just) featured in the studies mentioned above.

This most recent analysis of the census reveals that the majority of wives 'left behind' were living in their own households. Among the wives with husbands explicitly stated to be abroad this proportion is remarkably consistent across the whole period 1851-1891 ranging from 77 to 82%. The wives with absent husbands in the individual parishes of Camborne, Gwennap, St Agnes and St Just produced similar, albeit more variable, results, with in a minimum of 59%, and frequently over 70% of the wives 'left behind' living in their own households. This belies the image of these being 'deserted' wives reliant on the charity of family for their accommodation.

It was unusual for the married women heading their own households to be living alone, regardless of whether their husbands were definitely stated as abroad or simply absent. The majority had their own children living with them, while an additional number had extra individuals in the household, often identified as relatives. However, it is not always possible to distinguish between relatives and non-relatives as some blood relationships are hidden by census descriptions of relatives as lodgers, boarders and even servants and employees.

There is a perception that it was common for the wives to take in lodgers or boarders in order to raise additional income while their husbands were away,[12] but this does not seem as widespread as supposed. Analysis of the census shows that a generally low proportion of the wives with absent husbands in Cornwall had done so (less than 6% in most census years) but reveals a clear peak of 10% or more in either 1851 and/or 1861. Camborne also exhibited a higher percentage in 1891. This is a similar pattern to that for the numbers of wives apparently lodging themselves, which might indicate a greater lodging culture in those years, but might simply reflect a possible artefact of changes in census recording. The social consequences of the wives taking in lodgers, and why they might have been deterred from doing so, is discussed in a later chapter.

There is no indication of an increase in the proportion of wives with husbands stated as being abroad in the census giving up their homes to move in with relatives during this period, although there was a peak in the actual numbers in 1861 that corresponds with the peak in the number of husbands recorded as abroad in that census. Similarly, looking at all the women whose husbands were absent in the parishes of Camborne, Gwennap, St Agnes and St Just, there is no notable increase in the proportion of wives not heading their own households. On the contrary, other than the very small rise in St Agnes, the percentage of wives living with others falls or remains steady in all the parishes between 1851 and 1871. In Camborne, although the proportions co-residing changed little, there was a large increase in the actual numbers of wives not living in their own households between 1851 and 1871 (from 44 to 132) and less so in St Just (from 25 to 41) but this reflects the increasing numbers of households in these parishes over this period. So it is true that increasing numbers of wives with absent husbands from these parishes were living with relatives between 1851 and 1871, but not that an increasing proportion of the wives were forced to move in with relatives over that period. Therefore the increasing number of extended or collapsed households can partially be attributed to wives 'left behind' co-residing with relatives, but this is simply reflecting the increased numbers of such women. There is no evidence to suggest that any greater proportion of them found it necessary or desirable to give up their own homes between 1851 and 1871.

There are greater differences between the parishes in the following years to 1891, with a slight increase in St Agnes, a fall in Camborne, while numbers fluctuate in St Just, and remain constant in Gwennap. This variation may reflect the differences in the economy and housing stock at local level. Factors such as the size and affordability of accommodation and availability of employment opportunities are likely to have affected whether or not a wife maintained her own household. Most traditional miners' cottages, whether rural or in the more urban terraces known as rows, were too small to house a large extended family without overcrowding. Perversely this could mean that the slightly better off families dwelling in larger houses (whether rural farmhouses or urban villas) might have been more likely to be living as extended or multiple families than their poorer counterparts.

Those wives who lived in the more prosperous and populated towns would be better able to earn enough to maintain an independent household than those in the smaller rural communities. As the work available to many of the wives was of a domestic nature, as charwomen or laundresses, they could only earn money if there were enough people able to pay for their services. Unlike their husbands, the wives, especially if they had children, had far fewer options. Not only were they limited in the types of work they could do but also in their mobility to find it. These mothers would have to weigh up the benefits of moving to somewhere with better work opportunities against the loss of their familiar family support and child care networks that enabled them to be able to work outside the home in the first place. Similarly, as we have seen, some wives were able to take up positions in domestic service that required them to 'live in' away from home by arranging for their children to live with grandparents or other relatives.

The complexity of these interacting factors makes it impossible to find an unambiguous direct association between household collapse or huddling and the economic position of the wives. Only around a third of those whose husbands were absent (and a fifth of those whose husbands were recorded as being abroad in the census) were living in the households of others, and there was no significant increase in the proportion opting to move in with relatives despite economic decline in Cornwall.

Of those wives who were, for whatever reason, not living in their own home more than half (55-69% of those with husbands explicitly stated to be abroad) were living either with one or both parents. If living with just one parent it was far more likely to be the mother than the father; of the 'husbands explicitly abroad' group 28-47% were in their mother's household with no more than 6% living with their father. There is some indication that the proportion of wives living with their mothers appears to rise decade by decade between 1861 and 1891, while the proportion living with both parents falls over a similar period. Generally, a similar picture emerges for all the wives with absent husbands in Camborne, Gwennap, St Agnes and St Just.[13] The tendency for the wives to be living with their mother rather than their father reflects the large number of female-headed households in the community. With reduced longevity in the male population engaged in mining, the mothers were more likely than the fathers to have still been alive. In each of the census years 1851-1891 there are only around 3,000-3,500 male widower heads of household in Cornwall compared with 9,000-12,000 female widowed heads.

Establishing the status of some the wives who were enumerated in the census without their husbands in households other than their own is, however, problematic. If a wife was not in the parental home, the next more common scenario found was where there was no indication of any family relationship between the wife and the head of household. As with the situation of wives living in their own households, the absence of a specified relationship doesn't mean the individuals were not related. Those recorded as visitors were sometimes just that, with husbands to be found at their own home elsewhere in Cornwall. However, closer inspection reveals that some 'visitors' as well as 'lodgers / boarders' were in fact married daughters of the head of household staying with the family while their husbands were abroad. Similarly it is not possible to establish whether a married woman described as 'mother' or 'sister' to the head of household had moved in or was merely visiting. Therefore hidden within this group are an unknown number of family relationships of varying degrees of closeness.

In 1881 in St Blazey Christiana Clemence and her small son were staying in the house of a Christiana Trewen. The relationship between the two women was not given in the census, but other sources revealed that the two Christianas were in fact niece and aunt. Christiana Clemence and her son are described in the census as being "under sailing orders for Africa" so her stay with her aunt may have been a temporary measure between giving up her own home in preparation for her emigration and her departure.

Lodging could be a short-term solution rather than a long-term necessity. For example, Honor Tyacke Pope maintained her own home in Breage while her husband was away in 1881 and shared it with her married daughter whose husband was also away. After the daughter remarried Honor could be found in 1891 boarding at a hotel in Helston, before her husband returned and they moved back to Breage.

Much smaller proportions of the wives were found in the homes of siblings, adult children or other known relatives. Very few were living with their husband's parents or relatives before 1891. There are, however, some problems regarding the relationships within this group as it is not always possible to determine without detailed research whether a married woman in a parental household is a daughter or daughter-in-law. If she has the same surname this would normally suggest that she is the wife of a son. However, cases have been encountered where a married daughter was enumerated under her maiden name. This could be the head of household's mistake or a copying error by the enumerator, but it has also been stated that some Cornish wives continued to be known by their maiden names after marriage.[14] I have found little evidence of this in my research, other than when married daughters were living with a parent. It is possible that the practice arose in these cases because, in the absence of a husband or establishment of an independent household, the wife's identity as a member of her birth family persisted within the community; her transformation from her father's daughter to her husband's wife was incomplete.

The reason suggested by Brayshay for the wives to be living in a relative's household was that they were unable to afford their own accommodation. This places the phenomenon firmly in the context of the wives being in receipt of charitable help from their family. "The willingness of the Cornish to take in their needy relatives during this crisis is certainly remarkable", he notes, and although acknowledging that household collapse or huddling has been observed elsewhere as a means of deriving mutual benefit, states that "in the Cornish case it is not easy to see the advantages which might be afforded to the welcoming household".[15]

However, this is failing to consider the family as a whole. The remittances of married men working abroad were not just supporting wives and children, but in many cases contributing to the maintenance of elderly parents, and especially the large numbers of widowed mothers. Therefore decisions about living arrangements should be seen in the light of the wider family economy. A clear illustration of this is given in the correspondence between Joel Eade and his wife, Mary. In February 1864 Joel wrote from Michigan to Mary back in Cornwall, responding to the question of her going to live with his mother. "I think it is best for you to go to live with mother", he wrote: "if you think you can accord. It will stop one of the house rents for I think it must be hard for mother to raise the house rent by herself".[16] Joel is clearly thinking in terms of the overall saving benefit to his wider family, not only his wife.

Regardless of any financial gain or savings, combining households would have had other mutual benefits. It is noticeable that those women with children are more likely than those without to have additional relatives or non-relatives living with them. It may well be than the advantages of having another pair of hands to assist with child care and the greater burden of household chores would have made these individuals welcome additions to the household.

'If You Can Accord'

When Mary Eade contemplated moving in with her mother-in-law she had just given birth to a baby, bringing the number of her young children up to four, while Joel's mother, Christiana, was a widow in her mid-sixties, who had lived with the couple before. Sharing accommodation would not just have reduced costs for both women but created a supportive household where housekeeping efforts and child care could be shared, and loneliness alleviated, provided as Joel wrote, the two women could 'accord'.

Married daughters could also provide domestic labour. Elizabeth Ann Champion lived with her widowed father Philip Stapleton, a farmer in Breage, while her husband Joel was in California in the 1870s. Philip would have been on his own without his daughter and she would have made a valuable contribution to the domestic running of the household, so both parties benefitted from the arrangement. After Elizabeth and the children joined Joel abroad around 1886, it is perhaps not surprising that Philip in his mid- to late sixties remarried and thus another woman was on hand to take care of his domestic arrangements.[17]

Such examples illustrate that although financial constraints would have been important they would not always have been the dominating factor, so collapsed households should not just be interpreted as a 'deserted' wife needing charity. Nor should household collapse be seen as necessarily a negative experience from the wife's point of view. Sarah Glasson moved with her four young children into a house on her father's farm while her husband was in California. Her daughter later recalled the years (1867-1871) that they lived on the farm as a happy carefree time enjoyed by Sarah as much of the child care was taken over by her four enthusiastic unmarried sisters.[18]

As shown above, many wives were found to be living with one or both of their parents and in some cases the parental home contained more than one married daughter whose husband was absent. For example, in 1851 the household of carpenter Thomas Reed and his wife Elizabeth contained their two married daughters, Ann Jones and Jane Rapson, along with their respective children. However, as the household also included five adult males, sons and grandsons, all employed as copper miners it seems likely that the overall household income would have been sufficient to support the whole extended family, especially if the two absent husbands were also contributing.

The Married Widows of Cornwall

Two sisters, Jane Hocking and Mary A. Roberts, together with Mary's daughter, were living with their parents in Illogan while their husbands were abroad in 1861. At the same time in Madron, mine agent Richard Grenfell and his wife Elizabeth were accommodating two married daughters, Elizabeth Hall and Peggy Hall, both of whom had two-year-old daughters of their own. One son-in-law, William Hall, was a tin miner in America, the other, his brother Thomas Henry Hall, a blacksmith in Australia. As the parents were 77 and 65 respectively, they may have welcomed the help the sisters could give in running the household. Similarly, sisters Eliza Ann Axford and Elizabeth Pollard, together with Elizabeth's two young children, were living with their parents in Gwennap while their miner husbands were abroad.

Sisters with husbands abroad were also found living with their widowed mothers. In Redruth in 1861 sisters Catherine Williams and Elizabeth Annear, whose husbands were in America, were in their mother's home. In 1871 Amelia Toy and Mary J. Sweet were both living with their widowed mother and two unmarried sisters in Gwennap, providing plenty of carers for Mary's two-year-old son, the only male in the household.

Some sisters with absent husbands combined their households. An examination of some examples drawn from the census returns indicate a range of possible motivations, practical and emotional as well as financial. Sisters (as well as mothers) would have been able to provide invaluable support to wives who were pregnant when their husbands departed. In Gwennap in 1891 Joanna Trenberth was on hand to assist her sister Emily Annear with her new baby, while Rosina Treloar and her baby were living nearby with her older sister Mary A. Dower. There was good sense in sisters Jane Ford and Elizabeth White, each with a very young child, joining forces rather than maintaining separate, possibly lonely, households in Camborne in 1881. Similarly sisters Grace Penrose and Caroline Veal, both with two children, had by 1891 joined together to form a single household in St Just. Likewise, 24-year-old Elizabeth Uren is likely to have welcomed the help with her three toddlers that her newly married younger sister Mary Bolitho would have provided in 1881.

In Camborne in 1891 Eliza Shears was on hand to help her sister Emma Trewin with her two young children but also brought in some income as a charwoman. By combining households the women could rationalise the distribution of domestic labour, especially child care, and optimise the earning power of the joint family group. In 1861 Jane Hill and her 11-month-old baby were living with her sister Charlotte Penaluna in St Cleer. Completing the household were Charlotte's own two children aged two and four, and three older children, probably stepchildren. Jane and the oldest stepchild, a girl of 14, were working as copper ore dressers and it seems likely that Jane was only able to go out to work because her sister could look after the baby along with her own young children. Similarly living together in Gwennap in 1871 were Eliza Polkinghorne and her sister Eliza Jane Angove with their respective children aged 8 to 12. Both Eliza Jane and the eldest boy were contributing to the household income with work at a mine.

Sisters Jane Barnett and Sarah Waters in Camborne had three boys aged 12 to 16 between them in 1871, two of whom had work as surface labourers at a mine while Sarah brought in some income as a dressmaker. The combined household had three incomes in addition to whatever money was being received from both the husbands. It was a different picture in nearby Centenary Street where sisters Ann Rule and Elizabeth Bodinar were living together with their combined offspring of five children under ten. Here the only income to supplement that sent by their husbands was the money Elizabeth earned as a charwoman. Both wives later joined their husbands in America so it is likely that they were in receipt of some remittances.

Combining two households where both wives were struggling to be both a mother and earner had the potential to create a more sustainable joint household in which the domestic labour could be shared or redistributed, freeing one of the women from child care and enabling her to earn more. Although the woman working outside the home could never replace the male breadwinner in terms of the amount she could earn due to the poorly paid work available to women, such arrangements would have offered greater financial security to both wives, as well as providing emotional support.

In some households there is no indication that anyone was bringing in an income to supplement what was being sent home by the husbands. Sisters Elizabeth Ann Dunn and Amelia Morcom were both married to engineers who were away from home and Amelia had moved in with Elizabeth and her young son in Gwennap while the men were away in 1871. Similarly, at the same time in Redruth Elizabeth Jane Merritt and her children had moved into the household headed by her younger sister Hannah Hicks, while both their husbands were abroad. The arrangement wasn't permanent as within ten years Hannah had joined her husband in New Zealand and Elizabeth had remarried. Mary Angove and her sister Amelia Rutter, living together in Camborne in 1881, possibly did not need to work as neither was listed with an occupation and between them they had four children in education, even though three were above the school leaving age and legally able to work. An additional older boy was working as a carpenter and would also have been contributing to the household income.

Other, often older, wives who would otherwise be on their own also shared homes, such as copper miner's wife Susan Darlington, aged 61, and her 50-year-old sister Johanna Rogers, a charwoman, living together in Gwennap in 1881. In St Cleer in 1871 Phillipa Keast had no children at home but her household included her older sister Elizabeth Trevarton, whose husband was also absent, as well as their elderly mother. Other co-residing pairings included Martha Trestrail and her Australian-born children who were living with her sister-in-law Joanna Langdon and her children in Redruth in 1861. Martha's husband was in Australia while Joanna's was in America. Their next-door neighbour's husband was in Chile. Meanwhile in another part of the parish Mary Dingle was boarding with Mary Powell and her young son, both working as dressmakers while their husbands were abroad. Likewise Grace J. Williams was lodging with Elizabeth Mathews in Ludgvan in 1881.

The examples given here suggest that in addition to financial savings, combining households would have enabled domestic chores to be shared, provided support during pregnancy and childbirth, facilitated child care and in turn enhanced ability to take up work opportunities, as well as alleviating loneliness. The same would have been true where wives were residing with other family members.

In some households more than one generation were living without their husbands, with mother and daughter (sometimes daughters) co-residing. The household in Breage of Elizabeth A. Cardew in 1891

'If You Can Accord'

included her two married daughters, Mary and Emma, and their children. All three husbands were in America; two were gold miners, the third a blacksmith. Similarly, young wife Eliza A. Richards lived with her mother Eliza Harvey in Illogan while both their husbands were abroad in 1861. Ten years later Eliza A. was still living with her, by then widowed, mother. Although her husband Charles, a mining engineer, was absent then and in 1881, he had been home as the couple had started a family, and they were reunited by 1891.

In some families, generation after generation of wives were 'left behind'. In 1861 the household of farmer James Hooper and his wife contained four generations, including their married daughter Mary Clemmow and married granddaughter Mary Pollard with her young children. The husbands of both Marys (mother and daughter) were in Chile. The younger Mary was to go on to have a daughter, Mary Jane, who too was to find herself managing on her own 30 years later while her own husband was working in America.[19]

Such living arrangements became a way of life for some wives. Georgina Beckerleg's tin miner husband was absent in both 1871 and 1881. Her daughter Elizabeth J. married stonemason Obadiah Tregembo in December 1880 and the newlyweds lived with her briefly in Breage before Obadiah went to America to join his father. In the 1891 census Elizabeth and her daughter (born not long after Obadiah's departure) were again in Georgina's household, with both husbands recorded as being abroad. Georgina's was a gold miner and Elizabeth's was an iron miner. Ten years later Elizabeth and daughter were still living with Georgina, by then a widow. Elizabeth's husband Obadiah was very much alive and had carved out a successful career as a mine captain in Michigan where he died in 1917. That he had a wife and daughter 'in England' is mentioned in his obituary published in Cornwall but it seems unlikely that the couple ever spent much time together.[20] Elizabeth appears never to have been able set up her own home as a married woman and, like many of the wives whose husbands emigrated shortly after the marriage, she remained in her parental home. In spite of being mothers themselves, one might speculate that they were caught in limbo between the developmental transition from dependent daughter to adult independence as a wife.

In some cases of mothers and daughters co-residing, it was the mother living in the daughter's household while both husbands were abroad, which might have resulted in somewhat different power dynamics within the family. Mary Ann Jenkins was probably used to her husband, a 'mecannick' or engine smith, being away as she was bringing up the family alone in both 1861 and 1871, at one point running a grocery business. By 1881 the arrangement had reversed and Mary Ann was living in the household of her married daughter Mary J. Werry and her four young children in St Blazey while both their husbands were abroad. Arrangements were to change again when the daughter's husband returned sometime before 1891 and the couple moved to Plymouth with their children, while the by then widowed Mary senior remained in St Blazey. This illustrates how living arrangements adapted over time to changing circumstances and individual needs.

More unusually, while Elizabeth Phillips' husband was away in 1851, it was her mother-in-law, Christian Carlyon who lived with her in Breage. Both their husbands had gone in search of gold and it is possible that the menfolk had travelled abroad together. Certainly it is known that many men emigrated as parties of relatives, friends and neighbours. This seems to have been the case with Francis Wallis and his son-in-law Arthur May who arrived in America on the same ship in 1870. Their wives, mother and daughter Jane Wallis and Elizabeth Jane May, remained in St Cleer with the younger couple's small children. Both couples had been reunited by 1881. Another party from St Cleer comprised brothers Henry and William Short, and their brother-in-law, Thomas Husband, who were all working at the Central Mines in North Michigan in 1876 while their wives, Mary, Cordelia and Emma, and children remained at Tremarcombe in their home parish. The knowledge that their husbands were together would have been reassuring to the women and have created more of a shared experience. Wives whose husbands were living and working among relatives and friends abroad are likely to have received more news of their partners than those whose husbands were more isolated, as information was frequently shared and greetings passed on by relatives and neighbours receiving letters from the same mining area.[21]

This pattern of extended families split between two very distant places is well illustrated by the Kemp family. Sarah (Sally) Kemp's copper miner husband was absent in both 1841 and 1851, leaving Sarah with the children. In 1861 Sarah and her daughter Harriet Hall were living together while both their husbands were in Chile, and co-residing in 1871 when Sally's husband was still in Chile and Harriet's absent. With them was another married daughter, Elizabeth Treweek visiting with her daughter who had been born in Chile in 1856. Here we have two generations of a transnational family, split on gender lines with the women largely, but not exclusively, in Cornwall and the men in South America.

In other families the husbands of co-residing mothers and daughters were more widely scattered, and the wives did not have the comfort of knowing that their menfolk were together, but nonetheless had a wealth of shared experience in managing without their husbands. Louisa Pascoe's husband was absent in 1861, returned around 1866, but was in Chile by 1871. Ten years later he was in the Cape Colony while Louisa and her married daughter, Louisa Dunstan, whose husband was in South America, were living together in Gwennap. By 1891 the younger Louisa had a two-year-old child but an absent husband; while her widowed mother was living nearby.

These case histories demonstrate how, when taken in isolation, the census can give a deceptive impression of the permanence of household structures. A census return only captures a fleeting moment in time. As Neil Howlett pointed out in his study of the maritime community of Appledore, North Devon, "where there is much temporary absence, this can present a misleading picture of the nature of households".[22] When the census information is placed in the context of the wider history of the individual or family it becomes clear that collapsed or huddled households in Cornwall were often a measure adopted for a few months or years until families were reunited.

Howlett concluded that the people of Appledore were living together in extended and multiple family households not because they believed it to be the ideal, but because "by living together they could mutually overcome the problems which faced all families and individuals. The ways in which they combined reflected the different problems which faced them." Similarly in Cornwall, families would have tried to devise living arrangements that were mutually beneficial and acceptable to all parties. Who moved in with whom would have depended on a range of factors, including the size of the individual families in relation to the size of the accommodation available. In Appledore, if the wife accompanied her husband to sea, the children would live temporarily with their grandparents, as this was more convenient than the grandparents moving into the younger couple's home, which would be remain empty in their absence.[23] It would be easier for a singleton to join a family household than the other way around, provided the family was in large enough accommodation. However, if the singleton was occupying larger accommodation than they needed (perhaps because their spouse had died and children had left home) and the family was planning to relocate to join the husband abroad in the near future, then they might move in with the singleton.

In the Eade family's case mentioned above, Mary and the children joined Joel in America within a couple of years, so when it was suggested that they move in with his mother Christiana, they may have been planning to give up their own home anyway. Some younger wives never seem to have set up their own independent households if their new husbands emigrated soon after the marriage. For Harriet Chenhall, who was living with her widowed mother and younger sisters in Chacewater while her new husband had joined the Californian gold rush, her life as a married woman while her husband was away may have been little different from that before her marriage.[24]

The Cornish examples above show the various permutations and ways in which household composition evolved and adapted to meet the needs not just of the individual wives whose husbands emigrated but of the family as a whole. Household collapse was one of a range of pragmatic solutions to changing family circumstances motivated not exclusively by the need to alleviate any financial problems for wife. Shared and reduced living costs could be beneficial for the wider family. It could also provide an environment for mutual support within the family. Family members were on hand to help the wives during pregnancy and childbirth and with child care, while the wives themselves could care for, or assist, elderly parents. Mutual benefit was not only financial or practical, it also came in the form of emotional support and empathic company.

Although sharing a home facilitated familial support, it was not essential. The tendency for extended families to live as close neighbours in separate households in communities in the 19th century[25] meant that the women did not need to move into the same house to support each other. In the tightly packed housing in the mining villages and towns, often with shared access or courtyards, it would have made little practical difference whether kin lived next door or in the same house.

In these close-knit communities neighbours were quite likely to include close, or more distant, relatives. For example, in 1854 Joseph Lance sailed to join the Australian gold rush leaving his wife Elizabeth and three children in Cornwall. Two years later his father also went to Australia. In 1858 the Lance men struck gold and by 1861 Elizabeth and her mother-in-law set up homes as neighbours in Blackwater, St Agnes. Between the two households were distributed Elizabeth junior's children, her unmarried sister, sister-in-law and niece.[26] Living on the other side of Elizabeth junior was Grace Truran, another wife with young children, whose husband was in the gold fields of Victoria with Joseph. Whether by design or accident, these women would have been well located to offer each other practical and emotional support over a period of many years; Joseph was not to return from Australia until 1872.

This is a pattern that is seen time and time again in the census returns for the mining districts in Cornwall. Of the 116 households in Buller Row, Redruth in 1861, twelve (almost 10%) were headed by women whose husbands are described as being abroad. In 1871 seven of the 26 occupied houses in White Stocking Row in Gwennap contained wives with husbands abroad. Another typical example is Fox's Row in Carharrack in 1871. Here Elizabeth Hawke, whose husband was in America, had moved in with her older sister, Catherine Penaluna (husband in California), and her two young children. Next door was 62-year-old Mary Gidley (husband also in California) and in the next house beyond her was Jane Michell caring for three young children while her husband was in Chile. The heads of household of other houses in this short row[27] included a Mrs Smith who was 'directed by' her absent husband, Mary Ann Dower, whose husband had died in Australia, and seven other older widows. Only five of the 17 dwellings in the row were occupied by households headed by a man. The 38 dwellings in nearby Albion Row housed ten women with husbands abroad, eight of whom were heads of household.

Therefore few of the wives would have been truly alone in their experience. Most would have had relations, friends or neighbours who were facing, or had faced, the same challenges. Louisa Woolcock was one of three sisters in Baldhu whose husbands worked abroad during the 1860s and 1870s. Louisa's husband William went to Victoria in 1866, a year after they married, leaving her pregnant. Living close by in separate households in 1871 were her sisters Mary Dunstan and Elizabeth Hollow, both of whom were also in sole charge of children, as well as the sisters' mother. Within the wider family each of the sisters had additional sisters-in-law, Sarah Woolcock, Catherine Dunstan and Grace Gerrans, who all remained in Cornwall while their respective husbands worked abroad around the same time.[28] Similarly the wives, Elizabeth, Sarah and Hannah, of the three Harry brothers from Breage had the shared experience of their husbands living in America without them.[29]

In addition to these numerous wives, the large numbers of widows heading households meant that the phenomenon of women managing on their own, often raising children as single parents, was not an unusual one in the mining towns and villages of Cornwall. It may, however, be an exaggeration to see these as matriarchal communities as has been suggested by Schwartz.[30] Although an unusually large proportion of households were headed by women either as widows or 'married widows', there were still far more male headed households. Nonetheless a wealth of experience of managing without the men existed within these communities. The wives and their husbands cannot be considered in isolation; although separated from each other, both spouses were likely to be living and/or working among people they knew well, often relatives. Fathers and sons, or brothers would emigrate together, while the womenfolk of the family remained in Cornwall. Therefore the phenomenon was often more one of extended families leading interconnected transnational lives than simply of two individuals, married but living apart.

The examples given above illustrate how in some families two or three generations of wives shared the experience of separation from their spouses as a result of temporary labour migration. This common experience within the close-knit mining communities would have produced an accumulation of knowledge and wisdom on managing in this situation, as well an empathy for the wives' emotional responses, that would have made the experience for individual wives more bearable. It might also be supposed that later generations of wives would have benefited from advice passed down their older relatives and may have been better prepared to cope while their husbands were abroad. A form of cultural acclimatisation may have evolved, with spousal separation of this type becoming a way of life, as has been reported in other communities subject to large-scale male emigration. For example, Duroux describes women of the Auvergne region of France as viewing the departure of their menfolk in the 19th century as part of a longstanding tradition rather than a crisis.[31]

However, not all family and community relationships were harmonious, or help always freely given. Mary Jane Collett, who had requested that her newly married daughter should live with her to help her milk the cows, tried suing her son-in-law for the cost of lodging her own daughter.[32] There is also evidence of both family support and disquiet in the relatively few letters exchanged between husbands and wives that have survived. Writing to her husband in America about their son's death, Ann Goldsworthy mentions that his mother, who lived nearby, had been there when the young boy had woken in the night and taken "him upon her lap", that "cousin Elizabeth have been a friend indeed" and his family had been very kind to her and had done their best. Ann's relationship with her own father, however, was strained: "My father behave very slight to me… he have never been here but once or twice since you have been gone nor I have never been home but once".[33] Problems with both her own and her husband's family appear to have made Mary Ann Dower's life miserable, as we shall see later.

Even wives who were well supported by their husbands abroad and did not have a pressing need for financial help or accommodation from family, would have required practical assistance on occasion with certain chores or household repairs. Margaret K. Nelson has considered this predicament in the context of modern day single mothers in the US, and how they negotiated the absence of the male contribution in domestic 'self-provisioning', defined as "the efforts that household members make to provide, through their own labor (and for themselves), goods and services they would otherwise have to purchase in the (formal or informal) market".[34] Although the details of the challenges facing the wives left in Cornwall are different from those of 21st century women, the concepts are transferable. For example, Nelson recorded how many women used to living as a couple "commented on how bewildered they were when they first found themselves responsible for the chores that their husbands had previously handled".[35]

This can be illustrated hypothetically by a 19th century wife 'left behind' in Cornwall presented with the dilemma of a leaking roof. Under normal circumstances, her husband would probably have carried out or organised repairs. Amongst the women Nelson studied four self-provisioning strategies were applied in situations like this: lowered standards and avoidance; purchasing the necessary service; acquiring the relevant skills, and reliance on others.[36] So the wife with the leaky roof would have had limited options: a) do nothing, b) pay a tradesman to fix it, c) attempt the repair herself, or d) recruit a male relative or neighbour to do it. Although the woman may have been physically capable of affecting the repair, she may have been reluctant to attempt it through lack of confidence or skills, or by perceived improprieties of the dress and behaviour involved. To hire a tradesman would have involved costs which, even if she could afford them, would have been an additional strain on the family budget, highlighting the monetary value of the absent husband's domestic labour.

The other option was to obtain free help from male relatives, friends or neighbours. Nelson noted that although the tactic of reliance on others solved some problems, it also created new ones, the most relevant here being obligations of reciprocity. For those with teenage sons or willing male relatives on hand this option would have been less of a problem, although as Nelson noted, reliance on family has been associated with psychological stress and even within kin groups repeated unequally reciprocated requests for help may result in family tensions and resentment.

As demonstrated by the experience of Mary Ann Dower, family help, even if promised, could not always be relied upon. For those without willing family the simple matter of whom they could call on to help out would have been more of challenge. To request assistance from those who might not feel any strong natural obligation towards the applicant had its pitfalls. The modern day women were aware that in asking male friends for help "they were risking an intimacy and creating expectations", with the men sometimes expecting sexual favours in reward for their help.[37] There is little reason to suppose that the wives managing on their own in 19th century Cornwall would not have been equally sensitive to this issue, making them cautious of asking for help amongst their male neighbours.

Victorian sensibilities and mores of behaviour also had to be observed. In December 1888 Elizabeth Jane Moore thought she saw her husband, Thomas, going into the house of Jane Bishop who had two married daughters living with her while their husbands were abroad. Mrs Moore objected, as she did not consider it proper that her husband should go into the house.[38] She went there looking for her husband and ended up in court for assaulting Jane. It is not revealed why, or even if, Thomas actually visited the women, but there was a perception, at least in Elizabeth's mind, that it was inappropriate for him to do so. It seems unlikely that she would have been receptive to a request from them for Thomas's help with a repair job. This is one of number of incidents that suggest that in the absence of their husbands the wives had to be mindful of how they behaved, or were perceived to be behaving, a topic explored in a later chapter.

In summary, although there is good evidence to indicate that many wives did receive a range of help and support from neighbours and relatives, family politics meant that this was not always guaranteed, and as Nelson's work suggests, might come at an unacceptable price. Help was also not in the form that has been predicted by past research on household structures that has associated collapse or huddling of households with the wives' financial inability to maintain their own homes in the absence of their husbands. By contrast, the majority of wives 'left behind' were living in their own homes, and indeed many housed other relatives in addition to their own children. It is likely that a more important way in which the wives found support from family and neighbours was through empathy and the accumulation of knowledge that came from a shared experience within the female community.

5

Deserted, Desperate & Destitute?
The wives and the Poor Law

We have seen how the wives 'left behind' in Cornwall managed financially using variable combinations of remittances from their husbands, the output of their (and sometimes their children's) paid and unpaid work, credit and rationalisation of accommodation costs, whilst accepting help from family or neighbours as necessary. When these multiple means of income and subsidence, dubbed an 'economy of makeshifts',[1] failed to meet the family's needs, the wives could turn to the parish, through the auspices of the relieving officer appointed by local union boards of guardians under the Poor Law.[2] Indeed it has been argued that parish relief was an integral element of an 'economy of diversified resources' used by the poor as a means to get by.[3]

Little has been written about the operation of the poor laws in Cornwall. However, it has been shown that the expenditure per inhabitant on poor relief was lower in the mining districts than elsewhere in Cornwall.[4] It is thought that the mining communities' culture of independent self-reliance and Methodist respectability made people more reluctant to apply for relief. Instead, at times of hardship miners emigrated to avoid pauperism and loss of social standing, and this would have been a motivation for some husbands to seek work abroad while their wives and children remained in Cornwall.

Establishing the level of under-support among the wives 'left behind', and the extent of their need for poor relief, has proved difficult. As discussed earlier, the use of the term 'deserted' is tricky. In the commonly accepted sense it implies that the wife had been abandoned by her emigrating husband, effectively ending the marriage. However, in the context of the wives 'left behind' it has frequently been used when referring to wives experiencing difficulties because the financial support they were receiving from their husbands was inadequate, rather than nonexistent. These difficulties, however, might only have been temporary and should not be interpreted as indicating a failed or failing marriage.

This distinction was highlighted by emigration campaigner Caroline Chisholm in a 1853 lecture on the Australian gold diggings. She explained that there "was no desertion in the ordinary sense" because the husbands left with the intent of improving their families' circumstances. The problem, she argued, was that it took so long for the men to travel to the gold fields and then accumulate enough gold to make it economically viable to sell and remit the proceeds home, that their families might be 'on the parish' before any funds reached them.[5] This wasn't just a problem for those with husbands in Australia; delays and difficulties in establishing and maintaining regular payments home could affect wives wherever their husbands went. Poor law officials, who took a dim view of husbands who failed to support their wives leaving them chargeable to the parish, referred to such wives as, at best, 'neglected' or 'half-deserted', but more frequently 'deserted'. Hence many wives who experienced temporary problems appear in poor law documents as 'deserted wives' even though in many cases this was far from the truth. As a consequence, evidence based on these sources potentially exaggerates the extent of true desertion and associated destitution amongst the wives 'left behind'.

Few wives are described in the censuses for Cornwall as deserted, or as paupers, the term most commonly used to refer to someone reliant on poor relief. In 1851 only twelve such married women are listed, including three whose husbands were in America: Ann Sluggett in Stratton, Elizabeth Hulf in Week St Mary, and Mary Hicks in Jacobstow. All three lived in the predominantly agricultural districts of East Cornwall (Mary was the wife of an agricultural labourer) so it seems less likely, but not impossible, that their husbands' emigration was connected with mining. Nine of the deserted women (including the three above) were described as paupers or in receipt of parish relief. The 1861 census for Cornwall lists eight deserted wives, none of whom are recorded as having husbands abroad. A further three women are described as being separated or living apart from their husbands. None of these women in 1861 are recorded in the census as paupers, but have occupations including washerwomen, charwomen, cap maker and labourer.

Similarly, nine deserted wives are named in the 1871 census, only one of which, Philippa Pascoe, a pauper from the mining parish of Gwennap, is known to have a husband abroad.[6] Of the remaining deserted wives, a further three were in Gwennap: Mary Magor, Jane Reed and Catherine Northey. Mary was employed as a schoolteacher and was later to take in a lodger, while Jane was living on 'interest of money' and Catherine was being supported by her sons. Only Philippa and another deserted wife from a different parish appear to have been reliant on relief.

In the 1881 census the single suggestion of desertion among the miners' wives is the entry for Mary Ann Berryman of Penzance whose husband John was "supposed to be at the Cape but does not correspond". Mary Ann was left to support herself and her three children from her trade as a greengrocer. The only other deserted wives recorded were one in St Clement "ill in bed" and another in Camborne being "supported by charitable visitors". Likewise only three wives are recorded in the 1891 census of Cornwall as deserted, two of whom were married to soldiers. The remaining wife, who is the only explicit reference in any of Cornish census returns to a miner's wife in extreme poverty, is Jessie Davey. Jessie, aged 32 and able-bodied, is listed in Liskeard Borough Workhouse as the deserted wife of a copper miner, along with her four children aged between 5 and 11 years. Where her husband William John Davey was is not known. It is surely certain that among the married women listed as inmates in workhouses there were other deserted wives, including some with husbands abroad, but their numbers are unknown.

Clearly the census returns are of little help in determining the levels of desertion or poverty among the wives left behind in Cornwall, unless we are to believe that it was extremely rare. It is more likely that the level of desertion is under-recorded in the census, either because wives not being supported by their husbands did not choose to identify themselves, or did not recognise themselves, as being deserted, holding onto the hope that their husbands would get back in touch and/or start sending money again. Others may have written off the marriage completely and presented themselves to the world as widows.[7] Susie Bullock appears on the 1901 and 1911 censuses as a widow, although her husband Richard 'Deadwood Dick' in America was still alive and maintained contact with his son in Cornwall.[8] Three of the four deserted wives in Gwennap in 1871 are recorded as widows ten years later in 1881, raising the question of how they could be sure that their husbands were dead. Only deserted schoolteacher, Mary Magor, still described herself as married.

Considering census evidence in the context of that from other sources is equally inconclusive. For example, in 1857 the Redruth Board of Guardians voted unanimously to order all deserted women receiving outdoor relief (help given while living in the community) to enter the union workhouse with their families.[9] At the time Redruth had very large numbers of wives whose husbands were abroad as demonstrated by the 183 explicit references in the 1861 census. It could be argued that if a significant proportion of these wives were not being supported by their husbands and were applying for outdoor relief, the board would not have made this decision as the workhouse would not have been able to accommodate them all. Alternatively, the board's decision may have been made because so many wives were applying for relief that they sought to deter them by only offering help via the dreaded workhouse.

Therefore precise levels of neglect and desertion amongst the wives 'left behind' is difficult to quantify. Nonetheless, there is evidence to suggest that cases of poverty amongst them increased as the century progressed, with the first widespread expressions of public concern in Cornwall emerging with the mining depression of the late 1860s. The primary causes of the distress at that time were difficulties in the mining industry combined with severe winters and high food prices rather than existing emigration levels.[10] It is notable that in a publicised account of an encounter with groups of women making their way to claim relief at Penzance workhouse in the summer of 1867, only two of the 15 women were noted as having husbands abroad, and the person describing the incident goes to pains to say that it was a sight that he had never seen before.[11] This hardly seems indicative of widespread destitution among the wives 'left behind' prior to the mining depression.

In July 1867 the High Sheriff and magistrates in Cornwall set up sub-committees to investigate reports of distress in the mining districts with a view to setting up a relief fund.[12] As we saw earlier, the work of these committees, drawing on interviews and local knowledge, provides a useful survey of the numbers of husbands who had emigrated leaving their wives and families behind. The figures produced by these sub-committees were for the numbers of husbands who had gone abroad, and it is not always clear from the reports whether all their wives were in need of help. Nonetheless, around 600 men reported to have emigrated from the St Austell, Helston and Penzance Union districts were said to be sending "meagre and irregular remittances" to the wives they left behind.[13] The distress caused by the 1867 depression appears to have been localised. In response to the committee's enquiries only five (Penzance, Helston, Truro, St Columb and St Austell) of the thirteen Cornish poor law unions felt that it had any impact on their districts. As mentioned previously, the Redruth guardians, at the heart of the mining district and with the highest confirmed numbers of wives with husbands abroad, reported some distress but did not perceive that they had a problem significant enough to warrant a public appeal, although some reference is made to private charity alleviating local distress.[14]

Where there was distress, including that acknowledged in Redruth, it was largely associated with the families of the men who had emigrated, with problems arising as much from depression abroad as at home. Remittances from North America as a whole had fallen dramatically due to the low wages, high taxes and the high cost of provisions there. Remittance orders that had been arriving in amounts of £8 to £10 had fallen to amounts of £2 to £2 10s. Only remittances from Australia and especially California were said to be 'keeping up'.[15] A commentator in the *Royal Cornwall Gazette* noted: "Altogether, it was clearly proved that either times are not flourishing abroad as they were, or that 'absence' does not 'make the (marital) heart grow fonder' and there is less thought for the shorn lambs at home". The result, however, was "not so much pauperism or extreme destitution as very straitened circumstances".[16]

The figures provided by the various sub-committees do provide some clues as to the numbers of wives receiving help from the parish.[17] In the St Just district it was reported that eleven of the 300 families whose heads had left the parish were being given parish relief, while all the others were getting by on their own resources, credit from shopkeepers and help from neighbours. The majority of these families (250) were said to be receiving "small and tolerably regular remittances" averaging about £1 5s per family per month. In the St Ives district ten families with absent heads, mostly from Lelant, were receiving outdoor relief, while there were none in Marazion. In Helston Union 43 of the 143 families of men who had left were receiving parish relief, with others relying on credit from shops and what help the relief fund could offer. Truro Union reported 30 deserted wives in the Chacewater district, many of whose husbands had left long before the depression. The majority of the men who had left St Agnes for California had sent money to their families, while the wives of those who had not were said to be having a hard struggle to maintain themselves and their families. "Some" of the 11 wives left behind in Newlyn were receiving relief. There were said to be 40 women and families in Camborne neglected or deserted by their husbands. Given the large numbers of men abroad, relatively few of the wives appear to have been receiving parish relief. In addition, the 1867 Distress Committee concluded that although there was evidence of severe distress in almost all the mining districts (not necessarily all associated with deserted wives), it varied from place to place. For example, in June 1870 it was said of St Just: "An evidence of prosperity, or otherwise, is found by the number of uninhabited houses in a place. Although emigration has taken many persons from St Just, others have filled up the vacancies, and there is hardly a house to let in the place".[18]

There were, however, cases of extreme poverty. Contrary to the report from the union officers, the Police Superintendent of Truro claimed that scores of the wives and families around Chacewater and St Agnes were almost starving because their husbands were not sending them money.[19] Cases were also noted in St Just of women and children "low from semi-starvation".[20] In one case it was reported that a mother and six children, whose father had emigrated to South America, had gradually retreated into a single room of their home and had been reduced to burning the wooden fittings and floor boards to stay warm. While the mother was out working, five of the almost naked children remained all day by themselves in a room where the only furniture was a wooden bedstead with a piece of canvas as coverlet.[21]

The depressions of the 1860s and 1870s led to increased emigration; the 'pull' of being able to earn good money abroad was superseded by the 'push' of needing to escape poor conditions at home. However, unlike the skilled workers carefully recruited by overseas mining enterprises in former years, many of the men who left their wives behind in the 1870s were thought to be ill-prepared and unsuited to work abroad, and even when they were earning good wages, they often failed to send enough money home.[22]

In the late 1870s Cornwall was hit again by economic depression, and the distress committee reconvened to assess the situation. In some respects the depression was not considered to be as desperate as it had been ten years earlier, with most of the problems put down to low wage levels and unemployment,[23] but was said to be more widespread throughout different industries and districts.[24] Unlike in 1867, the press reports do not reveal statistics for the numbers of wives needing help, but some general impressions are given. These suggest a variable and inconsistent picture. The representative from Camborne reported in November 1877 that they did not have much general distress but that "there were certain miners abroad who did not send home such large sums of money as formerly".[25] However, the following month he reported that "after a very close investigation, he had come to the conclusion that there was very great and general distress in the Camborne district", but that the number of wives and families of men who were abroad affected was "insignificant" accounting for only 12 out of the 243 cases of distress.[26] In Gwithian and Phillack there were reported to be only two women with husbands abroad in need of relief.[27] In 1879 only 10% of cases dealt with by a separate Wesleyan relief fund involved the wives and families of men who had emigrated.[28]

Nonetheless financial distress was said by some to be prevalent amongst the families of men who had gone abroad.[29] The newspaper accounts of the Distress Fund meetings are peppered with reports from vicars and other parish representatives noting cases of distress amongst the women in their parishes whose husbands were abroad. Some men from Crowan, especially those in America, were not doing as well as they expected and were sending smaller or no remittances at all.[30] Similarly, cases were reported from Chacewater where men abroad had "fallen into adverse circumstances" and were unable to send money home.[31]

As John Rowe notes: "Emigration only solved or ameliorated individual problems; in many places it only aggravated the social distress".[32] In some cases the separation of husband and wife was a direct consequence of well-intentioned attempts to alleviate distress by funding the emigration of the husband alone. In 1887 the Callington distress committee was criticised for sending the husband of Mary Ann Buckingham to America, leaving her and the children chargeable to the parish.[33]

In 1888 the numbers receiving outdoor relief from the Redruth Board of Guardians had increased from 1200 to 1277 over a two to three year period due, it was believed, to the numbers of wives being deserted.[34] By the end of 1893 they had more cases than they could remember for 20 years.[35] Four years later the need for outdoor relief in the union was still increasing "in a great measure due to men going to Africa and neglecting the families at home".[36] In 1898 Redruth guardians complained again that: "Men emigrate to Africa and America and let their wives and families live on the parish".[37] By this time the guardians for the union, which contained the major mining parishes of Camborne, Redruth, Illogan and Gwennap, "were in a fix about it".[38] "I don't believe there is any board who have people out of the country to such an extent as we have", complained the chairman.[39] The Truro Union, by comparison, only had eight deserted wives in 1898,[40] although a year later both Unions were said to be on a par, with 14-15 cases each.[41]

Redruth certainly felt that it was in a unique situation. It was seen as having one of the highest levels of pauperdom in the country, largely due to a demographic imbalance with extremely large numbers of old people. It was acknowledged that they "had a good number of deserted women", but equally that money was coming in fairly regularly from the husbands abroad for the maintenance of their wives and families.[42] Just as important a cause of pauperdom was the numbers of families left unsupported because the men had died or been killed abroad,[43] although the Penzance board noted that they were giving out more relief resulting from desertions than deaths.[44]

As in earlier years, factors outside Cornwall also had an impact on the numbers of wives that needed help. In 1893-4 unemployment and stoppages in the mines in America reduced the remittances arriving in Cornwall and increased the numbers of wives seeking relief.[45] Their numbers were swollen by additional wives and children being sent home from America by husbands who could not afford to support them.[46] A strike in Australia also prevented men from sending money home.[47] At the turn of the century war in South Africa had a major effect on the wives and children dependent on those remittances.[48] The manager of the

Redruth branch of The Cornish Bank recalled how, from a situation before the war when thousands of pounds of remittances were passing through the bank monthly, "shortly after the beginning of hostilities not a single draft came to them from South Africa". Instead he had to send out money to the Cape to support Cornishmen who had not come home.[49] However, by the beginning of 1902 the men were returning to work and remittances were flowing again. While wives reliant on South African remittances had been struggling, others with husbands elsewhere were less affected as "substantial" money orders from Lake Superior, Mexico, Brazil and many other parts of North and South America had continued to arrive.[50]

Compared with the thousands of wives estimated to have had husbands working abroad, the numbers indicated in the reports above suggest that a relatively small proportion received long-term relief through the poor law system. Contemporary reports appear to support this, balancing portrayals of the emigrant miners as largely supportive but sometimes neglectful. When the issue of deserted wives in St Just was discussed in 1878 it was said that: "A good many absent husbands have been faithful, though not a few have proved unfaithful".[51] In *West Barbary*, published in 1888, L.L. Price praised the emigrant miners' propensity to return for their wives, their families and friends as "one of the most pleasing traits in the miner's character", but added: "It must, however, be said that cases also occur where the poor law guardians discover that the emigrants have found it convenient to forget their families".[52] An anonymous, but recognised, 'authority' interviewed in 1896 about the situation in St Agnes was confident that: "No kind of distress exists as prevails in the west. Our miners go abroad and send home plenty of money to their wives and families, and we seldom hear of a case of distress".[53] The implication is that although all was well in St Agnes, other mining areas (he mentions Gwennap, Breage and St Just) had more of a problem.

The evidence suggests that the apparent levels of neglect and/or desertion of the wives varied across Cornwall and over time. The problem was firmly centred on the mining communities, especially those of the Redruth Union, but at any one time there could be considerable differences between mining parishes. The reports also indicate that the need for poor relief changed over the years, giving the impression that the overall situation became progressively worse from the 1860s through into the 20th century. However, it is possible that the paucity of evidence from the earlier years, combined with increased press coverage arising from the debate over outdoor relief, which as we will see vexed the boards of guardians from 1870 onwards, created an inflated public perception of the degree of neglect.

To understand the interaction between the wives 'left behind' and the boards of guardians requires consideration of the poor laws and how they applied to married women. The 1834 *Report of the Royal Commission into the Operation of the Poor Laws*, which led to the New Poor Law Act of the same year, had little to say about the treatment of women in general, and even less about married women. As Beatrice and Sidney Webb noted in their detailed and authoritative history of the poor laws: "With regard to the really baffling problems presented by the widow, the deserted wife, the wife of the absentee soldier or sailor, the wife of a husband resident in another parish or another country – in each case whether with or without dependent children – the Report is silent."[54]

The assumption, under the principle of coverture, was that a married couple could be always treated as a single unit; the wife would follow her husband in all things and the husband's liability for his wife's maintenance was taken for granted.[55] This did not mean that husbands were the sole breadwinners. Working class wives were expected to contribute, although it was seen as increasingly less respectable for them to do so.[56] However, any situation that did not conform to the principles of coverture was not addressed by the original poor law legislation. In addition The New Poor Law of 1834 was aimed at dealing with destitution rather than general poverty; it was specifically designed not to supplement low incomes, which included those produced by irregular and intermittent remittances from husbands abroad. For these reasons it struggled to accommodate the needs of the wives 'left behind'.

Applicants for relief with the ability to work, classified as 'able-bodied', could only be helped if they went into the workhouse, an institution run under a regime intended to deter all but the desperate. Outdoor relief given to those who remained in the community was reserved for those unable to work through age or infirmity. If an able-bodied husband working in Cornwall fell onto hard times, his wife would have to follow him into the workhouse; but the situation of the wives who were receiving

The Married Widows of Cornwall

insufficient remittances from husbands working abroad was more complicated. If these wives were classified as 'able-bodied' they came directly under the regulations laid down by the central poor law authority in London, initially the Poor Law Commission.[57] This meant they would be subject to the workhouse test[58] and excluded from receiving help as outdoor relief that enabled them to stay in their own homes and keep their families together. If they were not classified as 'able-bodied' decisions about their relief could be made at a local level as the central authority had more limited powers. However, as the Act did not address this issue, the women's position was not clear.

The Webbs suggest that Parliament did not intend deserted wives or those whose husbands were resident in another country (or widows) to be viewed as 'able-bodied' if they were "encumbered with very young children" as they would not be able to work. This implies that wives without very young children would be classified as able-bodied and subject to national rules, whereas those with small children would be covered by local union bye-laws.

The Poor Law Amendment Act of 1844 provided more guidance by stating that for the purpose of poor law relief the wife of a husband 'beyond the seas' should, regardless of coverture, be treated as if she were a widow.[59] Although the description of a husband 'beyond the seas', which perfectly describes the situation of the wives 'left behind', appears in law it was not widely used in poor law authority discussions about the wives in Cornwall, where the preference, as noted above, was to refer to the wives applying for relief as neglected, half-deserted or deserted.

In 1844 the Poor Law Commissioners issued an Outdoor Relief Prohibitory Order that reiterated that both deserted wives and wives with husbands 'beyond the seas' could be treated in the same way as widows.[60] It also clarified that outdoor relief could be given to able-bodied independent woman only for the first six months, or indefinitely while they had one or more dependent children, provided that all the children were legitimate. However, there was provision for the women to receive relief under exceptional circumstances defined as sudden and urgent necessity; namely sickness, accident, bodily or mental infirmity of any member of family or defraying burial expenses of any member of family. The Webbs point out that these exceptions were so numerous that the wives "may almost be said to have been expressly allowed to receive outdoor relief" with little regard as to whether or not the women were in paid employment.[61]

After 1847 views on relief were to change with the Commission's successor, the Poor Law Board, beginning to urge all local boards of guardians to be stricter regarding outdoor relief and offer applicants the workhouse instead. Nonetheless, outdoor relief continued to be allowed to widows, and by implication deserted wives, with children. However, by the time the Poor Law Board was replaced by the Local Government Board (LGB) in 1871 it was recommended that boards should refuse any application from a deserted wife for outdoor relief for the first year of her desertion.[62] This move foreshadowed what became known as the 'crusade against outdoor relief' in which local guardians were under constant pressure from the LGB and its inspectors to restrict the distribution of outdoor relief. The result, in the Webbs' words, was an "amazing diversity" of different local bye-laws on how applications from deserted wives and those with husbands 'beyond the seas' should be handled.[63] Some unions maintained that they should be treated as widows, who, if they only had one child, would be expected to support themselves after an initial period that might range from one to six months; some required any additional children to be taken in to the workhouse. As with widows, having an illegitimate child would exclude any real hope of outdoor relief.

Nationally, many boards refused to give outdoor relief to deserted wives at all, and among those that did, relief might be withheld for differing periods ranging from six months to five years. A handful insisted that deserted wives and their children should go into the workhouse for a specified period before they could be granted outdoor relief, despite the fact that this would have broken up the home anyway.[64]

That relief was denied to deserted wives for a year (or another specified period) highlights the difficulty for those involved in determining whether the wife had indeed been deserted. Given the delays and losses in the mail, and irregularity of remittances received by some women, complete desertion would only have become apparent when any money had failed to arrive after an extended period. In December 1870 the Penzance Board of Guardians were pleased to hear that: "In one or two instances 'deserted' wives had received remittances, shewing that they were neglected and not exactly deserted, to their own comfort and the relief of the rates."[65] As this illustrates, more often problems were caused by the wives not receiving sufficient money, or not receiving it regularly enough, to meet their needs. The telling entry for Elizabeth Prowse of St Buryan in the 1871 census that she was receiving "some income" from her husband abroad is probably an apt picture of the wider situation.

This presented the Cornish poor law unions with a distinctive challenge; they understood that in many cases the wife's 'desertion' was not permanent and that her need of relief might be temporary or intermittent. For example, Honor Hosea from Tregeseal, St Just was given relief by the Penzance guardians when she stopped receiving money from her husband in Colorado, but he "was a good husband formerly" and she offered to tell the guardians if he sent to her again.[66] Relief would start and stop as remittances ebbed and flowed. Individual circumstances could change rapidly for the better making the guardians reluctant to stigmatise the wives as paupers or break up the family by refusing outdoor relief and insisting on the workhouse. For example, a young woman with three children from St Day whose husband had been in America for 12 months and had sent when he was able, was given relief but as soon as she received money from her husband she "took herself off the parish".[67] Similarly, the relief granted by Helston guardians to a St Keverne family was not taken up as the husband arrived home from abroad.[68] Other wives were able to reimburse the guardians, like the recipient of outdoor relief from the St Austell Union who in 1864 "honourably refunded all she had received", money having arrived from her husband in America.[69]

Lending the wives money to tide them over was a way the Cornish unions often used to accommodate these changing circumstances, and there are many reports of the guardians deciding to grant cash and loaves 'on loan'. Hence, when in 1895 a St Just wife was granted relief, "It was thought by one of the board that she ought to sign the loan book, as her husband is in America and may be able to send money soon".[70] In fact the Poor Law stipulated that where outdoor relief was given to the family of an able-bodied man it should be given in the form of a loan to be legally recoverable from him.[71] As recovering any money loaned helped to relieve the burden on the rates, the guardians were understandably keen to see the money repaid. Hence there are records of guardians deciding that it would be expedient to write to the husband's employers asking them to "do their best to secure the repayment to the board of any money advanced to the wife on loan".[72] Relief might also be given to wives as loans if their previously reliable husbands abroad fell ill, as in the case of Camborne mother of four, Bessie Rule, whose husband was hospitalised in South Africa and hadn't been able to send any money home for six months.[73] The use of loans for relief is a little researched aspect of the poor laws and there is the potential for such Cornish examples to provide useful case studies to contribute to this field.[74]

Across the country, bye-laws imposed by local boards of guardians also placed inconsistent restrictions on the women's living arrangements. Outdoor relief might be refused to a woman in 'unsuitable' accommodation, viewed by various Boards as 'not good enough' by being in insanitary or immoral surroundings, such as lodging houses or licensed premises; or 'too good' by being furnished, with rent above a certain value, or with a smallholding. Possession of any assets such as a cottage, or small savings account or investment, would disqualify an applicant in some unions. Others variously prohibited the taking in of lodgers, sharing a home with another woman who had any illegitimate children, or with anyone of wage earning age, as well as the keeping of dogs, poultry, other livestock or an allotment.[75] Given that the taking in of lodgers and the produce of a smallholding were often important parts of household economies in the mining districts, such conditions would have had a particularly negative impact in Cornwall. As the Webbs note, the bye-laws represent "a hopeless confusion of policy on the crucial questions of how far outdoor relief should or should not be restricted to those who have been thrifty in the past, or who are still exerting themselves to earn a partial livelihood".

As the above suggests, there was an element of moral judgement applied by the guardians in their assessment of the cases before them. Women with illegitimate children could not, under poor law rules, be given outdoor relief and help for them was conditional on their entering the workhouse. The implications of the birth of a baby after the husband had departed depended on reputation and rumour. For example, Mrs Rogers who had a baby two months after her husband had gone abroad and had not been heard from since was described as 'Poor soul - must have help'.[76] However, there was "loud talk" about another wife who gave birth after her husband had left for America, and despite her having three older legitimate children, the Redruth guardians would only offer the workhouse.[77]

The decision to give or withhold relief could also be influenced by a more subjective assessment of the applicant's character. When a woman in Lanner, deserted by her husband in America, applied for relief in 1889 she was only offered 'the house' by the Redruth guardians, "as her termagant [shrewish] tongue was said to be a poor instrument to reclaim a wayward husband".[78] The very same guardians decided to continue helping Mrs Tucker of Buller Downs and her two children (deserted by her husband then in South Africa), because she was "a most respectable woman and the fault is not on her side".[79] Similarly a woman from Camborne, whose husband drank his pay rather than send it home, was allowed outdoor relief because an officer assured the board that she "goes out to wash and is hard working and respectable".[80]

Although generally equated with widows, there was one area identified by the Webbs in which the wives 'left behind' were in a better position. A widow could only obtain relief for her children if she too claimed relief and therefore became a pauper. However, a wife not living with her husband, they point out, could insist on relief for her children without applying for relief for herself. This meant that, if necessary, she could send any of her children over seven years old to the workhouse without being forced to go with them, thus avoiding becoming a pauper and enabling her to work and hopefully earn her way out of the family's problem. In addition, as any children under seven could not lawfully be separated from her, even if she consented, help had to be given in the form of outdoor relief as offering the workhouse would involve separating the child from its mother.[81] Therefore wives with absent husbands were more likely than widows to be able to keep their families together, and had more options to escape pauperdom.

Despite the LGB applying pressure on local boards of guardians throughout the 1870s for outdoor relief to be denied, at least for the first year, to deserted wives, they eventually had to admit that such a policy was not legally justifiable. In 1880 they advised guardians that regardless of the woman's character, the cause or duration of the husband's absence or any possible collusion with him, they could not withhold outdoor relief for young children.[82] Hence in 1891 the Redruth guardians initially refused relief to an Illogan women whose husband was in Michigan because she had had a child by a married man, but then changed their minds as the family was said to be living in a "half-starved state", and granted three loaves a week and boots for her other children.[83] Similarly, when approached in 1894 by a woman whose husband had been in America for nine years, and who was "said to be pregnant", the same board thought that "many more deserving cases will come forward", but did supply help in the form of boots for her older, legitimate child.[84]

The granting of boots to the children of these women was as much about education as keeping small feet warm and dry. The Education Act of 1870 introduced a legal requirement for parents to send all their children aged between 5 and 12 to school, but inadequate footwear made this difficult for poorer families and as a result relieving officers were frequently approached by mothers, needing not only the modest school fee, the 'school-pence', but boots for the children in order to comply with the law. For some guardians enabling the children to go to school was good cause to make exceptions to the rules regarding the relief of deserted wives.[85] Other felt that too many boots were being handed out,[86] or that children should leave school as soon as they could, rather than being made paupers by being given boots.[87]

The 'exceptional circumstances' clause in the Poor Law combined with the adoption of local bye-laws gave the Cornish boards of guardians a great deal of discretion as to whether and how they could help the wives not being adequately supported by their husbands abroad. However, from 1870 onwards two factors combined to create a great deal of angst amongst the unions in Cornwall on how they should deal with requests for help from these women. One was an increased awareness, probably arising from the discussions of the Distress Committee of the late 1860s, of the real and potential social problems caused by wives and children relying for their support on men working abroad. Typical of the concern was the public expression in 1870 by one of the Penzance guardians of "his regret that so many Cornishmen abroad are unable or unwilling to contribute to the maintenance of their wives and families at home".[88]

Secondly, these concerns coincided with, and were exacerbated by, pressure from the central poor law authority to reduce expenditure on relief, in the 'crusade against outdoor relief'. As a result 1871 saw a major clamp down on the help that the Cornish guardians were prepared to give the wives. The St Austell guardians, having previously decided to grant outdoor relief "to women who had not heard from their husbands for a considerable period, as such women were virtually abandoned by the head of the family", changed their policy and announced that these wives would only be offered admission to the workhouse and would not have the option of outdoor relief.[89] The boards of guardians at Penzance, Liskeard, Helston, Redruth and Truro took the same line in refusing outdoor relief to deserted wives.[90]

The Penzance guardians, however, soon reconsidered their resolution (described as "somewhat hasty and sweeping") not to grant any more outdoor relief to the wives and children of men abroad as they realised that rigid application of the new rule would fill the workhouse, cost more and militate against their existing efforts to "rid children of workhouse associations".[91] The St Austell guardians had taken the precaution of assessing whether their workhouse could accommodate all their cases before making the decision. At the time they were supporting 29 wives and 89 dependent children, left destitute by men in America and elsewhere, with outdoor relief. However, it is likely that they did not anticipate that all these families would actually go into the workhouse; when the rule was imposed at Helston 24 wives were receiving outdoor relief but only two went into 'the house'.[92] This reinforced perceptions amongst the guardians that if they refused outdoor relief to deserted wives in favour of applying the workhouse test more rigidly, the women would "struggle hard to avoid the House",[93] and their husbands would act more responsibly.

There is evidence for a reduction in the numbers of wives receiving outdoor relief over the following twenty-year period,[94] but whether this was down to a change in the behaviour of the husbands or determination to avoid 'the house' on the part of the wives is debatable. Nevertheless, in using the workhouse test in their enthusiasm to apply pressure on the husbands, few seem to remember that it was the wives who had to live with the consequences. When it was pointed out to a Redruth guardian that refusal to give deserted wives a little relief would also break up their homes, he retorted: "The man has broken up the home when he left his family". A lone voice responded: "But the woman has not".[95]

Even when the guardians had decided against outdoor relief in principle, they frequently made exceptions when faced with the facts of individual cases.[96] The chairman of the Penzance board had to remind the guardians there that "he had again and again deprecated their breaking through" their own rule regarding helping deserted women, and "his difficulty had been in preventing them from finding special circumstances in connection with every case".[97] Reflecting on his term of office at Redruth an outgoing guardian cautioned against short-termism: "he feared that they, as well as nearly every other board, are too much inclined to look to the single case before them rather than to the general aspect of the relief in question". Another noted: "Much waste may occur in the method of granting relief and in a false sympathy, with the result of increased pauperdom out-of-doors and a lessening of the valuable house-test. The more the Poor-law board's rules and suggestions are acted on the better".[98]

Over time the Cornish guardians became entangled in their own efforts to deal with the problem and practice bore little resemblance to policies, of which the guardians themselves were not fully cognisant. When presented with the case of a deserted woman from Illogan asking for boots for her children in November 1886 the clerk to the Redruth Board of Guardians had to remind the board that they had the power to relieve such cases under the Local Government Board regulations but had passed a local bye-law many years previously forbidding it. He intimated that the guardians were probably not well enough acquainted with the Poor Law to know to what extent these local rules agreed with it.[99] In 1892 the same clerk pointed out to his board that the bye-laws to give outdoor relief to deserted wives that they were questioning again "had been passed in 1886 and you have altered them every year since".[100] They had, for example, in 1888 rescinded their resolution that allowed deserted wives to be relieved 'under exceptional circumstances' in the face of rapidly rising costs of outdoor relief for the women.[101] When the Helston guardians discussed the matter in 1895, the chairman ruefully noted that they once had a hard and fast rule refusing relief in such cases.[102]

Although in some unions, notably Redruth, the demands for poor relief were exceptionally high in the later years of the 19th century,[103] there were other times when it was surprisingly low, such as during the depression of the late 1860s, especially in the context of the large numbers of wives estimated to have been 'left behind'. However, it should be remembered that the numbers receiving poor relief is only a measure of destitution, as opposed to poverty. Some of the reported cases of wives requesting outdoor relief refer to the wives having not received any remittances from their husbands for months or even years, raising the question of how they had been managing all that time. In 1893 a young wife living in Gwennap, whose husband in the USA had not sent her any money for 12 months, was described as having "struggled hard during the last year and it was considered surprising that she had done so well for her children".[104] Among the cases outlined in the press reports some wives were stated to have been working, while others got by on credit from shopkeepers or money from friendly societies or clubs,[105] but there are also references to help from neighbours,[106] informal handouts and practical help from relieving officers and poor law guardians,[107] while during the depression years help sometimes came in the form of clothes and bedding from the distress funds[108] and assistance from local worthies.[109]

There is also evidence that many wives were reluctant even to apply for relief, especially as the process exposed them to subjective judgement of their character and behaviour. Families were said to be prepared to suffer great privations before appealing for relief, even to the point of starvation.[110] Those who did apply could fall foul of changing national, and sometimes mercurial local poor law policies that denied or delayed relief. This implies that although neglect and desertion of the wives appears to have been far from universal, there must have been an unknown degree of hidden poverty among the women, and many probably had to cope with straitened circumstances either intermittently or for long periods.

Although in many respects the poor law treatment of the wives 'left behind' was harsh, the power devolved to local unions produced a more flexible system than is often supposed, enabling them to supplement the wives' irregular and intermittent income from their husbands abroad as required. Nevertheless, the diverse and changing interpretations of poor law policy led to variations in the wives' access to relief and they were not always guaranteed help outside the workhouse. Further research would be required to ascertain exactly which bye-laws were in operation at different times within each of the different poor law unions in Cornwall,[111] but it is clear that not all the Cornish unions adopted the same bye-laws, or were subject to the same Orders from the Poor Law Commission and its successors. Therefore wives in different mining areas or applying at different times could get very different responses from the relieving officers.[112] One of the drivers for such inconsistent local policies was concern over misuse of the poor law relief system, as explored in the next chapter.

6

'Unworthy' Wives and 'Forgetful' Husbands
Deceit and collusion

The debate about whether the 'deserted' or 'half-deserted' wives should be given outdoor relief resurfaced time and time again at the fortnightly meetings of the Cornish boards of guardians. Opinion oscillated between taking a hard line to deter men from leaving their families chargeable to the parish and a more sympathetic approach to the wives and children.[1] One factor influencing the guardians' attitudes was the realisation that some wives, as well as some husbands, were manipulating the poor laws to their advantage.

The rulings against outdoor relief for deserted wives had been introduced largely to curtail poor law expenditure by better motivating husbands to maintain their wives. As the chairman of the Penzance guardians noted, "when the husbands knew that the Board of Guardians would maintain the deserted wives out of doors they would send no maintenance whatsoever, but when they knew that no relief, except the House, would be granted for 12 months they would be more likely to contribute towards the support of their wives".[2] There were also fears that the knowledge that the wives and families would be supported by the guardians would encourage husbands to leave. A Penzance guardian "denounced the conduct of men who migrate and who leave their wives and children to the tender mercies of other people; but at the same time hinted at occasional connivance of the said wives to let their husbands go, in the belief that the rates can support everybody".[3] Why should hard working rate payers support "unworthy objects - women who had driven their husbands away, or had agreed for them to leave and risk their and their children's coming on the parish", he demanded. Some years later another noted that "These cases were extremely difficult to deal with, and it was almost impossible to escape deceit and collusion in many of them".[4]

Some wives, it seems, were deliberately playing the system. One of the reasons that Redruth had passed a local bye-law forbidding outdoor relief to the women was "because it was found that several women were receiving relief and also money from their husbands at one and the same time".[5] In 1876 a St Austell guardian recalled that some years previously a woman had been denied relief under the rules "but the Board, considering the hardship of the case, gave her money privately, and yet it subsequently transpired that she was in receipt of money from her husband, this coming by the post office".[6] A Helston wife in receipt of outdoor relief was found to have been receiving money from her husband but was saving it so she could join him abroad sooner.[7] The Chairman of the Helston Board of Guardians was later to note: "Some years ago they were in the habit of giving relief to families where the husband had gone away and left the mother with five or six children behind. They found, however, that they were imposed upon, because many of these families were receiving relief from abroad".[8]

In 1881 the *Royal Cornwall Gazette* carried an item entitled 'A Nut for the Board of Guardians'. This related how a "poor widow woman, about 60 years of age, industrious, and whose pride was to avoid being a burden to the parish" complained that "she is constantly assailed by young women and called a fool for not pulling a long face and asking for parish relief; that amongst her assailants are those who regularly receive remittances from America, and conceal such sources of income from the relieving officer; that these persons are well able to work but resolutely decline to do so".[9] The belief that some wives were cheating the system was also fuelled by rumour and hearsay. When a woman who claimed she knew persons in receipt of relief who received money from abroad, was challenged to name them, she "whispered that she heard from Mrs A that Mrs B had said that Mrs C thought that Mrs D had seen Mrs E receive a letter from the postman on a day that foreign letters are due".[10]

The extent to which Cornish wives concealed remittances in order to claim relief can only be guessed at, but the number of 'impostors who ought not to be relieved' was certainly a concern for the Cornish poor law officers who realised that they could not take applicants' claims at face value. A Redruth guardian stressed that "the fullest enquiry ought to be made in each individual case, and that the clerk to try communicate with the husbands".[11] The relieving officer for St Ives tested one applicant by

The Married Widows of Cornwall

asking to see her letters from abroad, which he understood contained money. He felt his suspicions were confirmed when she refused to show them to him and did not trouble him again with her application.[12] When a union prosecuted one such 'impostor', 19 other recipients of relief took themselves off the books rather than face an enquiry.[13] In a much later case, the suspicions of one guardian were aroused when he had heard that the child of a woman from Newquay, who had been receiving outdoor relief for some time, was having expensive piano lessons. On investigation it was found that the mother had been receiving over £1 a week from her husband in America all along.[14]

Guardians became convinced that deceit was commonplace, one claiming "I believe it can be shown that the wives of these men do not care two pence for their husbands so long as they can get relief from us, and also that they get money from their husbands in addition to what they receive from this Board. This has been a vexed question for years".[15]

In 1885 the Editor of the *Cornishman* spelled out the guardians' dilemma:

> "A few years since, when miners quitted the west in shoals, the Penzance guardians decided that no wife left at home by a husband should receive outdoor relief until 12 months had elapsed. The workhouse, of course, could always be claimed. The rule worked well and has not been formally abandoned. We do not say that its strict observance did not inflict some hardships, ... but the regulation, doubtless, was mainly based on discoveries.. that relief is often openly received, while aid from friends abroad is carefully concealed. Postmen and neighbours do not, as a rule, know the contents of letters. Banks and post offices are reticent, very properly so, about drafts or orders they cash. And so the relieving officer and the guardians are in a dilemma - unmerited assistance, a refusal which may be harsh, or the breaking up of a home for that house which is so unhomelike."[16]

There were two things, he suggested, that influenced the guardians' decisions: "the character of the applicant for truthfulness, or the opposite" and the behaviour of past recipients. "One honest deed by a pauper and the board shew that they have a heart; and for some time their trust in their poorer fellow-creatures is enlarged and warmed: one subterfuge or trick and that heart contracts and hardens." He concluded: "Guardians must occasionally find themselves in such a fix that they scarcely know what decision to give."

The other concern troubling the boards of guardians was that to give outdoor relief would be "an encouragement to men to go away and leave their wives and children to shift for themselves, with the assistance of the Board".[17] This argument was offered in 1886 when the Redruth guardians debated their bye-law forbidding outdoor relief to the wives, "for if wives were getting relief from the union, the husband was not so anxious to send her money".[18] Despite this argument the bye-law was rescinded and outdoor relief allowed, but two years later in the face of rising expenditure Redruth guardians changed their minds. To give outdoor relief to the wives "was a great inducement for husbands, who did not care much about their wives and families, to leave their home; and, if they got a little nest of eggs afterwards, they thought their wives were being cared-for at home and that they need not trouble anything about them".[19]

This notion was confirmed when a Redruth official was informed by a man in South Africa in 1890 that "there was a man there who is saving up all the money he could and was not maintaining his wife at home, as he thinks that if the guardians take care of her he will have more money to live on after he returns home". It was becoming all too common, it was reported, "for husbands to go off and leave their wives unprovided for, as they are sure their families would not be allowed to starve".[20] Fears that this was a growing problem for the guardians and the rate payers were expressed again in 1892 when a Redruth guardian argued that it was "an act of injustice on our part to saddle the rates unnecessarily and encourage people to come here while their husbands are away doing we don't know what". His words being met by cheers and cries of: "That is the truth of it." He predicted that they were going to hear a lot more about this problem from the other various parishes in the union.[21]

In the face of the increasing cost of outdoor relief, which was ascribed to wife desertion,[22] what could the guardians do? One idea, put to the Penzance guardians in the winter of 1873, "to suppress these sad cases of husbands going abroad and leaving their wives and families dependent on the untravelled, less adventurous, but burdened taxpayers" was to petition Parliament to introduce legislation to prevent husbands from going abroad without taking their wives and families with them, or leaving a guarantee for their future maintenance.[23] Although this was thought to be rather impracticable, the guardians referred the matter to a committee. This agreed "that the desertion of families by those leaving the country is a great, and they fear an increasing, evil; that it inflicts a double wrong - first, in driving the family deserted to pauperism and possibly crime; and second, that it imposes an unjust and additional burden on an already heavily-taxed community".[24] The Penzance board decided to approach the Local Government Board (LGB) in London to see what could be done, suggesting that other boards of guardians should do likewise. However, this did not produce particularly helpful results as the LGB simply replied that they would "be glad to adopt any remedy, could one be found".[25]

Some wives also felt that the government should do more. The wife of a stonemason, who was in the Cape and not sending home sufficient funds to support her and their ill son, told the Helston guardians in 1882 that she "thought that the Board might represent affairs to the English Government, who would make her husband maintain".[26]

Others felt that the emigration agents were at fault. In 1883 concern was expressed by a Redruth guardian that agents in Redruth and Camborne were sending away men who left their wives and families with no maintenance, and argued that "both agents and wives should see that some provision is made". However, both agents and wives could be deceived. An emigration agent by the name of Piper had recently been blamed for sending away a man whose delicate wife soon wanted relief, but the man had told Piper that he was single and told the wife that she would receive £4 a month. Captain T. Angove reassured the Board that as representative of the huge Rio Tinto mines he "had never sent out a man (and would not send one, if he had to deal with ten thousand) who did not leave behind a proper provision for his family".[27]

There was a well-established procedure for dealing with husbands who failed to maintain their wives and families, leaving them chargeable to the parish, i.e. to be supported by the ratepayers. Deserting husbands were subject to prosecution at the instigation of the boards of guardians, who would arrange for the men to be apprehended and brought before a judge.[28] Those convicted were usually committed to prison for periods of one to three months with hard labour, often on the treadmill at Bodmin gaol.[29] The variation in length of sentence reflected the circumstances; one received six weeks hard labour because it was his second offence.[30] On occasion the matter could be resolved without resort to imprisonment; in 1840 William Bunt avoided prison after he deserted his wife and children by promising to pay all the parish expenses incurred and live with his family in future.[31] The guardians took a dim view if men failed to honour such arrangements, as Charles Rule discovered to his cost. When he failed to abide by an order to pay his wife ten shillings a week in the summer of 1893 he was sent to Bodmin gaol for 21 days, and a year later when he had still failed to pay the money he was jailed again and the guardians advised to seize his furniture.[32] The aim of these punishments was to deter other men from abandoning their dependants and minimise further calls on the public purse. As such they were publicised in the press; details of two cases were printed in 1844 under the heading: 'Caution to persons deserting their families'.[33]

The problem was catching the men. In 1871 the *Royal Cornwall Gazette* suggested that Cornish boards of guardians might learn a lesson from their counterparts in Birmingham in dealing with truant husbands. There they had a dedicated officer tasked with tracing and seeing the men captured and brought to book. The Birmingham guardians were also of the opinion that imprisonment was insufficient punishment and the magistrates should be able to order the men to repay the relief expended on their wives.[34] If the man had not gone too far they could be found and prosecuted, like the husband of a charwomen in Praze who was brought back from Wales in 1893 and sent to jail for three months.[35] Men who had gone further afield were harder to catch. Under the headline 'Gone to earth', the *Cornishman* reported that the attempts of guardians to trace a man who had left his wife in Redruth eight years previously had failed despite searching for him as far afield as Wales and Lancashire.[36]

Some guardians felt that the deserters abroad should be pursued with equal determination. Speaking of a man from St Ives whose wife had been taken into the workhouse, a Penzance guardian argued that: "he has promised to maintain her and we ought to find him. If he was a burglar we should find him fast enough." In that case the clerk thought that they might arrest the husband if he was in Canada (subject to British law) but not in the United States.[37] When a guardian suggested they find out something about another man who had deserted his wife after going to Africa, it was pointed out that he was in the Free-state not a British colony, to which the response was "If he were in Mount Ararat I think we ought to find out something about him".[38] In 1894 the *Cornishman* proclaimed 'An Extradition Treaty Wanted for Faithless, Cruel, Husbands' when the Redruth guardians were again wondering what to do about the cost to the ratepayers, running at £10 a week, of supporting deserted wives. Stressing what a serious matter it had become, one guardian proposed: "We ought to try to get at these men and not let matters go so quiet." It was suggested that: "it would be worth spending a little money to reach a man who has not been contributing to his wife's maintenance". However, there was also a feeling that "many women will shield their husbands and come on the rates".[39] In reality there was little hope of prosecuting the husbands unless they returned. An editorial in the *Cornishman* warned a man whose wife had been receiving relief despite him being reported to be "in good employ, with excellent pay" that as "he nears the English coast" a warrant awaited him "ere he can waste his pay".[40]

The difficulty in dealing with emigrating men deserting their wives was not a uniquely Cornish issue. Historian Marjorie Levine-Clark has drawn attention to references in newspaper reports and poor law records to wives 'left behind' in the Black Country, where they were also discovering that the empire (and beyond): "created space for neglectful husbands to make themselves invisible to the authorities back home".[41]

Unable to ensure that emigrating men left provision for their wives before they departed, or to prosecute the deserters, the boards of guardians could only try to alleviate the problem by exerting pressure from afar. This was the rationale behind withholding outdoor relief from the wives and only offering them the workhouse. In 1885 Helston guardians refused relief to a wife from Four Lanes whose husband in Australia "remits money to her but irregularly" with the simple reasoning that "the husband should maintain his wife".[42] However, this relied on the premise that no husband or father would want to see his family broken up and in the workhouse, and would therefore send adequate maintenance. Some guardians questioned whether the threat of the workhouse had any power to influence the behaviour of men who were neglecting their families anyway. When one Redruth guardian argued in 1892 for the application of the workhouse test in the case of a deserted wife because "if we maintain them outdoors the husband abroad is as happy as a lark", another pointed out that "He is just as happy if they are indoors, and it afflicts an additional burden on a poor woman and children. You may have a rogue in America but you have the family here".[43] It was an ongoing concern that applying the workhouse test had little effect on the men, but inflicted punishment on often blameless wives who were effectively treated in the same way as those who had illegitimate children.

The welfare of wives and families remaining in the mining communities in Cornwall depended on "the good conduct of those who have emigrated".[44] However, in the last decades of the 19th century there was increasing feeling that this could not be relied upon, and the boards of guardians and the press became increasingly vocal in their criticism of the husbands abroad. The behaviour of a husband in California who had not sent his wife and four children any money for a year, and who had returned her letters, was described in 1889 as 'Rather American'.[45] In 1893 a husband who had failed to support his wife and five children for more than five years was referred to as "A Cornish 'gentleman' in Africa".[46] Reports of other cases appeared under headings such as "Forgets to Love and Cherish",[47] "Australia's Forgetful Climate",[48] and "Absence causes forgetfulness".[49] "Another Disgracefully Negligent Husband" in the USA, who had reportedly "picked up with the meanest company and spends his money as he ought not to do", neglecting his wife and three children, was named a 'blackguard' by the guardians.[50] Under the headline "A serious indictment against absent miners" another man was described as "an able man but a negligent one" who too had "acted the blackguard in not sending home money".[51]

Given the number of cases coming before them (in November 1898 the Camborne district had 50 children not being supported by their fathers abroad), the guardians frequently vented their displeasure at the men's behaviour and wished they could punish them.[52] Feelings sometimes ran high. In February 1892 under the heading 'Down upon wife deserters', one guardian was reported to have said: "I am warm on this subject and, therefore, can scarcely trust myself"; his colleague commented that he "would not kill them, but he would beat them so that they couldn't live".[53] In one 'wretched case', a Redruth guardian thought the husband in question "ought to be flogged for neglecting a delicate woman in this manner".[54] On hearing yet another case of a wife whose husband in America had not sent her any money for two years, some Camborne guardians are reported as "wondering why some of these men are not drowned".[55]

The rhetoric increasingly blamed the men and exonerated the wives, casting them as the victims. On 15 September 1892 the editorial column of the *Cornishman* commented on the serious increase in demands being made on the union for outdoor relief, noting that: "a considerable portion of this heavy burden is caused by the neglect of husbands who have emigrated". A guardian was reported as thinking:

> "that even the poorest ratepayers will cheerfully bear some heavier burden rather than that wives, who have suffered by the neglect of those who have solemnly pledged themselves to safeguard and succour them, and innocent children, should be forced into the workhouse or starved…This speaks very well for the Cornish folk who are not tempted to wrong, as are some of the absentees, though these last are in receipt of ample wages… Of course the closest inquiry abroad as well as at home, should be made into each case."[56]

There was a growing feeling that it was not lack of work that was preventing the men from supporting their wives. Speaking at a meeting at Wheal Owles mine St Just in 1870, Mr William Bolitho complained that: "even when miners were abroad earning good wages, they too often failed to make any remittances home for the maintenance of their wives and children". He had known "numerous instances in which the greatest amount of destitution prevailed from the above-mentioned causes, and such a state of things was much to be deplored".[57] In 1895 the Penzance guardians were told that a man had left his wife and four children destitute in Madron, while it was known that he was getting £25 a month in Africa.[58] Similar complaints were made in 1899 when it was reported that when a large contingent left Redruth for the Transvaal by a special train, "a problem was created for the Redruth guardians with 42 children having to be supported as the emigrants were not contributing to their maintenance".[59] There was a perception that while the husbands went abroad, 'to better themselves', the wives were worse off than when they were at home.[60]

An insightful commentary in the *Cornishman* provides a useful summary of marital breakdown arising from the strains of transnational marriage and its consequences for the wives in Cornwall:

> *"Sheer neglect comes over some who were good husbands or sons at home. Or improper relations spring up between the absent ones and sirens in the strange land; letters and remittances grow fewer; then utter silence. Gloom and fear, then (as some whisper comes that the traitorous absentee is alive and well) distrust, and, lingeringly but finally, no hope - these haunt many a household. Some grieve silently; for others the public tale is compulsory; that the children may not starve the relieving officer has to hear the tear-stained story and the rates suffer for the shameful drunkard or shameless adulterer abroad. On the other hand queer stories crop up of the bad conduct of wives at home, well provided for by faithful husbands who toil for them in distant lands."*[61]

Drink was frequently believed to be the root cause of neglect. Asked by the Redruth guardians in 1898 why her husband in Africa did not send her money, a 'very highly respected' woman told them that he spent it on drink.[62] Another wife, whose husband was also in Africa, told the Penzance guardians that "last time she heard from him he said he would not give up his drink for anyone, and she should not think anymore about him".[63] Concerns were expressed that by relieving the families outside the house guardians were "encouraging drunkards and their wives" but "bad wives sometimes drive men abroad".[64] On hearing that a man in Africa who had not sent any money to his family in Camborne for five months had written home saying he was in hospital, a suspicious Redruth guardian commented that: "A saloon is the hospital".[65] Yet another wife, Minnie Hocking from Camborne, who was receiving very irregular remittances from her husband supposedly working at the Simmer and Jack Mine in

Africa, heard via her brother that he had left the mine and gone on a drinking spree.[66] Referring to a later case concerning a husband in California, a guardian quipped: "Thus Cornish ratepayers prop up Grass Valley's institutions, of which bar and saloon are not the least".[67]

Some of this emphasis on drink may simply reflect the growth of the temperance movement in Cornwall,[68] although as neglect due to drink was a driver of that movement it is difficult to determine whether the extent of the migrant men's drinking was overstated or not. Certainly, the conditions and rough culture of many mining camps were not conducive to temperance. Writing of the Cornish miners in Chile, Sharron Schwartz suggests: "It is not hard to understand why, in these forsaken camps, the small numbers of Cornish, denied access to regular sermons or prayer meetings, soon turned their backs on Methodism and sought solace in drink". Under these circumstances even the most devout could become 'backsliders'.[69] However, temptations for some started closer to home. Having recruited a group of carpenters and despatched them to Wales to await a ship for Cuba in 1837, Alfred Jenkin warned: "It is very undesirable that they should be supplied with much money to spend in intoxicating liquor whilst at Swansea".[70]

The local press also took a critical stance of neglectful husbands. In 1894 W. Herbert Thomas of the *Cornishman* wrote:

> "Cornishmen abroad, many of them unworthy of that name, who neglect wives and their own little children at home, ought to be proclaimed in every newspaper, placarded on each hoarding, refused work and companionship, and treated generally as disgraced men. Especially should mine-managers discourage, even to discharging from employ, such workers. Let better men take their places. A resolute course of action like this would do more to recall Cornishmen to their duty than reams of Board talk and home newspaper reports. There are many Cornishmen abroad, not all miners, who richly deserve gaol and a cat-o'-nine-tails for their conduct to unimpeachable wives and children who would do credit to any parents. Yet these poor souls are left to misery and semi-starvation, while prodigals spend pounds weekly in self indulgence."[71]

'Unworthy' Wives and 'Forgetful' Husbands

Thomas knew that the Cornish newspapers were widely read amongst the emigrant Cornish communities around the world and could be confident that these entreaties would be seen, even if not heeded. Having appealed to the husbands' consciences, he returned to the subject again the following year under the headline 'Negligent absentee husbands':

> "One of the South Africa 'gentlemen', who spend money and make a big show abroad, sometimes in dissipation and almost always in the selfish gratification of whim as well as want, has neglected his wife for six months. Her last £4 was half-a-year ago. The neglected wife, for children and self, has had to apply for poor-law relief. It is not granted. She has not been deserted a year, and she can shelter in the workhouse. Who can describe the anguish of vanishing means, of anxiously-waited mails, of the sale of household treasures to get bread, of the oft disappointment which makes sick hearts? If it should meet the eye of anyone who causes these home sufferings let us entreat him to think of that home and be merciful, as he hopes for mercy."[72]

Four months later Thomas decided that pressure from those around them might be more effective in influencing the men:

> "I hear that it costs Redruth Union fully £12 a week to maintain the wives and families of men who have either deserted them or are unable to send money from foreign countries to which they have emigrated. Some guardians would like to force the women into the workhouse in order to check the depravity of the heartless and negligent husbands and fathers. Such action would be unmerited by the wives and children and would have not the slightest effect on the scamps who prefer foreign liquor and women to sobriety, industry, and the welfare of their families. If a man would allow his family to appeal to the guardians for outdoor relief he would not be stimulated to manly conduct by his family having to endure the additional hardship of becoming inmates of the workhouse. Such wretches ought to be drummed-out of every mining camp."[73]

The guardians too realised that harnessing community pressure might be a way of getting negligent husbands to do their duty. Clerks were frequently instructed to write to the husbands concerned.[74] However, it seems this met with little success. When asked whether he had ever had any response to the letters he sent to men abroad, the clerk to the Penzance board could only remember having received one reply.[75] If direct appeals from the guardians fell on deaf ears it was hoped that family or friends might have more influence. In the case of a woman in Bodmin asylum, whose husband abroad was said to be able to afford to contribute towards her support, it was hoped that "relatives at home will try to get him to do so".[76] When the husband of a Mrs Stephens, with five children from Baripper in Redruth Union, had failed to remit for six months, the guardians could not understand why her relatives who were known to be working with the husband every day did not see to it that money was sent home.[77] Some attempts to put pressure on the men failed spectacularly. It was reported to the Penzance board that a husband in America who had deserted his wife for 16 or 17 months had been spoken to by "some mutual friends" who knew that he had earned £20 for a month's work. However, when they followed up and "bothered" him a bit about his neglected family in Cornwall, he left his occupation and fled to "unknown regions".[78]

Another tactic was to contact the men's employers abroad. This had been used in 1813 when several men from Redruth employed on the construction of the Plymouth breakwater were failing to support their families.[79] The overseers of the poor had not only informed the men that they would stop relief to the families, they had contacted their employers asking them to let them know how much each man was being paid and how much he was sending. In the 1890s there are numerous references to union clerks being instructed to write to the managers of the mines where the men concerned were employed and make them aware of the facts.[80] The newspapers joined in with direct appeals for action from the employers of named men. In 1899 the *Cornishman* publicised another case of neglect, this time of the wife of St Day man Joseph Ham. Although not named in the press, Joseph's wife can be identified from the census as Bessie Ham (née Tiddy). Joseph had been last heard of working at the Simmer and Jack mine in Johannesburg and had only sent home £21 in the previous 18 months to his wife and three children, about a twentieth of what he was paid, claimed the paper, which asked "Can the wail of the deserted reach the proprietors of the Simmer and Jack?"[81]

Some guardians could attest from personal experience that employers could be useful allies. A mine agent told his fellow Redruth guardians that when he had been abroad and had been informed that the wives of some of his men were receiving relief: "We told the men we were astounded at their conduct and that they would not get another day's work with us unless they left money with us to send home. They never deserted their families after that".[82] The problem, as pointed out by the clerk, was that he could only write to the mine agents asking them to get the men to send money to their families if he knew where to send the letter. All too frequently the wives could only give the last known address, which might be several years out of date, and did not know where their husbands were. A Redruth guardian recalled that "he had known cases where the name of the deserter had been sent to the agent of the mine in which he worked and the amount of relief had been regularly deducted from his earnings". The Chairman wryly responded, to the board's amusement: "When they know that, they generally move to a more convenient spot". It was the board's duty to look for the husband if his family became chargeable, "but the difficulty is to get to know his whereabouts".[83]

The solution, many of the guardians felt, was to use the newspapers to 'find them out'. There was an established practice of poor law unions publishing the names of men who had deserted their wives so that they could be found and arrested. The Redruth board had subscribed to one of the papers that carried these notices, but this was only for men who had gone to parts of England.[84] The guardians wanted to find a way of exposing the married men abroad who were not adequately supporting their families. The answer, they decided, was to publish their names in the places where they might be "to show up their bad conduct to their friends and employers"[85] and "if the facts were mentioned in the *Cornishman* and other papers they would soon reach Australia, Johannesburg, etc".[86] In reporting calls from the guardians that the husbands should be "shown up" in the press, the Editor of the *Cornishman* reminded readers that they frequently did give publicity to such cases.[87] Indeed in January 1895 the *Cornishman* reported a case where relief had been granted to a wife whose husband in America had sent her nothing in two years. The wife was named as Mrs Sowden of Rosewarne Road, Camborne. This clear identification and the publication of the item under the heading "Nothing for two years - Where is Sowden?" was a deliberate attempt to name and shame the husband.[88]

This strategy was not without risks. In October 1897 the 'Local Miscellany' correspondent of the *Cornishman* suggested that the newspapers in America, Johannesburg and Coolgardie, or wherever the men might be, should be supplied with, and asked to publish, the names of "neglectful or forgetful husbands", so that "the many honest Cornishmen may find out their less moral countrymen's doubtful doings and make them remember those at home with a little more regularity of remittance or leave the district they are in, banished by Cornish contempt, to find work nowhere." However, a note appended to the piece by the paper's editor pointed out that no paper would publish the names for fear of prosecution. "There are cunning Cornishmen and unscrupulous lawyers in every city, town and camp. The one would suggest, the other bring (for costs) libel-actions against the newspaper that sought to remind of neglectful duties. How can the paper justify publication, except at a ruinous cost of evidence fetched from Cornwall?" He was speaking with the voice of experience: "We have known of such threats abroad: indeed for that matter, at home", referring to a lawyer in West Cornwall who had made it known that he was keen to prosecute a newspaper on behalf of any client on what would now be called a 'no win - no fee' basis.[89]

The clerk to the Redruth board also urged caution pointing out "that in some cases it might be that the husbands were sending over all they could, and that the wives might be concealing that fact from the relieving-officers, and the men lose their situations when the fault was with the women, who had been sponging on the husbands and the rates".[90] The guardians were also worried about prosecution. If they published a list of men who had 'deserted' their families, and one of them had not deserted in the strict legal sense of the term, the board would be liable to an action for libel.[91] Their fears proved correct and the Redruth clerk stopped contacting employers abroad after the High Court of Justice opined that the mere statement to an employer or any person in power over a man that his wife and family were receiving relief was in itself a libel calculated to damage the man, who could sue the board, or more specifically the

'Unworthy' Wives and 'Forgetful' Husbands

clerk, on his return.[92] Although the problem was most acute in Redruth,[93] other unions such as Truro and Penzance were having very similar discussions exploring the merits of exactly the same strategies for trying to compel "these heartless men to support their families and to prevent other men from following their example".[94]

By December 1898 'the deserted wives question' was becoming increasingly serious. Guardians from both Redruth and Penzance were complaining of the numbers of cases on their books of wives and families deserted by men who had gone out to Africa, including ones where men were in full work and doing well, but leaving their families dependent on the rates at home.[95] The Redruth board decided that they had to take action. The clerk had come up with a plan for naming and shaming the negligent husbands without being sued; the board would not advertise the men as deserters, but simply make sure full details were given about each relief case at the full fortnightly board meetings, which were attended by the press reporters who had agreed to include them in their reports.[96]

The existing practice up to that time was, in most cases, to maintain the anonymity of the woman or family receiving relief:

> *1891 August – "A married women living at Wheal Harriet" - "has a husband living abroad who sent her £19 in 12 months. She has three children. It was decided to grant her 3s a week and three loaves on loan".*[97]

> *1891 December – "A young married woman from Stithians" - her husband had gone to Michigan 18 months earlier and since the previous June had only sent her 40s. She was granted 3s a week and three loaves for three months.*[98]

> *1892 February – "A woman named Tucker" of Buller Downs and her two children. Her husband was in Kimberley, South Africa. For the 12 months, while he was working for a company there he had sent money home to his wife at regularly, but now he had 'deserted' her sending "only trifles at long intervals". "It was stated that the wife was a most respectable woman and the fault is not on her side; so relief was continued for her".*[99]

1892 December – "Relief was continued to a Camborne woman whose husband, in America, has not sent her anything during the last four months".[100]

1893 January – "Forgets to Love and Cherish" - "A poor woman living at Beacon, Camborne, has two children, and her husband, in Montana, has not sent her money for 12 months. He wrote in April saying he would write again when he got work. He has not done so. He has been abroad five years and sent regularly until a year ago. His neglected wife works a little." Relief granted.[101]

1893 September – 'Australia's Forgetful Climate' – Ellen Thomas of Brea was maintained by husband but he hasn't written from Australia for two years. Granted 5s and six loaves per week.[102]

1893 December – "Poor soul - must have help" - "Relief was granted to a Carnbell woman named Rogers whose husband went abroad, two months ago, and has not been heard from since. She has been confined since he left".[103]

1894 April – "A woman from Ventonleage has received nothing from her husband in America during the last 18 months. Relief continued for three months".[104]

1894 April – "A woman, living at Brea, said her husband in Minnesota, USA, works for a dollar a day, as the distress is so keen. She has four children, and was granted 2s and two loaves." Extra loaf added when guardian commented that he couldn't see how the family could live on that.[105]

1895 February – "Sad neglect or inability" – "The wife of a once well known Camborne singer, who has had nothing from her husband (now in America) for two years, again desired relief from the Redruth guardians, on Friday. It was said to be a sad case." Allowed boots and continued relief.[106]

'Unworthy' Wives and 'Forgetful' Husbands

1895 May – "Absence causes forgetfulness" – "A woman called Tresawna, at Penponds, has a husband in California, who has not sent to her for two years. She does not know his address. Relieved".[107]

1895 July – "Where is the husband?" – "A woman at Polgear, Wendron, deserted by her husband three years ago, when he went to America, was granted relief".[108]

1897 February – "A Copperhouse woman, with two children, was obliged to apply for relief, as her husband, who is in Africa, has not sent her any money for eight months. The guardians decided to give 1s 6d and two loaves for three months".[109]

After the decision in 1898 by the Redruth guardians to give full case details in front of the press, the tone of these reports changed. Highlighting the particular case of a husband in Africa, said to be getting £35 a month but not sending anything to his wife, who was forced along with one of her children to go out to work, the Editor of the *Cornishman* stressed:

"Such men ought to be shown up in the papers. So any man - in the Transvaal from Camborne (and this negligent one is from here and is there) - should have his eye on the man wanted: we can further inform him that the little woman is very industrious, is about 35, and it is well worth the effort of some Cousin Jack to ferret-out this earthworm and make him send to his family."[110]

Over the next few months the *Cornishman* published more detailed reports, giving the names and addresses of the wives who had received relief from the Redruth guardians. All pretence of retaining anonymity was abandoned in an attempt to shame the husbands:

1 December 1898 – Mrs Catherine Goldsworthy, of Gwinear. She had three children, and said her husband, who is abroad, had not sent her money for three years. Relief granted.

The Married Widows of Cornwall

Mrs Louisa Richards of Centenary Row Camborne given relief for herself and her two children. Her husband was is Africa and had not sent her any money for 12 months.

What started as a couple of cases turned into comprehensive lists:

> **"A SAD LIST OF DESERTED WIVES."**
>
> "A Beacon woman, named Grace Sincock has been granted relief by the Redruth board-of-guardians. She says her husband is in America has not sent her any money for five years.
>
> Mrs James Scown of Baripper, told the Redruth guardians, on Friday, that her husband is in America and has not helped with her maintenance for four months. She was given relief.
>
> Harriet Popham, of Phillack, was also relieved. She says her husband is in Africa and has not sent her any help for two years.
>
> Caroline Gay, of Stithians, reported that her husband had not sent any money for the last year. She was also relieved.
>
> Ellen Daddow, of Illogan, had a similar story. She was given help because she said her husband (in Africa) had not sent her any money for four months."
>
> *Cornishman,* 15 December 1898

W. Herbert Thomas, the Editor of the *Cornishman* drew further attention to the list, which he thought would "speak for itself. I can only hope that this method will achieve the object the guardians have in view".[111] He was keen to use the paper's influence in addressing the neglect of the wives, both in general and individual cases, as in this editorial:

> *"Her husband is now in Africa and won't send her a penny! The little woman is known to the writer of this article as a hard-working, honest wife, whose husband, after making great religious professions, married her as a professedly, model man, no doubt, but oh! the sequel. We will spare his name for the time, but if he continues his cruelty The Cornishman may speak in Africa plainer than he think, perhaps. But here is the main point. We hope to be in communication with persons in authority who will use all possible power to make indifferent, neglectful, unchristian sons of Cornubia send to their wives, or will send these scamps about their business."*[112]

'Unworthy' Wives and 'Forgetful' Husbands

The lists became increasingly detailed as the guardians included the husband's first names and locality so that the men might be more readily identified.[113]

> **"DESERTED WIVES."**
> *"A Heavy List."*
>
> Lillie Trezona, aged 34 of Penponds, with 2 children. Husband in America; not sent for 2 years. He had sent his wife a paper asking her to sign it so he could get a divorce but nothing more had been heard. It was reported that "the friends of this man are doing exceedingly well". (3s & 3 loaves a week)
>
> Emily Ball, 27, of Phillack East, with 2 children. Her husband left two weeks ago and has not been heard of since. There was no food in the house. - Mr Jones said this was not a Hayle family, but had been imported.
>
> Amelia Andrew, Lanner moor, Gwennap, 2 children. Her husband was in Africa and did not send for 5 years. He has since died. (2s & 2 loaves a week)
>
> Elizabeth Gray, with 5 children, St Day. John, the husband, is in Africa, and has had not sent for several years. (3s & 3 loaves a week)
>
> Emily Davey, with 3 children, Carharrack. Richard, the husband, is in America, and has not sent for 7 years. (3 loaves a week)
>
> Emma Jane Terrill, with 1 child, Vogue. Thomas, the husband, in Africa, has not sent any money for 8 months. Her husband writes; and a letter was received from him last week. (1s & 1 loaf a week)
>
> Elizabeth Andrew, with 3 children, Sparnon's Gate, Redruth. Her husband William Andrew, went to America, and has not sent any money for 3 years. (2s & 2 loaves a week)
>
> Mary Jane Watling, Falmouth Road, Redruth, has 7 children. Richard, her husband has not sent for 10 years. (1s 6d a week)
>
> Fannie Grenfell, West Tolgus, Illogan, no children. The husband is in America, and has not sent any money for 5 years. (2s a week)
>
> Susan Trethewey, Carnkie, has 4 children. Her husband, William D. Trethewey, 39, is in America, and has sent no money for 5 years. (3s a week)
>
> Sarah Uren, Carn Brea, with 2 children. William Uren, 34, the husband, went to America, and sent no money for 9 years. (2s & 2 loaves a week)
>
> Catherine Tonkin, Tregajorran, has 6 children. Her husband William Henry, 38, is in America, and has sent no money for a year.
>
> Ellen Daddow, 36, Broad Lane, Illogan, with 4 children. Her husband, William Daddow, aged 29, is in Africa, and has sent no money for 5 months. (5s & 4 loaves a week)
>
> Caroline Gay of Stithians, 5 children. James Gay, her husband, 35, is in Africa, and has not sent any money for a year. (5s & 5 loaves a week)
>
> Elizabeth Knuckey, Stithians, has been left unsupported by her husband, Hugh, who is in America, for 6 years.
>
> *Cornishman,* 12 January 1899

The Married Widows of Cornwall

"REDRUTH BOARD OF GUARDIANS"
"DESERTED WIVES"

"The following cases of women deserted by their husbands were brought under the notice of the board, and, after being commented on, relief was granted:

Mary Williams, Camborne, wife of James Williams, from whom she has not heard for 8 months. Williams was last known to be in Nevada.

Mary Eva, Camborne, 3 children, wife of John Eva, who went to America about 3 years ago, but who has not written for 12 months. He was last heard of at Bear Creek, Colorado.

Mary Goldsworthy, wife of James Goldsworthy, 2 children, not heard from her husband for 6 months. Last heard of at Newcastle, New South Wales.

Mary Rule, Trewithian Downs, 3 children, wife of William Henry Rule, who left home 21 months ago and had not been heard of since.

Grace Sincock, 2 children, wife of Charles Sincock, who left home about 6 years ago. Not sent to wife for 5 years. Last heard of in Montana, USA.

Bessie Sowden, Camborne, 2 children, wife of James Sowden. Heard nothing of her husband for 6 years.

Lillie Trezona, 3 children, wife of William Trezona, who has not sent for 2 years. Last heard of in Colorado, USA.

Caroline Webber, 3 children, wife of John Henry Webber, who is in Africa, but who has not written his wife for 12 months. He was last heard of in Fordsburg, near Johannesburg.

Louisa Richards, Centenary Row, Camborne, 3 children, wife of Richard Richards, who has not sent home for a year. At present in the Transvaal.

Mary Odgers, Camborne, 3 children, wife of James Odgers. Left his home 3 months ago and has not since been heard of.

Catherine Goldsworthy, 3 children, Carnbell, Gwinear, wife of John Goldsworthy, who has not sent to his wife and family for 3 years. Last heard of at Iron Mountain, Michigan, USA.

Jane Scown, 5 children, Bareppa, Camborne. Her husband, who was last heard of at Bear Creek, Colorado, USA has not sent home for 6 months.

Martha Norman, Phillack east, 2 children, wife of James Norman, who has gone on a voyage to Rosario, South America, without making any provision for his wife and family.

Harriet Popham, 4 children, Copperhouse. Her husband, who is in Johannesburg, has not written for 2 years.

Eliza Whitford, Ventonleague, 2 children, wife of Samuel Whitford, last heard of at Salt Lake City, USA, and who has not communicated with his wife and family for 2 years."

Cornishman, 9 February 1899

[Catherine Goldsworthy and Jane Scown are both reported in the *Cornishman* as receiving relief a couple of months later (6 April). Although the earlier report says Jane's husband hadn't sent her any money for 6 months, the second reveals that he left three years earlier and so must have been supporting her up to that point.]

'Unworthy' Wives and 'Forgetful' Husbands

> **"HUSBAND IN COLORADO"**
> "At the Redruth Board of Guardians' meeting, on Thursday, it was reported that six years ago Edward Gilbert left his wife and two children at Pool, to go to Cripple Creek, Colorado, and has not sent them any money for five years. Relief was given."
> *Cornishman, 6 April 1899*

The enthusiasm for naming and shaming the husbands was not universal. The Truro board, which had also decided to advertise the names of men abroad who neglected to maintain their wives and children, had not actually done so. Truro's clerk, after conferring with his counterpart at Redruth, "declined to take on any responsibility in the matter, as an action for libel would be brought against him and not against the board". At least one guardian had little faith that publishing the names would do any good, claiming that: "the men on the Transvaal did not care what people here thought of them".[114] This view was echoed when the LGB inspector, H. Preston Thomas, visited the Truro board a couple of months later and advised them "that when a man was really abroad they could not get at him. He was outside their jurisdiction, and there was nothing practical they could do. Only a small proportion of those who were willing to stay abroad and leave their wives would be ashamed by the chance publication of their names".[115] Even Redruth had second thoughts having mistakenly identified an innocent husband, Thomas Terrill of St Day, as a deserter.[116] After the publication of the February list the practice seemed to have been abandoned although some individual cases, such as the one above, still appeared in the press.[117]

The problem facing all the boards of guardians was that they usually only had one side of the story. As the Redruth clerk explained: "There are wives who sometimes, out of spite, a natural mistake, mental defect, or otherwise, make statements which are not strictly correct and will not bear the light of day".[118] When they were presented with accounts from both husband and wife it was hard to know who to believe. Their quandary is illustrated by a well publicised case before the Helston guardians that occurred while the other boards were wondering if naming and shaming in the press was such a good idea, and may have influenced their decision making. This case is worth looking at in detail as it illustrates not only the guardians' dilemma but also a number of other facets of the experience of the wives 'left behind'.

On 29 December 1898 the *Cornishman* published an item under the headline "A good for nothing scoundrel". This was how one of the Helston guardians had described the husband of Mary Ann Carlyon. She applied for relief because her husband had been away in Colorado for four years but had not sent any money for her and the children for some months, although she had heard from his landlady that he was quite well.[119] A couple of months later the board received an angry letter from the husband, Thomas Carlyon, complaining that his name had been advertised and claiming that he had been sending money home, a total of £93 since he had been away. "It was disgraceful and discouraging for a man to work and send so much money home to a Hoodwink", raged Thomas. "And before the guardians advertise his name he should like them to have some reason for doing so, and should hear both sides of the story before they started afresh. He hoped this would bring his wife a little more economy, for the sooner she got economical the better".[120]

The board wrote to Thomas asking him to repay the relief granted, and summoned Mary Ann to appear before them. She explained that Thomas had gone to Silver City, USA in May 1895 and initially sent money home regularly, but had then gone "on a spree in Utah" before finding his way to her brother in California, who had helped him and sent her money, after which Thomas had gone to Colorado. It had been mainly in the previous 7-8 months that she had gone short. Prior to that he had sent a total of £139, but they had been in debt when he left. She had paid the debts and had heavy expenses, including a confinement and a burial. Mary Ann explained that she had four delicate children aged between three and seven, and she had been ill several times. When confronted with her husband's claim that she was extravagant, she relied "But I am not. Of course he will say anything. He owes my brother £100 now." Mary was considered by the board to have "acted honourably with the money, her character was unblemished", and her relief was continued. The board wrote to the captain of the mine employing Thomas asking them to make him pay up, or leave the mine. Thomas' reply was to tell the board to reclaim their money by holding a public sale of the family furniture, and give any balance of the proceeds to the children, whom he would maintain and put with his mother. As for Mary Ann, she was to have no claim on the children and be left "to go get her living".[121]

By April Helston guardians had received a letter from Mary Ann's brother, James Dunstan, who having seen Thomas's first letter in the press was writing in defence of his sister. At Mary Ann's entreaty James had funded Thomas' emigration, reluctantly as he thought America "not fit place for her husband, knowing that he frequently indulged in the intoxicating cup". He claimed that the £4 that Thomas sent home still left him with $40 a month "which he spent on his own gratification". Thomas, he claimed, had repeatedly borrowed, and even stolen, money from him, spending it and most of what he earned on whiskey, before being robbed and travelling the railroad as a hobo. The debt was now $500, "his own countrymen were ashamed to own him", and family members in America had predicted "that from the way that Carlyon was conducting himself, the time was not far distant when he would forsake his wife entirely".[122] James' letter was endorsed as accurate by mine officials who had encountered Thomas.

This very public family dispute encapsulates many aspects of the phenomenon. Mary Ann was not 'deserted', at least initially, in the literal sense. In fact she had played a major role in facilitating her husband's emigration by arranging the finance. Thomas had sent enough money home for her to get by for several years before encountering some kind of crisis, in which drink appears to have played a role. Mary Ann had actively participated in the decision for him to go in the knowledge that it would leave her to care on her own for at least four children, and possibly knowing that another was on the way. She had competently managed the family finances in his absence, as well as dealing with young children, a new baby and a bereavement, and yet when things went wrong she was in a very vulnerable position, accused of being wasteful and threatened with losing her home and her children. Like many of the wives she only turned to the relieving officers when she had no choice. Whether they would help her depended on their judgement of her character and conduct compared with that of her husband's, and fortunately for Mary Ann she had family prepared to defend her. Others may not have been so lucky.

The problems caused by the number of deserted wives in Cornwall, especially those with husbands in South Africa, was to continue into the first decades of the next century. Summing up the situation in 1902 H. Preston Thomas, LGB inspector, said:

> "It was a crying evil that so many men should go abroad, leaving their wives and children chargeable to their former neighbours, and that the Boards of Guardians could not, in the present state of international law, and the law between the colonies and England, get hold of them. Cornwall felt this state of affairs especially. He would not suggest that Cornishmen were more addicted to deserting their wives and children than other people [laughter] but it was a fact that, from the particular nature of the industries of the county, a greater proportion of Cornishmen went abroad than the inhabitants of most counties. It was the most difficult thing in the world to find a remedy. They would have to make international arrangements, and it would work both ways, because we would have to look after Americans and others and send them back. The complication and intricacies were so great that, although he had often heard the lament that nothing could be done, he had never heard any practicable suggestion as to what could be done."[123]

The affected boards of guardians in Cornwall (including Redruth and Helston), and in other parts of the country, went on to raise the issue at national level with The Royal Commission on the Poor Law and the Colonial Office in hope of finding ways of taking action against the men in South Africa.[124] In 1911 the Cornish Association of the Transvaal in Johannesburg invited any union in Cornwall to contact them to see what could be done to induce men in South Africa to support their wives and families in England (although they would have preferred them to bring their families out to South Africa and settle permanently rather than return to them in Cornwall).[125] As a result, the Association was supplied with lists of men who were failing to maintain their wives and families at home.[126] In 1912 the Cornish boards of guardians were helping to fund the efforts of the Association in South Africa to persuade negligent Cornish miners there to send money home more regularly.[127] An editorial in the *West Briton* assured the Association that Cornishmen at home did not under-estimate "the services rendered both to the families of the defaulters and to the good name of the county by the way in which husbands who have neglected wives and children are brought to account".[128] The co-operation between the Cornish boards of guardians and the Cornish Association in the Transvaal appears to have become strained by 1923 when the Association complained to the Truro guardians that they were getting "fed up" with complaints from Cornwall and that "it seemed to be a habit of Cornishmen when they went abroad to desert their wives".[129] However, by that time new international legislation was in place under which maintenance could be enforced in South Africa and elsewhere in the British Empire.[130]

The boards of guardians appear to have had some justification for their concerns that some husbands abroad were controlling the amount of money sent home to maximise the benefit from poor relief, while some wives in Cornwall were colluding and concealing the remittances they received.[131] The evidence suggests that in their individual 'economies of diverse resources' these wives were shamelessly willing to combine remittances and poor relief simultaneously. They were probably a minority, but their actions influenced the availability of relief to other blameless wives who found themselves in desperate need of help. These concerns, counterbalanced by a desire to help the genuinely impoverished wives and children, were often behind the seemingly endless discussions and frequent changes in local poor law policy.

However, a word of caution. The main source for much of the above information is the discussions of the poor law guardians as reported in the press. These, and the newspaper editorials, may not have accurately represented the true situation, but instead been a response to changing social expectations of male responsibilities as sole 'bread winner'. It is also possible, given the association of neglectful husbands with drink, that the plight of 'deserted' wives in Cornwall was emphasised by contemporary commentators keen to promote the temperance movement. Parallels can be drawn with the way, highlighted by Christina Twomey, that campaigners for land reform and industrial schools co-opted the issue of deserted wives in Australia.[132]

The idea of great financial pressure on the poor law system caused by large numbers of deserted or neglected wives does not sit comfortably with Peter Tremewan's finding that mining district unions, such as Redruth, were spending less per head of population than those in non-mining areas.[133] However, Tremewan's analysis only extends to 1881 and the more intense concerns about non-support of wives appear in the press after this. Therefore it is possible that there were increased levels of neglect, especially by husbands in South Africa, towards the end of the 19th century. This would accord with the Gill Burke's suggestion of hardship in the 1890s,[134] and the variation between different times and places implied by the conflicting contemporary reports. It is possible that there was something about the nature and timing of the South African migration stream that saw a breakdown of the structures that had supported earlier generations of wives left in Cornwall. For example, the South African mine camps appear to have attracted less family settlement than other destinations,[135] reducing the potential for community and chapel influence on the men's behaviour. At the same time, employers may not have had the same paternalistic attitude to protecting the welfare of wives in Cornwall through compulsory home-pay, like the earlier South American mines noted in a previous chapter. Whether there was a genuine increase in desertion, or simply greater awareness and press coverage can only be resolved by further research.

7

Lodgers and Lovers
Facing the consequences

In 1910 experienced Cornish county court judge Thomas Granger told the Royal Commission on Divorce and Matrimonial Causes that two aspects of emigration had a detrimental effect on the generally "high standard of matrimonial fidelity in Cornwall". The first, he suggested, was "that so many Cornishmen go abroad and stay away for years. It is quite a common thing for them to stay away for 20 years without ever returning, and very often after only being married a few months". The second was the widespread practice in Cornwall of taking in lodgers to supplement low incomes, particularly when the wives who had husbands in South Africa took in lodgers where, in Granger's view, "there is no necessity at all for it".[1] His words were echoed by Sharron Schwartz in her study of the mining settlement of Lanner when she noted that: "Some women who took in male lodgers entered into adulterous relationships, or were forced to entertain gentlemen to eke out a living which, when discovered, sometimes led to further family complications and even divorce".[2] But is there really such strong evidence to link the wives' lodgers with matrimonial infidelity?

The taking in of lodgers was a recognised way of supplementing or replacing a lost income source, especially among working class families.[3] At times, largely in the 1850s and 1860s, up to 10-12% of wives whose husbands were abroad or absent were housing lodgers. However, the majority of these lodgers were women, children and elderly men. For example, in 1891 only 15 of the 445 wives 'left behind' in Camborne had taken in male lodgers, while in 1861, the census year with the highest percentage of lodgers in the households of women whose husbands were known to be abroad, only half the lodgers were adult males, and of these the majority were elderly men, or had their own wives with them. In some cases the lodgers were brothers and other close relatives of the landlady, and in others the landlady herself was a woman of mature years and considerably older than her lodger. Not that this necessarily precluded bad behaviour – as we will see, some mature wives were cast in the role of seductresses of young men. Nonetheless, 'lodger' is not synonymous with adult male, and not all male lodgers had the potential to be the cause of marital disharmony.

Clearly there is little evidence here to sustain Judge Granger's suggestion of it being a common practice for wives to take in male lodgers while their husbands were abroad, certainly in the 1850s to 1890s. It is possible, however, that by the time Granger gave his evidence in 1910 the practice could have become more widespread. He gave several examples of marital breakdown involving lodgers in his evidence but despite his assertion that marital infidelity in Cornwall was associated with emigration, he only cited one example where the husband was definitely abroad. In that case the husband had left for South Africa three years into the marriage. He never sent any money home, and his wife struggled to support herself and the children, eventually taking in a male lodger with whom she formed a relationship. The husband, who had deserted her years earlier, sued for divorce on the grounds of her adultery.[4] This wife had hardly taken in a lodger 'needlessly' and it seems odd that, after 19 years of hearing court cases, Granger did not cite a better example to substantiate his claim, if indeed it was justified.

It is intuitive that the presence of male lodgers combined with couples enduring long separations could be a recipe for matrimonial infidelity, but it can also be argued that it is for this very reason that there are so few lone adult men lodging with the women whose husbands were abroad. An affair with a lodger would have been easier to conduct discretely, but it was this very convenience that would have aroused suspicion. Therefore wives are more likely to have avoided taking in a male lodger who might elicit gossip in the close-knit communities where everyone knew everyone's business. It was too great a risk to take when, as we will see, the wife's support from her husband (and the poor law system) depended upon her reputation.

Evidence for sexual relationships between wives 'left behind' and lodgers is understandably rare and largely anecdotal. By their nature, there would be little or nothing in historical sources to record the unknown

Lodgers and Lovers

number of discreet affairs carried out in private. Nonetheless there is ample evidence that some wives did form new relationships with men other than lodgers while their husbands were abroad. Judge Granger cited an example where the wife's adultery was with the husband's cousin and a man "across the way".[5] In his description of St Day at the end of the 19th century, Richard Blewett, headmaster of the school, noted the "occasional 'sex triangle' when the two angles at the base deluded themselves that the angle at the apex was at infinity when it was no further away than South Africa and could be quickly brought to the base by a 'Castle' liner".[6]

Most affairs only came to light when something went wrong and as our window on these events is mostly provided by the newspapers of time, there is a bias towards the more shocking or scandalous events.

One such story, reported in October 1880, was the elopement of Elizabeth Clift who was living with her parents while her husband was abroad. Wilson Williams, a man "in easy circumstances" from Liverpool who was staying at her parents' hotel in Truro, showed so much interest in Elizabeth that her parents asked him to leave.[7] However, their intervention was too late and the couple eloped by cab and caught a train out of Cornwall. Although Wilson had a reputation of being "rather a wild 'un", the press was equally critical of Elizabeth's conduct as she was far from neglected by her husband who was in regular contact and remitting £12 every month, from which she had saved the "good deal of money" that she took with her. A search of the 1881 census taken around six months later reveals Elizabeth and Wilson boarding together in Plymouth as a gentleman and his wife, after which no trace has been found of the couple.[8]

Dramatic elopements like this probably caused such a stir because they were rare. More frequent are the glimpses of extramarital relationships provided by cases brought before local officials. When a woman applied to the Penzance Board of Guardians in 1847 for her husband to be taken into the workhouse it turned out that he was in fact her brother-in-law, with whom she cohabited since her real husband had gone abroad several years previously leaving her with children.[9] Another case, from 1890, shows a wife whose husband was abroad to have been cohabiting with a miner to whom the Helston Board of Guardians took exception because he was refusing to maintain his own wife in the workhouse.[10] In such cases, this is probably the only record of these living arrangements. More unusually, another wife's adultery was publicly exposed when her husband, John Keen, was sued for goods supplied to her while he was in America.[11]

The details of one affair emerged in the criminal courts and the scandalous nature of the case ensured lengthy press coverage. In 1880 John Sullivan appeared in court charged with breaking into the house of Richard Serpell of Camborne and stealing a watch.[12] John claimed that he had been given the watch by Richard's wife Catherine, with whom he had been having an intimate relationship since Richard had gone to California four years earlier. Catherine countered that they were neighbours and nothing more. The stakes were high; John's freedom against Catherine's reputation. John carried out his own defence describing, and questioning Catherine about, their alleged affair in such detail that his evidence and their exchanges in court give some insight as to how such affairs might plausibly have been conducted. Firstly, both parties already knew each other and had found themselves on their own; Catherine when Richard went abroad, and John when his wife, who was Catherine's sister, had died eleven years earlier. As neighbours and relations by marriage they had reason to visit each other's homes. John's young son wrote Catherine's letters to Richard for her and acted as intermediary carrying Catherine's messages to his father.

John's descriptions of the couple's attempts to keep their affair from the neighbours are so detailed, and in some cases comical, that it is difficult to believe that they are not true. Catherine was alleged to have walked across the fields to avoid being seen on the road to John's house, and when she arrived, John would send his daughter out to greet her to give the appearance that she was the reason for her aunt's visit. Once inside Catherine would hang a black shawl inside the window to shield the couple from view. John also claimed that she had put stockings over his boots so that he could leave her house at night without her neighbours hearing him go.

The judge viewed John's defence as "cowardly and ungallant", but conceded that by spending time alone with John in his house Catherine "had certainly acted in a very indiscreet manner for a married women". The jury, unconvinced that either party was being entirely truthful, acquitted John of the burglary but found him guilty of stealing the watch.

Catherine's reputation is unlikely to have emerged intact given the extensive local press coverage. The reaction of her husband can only be guessed at, and it is perhaps telling that Catherine is listed as a married woman without her husband in every Camborne census from 1881 through to 1911.

It has been suggested that 19th century Cornish couples took a pragmatic view of their marriage vows if they were separated by emigration. John Gillis likened their attitudes to those of sailors and their wives; of whom he writes that men were "generally very forgiving" when their wives took up with male lodgers while they were at sea. "Among Cornish miners, who were sometimes away in America or South Africa for years at a time, a similar pragmatism persisted", he opined. "The roving miners sent money home, but when this was not sufficient the lodger often took the position of the husband".[13]

As we have already seen, analysis of the census returns offers little support for Gillis' belief that lodgers were widely implicated in extramarital relationships, but there is evidence that some saw no reason why a wife's infidelity while the husband was abroad should lead to a permanent separation. One wife was confident enough in her husband's acceptance of her behaviour in his nine year absence to want to join him in America despite her being pregnant, and the husband having not sent her any money for two years.[14] In another case Elizabeth Jane Eustice and her husband were told by the Redruth Board of Guardians in 1893 that they "had better live together like man and wife ought to" despite Elizabeth having had a child while her spouse was abroad. Elizabeth's husband agreed to take her back and support the child, while Elizabeth told the guardians that "she would go with him anywhere".[15] How much of this was a genuine reconciliation and how much bowing to societal pressure is hard to judge; Elizabeth claimed that her husband had said "he had no love or respect for her", while her willingness to stay with him may have been motivated, at least in part, by her need for his financial support.[16]

That some husbands were indeed forgiving is illustrated by another case that came before the Redruth guardians. In 1892 an Illogan woman revealed that while her husband was away she had given birth to a child who had died, but "since that time her conduct had been good".[17] She had at once written to her husband to tell him what had happened and he had forgiven her and sent her money since. However, the husband may have been more inclined to forgive his spouse in this case for two reasons. Firstly, he had his own problems and was planning to live under an assumed name in Havana in Cuba, where "he hoped she would share his trouble with him". Secondly, and of wider relevance, the illegitimate child had died, and would not be present as a reminder of the wife's adultery, or a drain on the family's resources.

Sometimes arrangements could be made to facilitate smooth marital reunions even if there was a living illegitimate child. A wife from Falmouth paid a nurse to take in her illegitimate child, born while her husband was in America, so that she could go to her husband there "all right".[18] This case only came to light when the payments ceased and the nurse could no longer care for the child. Any number of more successful arrangements could have gone unrecorded enabling couples to 'forgive and forget'.

A more common response was for the husband to withdraw financial support for his wife, a course of action that was condoned by the courts if the wife's adultery was proven. When he returned from America Luke Bray escaped going to prison for not supporting his wife because he was able to show that she had been cohabiting with another man in his absence, leading him to believe that "his wife's conduct had severed her from him", thus freeing him from financial responsibility for her.

If there were legitimate children in the wife's care the matter was more complicated, as although the husband might be justified in refusing to support an adulterous wife he could not abdicate responsibility for his own children, and would send remittances for their support only.[19] However, these children were reliant on their mother for their care and without support for herself and the additional illegitimate child, the whole family would suffer. A case before the Penzance Board of Guardians in March 1879 illustrated the problem:

> "A miner leaves a wife and four children and goes to America. In time the wife has a fifth child, and it is not her husband's. The absent one writes and says he will send money for his lawful children, but not for his unfaithful wife and her unlawful child. The question was asked - How can the woman and the four children live?"[20]

A family's problems could be lessened if the father of the illegitimate child contributed. For example, a women from St Just was receiving money from her husband abroad to support her legitimate children and also money from the father of the illegitimate child she had borne two years into her husband's absence. While this lasted she was able to manage, but the husband stopped sending any money home and the father of the last child left the scene as well, leaving the family in financial distress.[21]

As husbands abroad could fail to send money home for a variety of reasons, it is impossible to say that the wife's adultery was the only reason for remittances to cease in these cases, especially as some husbands stopped supporting their own children.[22] In the St Just case above the husband ceased maintaining his Cornish children because he had married another woman in America. In another example, the husband of an Illogan woman stopped sending money for her and their three children because she had given birth to an illegitimate child, but he had also written to say that he was "doing slightly".[23]

Wives and children were not the only ones affected if the husband withdrew support as a consequence of his wife's adultery. Other dependent relatives also suffered. In 1891 a "weak" woman living in Gwennap with her married sister, whose husband was sending her "a good living from abroad", had to go into the workhouse because financial support was withdrawn when the wife had an illegitimate child.[24]

The appearance of a baby was the most frequent way in which extramarital affairs came to light and provided undeniable proof of the wife's adultery, and could mean she lost far more than just her husband. To give birth to an illegitimate child, she would not only have to face the dangers of childbirth, shame and loss of reputation, she also risked losing financial support for herself and her existing children not only from her husband but also any poor relief she might have received at a time when she had another mouth to feed and was less able to work. The result could be a spiral into destitution, the workhouse and separation from her children. The case of Esther Waters illustrates what could happen. In 1861 Esther was living with her husband Richard, a tin dresser, in St Just. The young couple had two boys, aged seven and one, and they were doing well enough to employ a servant girl. Another son was born in 1864. Then sometime in the next few years Richard went to America and in his absence Esther had an affair resulting in the birth of an illegitimate daughter in 1869. By 1871 Esther and her three youngest children, including the illegitimate toddler, were in Penzance Union workhouse, where Esther's fall from grace continued when in 1872 she was committed for trial at the assizes for purloining workhouse clothing whilst in charge of the laundry.[25]

Despite these risks, the number of cases in poor law records indicates that many wives accepted the birth of an illegitimate baby. Figures given for illegitimate births in Cornwall from 1861 to 1891 are higher than the average for England and Wales,[26] but these include all such births regardless of the mother's marital status and so offer little help as to how many were born to wives 'left behind'.

Although the workhouse was generally to be avoided, it did provide access to medical services, and many poorer expectant mothers requested admission to the house for the birth, and these included wives expecting illegitimate babies. A pragmatic acceptance of the situation is suggested by the report that when a member of Penzance Board of Guardians enquired whether a woman of 40 who had received food during her confinement was single or married, the Relieving Officer's response of "Well, her husband has been abroad many years", drew laughter, as well as the recall that this was her third illegitimate child.[27] As this case demonstrates, some wives had more than one illegitimate child in their husband's absence.[28] It is likely that these represent a range of scenarios from the wife establishing a new long-term relationship (as will be discussed in a later section), to serial adultery and a slide into casual prostitution.

As mentioned above, some wives with illegitimate children were helped to get by with support from the child's father. Securing this support could be vital to the family's survival and, if it was not offered willingly, some wives were prepared to face the public shame of taking their lover to court to obtain an affiliation order to ensure maintenance for the child. However, this process, more often used by unmarried women, presented a specific difficulty for wives. The law held that the husband was the father of any child delivered to a married women unless it could be shown that he could have had no access to her around the time of conception.[29] In many of the cases reported in the newspapers the alleged father's defence hinged on whether or not the wife could prove that her husband was abroad when the baby was conceived.

Proving non-access was a challenge. The wife's statement that the husband was abroad was not enough. This argument was made in the case brought in April 1886 against William Thomas by Elizabeth Eustice of Breage, whose husband had been away for five years. The defence lawyer "objected to any evidence being given by her which had a tendency to prove non-access by the husband, the law providing that such evidence should be given by an independent party". He maintained that: "she should have come there prepared with some person who knew the husband was in America at the time of conception".[30] In another case the only evidence that Johanna Wall from St Just could offer to show non-access was that her daughter who was two when her father left for Colorado 13 years earlier had never seen him.[31] The affiliation case brought by Mary Ann Richards against John Osborne, both of Towednack, failed because the court would not accept as proof the statement of the wife's sister that she had received papers from the husband sent from America around the time of conception. The court required that a witness be brought who had actually seen the husband in America at the time.[32] In 1883 Elizabeth Jennings of Sithney fared better as the court accepted the testimony of two men who had known her husband in America and had been receiving letters in his own hand from him ever since.[33]

Elizabeth was lucky to have such witnesses and documentary proof. The chances in most cases of being able to find someone who had seen the husband abroad at the right time, who was also able and willing to testify in Cornwall, must have been slight. Given the high level of proof required by the courts and the logistics of procuring witnesses in such affiliation cases, inevitably not all succeeded. Nevertheless an outcome that could be assured was that the wife's embarrassing circumstances were made public wherever in the world the Cornish newspapers were read.

A married woman with an illegitimate child could be left in the unenviable position of little expectation of support from her husband whom the law assumed to be the father, and unable to prove that he was not in order to secure support from the real father. Her situation was made more desperate as the help that she could obtain from that safety net for the destitute, the Poor Law system, was severely curtailed. As we have seen, poor law boards were technically precluded from offering outdoor relief to women who had illegitimate children and could only help them if they and their children entered the workhouse. As this involved splitting up the family, the wife, through her adultery, could be blamed for a broken home, even if the husband's absence also played a part.[34]

Even had the Poor Law sanctioned these women being given outdoor relief, some guardians were reluctant to do so. When the St Just woman let down by both the fathers of her children applied to the Penzance guardians for help in 1897 she was denied outdoor relief, not only because the law would not allow it but because they felt "it would form a bad precedent in view of other women in St Just similarly situated".[35] However, as described earlier, guardians would provide outdoor relief for the legitimate children, which inevitably could be shared amongst the whole household, including the mother and the illegitimate children.

Given the repercussions of having an illegitimate child, it is not surprising that on finding themselves pregnant with no way of passing the child off as their husband's, some wives took steps to prevent the arrival of the baby, or dispose of it. In her history of infanticide in Britain, Anne-Marie Kilday describes the range of strategies employed by women in the past to avoid maternity, namely: abortion, abandonment and exposure, wet-nursing and baby farming, and newborn baby murder.[36] There is evidence for all of these amongst the wives 'left behind' in Cornwall.

Abortion, especially in the early stages of pregnancy, was seen as an alternative form of contraception in the 19th century and is believed to have been widespread in Victorian Britain, particularly amongst the working classes.[37] In 1879 Richard Pascoe, well known in the Truro area as 'Doctor Dick', was sentenced to five years imprisonment for "the most serious offence of administering a noxious drug and feloniously using a certain instrument to procure the miscarriage" of Edna Chapman. It was not the first time that she had called upon the services of Pascoe, who had a "doctor's shop" at his home in Perranzabuloe and claimed to have "cured 2000 cases of this sort".[38]

In at least one case it was the father of the illegitimate baby who tried to terminate the pregnancy. Grace Blight's husband had been abroad for eleven years when she had a relationship with her employer's son, John Henry Ball. On discovering that Grace was expecting his baby, John "thought it a very bad job" and had tried to persuade Grace to drink some gunpowder and gin "with an unlawful object". She refused, gave birth to a daughter and secured an affiliation order against him.[39]

Knowledge of abortifacients was commonplace amongst the female community and various commercial and 'quack' products were widely advertised in the newspapers.[40] The substance used by 'Doctor Dick' to induce miscarriages was ergot of rye, one of a wide range of folklore 'remedies', including savin, heira picra, pennyroyal as well as gin combined with salts or gunpowder as above, that were used with varying degrees of success, and possible fatal consequences for the woman.[41] In her study of the subject Pamela Knight describes how, although condemned by the establishment, abortionists such as Pascoe and those who supplied abortifacients were "generally tolerated and protected by a conspiracy of silence" amongst the women of working class communities who regarded their services as an inevitable part of life.[42] As miscarriages were common and even legitimate pregnancy in the 19th century was viewed as a very private experience,[43] it is impossible to know how many unwanted pregnancies were terminated successfully. Only those instances that went wrong have left any record of the event.

As Kilday notes in her book, abortion in the 19th century was "a dangerous enterprise and something of a gamble in terms of the potential implications for the mother's health", as well as being illegal under the Offences Against the Person Act 1861.[44] Therefore it is not surprising that some women allowed their pregnancies to go to full term either because unreliable abortifacients failed or they chose the dangers of childbirth over those of abortion. They would then have the dilemma of what to do once the child was born. In some cases babies would be reared outside the family, or secretly and informally adopted,[45] but others were abandoned.

Historians have concluded that abandonment was carried out on a substantial scale in the 19th century. Leaving a baby in a place where it was unlikely to be found was a form of newborn murder. Kilday suggests of women expecting illegitimate babies: "many must have felt that once they had concealed their 'shameful' pregnancies they were on an inescapable and inevitable journey to infanticide".[46] Reports in the Cornish press suggest that the discovery of dead infants was not that unusual; in the space of a fortnight in 1880 there were two instances of babies' bodies being found in wells in Camborne.[47] The extent to which married women in Cornwall abandoned their unwanted babies, leaving them to be found by others or die from exposure, is impossible to quantify as, along with secret adoptions, a record of such events only exists if for some reason the story appeared in the newspapers. In most foundling cases there was nothing to connect the child with a specific mother and so cases involving wives 'left behind' would be indistinguishable from any other incidents of abandoned babies.

To be successful the wife would have to hide her pregnancy and the birth. Most cases involving married women were exposed because something went wrong during or just after the delivery. As some women attempted to give birth without help, either intentionally in secret, or possibly because they were in denial about their situation, they faced increased risks during childbirth.[48] In January 1871 Mary Lark of Callington, whose husband had been regularly remitting her money from America for two or three years, was found in an unconscious state by a neighbour, alongside the body of her newborn baby.[49] Similarly, Elizabeth Ann Allen, whose husband had gone to California some three years previously, was found by her mother "in a fainting state" having just given birth.[50] Again, the baby was dead. In 1898 Mary Jane Richards' reluctance to have a doctor or midwife attend her when she went into labour in St Agnes not only aroused suspicion when it was claimed that the baby was stillborn, but contributed to her own death several days later.[51]

Rita Barton, in her compilation of 19th century extracts from the *West Briton* newspaper concluded that concealing the birth of an illegitimate baby was a very common offence in the 19th century. "In most cases the mother delivered the baby herself and afterwards disposed of it by one means or another, often behind a hedge, in a river or down an abandoned mine shaft" or even buried it beneath the earth floor of her home, which meant she could do it quickly and secretly without having to leave the house post-partum.[52] Women also paid sextons to bury the bodies of their illegitimate babies secretly at night for a small fee.[53] How many of these were stillbirths or natural deaths is known only to the women involved. In many cases where the body of an infant was found it was difficult to ascertain the precise cause of death, and whether it had occurred before, during or after birth. The columnist, 'Whachum', believed that the incidence of infanticide in Cornwall was "larger than one knows". Writing in the *Royal Cornwall Gazette* in November 1867 he lamented:

> *"In the event of children dying unbaptized, no one stands between parent or midwife and detection, but the Registrar of Deaths, and his only chance of discovering anything amiss is by questions addressed to those whose tale he has no opportunity of testing. In the event of a child being announced to a sexton as still-born, he quietly inters it; if it has lived a few days, the Registrar gives a certificate and again the sexton privately buries. There is no public ceremony, or publicity beyond the circle of gossips of the hamlet."*[54]

A mother who attempted secretly to dispose of the body of a stillborn infant could be prosecuted for concealing the birth. If the baby survived for a brief while, the charge could be child murder. This happened in the case of Mary Ann Roberts, a 23-year-old mother of three from Calstock. Her husband had been abroad for three years when Mary Ann realised in the spring of 1856 that she was pregnant. She was also expecting her husband to return very soon. When the illegitimate child was found dead shortly after birth, Mary Ann was charged with its murder, although later found not guilty at the trial.

Even if there had been no attempt to kill the child, the wives were suspected of ridding themselves of the problem through neglect.[55] 'Whachum' cited a case in Wendron as typical:

> *"Here is a woman, with four children, who are alive and because there is no reason why they should not be so, a fifth comes into the world, the witness of her falseness to her absent husband, and altogether a very undesirable arrival. This one pines and dies. A country midwife doctors it with gin; no apothecary is summoned; and the hand's-breath existence is soon over. Does any one believe there was much anxiety or effort to preserve this flickering flame? ... In many instances there is no actual violence, but there is a well-founded suspicion of purposed neglect; and the result is the same in both cases - a badge of disgrace, or an unwelcome incumbrance disappears."*[56]

The Married Widows of Cornwall

In the 1870s Redruth was said to have become "somewhat notorious" for infanticide.[57] However, this statement should be put in the context of what Kilday calls "the moral panic about new-born child murder that gripped England during the second half of the nineteenth century". She suggests that, although largely unwarranted, it led to a peak in the number of prosecutions and public awareness in these years.[58] As she points out, infanticide is normally associated with single unmarried women, and it is possible that, as in Cornwall it was not unusual for courting couples to engage in pre-marital sex with pregnancy preceding marriage,[59] some increase in infanticide might be due to the prospective grooms and fathers emigrating without marrying, leaving their 'fiancées' with the prospect of bearing an illegitimate child. However, Kilday also addresses the previously neglected involvement of married women in newborn murder, arguing that its extent is under-recorded in the historical record. In the eyes of the judiciary, a married woman would have no motive for concealing a birth or killing her child and therefore they were rarely suspected of foul play when a baby died. In addition, as the methods they used were often more subtle, allowing their infants to die from "neglect or passive cruelty" rather than more violent means often used by unmarried women, "infanticide by a married women was hard to uncover and even harder to prove". Nonetheless, it is now accepted that some married women did have two clear motives for newborn murder: limiting family size and to conceal adultery.[60]

In the absence of reliable forms of contraception, abortion and infanticide were used by married women to avoid the never-ending cycle of childbirth with its attendant health risks and the economic consequences of adding to the number of children that the family had to support.[61] As Kilday states: "Many Victorian women may well have regarded infanticide as a sure form of late birth control, when there were few other viable options whereby a pregnancy could be prevented or terminated. Infanticide may, therefore, have been seen as a pragmatic and necessary activity, resorted to when no other solution was possible and when control over social and economic destiny was tantamount".[62] For a wife in receipt of inadequate or unreliable remittances from her husband the imperative not to add to her financial and practical difficulties would have been significant; for those facing the marital and social penalties of bearing an illegitimate child it was even greater.

The potential loss of outdoor relief would have further increased the likelihood of desperate women resorting to infanticide, Kilday suggests. This view was supported by contemporary criticism of rules excluding women with illegitimate children from claiming outdoor relief. In 1894 after the Penzance guardians refused to relieve a mother of illegitimate twins, one of whom had died, unless the second twin also died, it was called "a very bad law as it encouraged ill-treatment of children".[63] By contrast, further demonstrating how a woman's treatment by poor law officials depended on where she lived, the Redruth guardians a few months earlier had cut off relief to a Stithians woman, deserted by her husband abroad, when it was found that she had given birth to twins, despite the fact that one was still-born and the other died not long after.[64] These women would certainly fall into the group Kilday identifies for whom, "faced with a lack of options to resolve their precarious situation and contemplating penury in the longer-term, infanticide may well have been regarded as a means of survival". Those with older children could also have had the additional altruistic desire to prioritise the health and wellbeing of their existing children over the survival of the illegitimate additional mouth to feed.[65]

Infanticide by married women was regularly under-reported, Kilday suggests, "because an unexpected fatality could be more readily explained away as a death by natural causes if it was non-violent and occurred within the context of a stable and formalised relationship". Nevertheless, there are many examples in the Cornish press of wives suspected of infanticide, and inquests into the deaths of illegitimate babies born to wives whose husbands were abroad appear routine unless a doctor was present. When the mother of two-month-old Georgiana Gray (a married woman whose husband had been abroad for some years) awoke to find Georgiana dead in her arms, the circumstances were felt suspicious enough to warrant a post mortem. This showed that the baby had died of natural causes, disproving the rumours that had been circulating to the contrary.[66] Similar verdicts of stillbirth or natural death were given in the cases of the illegitimate babies born to other wives whose husbands were abroad.[67]

In some cases, however, the inquest juries were convinced that the mother was responsible for the baby's death. Mary Daniel was committed to trial at Bodmin assizes in 1856 for concealing the birth of a child while her husband was in Australia when an inquest was unsatisfied with the circumstances surrounding its death.[68] In Camborne in June 1873 the jury at the inquest on the baby daughter of Elizabeth Ivey returned a verdict of 'death from suffocation'. The baby was Elizabeth's second while her husband was in Mexico.[69] The coroner's jury at the inquest of a baby boy found at the bottom of an abandoned shaft near Chacewater had no doubts as to what had happened to the child. Around the time the child was believed to have died a young woman called Emily Richards, whose husband was in America, asked for directions to the well. She was carrying a baby, but less than a hour later she was seen again nearby, this time without the baby. The inquest jury had no doubts that Emily had wilfully murdered her baby son, especially when it emerged that she had given birth in Penzance under a false name, and subsequently gone on the run. The story of 'the Chacewater Murder' became a news sensation reported throughout the country and beyond, with detailed descriptions of Emily's flight and eventual capture in Paris. However, when the case went to trial at the assizes, much to the astonishment of practically all concerned, Emily was acquitted. The circumstantial evidence was overwhelming but insufficient to prove, in the jury's minds, that Emily had murdered the particular baby whose body had been found.[70]

By their secretive nature, abortion, the concealment of stillborn infants and infanticide are practices that are impossible to quantify. As Kilday concludes: "If a woman successfully concealed her pregnancy, gave birth in secret and then subsequently killed her offspring, there was still a strong possibility – even in the nineteenth century – that this episode would go undetected by the authorities".[71] Other authors have speculated that married women were just as likely to dispose of unwanted babies and had greater chance of keeping it secret in the privacy of their own homes.[72] However, there is a case to be made that wives whose husbands were abroad came under greater social scrutiny than those whose spouse was in residence. Kilday points out that "Single women and widows of childbearing age were regularly seen as a threat to the stability of families and communities" for their potential to produce illegitimate children likely to be a drain on community finances. They were therefore subject to close scrutiny of their moral conduct and their physical appearance, especially by the other women in their community.[73] As wives whose husbands were abroad were often viewed to as semi-widows it seems likely that they too would have come under the same scrutiny.

Evidence that society was generally distrustful of wives with absent husbands has emerged from research outside Cornwall. In her study of wives 'left behind' by miners emigrating from Sicily in the same period, Reeder notes how such women were considered a danger in the community: "popular belief held that marriage awakened the powerful force of female sexuality, and once roused the only curb on a woman's lust was her husband".[74] Thus a married woman outside the control of her husband was a liability. Widows could remarry and therefore be rendered 'harmless', but wives caught indefinitely in the limbo of separation were a different matter. In Reeder's words "They did not fit into any of the well-defined social roles, and this may have made them more dangerous than other single women and caused the neighbours to be even more suspicious". It was commonly believed that in the absence of their husbands, such women would give in to their physical and emotional weakness and find another sexual partner, succumbing to another man's advances or potentially seducing their neighbours' husbands. In Sicily "politicians, doctors, social critics, and emigrants commonly agreed that women left behind, bereft of male guardianship, would surely sink into prostitution or commit adultery", meaning wives 'left behind' had to adopt the strictly confined lifestyle of a widow to avoid arousing suspicion.

Although we should be cautious in the comparison given the cultural differences between Sicily and Cornwall,[75] especially the Mediterranean concept of family honour, similar concerns were expressed about a closer parallel to the Cornish wives, namely the women living in the young cities of Australia while their husbands prospected for gold in the bush. Christina Twomey points out that while there was public sympathy for these women, it was "always tinged with concern about the absence of male protection and control". Echoing the views in Sicily, it was assumed in Australia that husbands were their wives' moral as well as financial guardians and so "helped to guide women's choices, contained their waywardness, and provided a bastion against female vulnerabilities". The absence of that guardianship "threatened to unleash that which was disorderly and unruly in femininity".[76] The great fear concerning these wives in Australia was that the poverty brought about by their husbands' neglect or desertion eroded the moral courage of these previously virtuous wives and mothers until "unable to remarry, but needing the strength and solace of a man, the woman 'seeks relief in some illicit relationship'". Once 'tripped', it was believed, the woman's descent into prostitution would be inevitable and rapid.

There is little to distinguish these wives of gold diggers in Australia from those left behind by men joining the gold rush from Cornwall; indeed the former very likely included Cornish women who had followed their husbands abroad. Therefore, although there is less evidence, the essence of these ideas may have been present in 19th century Cornwall.

As we saw earlier, some women did not like the idea of their husbands entering houses occupied by, or being "too familiar" with, young women whose husbands were abroad.[77] Other wives were cast in the role of experienced seductress. When 20-year-old farmer Arthur Thomas Hollow was tried at Bodmin Crown Court in July 1879 for theft, the judge agreed that although his "loose ways and infatuation" for his co-defendant, a married woman called Janie Lavers whose husband was abroad, had been "notorious for many months", he was a respectable man who had been "led astray by the female, who was ten years his senior, and who had a certain power over him".[78] Similarly, in a bastardy case in 1883 the lawyer defending the admitted father of Elizabeth Jennings' illegitimate twin sons argued that the court should consider that he had been "led into this by Mrs Jennings, who was nearly double his age".[79]

Among the wives who lived with their parents while their husbands were away, some fathers stood in for their absent sons-in-law, resuming their patriarchal control over their daughters' behaviour, as in the elopement of Elizabeth Clift, described above, whose parents had tried to thwart her relationship with Wilson Williams. Similarly Frederick Jones of the Railway Hotel in Grampound Road kept a close eye on his married daughter, a Mrs Mitchell, especially when she was discovered to be meeting 'friends' in the middle of the night.[80] The newspaper report took care to point out that "no impropriety was suggested", although the daughter's later disappearance and Jones' actions in threatening a local man seemed to imply otherwise.

Wives were frequently under continuous scrutiny from family and neighbours, not only in their interactions with the opposite sex, but in all aspects of their behaviour. Collectively, the wives were sometimes criticised for frivolously spending their husband's remittances, particularly on fine clothing,[81] but above all the wives were judged on whether or not they met expectations of respectability. Elizabeth Rodda, charged with stealing a hat in August 1878, was described as being of poor character: "Her husband went abroad some years ago and frequently remitted her money, but she has not behaved herself discreetly nor attended to her children as she ought."[82]

The volume of correspondence between those in Cornwall and their emigrant relations and friends around the world meant that gossip about the wives' behaviour could easily find its way to the husbands abroad. Writing to his son in Canada in 1856 Thomas Hockin revealed: "William Salter is gone to America… His wife is living with R. Havis. It would have been a good thing if she had never come in St Tudy".[83] John Lean, mentioned earlier, was made aware of his wife's adultery only when her father wrote to him in America to tell him that she was expecting another man's child.

The ease with which rumour and lies could reach the husband's ears made faultless wives vulnerable to accusations of misbehaviour. Under the heading 'How soon is strife made', the *Cornishman* noted that:

> *"There is reported to be a good deal of mischief done at Camborne of late by parties sending letters abroad to husbands concerning certain supposed extravagances of wives at home, much of which is, no doubt, greatly exaggerated. As a result of the efforts of mischief-makers money is stopped, children and mothers are almost starved, and wives cannot tell whether the breach made will ever be healed. Just a ride on Hancock's switchback railway for a young married woman and her child, and a letter is sent off to the husband and the mischief-maker has scored a triumph of parting man and wife!"*[84]

Local gossip proved damaging, even for blameless wives. Informants, however well-meaning, could be mistaken, with dire consequences. Judge Granger described a case that occurred around 1900 in which a miner had married a girl in the morning and left for South Africa that evening, the couple having never cohabited or consummated the marriage. The husband had sent money every month until he received a letter from a friend in the village informing him that his wife was pregnant. In reality she had developed a tumour, and despite being sent a certificate produced by two doctors who examined his wife and confirmed she was a virgin, the husband refused to believe that she was innocent of adultery and deserted her.[85]

Grace Tregonning suffered a similar fate. Her husband Thomas had left for America two days after their wedding in May 1879, sending her money regularly before returning in July 1882. At that point, "after making some inquiries" he refused to live with her. She had been ill and "a mischievous and false rumour" had been spread about. Despite proof that the allegations were untrue and appeals from Grace's solicitors, Thomas would not relent.[86] Another husband returning from abroad "went to his own people first and there heard something to his wife's detriment". He stopped maintaining her, refusing to believe her claims that she "had behaved herself well and discreetly" during his absence. Even with the help of a lawyer the wife "could not run the scandal to earth" and was forced to turn to the Penzance guardians for help.[87]

So, although theoretically the wives had more freedom while their husbands were abroad, their lives were constrained by the need for their behaviour to be seen as beyond reproach in order to preserve, not just their marriages and reputations, but the means to support themselves and their children. Writing home to his wife, Mary Anne, in 1866 John Dower reassured her "as long as you behave yourself and I am certain you will and keep the children and yourself respectable you shall never be forgot or neglected by me".[88] Although kindly meant, Mary Anne would have been in little doubt what might be at risk if she failed to meet expectations.

Given the social scrutiny to which a wife would have been subjected while her husband was away, and the potentially disastrous consequences should she be, or even be rumoured to be, unfaithful in his absence, it seems unlikely that many wives would have risked taking in male lodgers who might incur suspicion. This fits with the evidence from the census showing that the lodgers accommodated by the wives were mostly women, children or elderly men. In the popular perception of the period the link between lodgers and adultery among the wives has been given precedence over other potential explanations for adultery. It seems more probable that the lengthy separations that many couples endured played a larger part in the lapses in marital fidelity than the presence of lodgers. However, a long absence would not have been viewed at the time as any justification alone for adultery, especially that of a wife. Therefore the association with lodgers provides a rationalisation for the incidence of marital infidelity that fits with the 19th century gendered stereotype of the weak wife prey to sexual temptation when not under her husband's control. It also absolves the husband from any responsibility. As John Gillis points out, if their wives took up with lodgers, "Cornishmen felt justified in living with other women while abroad".[89]

Nowhere did the double standards in Victorian marital relations have greater impact of the lives of women than when it came to ending the marriage as we shall see.

8

Double Standards and Five-Dollar Divorces
Ending the marriage

For some of the wives 'left behind' the emigration of their husband was a temporary interlude before the couple were reunited in Cornwall or abroad, but for others it was the precursor to the end of their marriage; for those whose husbands left days, even hours after the wedding, it had barely begun. Historian John Tosh writes of the significant social impact that emigration had in terms of "the drastic realignments of family" in 19th century England,[1] and among these realignments were the dissolution and reforming of 'marriages' in a variety of forms. Despite this, few historians have considered the subject of marital breakdown associated with emigration. A notable exception is Olive Anderson's work on partial separation orders sought by deserted wives in South London and North Lancashire in the mid-1800s.[2] Anderson focuses more on emigration as a means for the husband to deliberately escape marital or financial responsibilities. However, she also gives examples where the marriage had broken down because the wife had refused to emigrate with her husband or join him when sent for, although even in these cases, not surprisingly given the source bias, the man's behaviour is portrayed as being unreasonable, using force and threats of separating the wives from their children to get them to agree to emigrate. Because the wives in these cases are all trying to prove they have been deserted, the husbands' emigration is portrayed as permanent, therefore Anderson does not touch on situations such as that in Cornwall where much of the male emigration was intended as temporary.[3]

Where the wife was in regular communication with her husband and receiving an acceptable level of financial support the couple had, by Victorian standards, a functional marriage, especially if the union had produced children. Both partners in the marriage were seen as fulfilling their respective sides of the marriage contract; he as the provider and she as the mother and homemaker. Nevertheless, this condemned the wife to a celibate and possibly lonely existence, unless she was prepared to face the risks and consequences described earlier. By contrast, the sexual double standard of the day left the men abroad comparatively free to meet their needs as they wished in this respect.

Recalling his childhood in 1942, A.L. Rowse included the "queer sex-life of the miners" in a quasi-nostalgic celebration of Cornish emigration.[4] That the men would not remain faithful while away was met with a degree of acceptance in some quarters, even at the time. Writing about sexual relations between married miners and the native cooks in the mining camps of Latin America, Sharron Schwartz quotes the views of 'Don' Martin Griffin, a Cornish veteran of the Venezuelan mines:

> *"Maybe one should make allowances, both for married men separated from their wives and young wives enjoying their husband's company. The formerly certainly, although you will rarely get women to see it. They shut their eyes deliberately to the physiological needs of men which I guess are fundamentally different from their own. Or perhaps it is because they themselves are different and the women's needs are less exigent, that they can't understand.... I guess the average woman at home would rather see her man go loco abroad than permit him to retain mental and physical health as Nature intended him to do. It's a problem, but whilst woman is monandrous by instinct and man is polygamous, and the social conventions clamp monogamy equally on both, then something is going to bust."*[5]

As Judge Granger acknowledged in his evidence to the Royal Commission: "I am afraid the men are not immaculate sometimes when they are abroad; I am afraid not; but they keep it very close, and they do not tell on each other when they come home".[6] Even if a husband's adultery was discovered the worst he could face was social disapproval. Adultery by either party however, carried far greater risks for the wife. Although she was likely to have an awareness of contemporary contraception/abortion practices as this knowledge was mainly shared amongst married women with families,[7] she would have to contend with the possibility of a resulting pregnancy. Even if a wife remained faithful, her husband's illicit sexual relations abroad could endanger her health. When they did come home, it seems likely that some errant husbands brought unwanted infections to their unsuspecting wives. Travellers reported that syphilis and other venereal diseases were common among the labour force of some mines in South America.[8]

Many women may have accepted their husband's absence and behaviour as their expected lot, or enjoyed a form of union that gave them the financial security and status of marriage whilst being able to live more independent lives without the burden of regular pregnancies. Others could, or would, not tolerate living without the solace of male company.

Regardless of how the wife felt about her situation, or how her husband behaved whilst abroad, she was powerless to end the marriage and legitimately start a new relationship. Prior to 1857 divorce was only possible by Act of Parliament and even after the Divorce Act was passed the costs involved with a hearing in London made the process prohibitively expensive for many people, especially those in distant Cornwall. Irrespective of cost, the Divorce Act had little to offer the women. It has been suggested that the only provision in the Divorce Act that could possibly be of any use to deserted women of the poorer classes, was that it allowed her to obtain an order from a local magistrate giving her control of her own earnings as a 'feme sole'.[9]

Even if a wife could afford to instigate a divorce, she could only obtain one if she could prove her husband's adultery was aggravated by desertion for more than two years, or he had committed incest, bigamy, or gross physical cruelty.[10] Thus as long as the husband supported his wife in Cornwall, even intermittently, he could act as he pleased abroad while the wife had little or no recourse. However, the inequality of the law meant that a husband could divorce his wife on the grounds of her adultery alone and, despite the costs and distances involved, divorce cases were brought by emigrant Cornishmen. The case studies below illustrate the range of outcomes.

Eliza Elizabeth Datson and her husband Richard married in 1868 and spent some time in America together before Eliza returned to Cornwall with their sons.[11] In 1876 Eliza gave birth to an illegitimate daughter and by 1881 her legitimate sons were living with Richard's parents while Eliza

Double Standards and Five-Dollar Divorces

worked as a domestic cook. Throughout this period Eliza was alleged to have committed adultery on "diverse occasions" with "persons unknown" having further illegitimate children (by the same father) in 1885 and 1891, after which Richard divorced her in 1893. In both the 1891 and 1901 censuses Eliza was an inmate of Falmouth workhouse.

Another wife whose life appears to have spiralled downwards was Elizabeth Jackson.[12] She married James, a miner, in 1850 and they lived together for three years before James went to America leaving 20-year-old Elizabeth with two young children. Elizabeth reportedly "went about very neglectful of herself" leaving the children dirty and starving. James on hearing that Elizabeth "had gone wrong", stopped sending her money and instructed his parents to take the children from her, which they did. Between 1857 and 1861 Elizabeth was working as a servant and was observed "romping and playing" with her employer's son. When cautioned about her behaviour, Elizabeth retorted that she would "do as she liked", and boasted when she became pregnant that it "was not first time she had been in the family way and would not be the last". The baby, clear proof of Elizabeth's adultery, was born in Redruth workhouse in December 1861,[13] but it was not until James returned to Cornwall in 1868 that he filed for divorce. By 1871 Elizabeth was living alone as a seamstress.

Both Eliza Datson's and Elizabeth Jackson's behaviour may have been reprehensible, but was it in some way understandable given their situation? Although financially supported, they had been left as young mothers to manage on their own, condemned to a potentially indefinite life of lonely celibacy. Even the judge at the Jackson's divorce hearing had some sympathy; on being told that it was a common custom for Cornish miners to go away shortly after the marriage and not return for many years, he said: "It is a very hard custom for a man to go away and leave a woman without anyone to take care of her. As a rule, if a man is obliged to go away, he makes some provision to come home at some time or for the wife to come out after him".[14]

Wives divorced by their husbands for adultery almost always lost their children.[15] For example, Arthur and Elizabeth Hodge married in Cape Town in 1885 but came to England and had two children before Arthur, a mining engineer, returned to South Africa at the end of 1889. Over the next five years Arthur took a series of jobs in South Africa, returning home

The Married Widows of Cornwall

every year or so. During the last of these absences, Elizabeth started an affair with a newly widowed local man, eventually moving in with him. When word of this reached Arthur in Africa he obtained a divorce in 1895 with Elizabeth losing custody of her daughters who were placed in a boarding school in St Austell.[16] (Elizabeth was the wife encountered in a previous chapter who spent the remittance money she received on shoes from Paris rather settling the butcher's bill.)

The wives' desperation at the prospect of losing their children is well illustrated by the letters written by Susan Biddick. Susan's husband George went to South Africa in 1896, leaving her caring for their three children in St Erth. George sent money home and the couple exchanged regular letters. However, in a letter dated August 1897 Susan made a painful admission: "My Dear George, I know you will be wondering why you didn't have a letter last week. I couldn't write George I have been unfaithful to you & have got myself into trouble". In a second letter, Susan begs George: "Do not to divorce me for the children's sake, do not do it. I know I have done you the greatest wrong a woman can ever do to her husband but spare my children… No one can take the children from me but you & if you were to see us you wouldn't do it. George have mercy on me & try to forgive for the children's sake if you cannot take me back as your wife again come home and see me & let me keep the children".[17]

Susan Biddick's letters, which survive as certified transcriptions in the divorce papers, provide a rare first hand insight into the emotional complexities of the situation the wives found themselves in, and offer a more nuanced image of the adulterous wife as a vulnerable victim of circumstance. For example, Susan had wanted to accompany George but had reluctantly acquiesced to his view that Africa was not a suitable place for the family: "George if you only let me go to Africa when I wanted to this disgrace would have been saved for I made up my mind to go & I was careful over the money until you said I was to stay at home. I felt mad & disappointed then & now this is my reward." In her hurt and disappointment, Susan had become involved with the local stationmaster who, in an account that reads like a Victorian melodrama, she claimed raped her: "He came in & locked the door after him I told him to go out & begged him to go but he got the upper hand of me & blew out the light & threw me down & done what he wanted". Susan's version of events has to read in the context of other evidence. Witnesses had observed her spending time alone with the stationmaster in his private office, and he had often visited her at home. Were Susan's pleas the words of a loving and contrite wife or an accomplished attempt at manipulating George's emotions? Either way they fell on deaf ears and he divorced her in 1899 taking custody of their three sons. Whether Susan was hiding a consensual sexual relationship, or whether this was the flirtation of a lonely woman that got out of hand resulting in rape, is impossible to tell. Nevertheless, it does seem probable that without their husbands' protection and, as we saw in earlier chapters, often reliant on largely male-controlled credit and male assistance for heavier domestic repairs, the wives 'left behind' were vulnerable to sexual exploitation.

Unlike Susan Biddick, some wives' adultery came about through the formation of a new long-term relationship. One such case was that of Edith Quick of Camborne who was divorced in 1899 for adultery while her husband was in Alaska, losing custody of her children.[18] She and her lover lived together as husband and wife in Wales where they had four further children before returning to Camborne. In 1911 they claimed to have been married for 12 years, a ceremony that would have predated the divorce. As no record of a marriage has been found it is uncertain that they ever took advantage of the divorce to formalise their union.

Divorce released some young wives from marriages that had barely begun before the husband went abroad. Thomas and Sarah Ann Wearne were only married for four days in 1866 before Thomas, an engine smith, left with Sarah's consent to join his father in Australia with the intention of coming back to fetch his wife later.[19] Sarah received letters and money from her husband but formed a relationship with Robert Noakes and bore his child. The divorce granted in 1870 brought the ephemeral marriage to an end freeing all concerned to remarry. Sarah married in 1872 and brought up her illegitimate daughter along with children by her second husband (not Robert Noakes), while Thomas too remarried and raised a family in Australia.

One possible explanation for these post-nuptial emigrations is that men who were planning to go abroad felt obliged to marry girls they were courting who had fallen pregnant.[20] Samuel John Tonkin was about to leave for Mexico when he was asked to marry Eliza Ellen Matthews who was expecting his baby. They married in June 1889, after which he left with the consent of her and her parents. In 1891 Eliza and their baby son were living in her parents' home, where she received letters and money from Samuel until, in 1892, he found out that she had given birth to another child, and consequently filed for divorce.[21]

The gendered double standard of the divorce laws create a bias in the record towards the adultery of wives while that of the men remains largely hidden. This is illustrated by considering James Jackson, mentioned above. His wife Elizabeth was condemned for having 'gone wrong', neglecting her children and seducing her employer's son. However, what of James himself, the wronged party? By his own evidence he was living in America without his wife for 15 years. Is it to be supposed that he was faithful to her for that entire time? Court papers show that between 1853 and 1868 James worked at silver-lead mines in North Carolina, locating him there at the time of the 1860 US Federal census.[22] A search of that census revealed only one possible match for him; James W. Jackson, born in England, sharing the same birthdate of 1831, and middle initial (for Walter), and employed cleaning ore in Silverhill, Davidson county.[23] However, the James in America is listed with an Agnes Jackson, and a six-year-old boy William T. Jackson. Agnes and her son are listed without James in subsequent censuses, which also confirm that William's father was English. Although not conclusive, this is strongly indicative of this being the same James Jackson, in which case his criticism of Elizabeth's behaviour was somewhat hypocritical. This case illustrates the power imbalance that allowed the men abroad considerable freedom in relationships, whilst similar behaviour amongst their wives was castigated and carried far more damaging consequences.

Even if James was equally unfaithful, Elizabeth would have had no redress unless she could prove he had committed bigamy as it was far harder for a wife in Cornwall to divorce an adulterous husband abroad. A rare example was that of Jemima Rowe. She knew that her husband, John, was having affairs with women in Helston where the couple lived in the late 1870s. When confronted, he eventually admitted it, but announced that he was "going to America, and that she would have to do the best she could for herself".[24] In 1880 Jemima was left behind with two baby daughters. Word reached her that John was continuing his unfaithful ways and "leading a bad life" in Michigan, but she would not be able to get a divorce on the grounds of his adultery alone, even if she could prove it, or afford the divorce. However, in 1886 she was able to file for divorce on the basis of "adultery coupled with desertion of the petitioner for 2 years & upwards without reasonable excuse", supported by testimony from miners who had witnessed John's behaviour in Michigan before they returned to Cornwall. Shortly after the divorce was granted Jemima wed Thomas Jenkyn, a gentleman over 30 years her senior, which may explain how she could fund the divorce. With Thomas she was able to provide a home for both her daughters and when he died in 1893 leaving an estate of over £1100 she would have found financial security as well.[25]

The cost of divorce in the British courts was prohibitive for most husbands and wives; Judge Granger described the case of a labourer who, finding that his wife "had gone wrong", had worked in America for five years in order to earn the £50-60 that it would cost him to divorce her in Cornwall.[26] In addition to legal fees, the men had the costs of returning from abroad for the proceedings,[27] although some were able to avoid this by giving depositions via a British Consulate.[28]

Faced with the cost and logistical difficulties of obtaining a divorce in England, some husbands found the American courts easier to deal with. Judge Granger cited the example of a miner who, having discovered that his wife had been unfaithful and not being able to afford a divorce in Cornwall, went to America, became naturalised and obtained a divorce there.[29] There was a perception that it was far simpler to dissolve a marriage in America.[30] "The ease with which divorces are procured in America is proverbial", reported the *Royal Cornwall Gazette* in 1867 reporting a case where a husband had divorced his "faultless" wife without her knowledge.[31] In June 1870 the *West Briton* drew its readers' attention to notices in the Chicago papers advertising: "Divorces legally obtained without appearance in court or publication in the papers. A common article five dollars".[32]

Incompatibility and a lack of understanding between the legal systems in England and the US caused further complications, and could result in men having different legitimate wives in both countries.[33] A divorce granted in the US was not necessarily considered binding in the next state, let alone in England. ("No rules of law are more perplexing to American jurists than those which regulate divorce… a good reason for divorce in one state may be no reason at all in the adjoining state", wrote a commentator in the *Royal Cornwall Gazette*.)[34] When Richard Henry Thomas wrote to the Truro Poor Law Union in 1894 to tell them that he no longer intended to support his wife in Cornwall because he had divorced her in Butte City, the Truro guardians "took a very serious view of the looseness of the divorce laws across the water, whereby men could on their own bare statement separate themselves from their wives and leave them chargeable to ratepayers of another country".[35] They refused to recognise the divorce and insisted that Richard Henry was responsible for supporting his wife, although, as we have already seen, they were powerless to enforce this.

In a similar case, the Redruth guardians viewed it as scandalous that when one wife eventually heard from her husband in Arizona after four years, instead of money to help support their three children, he had sent divorce papers for her to sign.[36] There was no evidence to suggest she was at fault and it was "thought perhaps that he had another woman out there". How many other wives simply received a letter out of the blue, or were divorced without their knowledge, is not known. This further illustrates the gendered power imbalance in controlling the future of the marriage. For the wives 'left behind' the idea that their marriages could be dissolved abroad quickly and cheaply, even without their knowledge, must have added to their feelings of vulnerability.

Marriages frequently 'ended' without the formalities of a divorce case. Indeed, many couples did not think they needed an official divorce in order to remarry.[37] From her study of cohabitation Ginger Frost concludes that "popular definitions of marriage and divorce were wider than the law allowed" and the idea of 'self-divorce' persisted well into the second half of the 19th century despite repeated official denials.[38] Self-divorce with a view to enabling remarriage could take a variety of forms. Some believed that the marriage was legally over if the wife or husband had been deserted for someone else. A common misconception was that because someone who had remarried after not hearing from their spouse for seven years could not be convicted for bigamy, it meant that the second marriage was valid. It wasn't. Others thought that they could draw up formal deeds of separation that would allow them to remarry, while some still insisted that 'wife sales'[39] were a legitimate form of divorce.[40] The notion of wife sales connected with emigration from Cornwall has been granted an unwarranted legitimacy through a re-enactment performed annually as part of a Cornish mining heritage festival but in reality there are no confirmed cases recorded that support this. In his extensive research on wife sales, Menefee was only able to locate ten cases, of varying veracity, in 19th century Cornwall.[41] Nearly all of these occurred in the early years of the century and none are associated with the need to raise money for emigration as suggested in the current popular mythology. Nonetheless, it is clear that some couples in Cornwall believed, or chose to believe, that they could be released from their marriage vows by mutual consent, and that this was a legitimate way of dissolving the union and being able to remarry. For example, when charged with bigamy in 1857 Ann Arthur claimed that she was free to marry because her husband had given his consent before a witness that she might marry any person she thought proper.[42]

So far we have focused on emotional and sexual motivations for wives forming new relationships in the absence of their husbands. However, 19th century marriage was a practical as well emotional contract. As Frost points out, poor men and women were interdependent: "Men needed housekeepers and women needed a provider, and neither could live well without the other".[43] Although the wives 'left behind' could not tend directly to their husbands' domestic needs while they were abroad, they did fulfil the role of housekeeper, caring for children and/or the family home in Cornwall. In return, the wives expected, and indeed needed, their men to support them as low wages and the demands of child care meant few women could earn enough to maintain themselves and a family. Therefore if a husband abroad failed to adequately support his wife at home, she had little choice but to find a new provider in order to survive. For some the role of provider might be taken on by the wider family or the Poor Law as described in earlier chapters, but for others, suggests Frost, a husband's 'misbehaviour' in failing to provide was justification for finding a new partner.

Both sexes used the rationale of their partner's 'misbehaviour' to end the marriage but what constituted unacceptable behaviour within marriage in the 19th century was split on gendered lines. Frost lists poor housekeeping, squandering a husband's pay, being too assertive (especially regarding control of her own income or property) and above all committing adultery, as 'misbehaviours' that a husband could cite as reasons to be free of his wife.[44] Wives, she suggests, were more tolerant of their husband's adultery. However, one could argue that they had little choice in the matter as the legal double standard regarding marital infidelity meant that there was little they could do that would not hurt them more than their husbands. As far as women were concerned the more important forms of male 'misbehaviour' in marriage were violence and failing to provide for the family. Wives whose husbands were abroad were safe from domestic violence but without day-to-day interaction with their husbands they were largely powerless to influence their husband's willingness to share his earnings. Failure to provide for her and the children, even complete desertion by a husband were not grounds for divorce (unless combined with proven adultery), even if the wife could afford one. Hence any relationship the wife formed with a man who would be a better provider for her family was unlikely to be a legitimate one.

It is believed that adulterous cohabitation was widespread amongst the working classes in general,[45] so it is logical to suppose that, given the difficulties that many of the wives 'left behind' faced, some will have given up on their existing marriages and found new partners; the adulterous couple living as man and wife. Cohabitation, when it was marriage in all but name, offered a deserted wife greater financial security, an emotional and physical relationship, and in some cases the only way of keeping her children. Offset against this was the fact that she could expect little sympathy or help via the Poor Law or charities should her new 'husband' die or desert her, as well as the risk, albeit small, that her legitimate husband might reappear with sufficient will and resources to divorce her and claim the children. As Frost notes: "The downward spiral of female cohabitees showed the difference in status between a wife and a 'mistress' most clearly; a woman could go from a pseudo-wife to a prostitute in an alarmingly short time". Such concerns might be reason for hesitation and delay but as Frost aptly points out: "With so many incentives, only the strongest-willed women could live for decades, eking out an existence with no hope for remarriage" so "eventually they chose to live with new mates".[46]

It is suggested that 'passing' as married was not that difficult especially

Double Standards and Five-Dollar Divorces

in urban areas,[47] although possibly not quite so easy in Cornwall where even in towns like Redruth and Camborne so many people were interconnected through family and work. Nevertheless, in some cases the Cornish communities do seem to have been tolerant of pragmatic, albeit unconventional, living arrangements.

One such case is that of Mary Hannah Phillips. Mary's husband Joel, a mine agent, had left to work in South America in 1853, just three years after their marriage. Mary and the couple's two young sons, William and Samuel, are said to have lived with Joel's mother in Blackwater, St Agnes where their received regular remittances. However, at some point in the mid- to late 1850s Mary went to live in the household of her uncle William Medlyn at Gregwartha in Four Lanes to help care for her ailing aunt, Jane. After Jane's death in December 1860 Mary continued living in the house as William's housekeeper. At the time of the 1861 census Mary and her two sons aged nine and seven were living with William, and visitors in the house included her mother, Elizabeth Berdiner. News of improper behaviour reached Joel abroad, who ceased sending remittances and returned to Cornwall to start divorce proceedings.[48]

Mary and her uncle William both claimed that Mary was simply employed as housekeeper, producing evidence of wages paid, and denied any adultery. However, the true nature of their relationship must have been common knowledge locally as two years after his wife's death the birth of a son, Joseph William Penaluna Medlyn, had been registered in 1862 using William's surname and giving Mary's (Berdiner) as the mother's maiden name. On 18 November that year, baby Joseph had been openly baptised in Carnmenellis parish church as the son of William and Mary Medlyn.

Despite any scandal associated with the divorce, which was reported in the local press in 1865, William and Mary continued to live the in same house and community, with William still trading and taking on local lads as apprentices in his shoe making business. The picture presented to the 1871 census enumerator portrayed Mary as William's unmarried servant, but the household included the couple's son Joseph, his older half brother Samuel Phillips and Mary's mother, Elizabeth. It was not until the 1881 census, shortly after William had died that Mary, as the widowed head of a household including her sons by both her 'husbands', calls herself Mary Medlyn. There is no evidence that William and Mary ever married after the divorce, and indeed any marriage would have been void as marriage between a widower and his spouse's niece was prohibited.[49]

It seems likely that unmarried cohabiting couples may have been tolerated or even accepted in communities that were aware of the difficulties of the situation, especially in cases where the wife had been deserted and divorce impossible. Such tolerance could also be extended to wives who remarried bigamously. In fact an attempt to 'legitimize' the union, in their own eyes if not in law, was seen by women as a prerequisite before agreeing to cohabit.[50]

The practice of bigamy[51] and cohabitation in the mining communities in Cornwall, and amongst the men abroad, was recognised at the time. In a commentary written in Cornish dialect, W. Herbert Thomas, 'reporting' a fictional local lecture wrote:

> *"Out in Alaska some ave the Cornish miners do live among the natives who do swop wives weth aich other, and do live weth thaise native women sa long, as they are in the country; and they do the same in Chili, Mexico, and other countries if they are'nt full ave religion. And I've knawed women here in Tolscadium to go awver to Truraw an marry another man, ef their husband es gone abroad, an doant send home to thum; an ave lived to theer death as the second man's wife, without taaken the trouble, or tryin to git the money to ave a divorce."*[52]

The clerk to the Redruth Union confirmed: "It is a very common thing for people - not only in America but within five miles of this house - to get married again and commit bigamy by making a false declaration".[53] References in the Cornish press to cases where a wife in Cornwall had remarried, or had found out that her husband abroad has done so, support the clerk's view.[54] A young married woman from Mousehole told the Penzance Board of Guardians that her husband, who had gone to Cardiff four years previously, "wrote a while but got tired" so she had remarried and had children with her new 'husband', assuming the first to be dead.[55] Another woman was alleged during an assize trial to have entered into a bigamous marriage in Cornwall despite having two living husbands, one in America and one in Australia.[56]

Examples of bigamy and of men having second (even third) families abroad are also preserved in family histories.[57] Grace Hannah 'Anne' Inch, wife of Captain William 'Guillermo' Inch, stayed in Redruth with the couple's daughter while her husband pursued his career in Latin America in the 1860s and 1870s. William remained in contact and is believed to have supported his family in Cornwall, but at the same time fathered and raised seven children with Josefina, a member of his employer's family in Bolivia.[58] Similar stories occur amongst Cornish communities worldwide. George Snow of Boyton had been married for less than a year in 1897 when he left his young wife and baby son in Cornwall, and emigrated to New Zealand where he married and raised a second family.[59] Likewise, Stephen Tyacke never returned to his wife Janie and their two children in Perranuthnoe, Cornwall because he formed a relationship with another woman in South Africa.[60] George Hicks is reputed to have married and started a second family in Australia because his first wife refused to leave Cornwall.[61]

Some women married in Cornwall not knowing that their new husbands already had wives and families abroad. When retired mine agent John Skewes returned from Mexico and married Katie Williams in Chacewater in 1880, he neglected to mention Luisa, his wife of over ten years, still living with the couple's seven children in Pachuca.[62] Many similar stories are rumoured, but they are often difficult to verify as families can be reticent about details of past events that have left a legacy of hurt and embarrassment that persists in some cases to the present day.[63]

Evidence suggests that only a small proportion of bigamists, even if exposed, were prosecuted,[64] and when added to the unknown number of couples passing as married, raises the question of how much trust can be placed in the census returns on this matter. It has to be wondered how many wives 'left behind' were omitted from the estimate of the scale of the phenomenon because they are 'disguised' as the wives of other men.

It is inevitable that some marriages could not survive the difficulties caused by lengthy separations and long distances. However, the suggested causal association between wives taking in lodgers in their husband's absence and adultery is unfounded. It should also be remembered that some of these marriages would not have survived anyway and as Olive Anderson points out, emigration often provided a means for men to escape unhappy unions. It also provided a way out for some wives. Provided they could survive financially, some may have been quite content for a husband that they did not care for to be on the other side of the world. In this way emigration destroyed some marriages and made others more tolerable at a time when legitimately ending the marriage through divorce was not an option for most couples. Whether the split was caused, or facilitated, by emigration, many wives saw no reason why they should be prevented from forming new unions whether through desire or necessity. To use Ginger Frost's words: "If the first spouse did not work out, they got another, whether the law recognised them as spouses or not".[65] However, such a course of action was fraught with danger for these women. Even if the wives, like the men, adopted a code of silence to shield their activities from their distant spouses, the high risk of pregnancy made discovery of any illicit relationships more likely, and once exposed they were subject to far greater and serious repercussions.

There is no way of knowing how many marriages failed as a result of emigration. However, some clues are provided by a comparison with more favourable outcomes of the separations these couple endured, a topic explored in the next chapter.

9

Meeting Again on Earth or in Heaven
Hope for a happy reunion

So far we have considered wives for whom the outcome of their husbands' emigration was desertion or marital breakdown. These are the wives who leave most trace in the historical record through their interactions with the Poor Law or courts. However, we need to ask whether the experiences of such women are typical. To answer this question recent research has balanced the qualitative evidence from sources such as newspapers, which focus on the more dramatic outcomes, with an attempt to identify less visible outcomes, such as the numbers reunited with their husbands either in Cornwall or abroad, or for whom death intervened; a possibility acknowledged in emigrant letters with the hope to meet again in heaven if not on earth.

By identifying hundreds of wives in the Cornwall census returns whose husbands who had gone abroad, and then tracing them in subsequent census years in a longitudinal study it has been possible to build up a picture based on multiple life-stories. Concentrating on five mining parishes (Camborne, Gwennap, St Agnes, St Just in Penwith and St Cleer)[1] it has been possible to trace what happened to at least 50% of the wives 'left behind' identified from the census. Generally more wives from later census years were traced than from the earlier ones, and in some of the later census groups 70-80% of wives were located ten years later. There are a number of inevitable biases in the success rate of tracing women from one census in the next. As well as an increased likelihood of finding those women with unusual names, or with children (as the presence of named children aids the search and confirms identification), there is also a bias towards finding middle-aged wives who are settled in the same location. Consequently, the bias is against finding those wives 'left behind' as young brides (less likely to have children or be settled in their own households) and the older women whose children had left home.

The Married Widows of Cornwall

It is also more difficult to identify wives who had remarried or died. An individual was only recorded in the research as having died if a family history led to a death or burial record, or her children were found with their widowed father. A small percentage (around 3%) of the wives could be shown to have died, but in most cases wives who had died would have fallen into the 'not traced' category, as it was not practicable to conduct full searches of the death records for so many women.[2]

Tracing wives who had emigrated was reliant on the online availability of overseas census returns, passenger lists and other emigration databases. As North America is far better served in this respect than Australia, and records for other emigration destinations such as South America and Africa unavailable, wives who joined their husbands in America were far more likely to be located. The US Federal censuses proved so useful in tracing wives that the loss of the 1890 one (destroyed in a fire) almost certainly depressed the figure for the number of wives from the 1881 census found to have emigrated.[3]

The outcome for which the results are most accurate is where the wife was located in the subsequent census living in Cornwall with her husband, because these wives were more easily identified with certainty than those who had moved or whose circumstances had changed more dramatically. One caveat is that among these women were the wives of husbands who were simply absent, and although evidence emerged that many of these men were indeed abroad, this group undoubtedly contained some whose husbands had not travelled far and therefore were more likely to have returned.

This research has revealed that 10-22% of husbands from St Just and St Agnes were back in Cornwall with their wives in the subsequent census year. In Camborne the range was narrower at 11-15%. These figures reflect the similar findings for the parish of Gwennap, in which 10-14% of the wives 'left behind' in the 1851, 1861, and 1871 censuses and 21% of these in 1881 were found reunited with their husbands in Cornwall. These results are in keeping with the more nuanced understanding of emigration that has developed in the last twenty years. Emigration has frequently been viewed in the past as a one-way process, with those who returned imagined largely as a limited number of 'failed' migrants. However, it is now thought that at least a third of all those who emigrated from Europe between 1824 and 1924 returned home. Estimates for return amongst British migrants range from just under 20% to as many as 40%.[4]

A phenomenon of temporary transoceanic emigration is believed to have evolved as a logical extension of the established practice of temporary labour migration within Europe. "Only the scale and distances changed", note migration historians Lucassen and Lucassen: "For many migrants, crossing the ocean was a less permanent and fundamental move than is often assumed".[5] Skilled workers could increasingly participate in an international labour market, creating multidirectional migration flows that operated alongside, and sometimes intertwined with, the traditional model of the emigrant seeking a permanent new life abroad. In the Cornish context the culture of local mobility required of miners as mineral deposits were discovered and exhausted in different locations within Cornwall, and elsewhere in the UK, was expanded to encompass the whole world.[6] As Payton points out: "this inherent mobility encouraged a degree of return migration, establishing the outline of a pattern which would reach its apogee in the relationship between Cornwall and South Africa at the end of the century".[7]

It has generally been assumed that transoceanic international labour markets and the associated long distance movement of workers only became established in the late 19th century. Examples of seasonal migrations at this time include the tens of thousands of Italian and Spanish workers who harvested grain and fruit in Argentina or worked in Brazilian coffee plantations annually from October to May between 1880 and 1914. The 1880s also saw the temporary migration of skilled building workers moving between London and New York,[8] and hundreds of English masons and stonecutters regularly worked in the United States from spring until autumn.[9] Among these workers were stonemasons and quarrymen from the Cornish granite quarries undertaking seasonal or annual migrations to America in the 1870s.[10] It is frequently suggested that such short-term labour migrations were only made possible by swifter sea crossings through the development of steamships,[11] and it was this that made temporary emigration an increasingly realistic option before the First World War. This implies that this form of temporary migration was a late 19th century development, epitomised by the easy movement of Cornish miners to and from South Africa "responding efficiently to the needs of each economy and in tune with their own priorities".[12]

While it is true that research has indicated a slight trend towards more couples being reunited in Cornwall in the late 19th century, in line with this increase in two-way migration, it has also shown that many husbands who emigrated much earlier had also returned to their wives before the following census. This is true for a fifth of the wives 'left behind' in St Just in 1851, close to the proportion of the 1881 group whose husbands had returned. Among the wives 'left behind' in Gwennap in 1851 there was a similar peak in the number of husbands back with their wives ten years later.

This means we have to question the notion of temporary migration being limited to the last decades of the 19th century. Historians have already pointed out that the lack of official statistics for the earlier period obscure our view of the numbers involved, and have noted the frequent references to early return and repeat migration in collections of correspondence.[13] Certainly, in Cornwall involvement in an international labour market can be traced back to the immediate post-Napoleonic era with the recruitment of skilled miners and engineers to work on fixed-term contracts in the mines of Latin America from the 1820s. The well-travelled returned migrant was already a presence in the Cornish mining communities in the 1850s; George Henwood described Chacewater at the time as a "colony of miners" who had worked in mines in various parts of the world, many having worked abroad more than once.[14] That so many husbands absent in 1851 were found to have returned to their wives by 1861 adds weight to an argument for the earlier establishment of temporary labour migration from Cornwall.

In the discourse of one-way migration, return is often interpreted as failure; if the aim was to escape from an unsatisfactory old world to a better new one, success equates with permanent settlement abroad. However, the aims of temporary labour migration are very different. Henwood noted that nearly all the returned miners in Chacewater had come back with "a little competency, to enable them to get into some way of business, a public house or beer-shop being the principal and favourite speculation". Migration as an investment in the future might also take the form of career development; the Cornish stonemasons working temporarily in America were taking advantage not only of higher wages but acquiring new skills in the technologically more advanced American granite industry.[15]

There is a wealth of anecdotal evidence for married migrants returning to establish a new or revitalised business or career in Cornwall. For example, amongst the family group comprising Louisa Woolcock, her sisters and sister-in-law, five of their six husbands returned to Cornwall having worked abroad. At least two of these had achieved their aims of coming back having made enough money to fund a change of career. Stephen Woolcock, a copper miner who went abroad briefly in 1870-1 leaving his wife Sarah in Cornwall with their five children, is recalled as having saved a substantial sum of money, sufficient to set himself up as an innkeeper and later tea dealer. Fellow copper miner and neighbour, Nicholas Gerrans (abroad in 1861) returned to his wife, Grace Louisa, and children with enough money to establish himself as a farmer by 1871.[16] Another returnee was tin miner turned grocer and draper, James Bennetts Williams. He left his new wife, Mary Ann, and baby daughter in 1883 in order to pay off accumulated debts by working in the Bolivian silver mines but had returned by the late 1880s and had re-established himself as a grocer and general dealer.[17] Therefore the migrant's return to Cornwall was far from synonymous with failure. The husbands of many of the wives who were 'left behind' in Cornwall were among those whom Marjory Harper describes as having gone abroad with "no intention of settling permanently in the new land, but with the goal of repatriating the profits they hoped to make in a range of enterprises".[18]

Contemporary reports also noted that among the returned miners were some who had "realised sufficient to maintain themselves in a state of independence".[19] For many wives dreams of such financial security would have made the prospect and risks of separation more acceptable, especially when the husband's emigration was of a more speculative nature as in the gold rushes that offered the perceived potential of fortunes being made very quickly. Such dreams were fuelled by reports of local men finding large gold nuggets or returning home with parcels of gold dust.[20] Many a wife managing alone would have had her hopes raised by the story of the wife of Nicholas Thomas of Northill. Nicholas had left his family penniless and destitute to go to America in 1849 where he joined the Californian gold rush. His wife had managed to support herself and the three children "by industry of her needle, with the help of some good friends" and they were just finishing a "frugal dinner of red herrings and potatoes" when Nicholas unexpectedly walked in after an absence of three years bringing with him over £1500.[21] In 1858 Maria Walters would have been equally delighted to receive the letter from her husband Henry enclosing a £200 banker's draft and the news that he was on his way home from Australia. These financial rewards may have been seen not only as ample return for the men's labour abroad, but for the wives' 'investment' of their dreams in agreeing to and/or enabling their husbands' departure.

Nonetheless, such success stories should be tempered with those more closely aligned to the idea of return as 'failed migration'. Individual strategies for working abroad were thrown awry when the men's destinations did not meet their expectations. A realisation of the true likelihood of success in the gold diggings undoubtedly brought some husbands home, and intelligence about more regular job opportunities overseas sometimes also proved inaccurate. In 1866 an advert placed in the Cornish press promoted constant employment and high wages to be had in Nova Scotia,[22] but the following year miners who had been "lured by some misrepresentations" and had gone there, many leaving wives and families behind, found once they arrived that there was no work.[23] In some cases life in a different country simply did not suit: "Dick Rabey did not like it and is home again, he came home all unexpected to his wife", wrote a neighbour from St Eval in 1888.[24]

Unplanned return was also triggered by ill health or accident. It is estimated that 20% of the workforce in the Brazilian and Cuban mines were lost to illness or death in 1841, and exposure to tropical diseases meant men were discharged early from their contracts in Latin America.[25] One of these was the husband of Ann Whitburn. James Whitburn, along with his brother William, was contracted to work as a mine engineer at Cobre Mines and arrived in Cuba in July 1836. Ann was one of the more fortunate wives who routinely received part of James' wages directly from the mine's agent in Cornwall. However, within 18 months James was too ill to work and was sent home in January 1838. Tragically, the family's high hopes for James' time working abroad were further shattered by the loss of the couple's only son. Eleven-year-old James junior had accompanied his father and uncle to Cuba but had also fallen ill and been sent home on an earlier ship. Ann knowing that her son was on his way, and that his ship had arrived in Swansea, made repeated trips to Portreath on the north coast of Cornwall expecting to meet him. It fell to the mine company's agent, Alfred Jenkin, to let her know that young James had died at sea, and arrange for his possessions to be sent to her. James senior only found out about his son's death when he arrived home.[26]

Work abroad could be brought to a premature end for a wide variety of health-related reasons. A Penzance man had to give up work in America due to failing eyesight,[27] while another returned to Redruth having been paid off after getting frost-bite.[28] In the late 19th and early 20th century numerous miners had their working lives in South Africa cut short by the debilitating effects of 'miner's lung' (phthisis) and many husbands returned to Cornwall broken men.[29]

Getting home under these circumstances was sometimes far from straightforward as husbands had frequently exhausted their funds and struggled to make their way home to their wives. The men who made the fruitless trip to Nova Scotia suffered great privations to get back as far as New York and then had to earn their passages back to Cornwall.[30] A Gwennap man in Australia, who found that he could scarcely feed himself, let alone send remittances to his family, appealed for friends to send out money to him to bring him home,[31] whilst a "steady and industrious engine-man" from St Day also requested a collection be made to help him return after having 'bad luck' in New Zealand.[32]

Even those who worked for generally paternalistic mine companies, might see little sympathy if they fell ill before their employers could recoup the costs of their voyage out. James Whitburn's boss in Cuba, John Hardy junior, was very reluctant to discharge him from his contract, and gained a reputation for a callous attitude to sick employees, cutting their wages and reportedly saying that it was cheaper to bury a corpse than pay for the men's repatriation. In other cases, employers were only too happy to send home men involved in industrial disputes and unrest.[33]

However, return migration to Cornwall should not be viewed through the polarized lens of success or failure; for many families in Cornwall it was simply one half of the temporary migration process.[34] In the same way as a dynamic interaction of push and pull factors influenced the decision to go, similar factors influenced the decision to return. An important one was fluctuations in the international labour market. As Marjory Harper points out with regard to migration to and from America in the 19th century: "For the first time skilled craftsmen could compare wage rates on either side of the Atlantic with the knowledge that they could easily, and quickly, return home if the opportunities in the labour market so dictated."[35] The proportion of husbands returning to wives in St Just and Gwennap dips in the 1860s and 1870s corresponding with the depression in Cornish mining that may have made return a less attractive prospect. The evidence for men returning in response to changing conditions presents a picture of the families constantly weighing up their options, deciding whether the men would be better off working at home or abroad as the balance of economic opportunities shifted.

The temporary migrations of numerous Cornish husbands can be reconstructed from public records and private family histories. One of the best documented, in that a diary survives offering some insight as to the feelings and motivations of the individual concerned, is the career of mine captain John James. Born in Sithney in 1822, John spent time abroad working in, amongst other locations, Norway, America (Tennessee), Newfoundland and Ireland, returning in between to Cornwall, which he regarded as home. In John's case each move overseas was undertaken reluctantly as he would have preferred to stay in Cornwall but was unable to find suitable work closer to home. John's wife, Joanna, accompanied him on some of these interludes abroad (to Newfoundland for two years, for example, albeit leaving three of her six daughters in Cornwall), but on other occasions remained in Cornwall or joined him later, as in his final employment in Ireland that lasted ten years.[36]

At times these individual family decisions accumulated into larger scale movements, both into, as well as out of, Cornwall. In a summary of the causes of 19th century migration Robert Woods notes the influence on emigration of the economic cycles either side of the Atlantic being out of phase.[37] It is clear that the international mining industry was extremely volatile during the 19th century, fluctuating between boom and bust in different places locally and globally in quick succession. This created very rapid changes in circumstances that would challenge modern intelligence and communication networks, let alone those relied upon by miners in 19th century Cornwall trying to decide what would be best for their families. Sometimes, intelligence on employment opportunities outside Cornwall was wrong or simply out of date, causing the men to come home.

In 1867 the Helston Union reported that: "Many of the miners who went to Scotland for work have returned, in a state of greater destitution than when they left home".[38] At the same time many men were coming home to Lelant from abroad, the North of England, and Ireland, worse off than when they departed.[39] In 1873 thousands of miners were reported to be returning to Cornwall because of economic depression in North America.[40] Similarly, large numbers returned from South Africa in 1906 as they were "dissatisfied with the conditions which prevail in the Transvaal, and are attracted by the mining boom at home".[41] Wars abroad and their associated economical upheaval also triggered decisions to return to Cornwall; so many people were returning to Cornwall in the summer of 1862 during the American Civil War that a housing shortage was reported in Redruth.[42] Likewise, at the close of the century the Boer War was to bring many Cornishman back from South Africa, if only temporarily.[43]

For married men, evaluating the economics of working abroad was more complicated than for their single counterparts and many underestimated the cost of living apart from their wives. In 1837 Alfred Jenkin advised the Cobre Mining Association: "It appears that the necessary expenses in Cuba exclusive of lodging require from £5 to £6 per month, so that if a man has an establishment also to support in this country [Cornwall] there is very little left to be laid by. Even at £9 per month men with families cannot do much for themselves and it will therefore be best to give a decided preference to young unmarried men".[44]

The men returning to Lelant in 1867 said that they found it "impossible to earn sufficient wages anywhere to support themselves and to remit a maintenance to their families".[45] In January 1873 it was reported from Hayle that:

> "Married men say they did not find it better for themselves or families to be abroad, and not half so comfortable, for by the time the high rate of board is paid in America, and the fatherless family at home goes through its little sicknesses, and the dozen necessities are paid for, which the father's presence would obviate, there is no

gain. So the "glorious dollar" becomes worth but an old fashioned shilling! and after the balance-sheet is drawn there is no real profit for the married man. If he takes his wife across, unless she is willing and able to rough it, to forgo her quiet and comfortable house at home, it is still worse, for if she expects to live in style in America, and dress herself and the children neatly, the cost will be more than her husband's gettings will provide. This is the married man's version."[46]

As a result some husbands decided that the costs outweighed the benefits and returned home.

Alongside these economic factors, decisions to return were influenced by emotional factors and changing personal circumstances.[47] A death in the family might mean an unplanned or premature return, as in the case of James Williams, who came back to Perranzabuloe from California in 1863 to be with his wife Catherine after the death of their young daughter.[48]

Running as an undercurrent to the practical drivers for return was an emotional one, the desire for 'home'. "A Cornish man always has the idea he is going to return to Cornwall; it does not matter how long he stops out, he always has it at the back of his mind that he wants to end his days in his own delectable duchy", Thomas Granger told the Royal Commission on Divorce and Matrimonial Causes in 1910.[49] These sentiments echoed an earlier article of 1901 that noted how "the Cornish miner, who, after several years' residence abroad, becomes possessed solely of one burning desire, which is to return to the place of his birth, and there spend some years of his life as well as some of its savings".[50] It was not unusual, however, for emigrants of any origin to profess a longing to return. As migration historian Eric Richards points outs: "In the unsentimental words of modern geographers, 'one never finds so much philosophising about returning as amongst migrants who will never in fact return'. This they bluntly term 'the return illusion'".[51] It is testament to the Cornish determination to make return more than an illusion that there are so many houses in the Cornish mining towns named after the places where their owners earned the funds to purchase or build their homes.[52] These are the Cornish equivalent of 'the American House', the badge of successful temporary labour emigration that appeared in other European emigration centres.[53]

The traditional idea of 19th century emigration as a daunting and expensive 'once in a lifetime' experience leaves little space for the notion of transoceanic visits home. Nonetheless this appears to have been a relatively common occurrence within the international Cornish community, with visits by named individuals reported in the local press. It has been estimated that around a quarter of those who went to Latin America returned to Cornwall at least once, with 6% of Cornish-born migrants making multiple trips abroad.[54]

Therefore migrant men who appear in the census with their wives in Cornwall may not all have been returnees but visitors. Even some of those who had emigrated to Australia made fleeting trips home at a surprisingly early date. A Dr George Witt wrote from Sydney in 1851: "People here think nothing of what they call running home; one man, it is said, went home to hear Jenny Lind, stayed in London a fortnight, and then returned to Sydney". The International Exhibition in London in 1862 also attracted visitors from Australia.[55] Christmas was an understandably popular time for a visit with many Cornishmen from the United States, Canada and South Africa coming home for the holiday in 1895.[56]

The husbands who returned to their wives may have done so for a wide variety of reasons. As Eric Richards suggests, failed migration, repatriations, and circulating labour all form part of the migrant experience.[57] The dynamic culture of mobility means that the 'outcome' revealed by the study of the census returns was frequently not a fixed one. It only reveals whether the couple were together or not at a single point of time. Therefore, whereas the presence of the husband could denote a permanent reunion, it could equally signify a spell between periods of work overseas or simply a visit home. When the information from the census is supplemented by family histories complex life stories are revealed. To give just one example, Margaret Roberts' husband, William, returned from working abroad in 1873 with enough money to buy a farm and inn at Morvah but, instead of settling there, went out to South Africa again some nine years later where he was killed in a mine accident in 1884.[58] A snapshot of the situation, as in the census, at different points during this story would have implied quite different outcomes.

Just as it can't be assumed that husbands who appear in the census to have returned to their wives in Cornwall were back to stay, the census can be equally misleading about their absence. In most of the mining parishes where census returns have been examined 20-28% of husbands who were absent in one census year were still absent, or absent again, in the subsequent census ten years later.[59] But this doesn't necessarily mean he was away continuously for a decade or more. Many husbands may have returned home and left again in the interim years between censuses. In many cases, as shown above, it was an interlude between contracts or working expeditions abroad, but in some cases the men found it difficult to settle and reintegrate into their old lives in Cornwall.[60] Given the period between censuses, such reunions may have been as brief as a day or two, or could have been for as long as nearly ten years if the couple were reunited just after one census and parted just before the next. Ample evidence for such reunions is provided by the numbers of legitimate children whose ages indicate that they could not have been conceived before the couple first parted.

Among those husbands who did not return for more than a decade there would have been some who simply could not afford to do so, or kept postponing with good intentions of earning more for their families' future. However, there were others whose motivation was more suspect. Emigration has frequently been viewed as a means of desertion, escaping from the responsibilities and constraints of married life.[61] Mr Boyns of St Just certainly thought so: "I am sorry to say that I think some few of our miners, but they are the exception, have gone away for the express purpose of leaving their wives and families, and I am equally sorry to say, though these cases are rare, that some of the wives almost deserve this."[62] Even if the husband left planning to return, the failure to do so in some cases must have been deliberate, turning as Roderick Phillips suggests in his work on the history of divorce, "an intended temporary absence into a permanent one".[63]

Phillips also points out, however: "Of those who did not return, no doubt many died while away, and the lack of systematic methods of identification meant that their families were never informed. The loss of a ship at sea might be notified only by its being long overdue." Thus, for some couples, death precluded any reunion. Of the wives followed in research on Camborne, Gwennap, St Agnes, St Just and St Cleer the proportions who were described as widows in the subsequent census are broadly similar for most years, in the 10-19% range (Gwennap was 17-19%), although some produced higher proportions closer to a quarter of all the wives (e.g. Camborne 1891; St Agnes 1851; St Cleer 1861 & 1881; and St Just 1881 & 1891). As these higher figures mostly occur in the later years this may indicate a slight upwards trend, but the significance of this, if any, is not clear. That either party were found to have died when the next census was taken does not, of course, preclude the couple's prior reunion.

As Phillips implies, some wives may never have known that their husband had died while abroad. This uncertainty inevitably leads to the need for caution in interpreting research based on the census alone. Some widows would have remarried and become untraceable as those who had remarried could only be identified if the children of the first marriage were living with them. An unknown number of the wives whose husbands were recorded as absent may have been widows without knowing it. An equally unknown number of those who described themselves as widows may simply have given up on their husbands and found it convenient to be thought of as such. It was also widely believed that if the husband had not been heard from for more than seven years he could be assumed to be dead.[64] One woman claimed that although she had not heard of her husband's death, "she knew it as a fact". After not receiving any letters for some time, she went to bed one night as usual but on getting up in the morning she "had found the house turned upside down, a sure token from the Lord that her husband was dead". Her story was sufficient to convince the Redruth Board of Guardians that her subsequent second marriage was valid.[65] Given that widows had more rights than married women there was a clear advantage in being accepted within the community as a widow.

When asked about their marital status by the census enumerator, some women would have found it hard to know what to say. If they had not heard any news from, or of, their husbands for some time they genuinely did not know if they were widows or not.[66] Even those who had received a recent letter could not be entirely sure. The time taken for mail to arrive meant that comforting letters received by wives from their husbands could be out of date. Only hours after opening a letter from her husband in Montana, reassuring her that he was well, the wife of Thomas Richards of

The Married Widows of Cornwall

Redruth received a visit from a friend breaking the news that he had been dead for more than a week, having been killed two days after writing the letter.[67] It is not surprising that word of a husband's death in a remote mining camp or at sea may take a considerable time to, or may never, reach his wife in Cornwall. Even towards the end of the 19th century it took four weeks for news of their husbands' deaths in Johannesburg Hospital in South Africa to reach some wives.[68] The mortality amongst Cornish miners in South Africa at the turn of the century gained it the reputation as 'the graveyard for lost husbands'.[69] Some wives were informed of their husband's death by telegram but then had to wait weeks to learn the full details.[70]

Even if death could be confirmed there was little emotional closure for the women. The funeral would have probably occurred long before she was aware of the death, and she would have no grave to visit. Although it was possible to bring bodies back to Cornwall for burial,[71] it was very uncommon and few would have been able to afford to do so even if they had the option. Some wives wouldn't even have had the comfort of knowing that their husband had received a decent Christian burial. In Catholic Latin America the church would not allow Protestants to be buried in the cemeteries and for much of the 19th century would not allow any display of nonconformist ritual. Although some separate burial grounds were established in some mining centres, an unknown number of Cornishmen were discretely interred by their countrymen in spare ground without the rites and ceremony that their families would have wished.[72]

Deaths of husbands abroad, as with that of others who died overseas, would sometimes be included on the memorials to family members buried in Cornwall. One example sits just inside the gates of the churchyard of St Hilary near Penzance, dedicated in loving memory of John Bawden who died at Kernville, California on 23 June 1882, aged 38. John, a gold miner, had left Cornwall sometime before the 1881 census, leaving his wife Martha and four children in St Hilary. Martha remained a widow until her death in 1925, aged 81, and is commemorated on the same memorial.

The dead husband's colleagues abroad often auctioned off his possessions or made collections to raise money for his family. In 1836 Alfred Jenkin, the Cornwall-based agent for Cobre Mines, liaised with the company and the family of Captain John Hocking in the decision that the £60 raised after his death should be best spent in building a small house for his widow so that she wouldn't need to pay rent. Friends and agents like Jenkin endeavoured to return money and personal items, such as watches, to the bereaved wife at home, but there were inevitable delays, and occasional mix-ups. In 1838 money raised after the death of the Mackinny brothers was mistakenly paid to the widow of one, instead of their mother. "I fear that it will be very difficult if not impossible to get it back from Martin Mackinny's widow", admitted Jenkin.[73]

The death of a husband and breadwinner abroad could leave the wife and family in Cornwall with financial difficulties even if he had accumulated some wealth. The wife of a Mr Peters, who died in hospital in South Africa in 1897, never saw any of the large fortune he had amassed there as it was 'lost' and she like many others was forced to turn to the parish or charity for help.[74] Even if money or property could be located, proving a dead husband's will at a distance, should he leave one, provided the widow with an additional challenge. Mary Ann Scoble, whose husband Joseph died in Cuba in 1867 had a three-year battle to prove his will.[75]

By following what happened to a large number of individual wives research has been able to demonstrate the extent of return migration among married men, and that these levels are consistent with large-scale temporary labour migration at a date earlier than previously acknowledged. It has also shown that far from being permanently 'left behind' many wives were able to join their husbands abroad throughout the second half of the 19th century. In the next chapter we will look at the trials and tribulations they faced in doing so.

10

Under Sailing Orders

"I will endeavour to give you all the instructions I can"

The mobility required by the men's occupation meant that even when husband and wife were shown to have been reunited, they were not always in Cornwall, but were living elsewhere in the UK or abroad. In each of the parishes studied a small proportion of couples were found in other parts of the UK. In most cases this represented only 1 or 2%, the exception being St Just where eight couples (6.6%) from the 1871 group had moved to other parts of the country by 1881. A similarly raised number of the reunited couples from the 1871 and 1881 St Cleer and Gwennap groups were also found elsewhere in the UK.

Not surprisingly, some couples were in neighbouring Devon and Wales but the majority of those who had moved within the UK, especially towards the end of the 19th century, were found in the north of England: in Yorkshire, Durham and Northumberland as well as Barrow-in-Furness in Lancashire; Millom in Cumberland; and Liscard in Cheshire. Significantly all these places are mining areas for either iron ore (Pennington, Barrow-in-Furness, Millom, Brampton, Brotton, Farndale) or coal (Shincliffe, Seaham, Penkridge, Glamorgan) or both (Tipton). Clearly couples were following work opportunities in the wider mining industry. These findings are in line with what Bernard Deacon has described as the crisis migration of the 1870s, a time when migration to other parts of the UK exceeded emigration overseas because the depressed state of Cornish mining meant those needing to look for work elsewhere could not afford to fund emigration.[1] However, lack of funding is only a partial explanation because, as noted above, the 1870s also saw periods of mining depression in America, which would have also deterred emigration, and made the move to northern England more attractive.

Also, at odds with Deacon's suggestion that at times migration from Cornwall within the UK outweighed emigration, recent research has found that for every parish studied more wives had emigrated to join their husbands overseas than had joined them elsewhere in the UK. This is despite the figures for wives emigrating being a significant underestimate as they were considerably more difficult to trace than those remaining in the UK. The traceability of the wives was heavily dependent on the records available for searching within the limits of the research, producing a significant bias towards finding women who had emigrated to America, as noted earlier. Indeed most of those located abroad were found in the United States. Emigration of wives to other places (mostly Australia, but also New Zealand, Canada, Mexico and Brazil) was represented in smaller numbers with evidence coming from less comprehensively searchable sources such as family histories, passenger lists and Australian death records. Therefore the wives found should be viewed as the minimum number reunited with their husbands abroad, with the likelihood of many more hidden among those not traced.

In her study of the parish of Lanner Schwartz suggests that the wives who joined their husbands "were the exception rather than the rule",[2] but more recent research suggests that it was far from uncommon. Of the wives 'left behind' in Camborne, St Agnes and St Just recorded in the 1861 to 1891 censuses 7-14% were found to have emigrated, as well as 14% of the earlier 1851 group 'left behind' in St Just. Nearly a quarter of the wives 'left behind' in St Cleer in 1861 and 1871 were traced abroad, but this may be misleading as the St Cleer sample was very small compared to the other parishes. The figures for subsequent emigration amongst those wives remaining in Camborne, St Agnes and St Cleer in 1851 were lower, which may simply reflect emigration to different, less well-recorded destinations.

The diary of Thomas Saunders of Gorran Haven mentions a number of wives who joined their husbands abroad after short-term separations: W. Luke Mitchell's wife and daughter followed him to Australia two years to the month after his departure, while Elizabeth Pomery emigrated less than two years after her husband.[3] Similarly, Mrs Abraham Roberts from Paul and her six children joined her husband Abraham in Bendigo, Australia in 1856 after a three-year separation.[4] For such women these separations were brief interludes in their marriages, in some cases, like that of Elizabeth Pomery, occurring at the very start of her marriage and forming a transitional period between marital states. For others such

The Married Widows of Cornwall

separations were part of a transnational life-style more usually associated with the 20th rather than 19th century,[5] in which the wives were often as mobile as their spouses. An early example was Martha Jenkins. She lived with her husband in Brazil for five years in the 1840s, returned to Cornwall before journeying with the children in 1848 to Mineral Point, Wisconsin, via New Orleans to set up a new home in preparation for her husband, who was mining in Mexico by that time, to rejoin the family.[6] Similarly, Emma Rouse accompanied her blacksmith husband, George, to Brazil where she was able to raise her children in a comfortable home with native servants before returning to Cornwall, after which George moved on to California, where Emma later joined him.[7]

These women, as W.E. Van Vught notes, are "a reminder that many were remarkably resilient, courageous, and equal partners in their marriages rather than servants to the husbands".[8] They are also further wedges in the cracks that B.S. Elliot describes as appearing in previously made assumptions that transnationalism was "characteristic only of the Age of Steam, or even of the late twentieth-century global village".[9]

The mobility of the wives may have been greatly underestimated in the past. In has been calculated that in 1851 alone, 17,250 British women aged fifteen and above emigrated to the United States. Of these 42% were travelling with husbands, but a further 11% arrived accompanied only by children, presumably to meet husbands, although some widows with children also emigrated. Another 28% arrived as lone immigrants but we have no way of knowing how many of them were joining husbands already in America. Sadly immigration records rarely record if a woman travelling alone or with children had a husband waiting for her.[10]

In a survey of 2500 records of Cornish migrants to Latin America, Sharron Schwartz found that the majority of the 11% with domestic occupations were married women joining their husbands.[11] And the large numbers of children in the Cornish census returns, including young babies, who were born overseas to Cornish mothers is proof that numerous women had spent part of their marriages abroad.[12] Very often this is the only clue that some wives had been reunited with their husbands abroad. For example, Harriet Rowse and Caroline Raby were among the women in Gwennap whose husbands were away when both the 1851 and 1861 censuses were taken, but the 1861 census reveals that Harriet's three-year-old daughter was born in Mexico, and Caroline's six-year-old daughter was born in Brazil. Similarly Amelia Spargo, whose husband was away in Wales at the time of the 1871 census, appears in the 1881 census of Gwennap without her husband but with a four-year-old born in Gwennap and a one-year-old born in Brazil. The existence in the census of young children who had been born abroad indicates that it was not unusual for couples to have spent time together overseas. Clearly not all these women were afraid to travel and the presence of infants and toddlers with overseas birthplaces means that some women were prepared to risk long and difficult journeys with babies.

The majority of the wives from mining parishes studied who have been traced abroad were found to be living with their husbands, for example, enumerated together in a US Federal census. In some cases, however, the evidence of the wife's emigration (for example, with her children in a passenger list) did not provide confirmation that the couple had been reunited. The possibility that she was emigrating as a widow could not be excluded. Alternatively some wives were found in the US census without their husbands; miners were just as mobile within their destination country and it was not unheard of for a wife to join her husband abroad, only to be 'left behind' once more as he took up work elsewhere. In America many wives remained in the East while their husbands went West,[13] or stayed in one mining region while their husbands sought more lucrative work in another.[14] In 1858, for example, John Coad's wife lived in Mineral Point, Wisconsin while he worked in Grass Valley, California.[15] Wives who had joined or accompanied their husbands in Australia often found themselves managing on their own in the city as their husbands spent extended periods at the diggings in the bush.[16] In 1845 Elizabeth Nankivell from St Agnes had emigrated to Australia to be with her husband but spent very little time with him as he followed different work opportunities.[17] Years later, in 1893, Julia Odgers had a similar experience as she was left with the children in Bendigo while her husband worked in the Kalgoorlie gold fields.[18]

Before setting off to join her husband abroad, it often fell to the wife to make all the domestic arrangements, although husbands, as well as friends and neighbours, provided helpful advice on what she and the family would need for the journey and at their destination.[19] "I will endeavour to give

The Married Widows of Cornwall

you all the instructions I can", wrote William Paynter in his last letter to his wife Sophia before she left to join him in Australia. His advice covered what food, bedding and utensils she would need as well as a suggestion that she bring some sewing "as you will be glad to have some thing to do on board otherwise you would find it tiresome".[20] In addition to the domestic tasks of packing, wives were also entrusted with disposing of the family's household goods, and sometimes property. "I think you had better agree for the house if you can make £30 of it", wrote William to Sophia.[21]

Once all the arrangements had been made, the wives awaited their sailing orders, the final instructions and details for embarkation. The 1881 census captures this moment in time for one wife, Christiana Clemence. She and her three-year-old son are listed as visitors "under sailing orders for Africa" in the household of her maiden aunt in St Blazey.[22]

The departures of wives and children leaving to join their husbands abroad was frequently reported in the Cornish press.[23] Hence readers were informed that in October 1895 Mrs Marks and family from St Just were departing to join her husband in South Africa,[24] while Mrs Leah and family of Market Place, Penzance were sailing on the *Oruba* in May 1897 to be reunited with her husband at Algoa bay, Africa.[25] In the same year it was reported under the regular heading 'Cornish Emigration' that, among many other departing, Mrs Lawrence and two children were returning to her husband at Butte City,[26] and "Mrs S. Williams and child left Fore-street, Goldsithney, on Friday, to join her husband, who is underground captain at the Guliowa mine, Yalgoo, Murchison, Western Australia".[27]

Departures did not always go smoothly. The wife of Thomas Rouse ran into problems in August 1844 when she tried to embark at Liverpool to join her husband in Mexico. She believed that she would be able to pay for her passage out of the home-pay due to her that month only to find that, because she was joining him, the company treasurers had already cancelled the payment, leaving her short of the fare.[28] In a later case problems embarking proved fortunate. Elfrida Hoskin had a narrow escape when she and her children were not allowed to sail with the ship on which they had booked passage to join her husband in America because their papers were not in order, a new baby having been born since the family passport had been issued. The ship was the *Titanic*.[29]

The voyage itself was a daunting challenge for the wives, especially if travelling with small children.[30] After encountering a woman at Truro station with four children on her way to her husband in North America in 1883, James Bennetts Williams noted that is was "a great charge for one person".[31] Alternatively the children might be left with relatives who sometimes struggled to care for them,[32] or sent to boarding schools while their mothers were abroad.[33]

However, older children could be a great help to their mothers on the journey. William Paynter reassured his wife Sophia: "You are not like one with a family of small children, there are enough big ones to take care of the small ones so by that means you will find yourself more comfortable." Nonetheless, he warned her to "not allow the children to straggle away out of your sight and you will be wise enough to be careful of what you have got on board as there are generally thieves amongst a number of persons".[34] Rachel Carmen sailing on the *Vanguard* in 1864 to join her husband in Melbourne recorded that her Cornish friend and fellow passenger, Mrs Brea, had all her money stolen one night and was reliant on money lent by some Cornishmen who held her ring as security.[35]

Single-handedly minding a brood of children and the family's possessions under the difficult conditions of shipboard life would not have been the wives' only worries. Sea travel was not without its dangers. Mary Oates' voyage to join her husband in Uruguay in 1887 turned into a terrifying ordeal with the ship nearly sinking in the Bay of Biscay and drifting for three days after being damaged in a storm. Despite this experience Mary made the return voyage to Cornwall with her husband fours years later, only to be parted from him again when he took up and then extended another contract in South America.[36]

It is tempting to picture a heart-warming scene of husbands waiting on the dock to welcome their wives and children as they disembarked, but for many women the sea voyage was only one stage of the complex journey she would have to navigate in order to be reunited with her spouse. In 1862 Mary Anne Collins and her two children took three months to travel from Cornwall to California via the Isthmus of Panama, but when her husband came to meet her in San Francisco he struggled to find them in the city before eventually locating them in a boarding house. Mary Anne's journey was still not complete as it took another boat and a stagecoach to reach her new home.[37] If a husband had not arranged for anyone to meet his wife off the ship or train, she might be directed to a particular lodgings from where she would write to let her husband know that she had arrived. Sophia Paynter had instructions from her husband in 1860 that on arriving in Port Adelaide, Australia, she "must take the train at once for town and enquire for the Fenix Hotel in Hindley Street". There she was told she would find Mrs Martin, a sister to Betsy Williams at Hixes Mill (someone it is implied she was familiar with from Cornwall), who would "make you comfortable until I come down for you".[38]

Rendezvous did not always go to plan. In 1871 Jane Champion endured a sea voyage and lengthy rail journey with two small children to get to California, but when her husband was delayed and was not there to meet her, she is reputed to have been so angry that she immediately started preparing to go back to Cornwall.[39] Other reunions were more joyous. When the wives of John Thomas and Charles Smitheram arrived in Melbourne from Cornwall in September 1867 their husbands planned to surprise them by 'marrying' them a second time with the customary 'kettle band', the noisy accompaniment of tin pots, kettles and bells usually reserved for young newly-weds.[40]

It is interesting that so many wives were found to have emigrated to join their husbands during the 1870s, a period when according to Deacon's argument fewer families would have been able to afford the passage. Eric Richards pointed out: "the poor were not well placed to raise the costs of emigration" and there were a variety of emigration schemes that enabled those without funds to do so.[41] However, the position of wives who wanted to join their husbands abroad was viewed differently from that of the poor emigrating as complete families.

In the first half of the 19th century parishes would consider funding the passages of wives wanting to join their husbands. For example, in 1842 the Redruth Vestry helped a wife and five children to follow her husband to Ireland, and another family be reunited in Canada.[42] However, help from poor law boards of guardians was more constrained and as the poor laws grew stricter it became more difficult for local officials to help the wives. The poor laws took little account of the benefits of reuniting couples who had become separated through emigration (with the exception of sanctioning the sending out of convicts' families) taking the view that if a husband emigrated without his wife it constituted voluntary desertion, which it could not condone.[43] Nonetheless, the local boards of guardians could see the benefits to all concerned of reuniting these couples and they frequently wrote to the central authority in London arguing the case for funding the emigration of wives.[44]

One such exchange took place in 1842 when the Truro Poor Law Union wrote to the Poor Law Commissioners seeking approval for their spending £7 to assist Betsy Randall and her three children from Probus to emigrate to Quebec, Canada. When the commissioners enquired as to whether Betsy was a widow and if not, where her husband was, the clerk replied that her husband, Robert, was already living in Quebec and she wanted to join him there. This did not satisfy the commissioners who took the view that as her husband had left her behind, Betsy had been deserted. They deemed it "highly improper that when a man has deserted his family and gone abroad, that his wife or family should be sent after him at the expense of the parish", and if the husband had "prospered" he should pay for his family's passage. The guardians explained that Robert had not deserted his wife but had gone at his own expense, with the full approval of the parish, to gain employment so as to better support his family. In his absence the family had become chargeable to the parish, and the parishioners "had unanimously agreed" that it was right to help the family with an advance so that they could be reunited.

The commissioners, however, were resolute, replying that:

> *"They cannot approve of a man leaving his wife and family in this country in such circumstances as to require parochial assistance to enable them to join him and to sanction such expenditure would encourage desertion in different forms. The case may well be worthy of consideration by individuals but will not justify an expenditure from the public funds of the Poor Law Commission."*[45]

Even if the central poor law authority had been willing in principle to aid the emigration of wives they classified as deserted, those seeking help to join their husbands in the United States had another problem as public funds could only be used to fund emigration to British colonies.[46] This led on at least one occasion to a husband in America crossing a few miles into Canada in an attempt to secure funding for his wife to join him.[47]

The hands of the local guardians were effectively tied by the decision of the central poor law authority. If local guardians made a payment without it being sanctioned by the officials in London the auditors could disallow it, leaving a hole in the union's accounts, and there are examples of Cornish unions appealing such decisions.[48] The central poor law authority's resistance to attempts to fund emigration of the wives through the rates was a source of continued puzzlement to local boards of guardians, especially those in the mining districts of Cornwall who had a better understanding of the pattern of temporary labour migration that led to couples being separated without any intentional desertion on the husband's part. If the family fell on hard times it would be cheaper for them to live together, rather than maintain separate homes in different parts of the world, and paying the family's passage and reuniting the family seemed a more sensible use of the union funds than supporting them indefinitely in Cornwall.

In the periodic depressions of the Cornish mining industry those who sat on the boards of guardians were especially keen to find some way of helping the wives to join their husbands abroad. When the General Committee of Magistrates and Boards of Guardians' representatives appointed to inquire into the existence of distress amongst the mining population of Cornwall met in 1867, the representative from Redruth put forward his board's view that: "if a sum of money can be raised it may be cautiously and judiciously applied to meet their distress by assisting their husbands to send for them and their families".[49] The proposal was supported by other unions, such as St Austell, who also felt that: "much good might be done by enabling the families of those who have emigrated to leave this country and join their husbands and fathers".[50] The General Committee recognised that given the poor law rules this "great boon… the removal of the wives and families to the new spheres of labour to which many of the married miners have gone", could only be achieved by raising a large fund independent of the Poor Law, with this as its primary aim.[51] Therefore the focus of the County Distress Fund that emerged from this meeting was on helping reunite wives with their husbands. Top of the published list of ways in which the monies raised were to be used was: "Supplying the means whereby, when a labourer is separated from his family, they may be enabled to rejoin him". This took precedence over the other aims (including helping men to take up "remunerative employment offered at a distance")[52] and indeed in October of that year the fund's resources were restricted to this purpose.[53] This is at odds to the interpretation of the Distress Fund's activities provided by Payton that implies that they were keen to promote the cause of general emigration.[54] On the contrary, reservations were expressed at the time that sending wives to their husbands would encourage emigration, which it was thought should be discouraged as there would be a shortage of men should mining revive.[55]

Applicants for grants quickly came forward. By the end of October two wives from Redruth and nine from St Just had presented themselves as ready to go to their husbands. However, of the St Just women only two, travelling to the USA, could be considered right away. The other cases were more complicated; two wanted to go to Lake Superior but it was too late in the year to undertake the journey, while the other five had not received letters from their husbands.[56] This latter point was crucial, as the committee would only help the wives to leave if they were satisfied that the husbands were prepared to receive them. To test the husband's resolve on this matter a condition of the grant was that he should make some contribution towards his wife's travel costs. "Unless a husband contributed it would be better to keep the woman at home, for if a man could not give anything he would not be in a condition to maintain his wife when she arrived", reasoned the committee's chairman.[57] If emigration was involved the Fund's grant was restricted to no more than half the cost.[58]

By February 1868 the committee of the Distress Fund had approved over £300 towards the costs of 41 wives emigrating to join their husbands; nine had gone and it was expected that the rest would follow shortly.[59] Over the following months a small but steady stream of wives were funded to travel to their husbands and positive reports were being received of how well the families were doing once reunited.[60] In April 1868 the committee chairman noted "that undoubtedly much good had been done by sending families abroad". However, by that time things in Cornwall were getting better and there was a shortage of skilled miners so he warned that "whilst sending out the families, therefore, of those who had gone they should do nothing to encourage other men to go".[61] By November the situation in Cornwall was so improved that the last few applicants were allocated grants and the operations of the emigration fund suspended with money remaining. The chairman remarked that they "would greatly prefer to hear of the return of the miners to their wives than of wives going abroad to their husbands".[62]

When depression in the Cornish mining industry returned a decade later, the joint committee of the County Distress and Wesleyan Relief Funds took a similar approach,[63] complementing but not impinging on the work of the Poor Law.[64] Once again the committee was reluctant to encourage the emigration of men who might be needed by the industry in future and saw enabling the wives to join their husbands abroad as the best means of reducing distress, provided they were sure that the husband could support his wife abroad.[65]

A similar scheme was in operation in 1896 when the Miners' Relief Fund was providing financial aid to wives wanting to join their husbands in Wales. Again the grant was conditional on the husbands making some contribution to ensure that they could or would support their wives, as otherwise there were fears of wives being sent back at the expense of the unions in Cornwall.[66]

Wives hoping to join their husbands abroad could expect little help from the Poor Law, and even in the most depressed times grants only met part of the costs. The balance had to come from the family's own resources. For example, a woman with four children wanting to join her husband in California in 1879 applied to the fund for £10 to supplement the £30-40 she could raise on own.[67] If the wife was unable to make up the shortfall, she had to rely on help from other sources. The story of two Illogan wives, Mary Dadds and Jane Tremewen, who successfully appealed to Queen Victoria for the £10 needed to release an emigration grant from the Cornwall Central Relief Committee, made the national press.[68]

Money was not only required for sea passages but for getting to the port of departure, and for fitting out the family for the voyage.[69] Although the poor law guardians were also prohibited from providing this where it might be seen as encouragement to emigration, they were able to help with essential necessities under certain circumstances. In 1867, for example, they were allowed to give a maximum of £2 10s worth of clothing, but only to those going to the British Colonies, despite petitioning the Poor Law Board for a relaxation of the rules.[70]

Local poor law and parish officials were frequently frustrated by not being able to offer more official aid but were supportive in other ways, writing letters to husbands and their employers, as well as encouraging friends of the family to help.[71] When those present at a parish meeting in Kenwyn found that the parish could not legally give a woman with five children the £5 she needed to fit out the family for the passage to Australia booked and paid for by her husband, they made a collection amongst themselves raising half the amount needed there and then.[72] Assistance also came from private individuals. In 1868 it was reported "Through the very benevolent exertions of Morrish Wilton, Esq, Spring Gardens, Egloshayle, the sum of £15 has been raised towards paying the passage of a deserving woman named Betsy Hamley, of Egloshayle, and her seven children to Coburg, West Canada, where her husband, who is a tailor, emigrated some 14 months since." Betsey's husband had sent enough money to secure the family's passage on a timber ship but none were available, so Mr Wilton paid for the family to travel in a steamer.[73] In 1892 Priscilla Kent, one of the wives from Gwennap whose husband was in Chile, was helped by her old mistress who raised the bulk of the money for her to go abroad.[74]

The restrictions of the Poor Law and the limited distress funds suggest that over the whole 19th century only a small proportion of the fares and expenses of the numerous wives who followed their husbands abroad would have come from these sources. The majority of passages were paid for by the couples or their families, or through other emigration schemes; for example, numerous records of husbands contributing to the costs of bringing their wives and children from Cornwall to join them in Australia can be found in the New South Wales Immigration Deposit Journals for the second half of the 19th century.[75]

Reunions abroad were not always successful and some wives regretted their decision to emigrate. A wife from Wendron joined her husband in America after three years of separation only to have him desert her after two days, leaving her to fend for herself and eventually return to Cornwall.[76] Another wife, Jane Goldsworthy, returned to Camborne because she had been ill and her husband had behaved badly to her while she was with him in Australia.[77] Other wives came back telling similar stories of not being able to stay with their husbands in Australia due to ill health and the hot climate.[78] In these and other cases the wife's return to Cornwall resulted in cessation of financial support by her husband.[79]

In America the conditions in the mining camps made some miners' wives desperate to return home. Soon after arriving in Mineral Point in the 1830s Mary Bennett was pleading with her husband James to go back to Cornwall, away from the "hardly discovered wilderness" with its numerous Indians and wild animals.[80] War also brought wives home. Redruth station was busy in 1900 with wives and children leaving to rejoin their husbands in South Africa having "unexpectedly and hastily" returned to Cornwall leaving their homes, household goods and furniture there at the start of the Boer War.[81]

In the census records women who joined their husbands abroad for periods between census years are indistinguishable from those who never left Cornwall (unless, as we have seen, one of their children is listed as having been born abroad). Similarly, those wives who did return alone may appear in the census returns as wives 'left behind' although this is far from the truth.

It is equally possible that some of the wives who were listed at their parents' homes in the census may have been on extended visits from abroad while their husbands remained at their workplace. There is ample evidence of wives bringing their children back to Cornwall for family visits but few of these will have been captured by the ten-yearly snapshot of the census. Cordelia Short who joined her husband William in Colorado in 1877 can be found with her children on the passenger list for the *SS Arabic* returning to America after a visit home in 1887. Similarly, Rebecca Varker returned to St Hilary with her children in 1899, having joined her husband Edwin in Idaho four years earlier. She probably came to visit her dying mother, and stayed for six months before returning to America. During their visit, Rebecca's youngest child, Leona who had been born in Idaho was baptised in St Hilary, and her eldest daughter, Nora, attended the local school. Their departure is noted in Nora's school record: "Gone to America October 27 1899".[82]

Rebecca was to return permanently to Cornwall with her surviving children after her husband's death in a mine explosion in 1902. Inevitably with their husbands working in such a dangerous industry many of the miner's wives who emigrated found themselves widows in an unfamiliar country. Ezekiel Williams of Camborne, who had left for a second visit to the US two years earlier, was killed a week after his wife and family had joined him there.[83] Tragically some wives made the journey only to find that their husbands had died whilst they were en route. Todd cites the example of a wife who made the journey from Blackwater near Truro to Mexico in 1880 expecting to rendezvous with her husband travelling from Chile, but he never arrived, having been killed in a mining accident, leaving her to make her own living in a strange land.[84]

Mary Grenfell from Carnyorth in St Just, who worked as a maid in Penzance while her husband was away, found herself in a similar position. A year after her husband, William, left for Colorado Mary set out to join him. Her third child had died shortly before she left or possibly during the journey and she arrived in New York with her two remaining children on 3 November 1879. A family story records that she also lost her trunk of best clothes en route. Mary then had to endure a tiring overland journey by train. Arriving in Denver, she was surprised to be met by her brother. Mary's granddaughter Lilian Harry recalled the story in a TV interview: "She immediately said: "Where is Will?" Her brother said: "Oh, you'll be alright, Mary." She said: "Is he sick?" "You'll be alright, Mary." "Is he dead?" Apparently her husband had been buried the day before." He had died of typhoid fever a week after Mary's ship had docked in New York. Knowing that she was on her way they had hoped to delay his burial until she arrived but it wasn't possible due to the climate. To add to Mary's woes her four-year-old daughter Martha Evelyn died of measles the following month. Mary found herself living in a log cabin built for her by family and friends in Bald Mountain, Nevadaville where she made a living by washing and baking for 24 men, working from 4 o'clock in the morning to midnight every day. The following year she remarried, and returned to Cornwall with her second husband and family in 1892.[85]

Mrs Veal, also from St Just, was in some ways more fortunate in that the news of her husband's death in America arrived before she set off to join him in 1892. Nonetheless she had already booked passage for herself and her two little boys, packed or sold the household goods and ordered a conveyance to take their luggage to Penzance when a telegram arrived to inform her that her husband was dead. As the newspaper asked: "Who will not sympathise?" as "the widow and the fatherless weep in the reoccupied but desolate house in St Just".[86] Two years later the wife of Charles Tregoning was to receive a telegram with the news that he had been murdered in Africa the day before she was due to leave to join him there.[87] In the words of the Editor of the *Cornishman*: "it is well that the rapid transmission of news has saved her from travel by land and sea which might have intensified the shock of learning on her arrival in a strange country that her husband had met this awful fate."

Such stories highlight once more the challenges that faced and were overcome by the wives, but also their vulnerability, especially if things went wrong.

"A CAMBORNE MAN SHOT IN THE UNITED STATES"

"A letter was received at Condurrow, near Beacon, Camborne, on Wednesday, having special reference to the murder in the United States of Mr. John Sanders, late of Condurrow, a married man, and the son of Mr. Stephen Sanders, who was shot by a Swede about three weeks since. Money, it is said was the cause of the Swede's murderous attack, he having made an unsuccessful attempt to rob Mr. Sanders. Mrs. Sanders is now left a widow, and it is reported that she left Tuckingmill a fortnight since to join her husband."

Cornishman, 3 March 1881

11

Two Lives Compared
Sophia Paynter and Mary Ann Dower

So far, in exploring what life was like for wives 'left behind' we have encountered many individual women whose stories illustrate different aspects of the experience. Very often these are only glimpses of moments of their lives salvaged from fragmentary evidence: a rudimentary census record, a mention in the newspapers, or a brief encounter with the Poor Law. But there are two women whose experience can be examined in more detail: Sophia Paynter and Mary Ann Dower. Their stories emerge from the two most complete runs of letters from emigrant husbands to their wives that have come to light. In the Cornwall Record Office there are copies of 14 letters to Sophia Paynter (née Gribble) from her husband, William, covering the period January 1859 to April 1860. Letters from John Dower to his wife Mary Ann are more scattered, with 23 surviving originals or copies dispersed in public, academic and private archives in Australia, Cornwall and Canada. They cover the period October 1865 to November 1868.[1] This previously neglected correspondence provides valuable insights into the lives of two wives 'left behind', and raises questions about a number of different facets of the experience of being a 'married widow'.

Regrettably, as is so often the case, none of the wives' letters have survived. Emigrant correspondence is a valuable source for migration history but unfortunately, the overwhelming majority of 19th century British emigrant letters in archive collections were written by men. Letters from women are rare and those from wives to their husbands have proved to be exceptionally so. Gerber attributes the under-representation of female correspondents in the collections to lower literacy levels among the women.[2] However, references in the letters written by the husbands indicate that they are receiving letters from their wives. A more plausible explanation for the gender disparity in these cases is that fewer of the wives' letters survived. One possible reason for this is that the letters sent to the husbands abroad were more likely to get lost or damaged as the men moved around or endured poor living conditions, whereas the wives settled at home were able to take better care of the letters they received. Although, with a few significant exceptions, it is only possible to examine letters written to the wives and not by them, these do provide useful information through their husbands' responses on a wide range of financial and family matters. Therefore by reading these letters against the grain it is possible to hear something of the wives' voices as they are reflected in their husbands' replies, and get an idea of their concerns and emotional states.

The stories of Sophia's and Mary Ann's time spent apart from their husbands can be teased from their husbands' letters supplemented by genealogical background research. What makes them particularly interesting and relevant is that their experiences were so different, despite the fact that their initial circumstances were very similar.

Sophia was the wife of William Arundel Paynter, an experienced miner in his late thirties. They had married in 1842 and by 1851 were settled in Gwennap with four children: Catherine (aged 8), Emily (5), John (2) and Samuel (4 months). Less than a mile away in 1851, at Ting Tang in Gwennap, was the home of newlyweds, Mary Ann Dower (née Benbow) and her husband, John, also a miner. In photocopied photographs of Mary Ann and John in the Cornwall Record Office the couple's appearance can just about be made out: slender John, dapper with his centre-parted hair and moustache; oval-faced Mary Ann looking straight at the camera, her expression and features ghostly and barely discernible.

Towards the end of 1858 William Paynter was contracted to go to Australia by the Wheal Ellen Mining Company. By that time the family had grown with the addition of two more children (William born 1853 and George born 1857). A few years later, in 1865, Mary Ann's husband John Dower borrowed the cost of his passage from her brother, John Benbow, and set off to work in the mines of Victoria. Mary Ann's family too had grown and she was left to care for two boys: William aged eight and ten-year-old John. So both Sophia and Mary Ann were in their thirties with children when their husbands, quite independently, left to work in Australia while they remained in Gwennap. Living so close together in the same mining community it is quite possible that these two women knew each other.

Initially both husbands wrote home regularly, every four or five weeks. Although written by husbands to their wives, they are not love letters as such, and the degree of intimacy was probably dictated by the level of privacy the couple could expect.[3] Emigrant letters often cannot be considered as private correspondence, not only because a third person might be involved as scribe, but because they were frequently shared amongst family and friends eager to know how those abroad were getting on.[4]

William Paynter's letters are consistently in his own hand, whereas John Dower's are more varied leading to the suggestion that although there is evidence that he was literate (he criticises his son's poor spelling), some of his letters may have been written on his behalf.[5] With regard to the wives, William's reference to being glad to see Sophia's handwriting confirms that she was literate, whereas Mary Ann was less so with John wishing that she "would sit down and try to learn to write".[6] It seems likely that Mary Ann's letters were written for her by the couple's teenage son, in the light of John's comments on his spelling. John's desire for Mary Ann to learn to write is indicative not only of his aspirations for the family to better themselves that emerge from the correspondence (for example, John's comment that he would rather his wife spend her time at 'tea meetings' than tending the family potato plot), but also of migration as a driver of increased literacy.[7]

Of the two men, William Paynter was the more adept writer and his feelings for Sophia are apparent in his letters. He asked her to give his love to others but to accept the "best love" for herself. After visiting Devil's Bridge in Wales on his way to Liverpool he wished she had been there with him to share "the most romantic place I ever saw".[8] Sophia would have been in no doubt that she was very much in his thoughts throughout his absence. He wrote: "I have been in all day weatherbound and think a great deal about you at such times you are seldom out of my mind long together at any time", and in another letter: "there is never a day or an hour when I am awake but that I think of you and I hope we shall meet again ere long I wish you was here with me".[9]

John Dower expresses a similar sentiment to Mary Ann when he writes while at leisure during his outward voyage: "I should like for you to be here to see the beautiful birds".[10] However, once in Australia, his letters are more concerned with practical issues. Communication between Mary and John was taking place through at least one intermediary and subsequently their letters are less private than those between Sophia and William, and there is a distinct sense of Mary Ann acting as a conduit, passing on messages and news between John and the rest of the family and community. However, counter-intuitively, John's letters are less formal than William's and provide more clues as to Mary Ann's emotional state, in particular, regarding the problems she was having with the family.

Mary Ann and the couple's two young sons had numerous relatives living nearby, and John had every expectation that after he left Mary Ann would have plenty of support from both sides of the family. In his first letter from Victoria he wrote that he hoped her brothers were helping and being kind to her, and enquired whether his own brother Peter had kept his promise to him to see her.[11] John's next letter contained a hint that perhaps good family relations were not taken for granted: "I hope that you are getting on very well with your family and my family and I hope that you are behaving as far as your abilities will allow to mother".[12] Sadly none of Mary Ann's letters have survived so the root of any disharmony is not known, although John's urging of Mary Ann to 'cheer up' makes it clear that she was not happy.[13] Things seem to come to a head when John's mother died: "Dear Wife I was very [sorry?] to hear you were so much put about with such ungrateful friends which ought to have acted better towards you on account by my being a way from you and my dear family… you say they treated you very cooley [sic] and put the boys last at the funeral because you had not deep morning but never mind we have better and be better off than them yet but I thought you and Sophiah were real good friends so I cannot make out what is the cause of it or what they mean". His brother Peter also seems to have let him down: "I was sorry Peter would not give you the money never mind do not ask him for it any more. You can tell him from me he has acted different towards you than I would have done if his wife and family were placed as you are but we will all meet again and I shall treat him as [he] deserves".[14]

In spite of John's hope that his wife and family become "more comfortable together", for some unknown reason Mary Ann was being snubbed, or felt she was being snubbed, by some friends and family. John tells her not to 'trouble' herself about people who are not calling on her, promising that things will get better: "for you will be quite independent of any of them for you [k]now that I never cared who visited or not. If the[y] do not like come or speak they can stop away".[15] John even writes to his eldest brother complaining of the way Mary Ann was being treated.[16] Without her letters it is impossible to determine all the rights and wrongs, and whether Mary Ann was blameless in the matter. Certainly by the following year, John had had enough: "And as for that Pound that Peter owes do not trouble yourself ab[o]ut it any more for a sovereign is not worth so much disagreeableness and as for my family if they do not choose to see you keep yourself to yourself for I want to hear no more about it for it is very disagreeable to hear of ye every letter on bad terms with each other you want nothing from them so let me hear no more about them unless it is pleasanter news".[17] Whether relations with John's family improved after that or Mary Ann just kept quiet is not known, however, the following year it is Mary Ann's own sister, who has upset her; "Dear Mary Anne as regards your sister Grace thinking herself above you she is quite mistaken you require nothing from her nor you shall not while I am alive so take no notice".[18] Although Mary Ann obviously did have some family troubles, John's letters contain numerous references to other friends and neighbours, so it is not suggested that Mary Ann was completely without help. Her younger brother, John, in particular was very supportive, having financed her husband's passage to Australia and is mentioned as jointly keeping a pig with Mary Ann. Nevertheless, her troubles are a reminder that the support of family and friends, even Cornish ones, could not be guaranteed.

Both Mary Ann and Sophia were left in no doubt that their husbands missed them, that they would rather they were with them to share their new experiences, … as well as to do the housework. "There is no one near to do anything for me so you may judge how much more comfortable I should be if you were here", wrote William after describing his cooking arrangements.[19]

In the Paynter correspondence William appears to acknowledge that coping with the family without him might not be easy for Sophia, hoping that she "will have a little patience with the children".[20] This is just after he referred to their meeting again "in better circumstances than when we parted", suggesting that Sophia may have been a little resentful at him going away leaving her to manage such a large family on her own. William seems mindful of this and is supportive with messages such as: "P.S. I hope the children will be good to their mother" and will "do their best to make you comfortable".[21]

At a time when a gendered view of parenting associated the mother with nurture and the father with discipline, there were concerns that wives might not be able to control the children in their father's absence. In Australia there was a strong perception at the time that the offspring of 'deserted' wives would inevitably turn into criminals.[22] James Bonwick helpfully included advice on the 'Management of Children' for mothers whose husbands were at the diggings in his monthly magazine for those participating in the Australian gold rush,[23] although his suggestion that "having more time and leisure during your husband's absence" a wife should devote herself to her children shows a marked lack of understanding of a mother's domestic workload.

The issue of transnational fathering (how men perform the role of parenting while abroad) has received very little attention from historians. It has only recently been addressed with respect to modern labour migration, where it is suggested that migrant men attempting to father from a distance via letters (and possibly the occasional visit) perform "a heightened version of conventional fathering" through "the display of authority and imposition of discipline".[24] Such remote authoritarianism, which is frequently associated with the austere Victorian father figure, is seen as damaging to his relationship to his children, whereas a more nurturing, communicative and less disciplinarian approach mitigates this effect. Neither William Paynter nor John Dower appear, from their letters, to have been fierce disciplinarians, preferring the carrot to the stick. William wrote to Sophia regarding their children: "tell them from me if they behave themselves well they shall fare the better for it".[25] John Dower, too, resorted to bribery in an effort to exert his paternal authority from afar by promising rewards and presents for good behaviour. Other letters reveal absent Cornishmen as indulgent fathers. Mat Hore, for example, penned a charming letter from California to one of his children in 1876: "My Dear Child, your Mama told me that you would like to get a letter from your Dada… I do wish that you could answer it for I should be so proud to get a letter that was written by your dear little fingers".[26] Similarly affectionate letters survive written by Richard Colliver to his young son.[27] However, in some families the father's desertion or second family abroad created resentment and insecurities that adversely affected the children, some of whom never knew their fathers.[28] This is a topic that warrants further research as given the number of families involved it could potentially have had a significant social impact on intergenerational relations in Cornwall.

Both William Paynter and John Dower were keen to support their wives in caring for their children, expressing an active interest in their behaviour and a desire to exercise some influence over their upbringing. Mary Ann is instructed by John to buy the boys a bible and hymnbook each, "any thing they require to assist them in their learning".[29] The reason he was working abroad was to provide a better future for the family, and his sons' education was central to this, so Mary Ann was urged to keep the boys at school. When he heard that the eldest boy, aged 12, was to start work, John replied: "I do not intend him to go to work for the next two years I mean for him to keep at school until he is able to write a letter properly".[30] William wrote to Sophia in a similar vein hoping that she was "keeping the children in school".[31]

Raising children in the 1850s and 1860s Sophia and Mary Ann did not have to deal with the demands of the 1870 Education Act that increased state pressure on parents to ensure that their children under 13 years old attended a certified school, with it becoming compulsory after 1880. The introduction of this legal requirement put an additional strain on family finances through school fees and loss of earnings for the mothers who could no longer call on the older children to look after the little ones while she worked. This brought some of the wives 'left behind' into conflict with the state when they were issued with summonses and fined for non-attendance[32] or non-payment of school fees.[33] The mother could apply for the school fees to be waived,[34] but this didn't always solve the problem as some mothers were not able to provide the footwear needed for the children to get to school and there were numerous applications to the boards of guardians for children's boots specifically for this purpose.[35] Local guardians sometimes ruled that they would help with the fees but not the boots, drawing the retort from one deserted wife that the school-pence was no use without the shoes as the children couldn't go to school without them.[36]

An editorial in the *Cornishman* of 16 July 1881 drew on the example of a wife who found herself up before the magistrates while her husband was in Australia to illustrate problems caused by the implementation of the education laws, which it argued "must be perplexing to, not to say tyrannical towards" women such as a Mrs Foss of Penzance who had received nothing from her husband in Australia for over two years. "Working hard all day she has managed to send four little ones to school, though not regularly, - a fact about which we need not feel much surprise if we take the trouble to imagine what one pair of hands can do to maintain, keep clean, and look after such a number of little ones."[37] The editorial writer was of the belief that the women of Cornwall had potential political power: "If all the widows and deserted wives of Cornwall, who are perplexed into savagery by this educational craze, could get to the House of Commons, they would produce the same effect on Mr Forster [the MP responsible for the Bill] and his friends as the match-sellers did on Mr Lowe".[38]

In spite of the difficulties faced by the wives left in charge of the children with frequently limited and uncertain resources, they were on occasion credited with doing a better job than those who had resident husbands. In May 1896, reporting on the school board's dilemma in knowing "how to deal with some Camborne mothers who will not rise in time to send their children to school", the *Cornishman* noted: "As far as our correspondent knew of those mentioned at recent meetings they are not the wives of husbands away in India, Africa, and America, but of too easy-going husbands at home".[39]

It is clear from their correspondence that both William Paynter and John Dower were devoted fathers and husbands. Being so far away the men expressed worries about the family's health. The regular correspondence between the Dowers was interrupted when Mary Ann suffered from a severe cold, leaving John to worry: "I beg of you to be more careful of yourself for the future for you are aware of the serious loss it would be to our beloved boys for there is no person can look to care for them like yourself".[40] Sophia Paynter had to deal with the two youngest children being ill and around that time William did not receive any letters from her; possibly she was too busy or reluctant to write for fear of worrying him until they were getting better.

The Paynter children recovered but other parents were not so fortunate and many women found themselves dealing with a family tragedy without the support of their husbands. The story of Ann Whitburn's ordeal of repeatedly going to Portreath Harbour meet her son, James, who had been sent home ill by his father in Cuba, only to find that he had died on the way home was told earlier, but she was far from the only one. Despite help from other family members, the loneliness and strain is clear in the words of another wife, Ann Goldsworthy from Skinners Bottom, near St Agnes, writing to her husband, James, about the days leading up to the death of their son Colon: "I have not had my clothes of[f] for one week... when he died I had no one to speak to but my children and they were all at sleep".[41] To add to Ann's emotional stress she believed another of her children was likely to die from the same illness. "I don't think you will ever see her again", she told James. The deaths of children back home must have been equally painful for the fathers so far away, who may have seen little of their short lives. James Williams in California in the 1860s must have been delighted to receive a photograph of his baby daughter Tryphena siting on his wife Catherine's lap. We can only imagine his feelings as he travelled back to Perranzabuloe in Cornwall less than a year later to be with Catherine after Tryphena died of 'teething'.[42]

Family deaths were not the only major life events that the wives had to face without the support of their husbands. As far as we know neither Sophia nor Mary Ann was pregnant when William and John left, but it was not unusual for a husband to emigrate knowingly or unknowingly leaving his wife with a child on the way. Many announcements of the births of these babies in their fathers' absences appeared in the Cornish press. For example, in January 1857 the *West Briton* announced the births: "At Carnbrea, near Redruth, on Sunday last, the wife of Mr. John Carpenter, late of Carnbrea, but now in Australia, of a daughter" and "At Camborne, on Monday last, the wife of Mr. James Rowe, late of Camborne, (now of Australia) of a daughter".[43] The news of the birth would have taken some weeks to reach the fathers abroad, who must have felt rather detached from the event. Joel Eade wrote to his wife in February 1864 to say how glad he was to hear that she was alive and well after giving birth to their son, but was slightly discomfited to be told that the baptism had been arranged but not his new son's name: "I dont know what he is caled [sic] and you did not say I want for to know".[44] It is interesting that Joel offers no suggestions or instructions regarding his new son's name, implying that he was content with his wife making the decision.

The Paynter and Dower letters, like much Cornish emigrant correspondence, suggest that couples called upon their religious faith to help them cope with the separation. "I dare say you feel lonely as I do myself but my Dear Sophia we must look to the strong for strength and if we trust in him he will bring us through", wrote William.[45] As Charlotte Erickson noted with regard to attitudes to migration: "The women who accepted their situation almost invariably expressed a simple faith that families and friends, separated by migration, would be reunited in heaven and the trials of this world were to be borne in that hope".[46] Phrases such as 'may we meet in heaven if not on earth' appear frequently in correspondence between couples and although undoubtedly they attest to genuine beliefs in many cases, it is also possible that their use, particularly in 'signing off' letters, might simply be explained by formulaic letter-writing practice.[47] For example, the influence of customary practice is suggested by John Dower's use of near identical phrases each time to express this and other sentiments. However, frequent references to activities associated with their Methodist faith, illustrate the importance that chapel attendance played in the lives of the Paynters and Dowers.

The role of Methodism, the predominant faith in the Cornish mining communities, in migration strategies and experiences requires further investigation. Methodist ideals of self-improvement align well with the model of migration for family betterment. However, it is hard to see how the investment of proceeds from successful emigration projects in pubs and beer houses described earlier, was compatible with Methodist teaching on alcohol consumption. Another area worthy of consideration is whether the perception that wives in Cornwall were not being adequately supported because of their husbands' drinking habits abroad (see Chapter 6) was a driver in the temperance movement.

Religious faith may also have coloured how couples viewed the sexual aspects of their separation. John Tosh notes how one Methodist husband whose work took him away from home suggested in a letter to his wife that his "passionate spirit" meant she was better able to serve God in his absence than when he was at home.[48] This concern for a spouse's spiritual health is displayed in the Paynter and Dower letters with both husbands urging their wives to mind 'the one thing needful'.[49] William, in particular, devoted much space in his letters to discussion of his wife's faith: "Dear Sophia you do not know what good it will do me to hear that you have been at the meeting and that you feel the need of a Saviour" and he was concerned that she was "in the narrow path that leads to life eternal", and "still determined to serve the lord".[50] John hoped that Mary Ann was able to get to chapel meetings, but also made several references to his wish for her to 'behave' and keep herself respectable.

These statements could be interpreted as evidence of distant husbands attempting to exercise a degree of control over their wives, but it is clear from John's letters that Mary Ann is responding in kind with enquiries about his chapel attendance and whether he was still teetotal (he teases that she would make a good missionary), suggesting an equality in the relationship. Neither set of correspondence suggests anything other than the husbands' respect for their wives' opinions, and their ability to manage the household on their own. William makes no reference to Sophia's financial management, and entrusts her with the disposal of the couple's house. John does express more interest in how his wife spends the money he sends home but he doesn't complain of Mary Ann being frivolous or wasteful. Instead, he always encourages her not to hold back in spending money on the family. He tells her not to stint over Christmas dinner, to buy whatever she needs to make herself comfortable.

In spite of all the similarities, there was one major way in which Mary Ann's and Sophia's circumstances differed, and one that led to dramatically divergent experiences. Sophia was among the wives in receipt of regular monthly home-pay direct from her husband's employers, whilst Mary Ann had to manage on what John could send home from his fluctuating earnings as an independent tribute miner. As a result Sophia appears to have had a degree of financial security while Mary Ann's income was irregular and became increasingly unreliable.

However, both men had every intention of being reunited with their wives. In Sophia Paynter's case this went smoothly, and in April 1860, after

The Married Widows of Cornwall

a separation of just over a year, she and the children sailed to join William in South Australia where they settled. John Dower had initially planned to return home, but within ten months of arriving in Australia he saw a better future for the family there and asked if Mary Ann would like to join him. This was a radically different proposition from what Mary Ann had been led to expect from John's earlier talk of coming home and a financially secure future in Cornwall. For reasons unexplained, Mary Ann did not go, a decision she may have regretted when her friends, the wives of John's workmates, left to join their husbands. When the issue was raised again nearly two years later the decision was taken out of her hands when John wrote: "You told Misses Thomas if I sent for you now you would not come but you must consider that what I do is for both our benefits … you may expect your sailing orders the mail after next."[51] However, the sailing orders did not arrive, as John delayed, trying to make things 'more comfortable' for her. There was then a six-month silence before John wrote again telling Mary Ann that he had tried working in New Zealand but had become ill and returned to Australia. He hadn't written sooner because "not able to send you good news I thought I would not send you bad".[52] John assured her that he would either come home or send for them. Sadly there was to be no reunion as two months later he died in Australia.

Sophia's and Mary Ann's stories are both representative of common experiences. Sophia was one of numerous wives reunited with their husbands after relatively short separations and who appear not to have suffered any significant financial hardship while their husbands were away. On the other hand, there are also many examples of separations where things went wrong, as they did for Mary Ann, and planned reunions were foiled by unforeseen circumstances. Had Mary Ann applied for poor relief she would have surely been regarded as a deserted wife, despite John's apparent good intentions throughout. However, neither Sophia nor Mary Ann was neglected by her husband, and their experiences act as a counterpoint to stereotypical representations of the wives 'left behind' as deserted and destitute.

12

Choice and Power
Perceptions and emotions

The issues discussed so far: financial support, the quality of relations with others, and outcomes, were major factors in how the wives in Cornwall experienced separation from their migrant husbands. However, they were not the only factors, and may not have been the most important ones for individual women. For example, we should be cautious in interpreting the wife's experience of the couple's separation solely in the light of its outcome. Just because something ended badly, with death or desertion for example, does not mean that it was not a more positive experience up to that point. A wife who received good emotional support within the community, with regular letters and remittances from her husband until his death is likely to have been more content while her husband was abroad than one who struggled on her own with little contact or money, but whose husband eventually returned to her. A wife's experience was defined not only by practical considerations but also by her perceptions of her position and her emotional inner life.

There is ambivalence in perceptions of what life was like for the wives 'left behind' in Cornwall. Even for those women who did receive money from their husbands, the very experience of separation has often been portrayed as overwhelmingly negative. Sharron Schwartz wrote in 1991 that the emigration of the men and being dependent on remittances was "doubly devastating" for many Cornish women.[1] A more optimistic picture is given by Gary Magee and Andrew Thompson's work on remittance flows to Cornwall from South Africa at the end of the 19th and beginning of the 20th century. They conclude that: "For many Cornish migrants, their departure from Britain was not so much a case of 'cut and run' as of run, remit and (eventually) return".[2] Deacon, however, suggests that remittances divided wives into the 'haves' and 'have-nots'; a situation conducive to division and jealousy within the community.[3]

The Married Widows of Cornwall

Gill Burke has suggested that "for Cornish women in the mining districts the 1890s were times of bitter and lonely hardship" when they were "deprived of the old ways of collective support".[4] But in communities where so many women over several generations shared the experience of managing without their husbands for long periods, new ways of collective support had the chance to develop: from the availability of practical advice from female relatives and neighbours who had lived through the same experience, to a degree of empathy and understanding from poor law officers.

Alongside the negative representations of the wives leading grim and desperate lives in the absence of their husbands sit suggestions of more positive aspects, such as greater control over family affairs and a freedom from repeated pregnancies.[5] In the absence of any detailed research on these women, such views have largely been speculation that does not take into account variation in the nature and duration of their husbands' absences, or the extent of the wives' involvement in the emigration decision. These factors are likely to have played some, if not a major, part in how the wife experienced separation. It is intuitive to think that those who approved of their husbands undertaking serial temporary labour migrations would have viewed their situation very differently from those whose husbands had left against their wishes with the aim of starting a new life abroad and intending to send for their wives at some later date.

Emigrants usually did not make the decision to emigrate in isolation, and the degree to which a wife had a say in whether her husband went abroad and whether she should or should not accompany him would have a significant effect on her feelings about the separation. Susan Biddick, whose marital problems were related in Chapter 8, attributed her unhappiness directly to the fact that her husband had not agreed to her desire to accompany him to South Africa.[6] The legally subordinate position of married women might imply that a wife had no option but to comply with her husband's wishes on this matter. However, in practice a husband ignored his wife's views at his peril, as William Cobbett conceded in his 1829 emigrant's guide; if the wife remained "obstinately perverse" in refusing to emigrate, he advised, the husband should not go because all the advantages of emigration would be negated by the couple living "in a state of petty civil war".[7]

Choice and Power

There is clear evidence that Cornish wives, even if not an equal party to the emigration decision, could attempt, and sometimes succeed, in changing it. Schwartz has drawn attention to instances of men who had agreed to employment in Cuba in the 1830s having to be freed from their contracts because their wives objected so strongly to them going. One example was William May, who was recruited to go to Cuba as a wheelwright by Alfred Jenkin, agent for the Cobre Mines. William, however, had not consulted his wife. We can only imagine the conversation between the couple when she found out, but the upshot was that they appeared at the agent's office where Mrs May made it clear that she opposed her husband's migration and begged Jenkin to release him from his contract. Likewise the wife of Captain Reynolds persuaded him not to go to Cuba, even if it did mean giving up the opportunity to earn £14 a month.[8]

Clearly, Cornish wives were not completely powerless in the face of their husband's decision to emigrate. In 1853 it was reported that a group of St Just miners heading to Australia had "injudiciously" allowed their wives to accompany them to the steamer at Penzance to bid farewell. Some of the wives became so distraught, with one threatening to throw herself and her child into the sea and be drowned if her husband insisted on leaving, that two of the men had to abandon their travel plans and return home.[9] There are also examples of husbands who left in spite of their wives' objections, but acknowledged their moral right to disagree. "I know I left without your consent", wrote William Toll to his wife Charlotte explaining that he had no option but to go.[10] Further testimony to an appreciation that a wife should have some say in her husband's migrations is provided by a letter written in 1874 by a miner in California to his friend's wife seeking her views as to whether her husband should go to Australia with him.[11]

In the same way that some wives were consulted and able to influence their husband's decision to go abroad, others exerted their own agency as to whether or not they themselves should remain in Cornwall. Describing his wife's refusal to join him in the Wallaroo Mines in Australia, Captain Dunstan thought that "a whim rope wouldn't be strong enough to draw her" from Cornwall to the Yorke Peninsula.[12] Such comments seem to substantiate the view of the English woman as a generally unwilling emigrant, reluctant to leave her homeland and face difficult ocean voyages.[13] In 1867 the chairman of the Distress Committee felt that one of the reasons why the wives did not go to their husbands was because they had "a natural affection for their homes".[14] Others attributed this reluctance to a lack of courage and fears of the dangers she and her children might face in mining camps abroad.[15] Matthew Hore, writing home from California noted that if his wife and children did join him there they would soon want to go home again.[16] Some wives were unwilling migrants because of the additional domestic duties entailed; one is recalled as delaying her departure for as long as possible because she realised that joining her husband would involve cooking and cleaning, not just for her husband, but for a houseful of his fellow miners as well.

On the other hand, some wives were equally adamant about going and refused point blank to be left behind. When Annie Jane Combellack and her husband discussed emigration, he suggested that he should go ahead and she should follow only if things were favourable. Her response, according to family tradition, was effectively "No way! We are in this together from the start".[17]

However, the extent to which the wife could exercise her own agency was constrained by structural factors. For example, a wife was more likely to be able to choose to accompany her husband if the destination was perceived as fit and safe for wives and children. Many were not, although couples did not always agree on this point. George Biddick, husband of Susan mentioned above, had refused to allow her to join him in South Africa because "the country was not suitable to her health and that of the children".[18] Into the early years of the 20th century it was still felt that the lack of acceptable family accommodation at many mines in South Africa was a deterrent to the men taking their wives out.[19] "Many men in Africa might think they would scarcely be doing justice to their wives if they brought them out", Frank Harvey told a large gathering of Cornish in Johannesburg in 1912, especially as the men often didn't expect to stay there.

Some mining camps were viewed as simply too dangerous for women and children. Those wives who did go to South Africa, and elsewhere, learned to use guns for their own protection, while the threat of attack and robbery in parts of Latin America led Cornishwomen to sew their valuables into their petticoats.[20] During periods of political upheaval in Mexico Cornish immigrants were caught in the cross fire and, as foreigners, were the targets of violence. A report in the Cornish press in 1862 told of a wife killed by a musket ball during an attack on the carriage in which she was travelling with her husband, and of another, a Mrs Stephens, who was dragged from her house by revolutionary bandits, forced to kneel at gunpoint and threatened with instant death if she did not reveal where the family's valuables where hidden. She managed to convince them that the cash, jewellery and clothing that they had already found was all she had, and "her painful lamentations prevailed in arresting the violence of the thieves, and her life was spared".[21] The women who risked joining their husbands in such places found their lives and movements severely curtailed. At times, simply going to the weekly market required an armed guard, as Bessie Rogers discovered when a shot aimed at her narrowly missed her head.[22]

Another factor was the attitude of her husband's employer. The drunkenness and immorality in the more remote mining camps were a deterrent for wives accompanying or joining their husbands, but at the same time led to some employers actively encouraging wives to go, as their presence would have a civilising and stabilising influence on the men. There were also employers, such the owners of the Brazilian Morro Velho mines in the 1830s, who had another reason for wanting couples and families to immigrate; it was cheaper to establish a colony producing a new generation of workers (as young as eight years old) in situ rather than repeatedly recruit and pay the passages of men from Cornwall. At the same time, employers could be sensitive to the demoralising effect if wives could not settle. When one woman at Morro Velho died in 1867 after pining away through homesickness, the company became so worried that another who was similarly distressed would die that they considered sending her home to Cornwall.[23]

There were reasons, other than consideration for the welfare of the woman and children, why it was not always in the couple's best interests for the wives to join their husbands abroad. Many mine companies preferred to employ single men, however, as Alfred Jenkin, recruiting agent for the Cobre Mines in Cuba, found in 1838, it was difficult to find men with the right skills and experience who weren't married.[24] Richard

Lingenfelter, writing about the American mines, noted that some mining superintendents felt that men with families were "less vigourous, less energetic and less daring". As they were therefore less willing to risk their lives for the company, married men were frequently the first to be laid off if a mine was in difficulties. Encumbered with a family, the unemployed married miners would find it harder to move on in search of alternative work.[25]

Therefore for the temporary labour migrant and those unsure of their long-term plans, the presence of wife and children could be a hindrance, potentially exposing the husband to employer prejudice and limiting his flexibility in moving around to maximise work opportunities. So, it is not surprising that many couples felt that it was better that the wife stay settled in Cornwall maintaining a home for the husband's planned or possible return. On the other hand, in some cases the wife's domestic labour was considered to be of more use abroad than at home with wives being sent for specifically because the men needed someone to do the cooking and laundry.[26] Additionally, as discussed in the previous chapter, living separately incurred extra costs, which could undermine the financial viability of the emigration project. Therefore the wife's decision making was limited within the needs of the family economy.[27]

These concerns were not the only possible constraints on the wife's options. Commitments in Cornwall would also have restricted her freedom of choice. In some families the fate of elderly relatives would have been a consideration. One reason that Elizabeth, the wife of Captain Dunstan above, might not have wanted to join him in Australia, is suggested by the 1871 census, which shows her 73-year-old mother living with her while her husband was abroad.[28] What might have happened to Elizabeth's mother if she had gone is illustrated by the case of a wife whose decision to join her husband in Mexico in 1894 meant that her ill, widowed mother had no-one to live with and had to turn to the poor law guardians for relief.[29] Fears for their daughters' welfare led to the parents of some wives strongly objecting to their going abroad. Catherine Williams' parents were so worried about her making the journey that they reputedly told her husband "You'll kill her!" when he planned to take her back to California with him.[30] It is not hard to imagine that concern for their children and grandchildren (and possibly their own futures) combined with fears that they would never see them again could lead to parental pressure for the wives to remain in Cornwall. This could come from both sides of the family as in-laws may have felt that their sons were more likely to settle back in Cornwall if they had wives to come back to.

A child's ill health could also reduce the wife's options. Harriett Trewin and her children were unable to sail to join her husband in New York as planned because one of the daughters suffered from such severe travel sickness that the family was advised that she would not survive the voyage, a situation that was ultimately to end the marriage.[31] Conversely, the death, or recovery, of a dependant relative could be the trigger for a wife to finally join her husband overseas.[32] Many a wife must have been torn between the desire to be with her husband and conflicting family loyalties in deciding what she should do.

For other wives, emigration could mean abandoning interests outside the home. Mrs Banfield left behind a successful career as the headmistress of Lelant School to join her husband in America in 1883.[33] Ellen Gray Lean didn't join her husband, William, in Chile, it is suggested, so that she could continue to manage her family's property interests in Lanner.[34] The persistence of the trope of wife as fearful emigrant versus one exerting her own agency is illustrated in this case by a family belief that she didn't go because she was afraid to travel by sea. Which of these reasons was uppermost in Ellen's mind is impossible to judge.

Dudley Baines wrote: "We cannot know what actually passed through the minds of potential emigrants. We can be fairly sure that personal motives, often connected with particular stages in the life-cycle, played a large part in the decision to emigrate. And we can be fairly sure that there were psychological barriers to emigration that had to be overcome".[35] His words apply equally to those who chose not to go. In order to, as Charlotte Erickson put it: "examine migration in a more holistic, nuanced fashion", the migrant has to be considered in the context of his immediate family, and especially his spouse.[36] This recognition that the migrant cannot be considered in isolation from family or community relationships has become more prominent in academic discussion of migration.[37] However, the focus has been, predominately, on the role of the family in the migrant's decision to go, rather than what influenced the decision of those family members who remained in the sending community to stay. More pertinent is the "holistic-material-emotional approach" described by Dirk Hoerder, which places individual choices in the context of an overall family economy that combines the "income-generating capabilities of all family members with reproductive needs - such as care for dependants, whether children or elderly - and consumption patterns so as to achieve the best possible results according to traditional norms".[38]

Put simply, in the transnational nuclear family, now known to be commonplace in the mining communities in Cornwall, the wife's role in remaining in the sending community was as important to the success of the family's emigration project as that played by the migrant husband himself. By staying in Cornwall, whether briefly or permanently, and providing the labour and shouldering the responsibility for the care of children, extended family, homes and sometimes business interests, the wives created the freedom that enabled their husbands to take advantage of the opportunities abroad in the same way it has been suggested that their counterparts did in other emigration centres in Europe.[39]

Viewed from this perspective, the wives 'left behind' are far from the passive victims of the Cornish migration narrative. Nevertheless, the wife's options were circumscribed by what was practical or advantageous in terms of the overall aim of the emigration project. The extent to which the wife could exercise her own agency and could accept any compromises required to accommodate the overall family's needs would have affected her mental attitude to the separation from her husband. A wife who felt that she'd had little say in whether her husband emigrated, either because her opinion was not respected or his departure was necessitated by economic crisis, is likely to have had a much more negative approach to her situation than one who had agreed to her husband going abroad for the benefit of the family, especially if she was in receipt of adequate, even generous, remittances. In the latter case, there is little reason to suppose that she saw the separation as an overwhelmingly bad experience.

However, resentments could have grown where a wife was left responsible for wider family for whom she had less of an emotional bond, such in-laws or stepchildren. Even amongst those wives who may have initially supported their husband's emigration without them, positive feelings and resilience could be worn down over time or if circumstances changed, for example, if remittances stopped or tragedy struck. Ann

Goldsworthy from Skinners Bottom, near St Agnes, whose husband had been in America for nearly eleven months, wrote to him in 1861 "with an aching heart and feeble frame" to tell him that one of their children had died during the night and another was ill: "I would not for you to [have] left this house for all the money that is in this world".[40]

It is intuitive to suppose that the wife would also have had regrets if the separation went on for longer than anticipated. The duration of the separation compared with the wife's expectations therefore would have had a material impact on the nature of her experience. Research has shown that in the parishes of Gwennap and St Agnes as many as a quarter of the absent husbands in one census year were also absent in the previous census. In the majority of cases there is no way of knowing if these couples had been reunited between census years. In Gwennap 23-37% of husbands absent in consecutive censuses were found to have been reunited with their wives in the interim period. Hence, at best, the husband's absence in more than one census can only provide a maximum length for the couple's separation. For example, a husband absent in two consecutive censuses may have been overseas for up to 30 years, or at the other extreme he could have travelled abroad twice for only a few months around the time of both censuses. Similarly, husbands absent or abroad in any one census year may have been away for 20 years or a couple of months, weeks or even days depending on how far they had travelled. Therefore analysis of the census can provide little conclusive evidence of length of separation.

Lengthy absences were not unknown. Jane Trevithick, mentioned earlier, didn't see her husband Richard, the mining engineer, for 16 years.[41] The census enumerator for St Just in Penwith in 1871 noted that Jane Tonking's miner husband "has been in Australia 17 years"; the only entry in the Cornish census that specifies how long the husband had been away.[42] Other separations had become, or were assumed to be, permanent as evidenced by the wives discussed in previous chapters who were genuinely deserted. As a counterpoint to the few documented cases of very lengthy separations, there are, as described in previous chapters, numerous stories of husbands who returned permanently after brief periods abroad or became serial migrants, or who sent for their wives to join them as soon as possible. Although it hasn't been possible to discover the proportion of wives who were subject to long as opposed to short separations, there was clearly a wide variation in their duration and regularity, which in turn adds to the diversity of the wives' experiences.

Distance, and the ease of travel and communications between Cornwall and her husband's work place would have influenced views on whether individual wives should go or stay.[43] For a wife who remained in Cornwall, these factors also influenced her perception of her situation: how long it might take to communicate with her husband in case of a family crisis, or if it was possible for him to come back relatively quickly if necessary; whether he was with relatives or friends who would ensure that she was informed if anything happened to him; was she party to an accumulation of knowledge concerning the community and living conditions in which he was living, or was it an unknown and frightening world to her? These factors changed with technological improvements and as pioneer settlements developed. Thus when, as well as where, her husband was abroad altered the options available to the wife and her experience of the separation. Further research might detect specific differences between the experiences of wives whose husbands had emigrated to different parts of the world at different times, but with so many factors involved it would be unwise to assume, for example, that a wife whose husband was in Africa at the turn of the 20th century necessarily had an easier time than one whose husband was in South America eighty years earlier. As demonstrated in previous chapters, conflict, economic depressions, politics and the destination's relationship to the British Empire could dramatically affect the wife's experience of separation from her husband and its outcome.

The wives would have been subject to fairly constant worry about their husband's, and by inference their own, wellbeing and security. Mining accidents were common, but a wife whose husband was working locally would quickly know if he was safe, or not, after an incident. It could be weeks before news of any accidents abroad reached Cornwall, and even then it may not be clear which men were involved. In 1895 it was reported that 13 men had drowned in a mine in America where men from Camborne were known to be working but no names were released, causing great anxiety in the town.[44] The local newspapers frequently carried notices of the deaths of Cornishmen abroad,[45] but to add to the wives' uncertainty, they occasionally reported the deaths of the wrong men, for example, in 1894, confusing John Bennetts in California with James Bennetts in Montana.[46]

Over and above the inherent dangers of mining, the men could fall prey to other accidents, injuries and diseases through travel and poor living conditions, as well as crime. In her work on *The Cornish in Latin America*, Sharron Schwartz tells the stories of many miners killed by natives, revolutionaries and robbers. Examples from the mid-1800s include a number of Cornishmen killed by a Comanche raid on the Santa Maria Mine in Mexico, whose remains in the mineshaft were not found until decades later, and others killed and wounded by renegade soldiers in Bolivia.[47] It is hard to imagine whether Sophia Paynter would have been reassured or alarmed on hearing that William had acquired a dog and revolver so should he be "molested" he "could make some resistance".[48] In 1889 the shock of learning that her husband had been shot in America left a St Just wife "incapacitated" and unable to work to support herself and her two children.[49]

Husbands might also find themselves caught up in conflicts, as in the American Civil War (1861-65) and the wars in Africa at the end of the century. In 1899 wives in Camborne (and presumably elsewhere) were anxious about their husbands in Kimberley, which had been shelled by the Boers;[50] other married men with wives in Cornwall enlisted in Cape Town to fight.[51]

The ultimate uncertainty was when the wives lost contact with husbands who effectively disappeared from their lives. In addition to the obvious emotional and financial impact on the family, there were legal implications centred around whether the husband was still living, including the wife's legal marital status, inheritance of any property and the continued use of tenure on three-lives leases.[52] In 1853 the Cornish press reported that Melbourne newspapers carried numerous adverts placed by wives trying to contact their gold-seeking husbands,[53] and in 1864 a Mr S. Morcom was advertising his services in tracing missing relatives in South Australia, supplying death certificates and recovering property if they had died.[54] Efforts to track down missing men continued into the 20th century via the press, such as the Moonta *People's Weekly* in South Australia and organisations such as the South African Cornish Association.[55] As discussed in earlier chapters, poor law guardians had a

The Married Widows of Cornwall

vested interest in tracing husbands who had disappeared and although they could not exert their official powers abroad, they had some success in locating men via informal networks within the international mining and Cornish communities.[56] For example, in 1899 the Redruth Board of Guardians found out that John, the husband of Priscilla Kent from Carharrack, was not dead as had been thought, but was working as the assistant manager of a mine in Bolivia.[57]

Some men clearly wanted to 'disappear' abroad, such as the husband of a Camborne woman who, after she had him bound over to keep the peace, took his pay and her savings, and left for Africa with the help of his mother.[58] Other cases are more ambiguous; a young women told the Helston guardians that her husband had been sending her money regularly from abroad but then had written that he was going to Columbia and that she had better not write to him again, as it was a strange country and the letters would not find him. She had not heard of him since and did not know if he was still alive.[59]

In many cases, however, it seems likely that the husband, like John Dower, left with good intentions, but these were subverted by distance, time and events beyond his control. In 1902 W. Herbert Thomas, the well-informed newspaper proprietor provided a contemporary description of the difficulties of Cornish transnational marriage:

> "I have met my fellow Cornishmen in far off mining centres and know something of the temptations that beset them. Sometimes they are out of work and unable to send home money. This worries them, until they become hopeless and desperate, and having no good news to send they stop writing - until they lose their self respect. Sometimes the loneliness of their life causes them to fall an easy prey to the charms or the wiles of women, with the result that among the Esquimaux in Alaska, or in Mexico, Chili, Peru, or the United States you may find a Cornishman with a wife and family who have never been introduced to the wife and family at home. Then again boon companions may cause a man to take to drink as a change from toil; or just as a man thinks he has some money in the Bank at home he finds that his wife has spent all on finery and cab hire, or that she has forgotten her marriage vows,

> or shown in some way that she prefers married life with the husband abroad. There are many cases in which even the erring and neglectful husband is as much to be pitied as blamed; while there are other cases of men who deserve horsewhipping for inexcusable treatment of worthy women and helpless children. As a rule the Cornishman who violates the unwritten laws is either given strong advice or the cold shoulder by his comrades, who realise that heartlessness of this kind becomes a blot upon the fair fame of Cornwall."[60]

W. Herbert Thomas' editorial provides a useful summary of the broad and complex range of experiences arising from marital separation associated with emigration, many of which have been discussed in previous chapters. However, common to all the wives was an uncertainty that must have been incredibly unsettling, even overwhelming at times. For those who felt they had some say in and control over their situation, who were well supported financially and emotionally, the uncertainty would have been more bearable; a necessary sacrifice to the overall family project.

However, if such uncertainty was exacerbated by lack of support and/or a sense of powerlessness, the result was despair, desperation and sometimes, suicide. Coroner's inquests reported in the Cornish press provide a small but sad litany of such cases throughout the period. Margaret Rowe (aged 29) hanged herself in 1842 at her father's home in Gwinear where she had been staying since her husband had gone to America. "It appeared that his absence, and the want of the means to go to him so preyed on her mind as to deprive her of her reason", concluded the coroner.[61] Mother of six Harriet Hick of Kea received regular remittances from her husband in Australia, but had been in "a low, desponding state" and afraid that she would never see him again. She too hanged herself.[62] In a similar case in 1861 Elizabeth Harris of Redruth used a borrowed razor to cut her throat. Her husband in Australia had not written to her for some years, which had "evidently depressed her mind". The Coroner heard how she "frequently complained of head-aches, which were worse every time the Australian mail arrived and brought no letter for her".[63] Likewise, according to her son, Elizabeth Tonkin of

The Married Widows of Cornwall

Chacewater had been depressed for months, having heard rumours concerning her husband in Chile, resulting in her suicide by hanging in 1889.[64]

Even more disturbing are the rare cases where despair drove a wife to take not only her own life but also that of her children. Around 1857 Joseph Trebilcock went to Australia leaving his pregnant wife Mary Ann and their young daughter in Cornwall. Five years later, Joseph asked Mary Ann and the children to join him abroad. Mary Ann, however, was unwilling to go and not hearing any more from her husband became "low spirited and dejected", telling friends "she did not care whether she lived or died". In December 1862 her body and that of her four-year-old son, William, were found in the river at Perranarworthal. Her seven-year-old daughter, Alice, who was seen with her earlier, was also presumed to have drowned as her hat was found floating in the river.[65]

A rare insight into one woman's state of mind was provided by the reminiscences of an elderly woman in Helston in the 1920s, recalling the despair she experienced on losing contact with her husband in South Australia:

> "Many times I have gone to the wash tray without breakfast, and my two dear children have had to stay until I came home without any food in the house. I have cried myself to sleep many a night. One night I lost heart, so I took my two children to a water shaft at Basset mines, with the intention of drowning them and myself; but the captain of the mine saw me just in time. I told him my trouble and he wrote to Captain Hancock in Australia, and found my husband working there. He could not do anything, but asked him to write. Captain Hancock's daughter sent me £1. I often wished I could write; I would thank her so much."[66]

In most of the suicide cases described above the inquest returned a verdict of 'temporary insanity', acknowledging the presence of mental illness but equally likely to be a pragmatic means of enabling Christian burial of the women concerned rather than an attempt at a true diagnosis.[67] The contribution of a possible pre-existing or predisposition to mental illness cannot be discounted. Sarah Mallet, a 37-year-old from

Duloe, was described as a "pauper lunatic" when she hanged herself at the County Lunatic Asylum. She had never heard from her husband after he had gone to America some years earlier but how much this contributed to her mental illness is impossible to say as she had already made one failed attempt on her own life.[68] Therefore not all suicides committed by wives whose husbands were abroad can be attributed to that fact. In 1887, while her husband was abroad, Ann Webb attempted suicide by hanging claiming that the devil told her to do it; she was hospitalised with 'religious mania'.[69]

Thirty-nine-year-old Elizabeth May from Newlyn East suffered an episode of mental ill-health after her husband Samuel, a miner, left to work in Turkey for three years in 1870. Elizabeth, who had recently given birth to the couple's seventh child was refusing to eat or drink, had wished to poison herself and had tried to jump out of a window. She was considered a danger to herself and her children and admitted to St Lawrence's Hospital, the asylum in Bodmin. Her doctors attributed Elizabeth's illness to grief for the loss of her husband and "probably the puerperal state". From Elizabeth's symptoms it seems likely that she was suffering from postpartum psychosis, unrelated to her husband's absence. Her baby daughter died while Elizabeth was hospitalised but her story has a happy ending. Elizabeth recovered and was discharged after seven months and could be found living with her husband and surviving children in the 1871 census, Samuel having returned early from abroad.[70]

As in Elizabeth's case, a causal association was made between male emigration and female mental illness in some other 19th century sending communities. In her study of the Sicilian 'widows in white', Linda Reeder describes the common assumption, endorsed by contemporary medical opinion, that the absence of husbands through migration (and therefore unfulfilled sexual needs) would inevitably lead to insanity amongst the wives.[71] This belief was closely related to the more widely held notions of the inability of women to control themselves in the absence of men that were expressed in 19th century Australia.[72]

Although some wives found their situation unbearable, there is no evidence of widespread extreme emotional distress amongst the thousands of wives identified as having remained in Cornwall, suggesting that the majority of wives had the support and emotional resources to cope in the absence of their husbands. Paradoxically, this ability to cope was probably boosted by the level of autonomy allowed the wife regarding emigration decisions, in that she had a sense of fulfilling her part in an agreed joint project but, once the husband had left, her role in strategic decision making was much diminished, and her autonomy constrained to more limited affairs in Cornwall.

13

The Worst Kind of Widowhood?
Conclusions

We started this exploration of the experiences of the 'married widows' with the observation in an 1876 issue of the *Royal Cornwall Gazette* that there were "considerable" numbers of wives 'left behind' by emigrating husbands. The finding that an estimated two to six thousand of these wives remained in Cornwall at any one time between 1851 and 1891 proves this to be the case. Accumulatively over that period some tens of thousands of married women and their children in Cornwall would have been affected. What is more, the social impact of the phenomenon would have been magnified because it was so concentrated within the mining districts, predominantly in the western parishes, although its distribution reflects the development of other mining areas within Cornwall. Its scale and prevalence in these areas mean that it must be viewed as an integral element of Cornish mining community culture.

Having looked at the practical aspects and provided some insight into the more intangible aspects of the wives' experiences, it is time to draw the different strands of evidence together, and to address the question of whether the wives' situation was indeed 'the worst kind of widowhood'.

An appreciation of the scale of the phenomenon is crucial in how we interpret the evidence of how the women fared in the absence of their husbands. Although there were individual cases of extreme financial hardship, there is no indication of widespread destitution amongst the wives 'left behind'. This conclusion is drawn from a combination of several findings. The first is the absence of any suggestion that, across the period studied, many thousands of married women in Cornwall were turning to the poor law officers for help. Only in the recognised period of mining depression in the late 1860s, when contemporary statistics were gathered at a local level, do the numbers of inadequately supported wives appear to approach the number estimated to have absent husbands. Even during this period of heightened awareness of distress in the mining communities, those parishes in which the highest numbers of absent husbands have been identified did not report problems on a scale consistent with a large proportion of the wives 'left behind' seeking relief.

Secondly, throughout the period studied the majority of wives maintained their own homes. Little evidence was found of household collapse or clustering in response to financial distress as suggested by Brayshay.[1] Where wives have been found to have been living in households other than their own, a number of alternative practical and emotional reasons that do not involve financial difficulties on the wife's part have been proposed. These include new brides remaining with their parents and postponing independent household formation until they join their husbands abroad, strategies for shared child care and emotional support, assisting relatives and temporary visits from abroad or stays in preparation for emigration.

If destitution on a scale matching that of the thousands of wives 'left behind' had occurred it is hard to believe that it would have not caused more concern and comment. Indeed the evidence appears to confirm contemporary views that the majority of wives were supported by their husbands abroad. Although a strong case can be made to exclude widespread destitution amongst the wives, there is insufficient evidence to assess the levels of less extreme poverty. Many of the women who did eventually apply for poor law relief appear to have done so some time after remittances from their husbands ceased, suggesting a lengthy period of struggling to get by. Many others may have succeeded in making ends meet without resorting to the poor law system but remained close to the poverty line. Therefore the possibility of considerable hidden hardship amongst the 'silent' majority cannot be discounted.

The 'economy of diverse resources' under which the wives managed has been shown to be broad indeed. Many of these resources, such as remittances, employment and collateral support from smallholdings, were to be expected from wider research on Cornwall. We need, however, to pay more attention to the previously under-considered role of home-pay. The impact of home-pay in Cornwall warrants further study. Its scheduled regularity offered those in Cornwall reliant on income earned abroad far greater financial security than the unreliable postal remittances more commonly associated with emigration narratives. As home-pay payments were generated within the British banking system they would also account for an unknown level of additional revenue into the Cornish economy over and above that previously estimated from records of foreign banker's drafts or money orders.

Delving into the stories of individual wives has highlighted the use made of poor relief, even on occasions when there was no entitlement to it. The extent to which married couples, either in collusion or independently, manipulated the poor law system to increase their income is a fertile area for further research not just in the Cornish context, but nationally. The Poor Law has such close association in the popular imagination with workhouses that the outdoor relief system that helped far more people in the past hasn't received the attention it perhaps deserves. There is scope to increase our understanding of the intricacies of the operation of this aspect of the poor laws at local level, especially in relation to temporary relief given in the form of loans. It would be interesting to know, for example, whether more relief was issued as loans by unions with a high proportion of wives 'left behind' than those without.

The improved access to 19th century newspapers may play an important role in this research, as they contain greater detail and a different perspective from that found in official boards of guardians' minutes. However, greater use of newspapers needs to be accompanied by a better understanding of the men who controlled them. The role of the press, and in particular of W. Herbert Thomas, proprietor of the *Cornishman*, in addressing the issue of the wives 'left behind' warrants further attention. Although a professional journalist, and therefore theoretically an objective observer, he writes with the insider's insight of one born in the heart of the mining district who spent time in the mining camps in America.[2] As the most predominant public commentator on the challenges facing transnational Cornish families, his output undoubtedly influenced not only contemporary opinion at the time but also how the wives have been perceived by later generations.

There were certainly contemporary perceptions that Cornish husbands abroad deliberately withheld funds in the knowledge that the poor law authorities had little real alternative but to contribute to the support of their wives, but whether these were justified, or a few cases exaggerated to fuel the crusade against outdoor relief, is a question that remains unanswered. Similarly, further work is required to ascertain whether the greater attention given to the issue of 'deserted wives' in Cornwall in the last decades of the 19th century arose from a genuinely increasing social problem, or raised public awareness and debate about the cost of poor relief and frustration with existing legislation that failed to ensure husbands abroad supported their wives in Britain.

The issue of not being able to enforce the maintenance of wives and children by men abroad was one of a number of challenges not encountered before the emergence of the transnational nuclear family with so many married couples living in separate countries in the 19th century. In Cornwall there is clear evidence that the authorities adapted to accommodate the tension between transnational marriages and a legal system based on a doctrine of coverture. The Poor Law, contrary to its original intent, was used to supplement low or irregular incomes of working families through outdoor relief, often given as loans. Similarly, the courts had to balance the difficulties tradesmen had in recovering debts incurred by wives for which, under coverture, husbands were responsible, with the need to keep open the credit channels on which the women relied to compensate for irregularities in income. In both cases authorities appear to have been willing to adopt a pragmatic interpretation of the law. There was little they could do, however, about international inconsistencies in divorce laws.

Compared with their contemporaries whose husbands were in Cornwall, wives 'left behind' had far greater interaction with the authorities, as illustrated by the many examples of dealings with poor law officers, courts, and school attendance officers, both as agents for their husbands and in their own right. Some parallels can be drawn with the transformation of the relationship between the Sicilian 'widows in white' and the Italian state described by Reeder.[3] Like the Sicilian wives, those in Cornwall learned how to negotiate bureaucracies to the benefit of their families. Similarly, Duroux describes how wives 'left behind' in Auvergne, France also had to take on more public roles.[4]

However, detailed comparisons between the wives 'left behind' in Cornwall and their contemporaries in other parts of the world are problematic. Historical studies of couples separated by emigration are few and cover different time spans and cultures. Most are only concerned with emigrations that appear homogeneous over a relatively short period; for example, Reeder covers emigration from Sicily to America between 1880-1920, while Brettell, although covering more of the 19th century, is primarily concerned with post-1870s emigration from Portugal to Brazil.[5] Others have a narrow focus on wives 'left behind' by specific events, such as gold rushes, or internal migrations.

Emigration from Cornwall was different, with both a longer time span and greater variety. The research behind this book has revealed the extent of early temporary labour migration of married men from Cornwall with sophisticated systems of overseas contracts and home-pay for families in operation in the 1820s. This provides the Cornish transnational nuclear family with a long pedigree, spanning several generations. Therefore, there was ample scope for the practice to become customary, with its own accumulated wisdom within the mining communities, well before the 'birds of passage' style migrations of the late 19th century normally cited as the exemplar of Cornish temporary labour emigration.

In this respect, a closer parallel is the varied 19th century migrations from Auvergne studied by Duroux.[6] Despite this similarity, important cultural differences limit the extent to which these groups are comparable. In contrast to ambiguities of the English doctrine of coverture, the women in Auvergne had the benefit of an established system of legal marital proxies that legitimised their authority to manage affairs in their husbands' absence.

Another factor differentiates the wives 'left behind' in Cornwall from their counterparts in other parts of Europe. Duroux, Reeder and Brettell all describe the effect on rural peasant women, whereas the Cornish wives lived in communities that had become industrialised in the late 18th century and were accustomed to women earning independent incomes. This makes early 19th century emigration from Cornwall unusual, if not unique, in that the movement was of skilled workers from an industrialised society rather than the large-scale emigration of agricultural workers from a peasant economy. This, and the earlier timing of mass emigration from Cornwall, suggests that any resulting transformation in the relationship between Cornish women and the state would have occurred at a much earlier date than in these other European sending communities.

Nevertheless, as we have seen, similarities can be identified. The tradition of smallholdings providing important collateral support for Cornish miners' families,[7] offered the potential for Cornish wives to have enabled the men's migration by maintaining these plots in the same way as their Portuguese counterparts.

The wide range of cultural and structural differences between Cornwall and the other sending communities where women have been 'left behind', or where women were numerically dominant, make comparisons complex and cast doubt on how far the consequences of separation can be considered universal. For example, the emigration of so many men inspires speculation on the matriarchal nature of the mining communities. So, for instance, can Cornwall be compared with Shetland, which was very much a 'woman's world' in the 19th century? In Shetland the demographic imbalance was far greater (only partly due to wives 'left behind'), as many women married very late, if at all.[8] In other respects there are similarities, with male occupational absence and mortality, resulting in early widowhood, in both communities. However, in Shetland women were at the heart of the local economy as producers through crofting and knitting, whereas in Cornwall it appears the women's economic role was as consumers channelling money earned by the men abroad.

We also have to consider the possible positive aspects to the wives' situation. In addition to the prospect of a better future for her family, the husband's absence created potential space for the wife's greater independence and personal growth. Lyn Bryant has drawn attention to Cornish women as workers in their own right with strong female kinship networks,[9] while Schwartz and Parker describe a resilient, near matriarchal society in 19th century Lanner, populated by women whose experience as independent bal maidens in their youth had "equipped them well to deal with the task of decision making and bringing up a family alone".[10] Schwartz suggests that: "many carved out powerful positions for themselves within the context of their economic dependency as the surrogate heads of household creating 'matrifocal communities' where socio-economic life continued successfully without their menfolk".[11] Freedom from childbirth and breast feeding, greater autonomy in how the family income they received was spent and children were raised are all ways in which it has been argued that the wives could have been liberated by their situation.[12] The actual realisation of these supposed positive aspects of life for the wives 'left behind' is, however, problematic on several grounds.

Firstly, was the claimed near-matriarchal nature of some mining communities really the result of so many husbands being abroad, as suggested by Schwartz? Detailed analysis of the Gwennap census, for example, shows that throughout the second half of the 19th century there were always more households in the parish headed by men than by women, that widows significantly out-numbered wives as heads of household, and although there were large numbers of wives 'left behind' in the parish, there were always at least 75% of husbands living at home with their wives in each census year.

Another potential positive aspect of the wives' experience is that the men's absence relieved the wives from repeated pregnancies. Gill Burke suggests that in the absence of their husbands these women were "released from the treadmill of annual childbearing that was the lot of so many women in the 19th and early 20th centuries". In the same vein, Schwartz wonders that: "no-one seems to have considered how liberating it might have been for women to be freed from long cycles of pregnancy and breast feeding".[13] This too needs to be re-examined, as it assumes that the norm was long-term separation. We now know that there was a high level of temporary/return migration with the husbands coming home after short contracts or spending time in Cornwall between periods abroad, or the wives joining them overseas after a brief separation, either temporarily or permanently. For these couples the interval between pregnancies may not have differed much from the norm.

It is logical to assume that longer-term absences of the husbands could have reduced the birth rate. Giving his annual report in February 1893 the Medical Officer to Helston Town Council did attribute the low birth rate at the time as being due to there being "many old people and wives with husbands abroad".[14] This does not, however, take into account the preference for smaller families that was developing in the late 19th century.[15] The evidence regarding fecundity from research on wives 'left behind' in other emigration centres presents a conflicting picture. Caroline

Brettell concluded from her study of Portuguese wives that all forms of migration of married men reduced the pregnancy rate, including temporary migration, which had the effect of lengthening birth intervals.[16] On the other hand Reeder found that the reproductive lives of wives left behind in Sicily were not disrupted by the migrations of their husbands and that the increased wealth created by the men working overseas enabled and encouraged them to have larger families.[17] In Russia peasant wives left behind in rural areas had a reduced pregnancy rate because the heavy and demanding agricultural labour they did while their husbands were away working in the city for periods of three to five years disrupted their menstrual cycles.[18] This variation suggests that it would be foolhardy, without further research, to associate any reduction in the birth rate in Cornwall, and therefore a liberation of the wives from the dangers of childbirth and demands of breastfeeding, solely with the emigration of the men, when other cultural, social and biological factors could be involved.

Any change in financial autonomy is also contentious. In the absence of their husbands the wives had day-to-day control over the household purse, but this was probably little different from what they had when their husbands were home. What they lost was influence over the size of that purse. Bernard Deacon has drawn attention to the fact that although the wives had more autonomy with regards to how they spent the money they received, they had no control over the proportion of their husband's earnings that was sent home.[19] Once the husband had left, distance lessened the wife's control over her circumstances. Without regular face-to-face contact and with only delayed intelligence about his situation, the wife's ability to influence her husband's decision making was reduced. Therefore, compared with a couple living together, these wives were less able to use their own agency with regard to the distribution of the family's resources, both financial (how much money her husband sent home) and labour (when/if he would return or she join him). Far from leaving the wives empowered, this loss of influence and control would have led to a greater sense of powerlessness.

Expressions of independence also caused problems in some marriages. It is said that Charlotte Lean's capable management of family and property affairs in Lanner so unsettled her husband, William, when he returned from working in Chile that he was 'not home five minutes' before he left again.[20] As we saw earlier, Amelia Tucker's attempts to make ends meet and save a little for the future were met with distrust and bitter complaints from her husband in South Africa, resulting in him tightening his control on the money sent home.

However, their husbands' absence brought the wives into greater contact with financial dealings at a higher level. Not only would they have had to negotiate international money transactions and, in some cases, running businesses, they were also exposed to more involvement in legal cases, especially concerning debts, which under normal circumstances would have been dealt with by their husbands. The wives also had to navigate the difficult path of contributing to the family economy whilst at the same time not undermining the family project designed to improve social circumstances and status, of which the badge of achievement was the domestic ideal of the non-working wife. They had to tread a fine line between managing the family finances frugally, avoiding criticism for 'mad spending', whilst at the same time displaying the husband's success through aspirational dress, household goods and their children's education.

It remains to be resolved whether the women in Cornwall had more in common with those in Shetland and other places where male absence/death was associated with maritime occupations, or those in other emigration sending communities across Europe. This book provides an overview of the phenomenon in Cornwall to inform such comparisons but additional analysis of the differences in family structure, land tenure and inheritance, and religious and social factors is required before meaningful comparisons can be made. In particular, the issue of wives 'left behind' needs to be disentangled from the extremely high numbers of widows in these communities so that the impact of emigration can be distinguished from that of high male mortality.

The long history of married Cornishmen working abroad is not a homogeneous one; there was enormous diversity of destination, length of absence, motivation and employment practice. Wives remained in Cornwall under a wide range of scenarios: postponed departure while husbands went ahead to test or prepare the way for emigration of the whole family, either permanently or for a limited time; temporary solo sojourns abroad by husbands intending to return; refusal to participate in emigration; and desertion by husbands. It is also clear that none of these scenarios were fixed, as the individuals involved changed their minds, circumstances altered and different options and opportunities arose.

The date, destination and nature of her husband's emigration, and even where she herself lived, all had implications for how a wife experienced the separation. This limits our ability to make generalised interpretations of what life was like for the wives 'left behind'. In addition, this already complex situation does not lend itself to a narrative of progressive improvement. Technological advances and development in transport, postal services and international banking, combined with accumulated knowledge shared by their mothers and aunts, would all suggest that life was easier for the wives managing without their husbands later in the century than for those of previous generations. However, this has to be offset by a decline in the practice of compulsory home-pay as employers became less paternalistic, more restricted access to poor law relief, and educational reform reducing the contribution of older children to the domestic economy through wages and help with child care, which in turn compromised the women's access to employment.

The seemingly endless permutations of structural influences on the lives of the wives 'left behind' might be taken as a sign that the wives' experiences were so varied that they had little in common at all. However, patterns and commonalities can be detected when the women's autonomy and emotional lives are examined. The qualitative evidence extracted from contemporary sources, such as newspapers, combined with the quantitative analysis showing high levels of reunions both in Cornwall and abroad, suggests that the majority of wives 'left behind' were not simply being abandoned to their fate by their emigrating husbands. Wilful planned desertion appears to have been rare. More often neglect of the wives arose from unforeseen circumstances: unemployment, illness, the unanticipated financial drain of maintaining two households and expense of fees charged for sending remittances home, or simply a drifting apart of a couple leading very different lives and unable to share the intimacies that reinforce emotional attachment. Instead, like the spouses 'left behind' in other labour migrations, past and present, the wives in Cornwall were partners in a family strategy to improve the family's circumstances, whether as a matter of survival or social/financial upward mobility.

Nor, it seems, were they 'silent' partners, in any sense of the word. They participated in decision-making, and were prepared to protest their right to influence who went and who stayed. Whether or not they were overruled depended on the dynamics of the marriage, but it was in the best interests of the emigration project that the wives should agree to the planned action, as their participation was, in most cases, essential to its success. Without the active contribution of the wife in shouldering the management of the family's interests in Cornwall (be it a home, property, businesses, the children, elderly relatives, or simply herself) a married man who was, at that time, legally and morally responsible for all of these would have found it almost impossible to have the freedom to take advantage of work opportunities overseas. As Sharron Schwartz has suggested, the wives were as actively and intimately involved in the migration strategy as their men who moved.[21]

This co-dependent model of transnational marriage sees an adjustment of the notion of separate spheres. Instead of a gendered division between the domestic and public, there is a geographical division with both spouses engaged in domestic and public activities in their respective locations; in addition to their traditional roles, wives in Cornwall represented the family in engagement with the authorities, while their husbands abroad tended to their own domestic needs.

Although there may have been relative equality in the relationship while the husband was at home, once he was out of the country the power balance changed. The husband's authority was enshrined in law irrespective of where he was, whereas the wife's power could only be exercised through face-to-face contact. Without that contact her ability to influence her husband or the overall family strategy was reduced. It has been suggested that the wives had more freedom while their husbands were away,[22] but the evidence is not persuasive. It can be argued that they had less behavioural autonomy. The wives' survival depended on their behaviour meeting acceptable standards; any lapse, real or perceived, could have dire consequences as the case histories presented here demonstrate. Therefore, the wives are more likely to have erred on the side of caution and been more inhibited in their behaviour in order to preserve their reputation, and along with it access to support from husband, family, community and the Poor Law. The men abroad were under far less scrutiny, and faced far less severe consequences if any misbehaviour was discovered.

Ideas of 'autonomy' in this context can become a euphemism for additional responsibility; true autonomy would involve the wife choosing when and for how long to take on this responsibility as opposed to it being left on her shoulders indefinitely. Whereas the men could 'opt-out', resolving their need for domestic labour and home comforts by sending for their wives, or in some cases starting second families abroad, the wives had little option but to 'stick it out' or risk everything by looking for a new relationship. On balance, there is little evidence that the majority of wives 'left behind' were especially liberated or empowered by their experience; any reduction in family size or increase in literacy cannot be attributed specifically to the absence of the men as opposed to other social drivers. Instead the wives shouldered greater and broader responsibilities, freeing their husbands to pursue work opportunities abroad for the benefit of the family.

This emerges as a common feature of all the studies of wives 'left behind'. Duroux, for example, describes the women in Auvergne as being involved in a migratory dynamic that granted them closely controlled freedom while requiring more self-sacrifice of them than of their husbands.[23] Reeder's description of wives seeing separation from their husbands as being an investment is apt, but for the women it was a risky investment, both practically and emotionally.

The individual case studies and correspondence examined here reveal the great diversity of ways in which wives could experience separation from their husbands, even if those husbands were participating in very similar migration streams. In the Paynter and Dower cases it was the husband's job security and health that ultimately dictated the outcome for the wives, but these outcomes were unknowable to the wives at the time and could not determine their initial experience of their husbands' absences. Dealing with practical issues such as household management, child care and wider family commitments, with at best remote help from husbands, would have been their primary day to day concern. The wives' greater autonomy in these areas in the absence of their husbands is similar to that of widows.

The Worst Kind of Widowhood?

So often the wives 'left behind' have been likened to widows. It seems ironic that all the 'positives' attributed to the wives' situation (financial control, freedom from pregnancy, etc) would apply equally to widows, whose change in circumstances is not normally represented as liberating or empowering, albeit that individuals might find emotional compensation for their loss in the greater autonomy and rights that accompanied their widowhood. A key difference is that the wives 'left behind' were put in the position of widows without the legal recognition of that status, which alone would support the view of their situation as being worse than widowhood.

However, there was another way in which the wives' situation differed from widowhood, one which surely made the experience even more difficult, and would have been universal to all the wives 'left behind'. A widow had the certainty of knowing her condition, her husband's fate was known and fixed. She could plan and adjust her life accordingly. Unlike widows, who could remarry, the wives 'left behind' would have been subject to a degree of uncertainty combined with little power to change their circumstances, which undoubtedly justifies the unfavourable comparison with the rights and options available to widows.

A wife 'left behind' was caught in limbo and unsure of her position. Was the money going to come? When would her husband return? Would he send for her to join him next month, next year, ever? Would she, at short notice, have to pack up her home, uproot the children from everything they had ever known, leave relatives and friends, and make a long, intimidating voyage to an unknown future with a man she may not have seen for years? The ups and downs of Mary Ann Dower's experience are a good illustration of this, and although Sophia Paynter's experience turned out well, she had no way of knowing, as she lived it, that it would. Of all the challenges that the wives 'left behind' had to face: feeding and managing the children on their own, dealing with money and property issues, weathering family crises, poor communications and loneliness, by far the most difficult must have been the uncertainty, wondering when, or if, another letter might arrive, and what it might contain.

Many aspects of this experience would have been familiar to wives 'left behind' in other parts of the UK, but the sheer numbers and concentration of 'married widows' in Cornwall may have meant that individual women there were better prepared and supported than wives in communities where it wasn't such a common occurrence. Although their individual experiences of separation may have varied in many respects, all the wives were vulnerable and faced uncertain futures while their husbands were away. Given the numbers involved in Cornwall, the lack of any historical record of major social problems arising from the men's absence suggests that these women faced the challenge with quiet and stoic dignity.

Opening a window into the lives of the wives 'left behind' poses other questions concerning the impact of emigration within sending communities in Cornwall and elsewhere. For example, what were the consequences for the children raised in female-headed households in the absence of their fathers? A hint to the psychological impact comes from the family of Harriett Trewin, broken apart by the ill health of one of her daughters preventing Harriett and her children joining her husband in America. Her son, William, who was only a baby when his father left, had in his possession a letter to Harriett in which the father he never knew asked her to "Kiss the dear boy for me." After William's death in old age, it was found, falling apart, in his wallet where it is thought he carried it throughout his life.[24] In the families that were reunited how did children adjust to the changes in personal and parental dynamics, perhaps only meeting fathers when they themselves were near adulthood? One can only wonder what residue of feelings of loss, abandonment or resentment lingered in those families negatively impacted by emigration of husbands and fathers.

On a possibly more positive note, with the high incidence of return migration throughout the century, including numerous women and children spending time abroad, what influence did it have on Cornish society that so many people had experienced life in other countries? Cornish women, and men, were exposed, for example, to more liberal American attitudes to female independence.[25] Particularly worthy of study would be the impact on Cornish society of the concentrated presence of a younger generation born overseas and exposed to diverse lifestyles, environments and languages. Did this endow those generations with worldviews very different from their untravelled counterparts in other parts of the country, and how did that contribute to Cornish difference and identity?

Furthermore, it would be wrong to consider the emotional responses of the women to spousal separation without extending the same courtesy to the men by exploring the male perspective. How did men feel about, and cope with the demands of being husbands and fathers at a distance? These are all questions that have resonance for the impact of emigration on any community.

Approaching the subject of emigration from a different point of view, that of one group within the sending community, highlights important wider issues in migration studies concerning the migrants themselves. In most studies migrants are categorised as families, males or females. Whereas the presence of children or the title of 'Mrs' enables some female migrants to be identified as married, there are no clues regarding the marital status of men travelling alone. Married men are therefore aggregated into the group commonly referred to as lone or 'single' male migrants, but the decision process regarding migration for a married man is very different from that of his unmarried counterpart. The married migrant has the greater responsibility of supporting a wife and possibly children at home, and has to earn proportionally more to offset the additional expense of maintaining two homes. Therefore, when examining the motivation and actions of lone male migrants it is essential that their marital status be taken into account. A more nuanced approach to examining gendered migration is required. Not only it is desirable to distinguish married from single men in the consideration of male emigrants, it is important to disaggregate married couples from the wider 'dispersed' family as the dynamics and responsibilities between husband and wife are very different from those between parent and child, or siblings.

As migration studies increasingly recognise that emigration narratives encompass those in sending communities as well migrants, there is also need to recognise that neither is homogenous or mutually exclusive, and that marital status is an important factor in determining the actions of, and impact on, both groups. The dispersed nature of Cornish families is well known, but by focussing on the wives (those who stayed, as well as those who went and returned) it becomes clear that the transnational nuclear family was a major feature of emigration from Cornwall throughout the 19th century.

Examining the complexity of experiences, motivations and outcomes of the Cornish 'married widows' offers an addition to the, so far limited, range of historical studies of women in sending communities, and a valuable case study for further comparison. It takes us beyond the simplistic stereotype of wives 'left behind' as the passive victims of crisis migration and has revealed the true importance of their role in Cornish migration history.

Notes and References

(References are given in full where first listed and abbreviated where repeated)

Introduction

1. *Royal Cornwall Gazette*, 15 July 1876.
2. P. Payton, *Cornwall* (Alexander Associates, Fowey, 1996), p. 236. The leading work on Cornish emigration is P. Payton, *The Cornish Overseas* (Cornwall Editions, Fowey, 2005).
3. A.C. Todd, *The Cornish Miner in America* (H.E Warne, St Austell, 1967), p. 19.
4. B. Deacon, 'Cornish Emigration', unpublished paper, 1993, p. 5 quoted in Payton, *Cornish Overseas*, p. 28.
5. Examples include: Worldwide: H.C. Blackwell, *From a Dark Stream; The Story of Cornwall's Amazing People and their Impact on the World* (Dyllansow Truran, Redruth, 1986); Payton, *Cornish Overseas*. North & South America: Todd, *Cornish Miner in America*; A.C. Todd, *The Search for Silver: Cornish Miners in Mexico 1824-1947* (The Lodenek Press, 1977); A.L. Rowse, *The Cornish in America* (Dyllansow Truran, 1991); S.P. Schwartz, *The Cornish in Latin America: 'Cousin Jack' and the New World* (Cornubian Press, 2016); J. Rowe, *The Hard-Rock Men; Cornish Immigrants and the North American Mining Frontier* (Cornish Hillside Publications, 2004); R.M. James, 'Home Away From Home: Cornish Immigrants in Nineteenth-century Nevada' in P. Payton (ed.), *Cornish Studies Fifteen* (University of Exeter Press, 2007), pp. 141-163. Australia & New Zealand: P. Payton, *The Cornish Miner in Australia; Cousin Jack Down Under* (Dyllansow Truran, 1984); P. Lay, *One and All - The Cornish in New South Wales* (Heritage 2000 Plus, NSW, 1998); C. Fahey, 'From St Just to St Just Point: Cornish Migration to Nineteenth-century Victoria' in P. Payton (ed.), *Cornish Studies Fifteen* (University of Exeter Press, 2007), pp. 117-140; P. Payton, *Making Moonta - The Invention of Australia's Little Cornwall* (University of Exeter Press, 2007). South Africa: G.B. Dickerson, *Cornish Immigrants to South Africa - the Cousin Jacks' contribution to the development of mining and commerce 1820-1920* (A.A. Bakema, Cape Town, 1978); R.D. Dawe, *Cornish Pioneers in South Africa - 'Gold and Diamonds, Copper and Blood'* (Cornish Hillside Publications, 1998); J. Naurighty, 'Cornish Miners and the Witwatersrand Gold Mines in South Africa, c. 1890-1904', *Cornish History*, July 2005 (2005).
6. C. Harzig & D. Hoerder, *What is Migration History?* (Polity Press, 2009), p. 3.
7. See for example B. Deacon & S. Schwartz, 'Cornish Identities and Migration: a multi scalar approach', *Global Networks*, 7 (2007), pp. 289-306; Schwartz, *Cornish in Latin America*.
8. B. Deacon, 'Communities, Families and Migration: some evidence from Cornwall', *Family & Community History*, 10 (2007), p. 59.
9. C.B. Brettell & J.F. Hollifield, *Migration Theory: Talking Across Disciplines* (Routledge, 2008), pp. 17-20.
10. There are numerous examples of work on wives 'left behind' in 20th century migrations. A sample include: China: S. Huifen, 'Engendering Chinese Migration History: "Left-behind wives of the Nanyang Migrants" in Quanzhou before and after the Pacific War', unpublished PhD thesis, National University of Singapore (2006). India: L. Gulati, 'Coping with Male Migration', *Economic and Political Weekly*, (1987), pp. WS41-WS46. Italy: D. Gabaccia, 'When the migrants are men: Italy's women and transnationalism as a working-class way of life' in P. Sharpe (ed.), *Women, Gender and Labour Migration: Historical and global perspectives* (Routledge, 2001), pp. 190-208; D.R. Gabaccia & F. Iacovetta, *Women, Gender, and Transnational Lives: Italian Workers of the World* (University of Toronto Press, 2002). Lesotho: E. Gordon, 'An Analysis of the Impact of Labour Migration on the Lives of Women in Lesotho', *The Journal of Development Studies*, 17 (1981), pp. 59-76. Morocco: H. De Haas & A. van Rooij, 'Migration as Emancipation? The Impact of Internal Migration on the Position of Women Left Behind in Rural Morocco', *Oxford Development Studies*, 31 (2010), pp. 43-62. Philippines: R.S. Parreñas, 'Transnational

Fathering: Gendered Conflicts, Distant Disciplining and Emotional Gaps', *Journal of Ethnic and Migration Studies*, 34 (2008), pp. 1057-1072. Turkey: A. Kadioglu, 'Migration Experiences of Turkish Women: Notes from a Researcher's Diary', *International Migration*, 35 (1997), pp. 537-557; I. Koc & I. Onan, 'International Migrants' Remittances and Welfare Status of the Left-Behind Families in Turkey', *International Migration Review*, 38 (2004), pp. 78-112.
11 S. Pedraza, 'Women and Migration: The social consequences of gender', *Annual Review of Sociology*, (1991), p. 311.
12 D. Baines, *Migration in a Mature Economy: Emigration and Internal Migration in England and Wales, 1861-1900* (Cambridge University Press, 1985), pp. 157-159.
13 For example see: N.M. Howlett, 'Family and Household in a Nineteenth-Century Devonshire Village' in D. Mills & K. Schürer (eds.), *Local Communities in the Victorian Census Enumerators' Books* (Leopard's Head Press, Oxford, 1996), pp. 298-305; L. Norling, *Captain Ahab had a Wife: New England Women and the Whalefishery 1720-1870* (University of North Carolina Press, 2000); L. Abrams, *Myth and Materiality in a Woman's World: Shetland 1800-2000* (Manchester University Press, 2005); D. Cordingly, *Seafaring Women (originally published as 'Women Sailors and Sailors' Women'* (Random House, 2007); J. Hurl-Eamon, 'The Fiction of Female Dependence and the Makeshift Economy of Soldiers, Sailors, and their Wives in Eighteenth Century London', *Labor History*, 49 (2008), pp. 481-501; H. Doe, 'Travelling by Staying at Home: Women in westcountry ports and their overseas connections in the nineteenth century', *Journal Transport History*, 30 (2009), pp. 183-199; P.B. Nutting, 'Absent Husbands, Single Wives: Success, domesticity, and seminuclear families in the nineteenth-century Great Lakes world', *Journal of Family History*, 35 (2010), 329-345; M. Lincoln, *Naval Wives & Mistresses* (The History Press & National Maritime Museum, Stroud, 2011).
14 Payton, *Cornish Overseas*, p. 270.
15 P. Payton, *Cornish Farmer in Australia* (Dyllansow Truran, 1987).
16 For a description of the micro-geography of Cornish mining, see B. Deacon, 'Mining the Data: What can a quantitative approach tell us about the micro-geography of nineteenth-century Cornish mining?' in P. Payton (ed.), *Cornish Studies Eighteen* (University of Exeter Press, 2010), pp. 15-32.
17 Payton, *Cornish Overseas*, pp. 17-19.
18 S. Schwartz & R. Parker, *Lanner: a Cornish Mining Parish* (Halsgrove, 1998), p. 163; J. Mills & P. Annear, *The Book of St Day* (Halsgrove, 2003).
19 Payton, *Cornish Overseas*.
20 M. Brayshay, 'The Demography of Three West Cornwall Mining Communities 1851-1971: A Society in Decline', unpublished PhD thesis, University of Exeter (1977); M. Brayshay, 'Depopulation and Changing Household Structure in the Mining Communities of West Cornwall, 1851-71', *Local Population Studies*, 25 (1980), pp. 26-41.
21 G. Burke, 'The Decline of the Independent Bal Maiden; The Impact of Change in the Cornish Mining Industry' in A.V. John (ed.), *Unequal Opportunities: Women's Employment in England 1800-1918* (Blackwell, 1986), pp. 179-204; S.P. Schwartz, 'In Defence of Customary Rights: Labouring Women's Experience of Industrialization in Cornwall' in P. Payton (ed.), *Cornish Studies Seven* (University of Exeter Press, 1999), pp. 8-31; S.P. Schwartz, '"No Place for a Woman": Gender at Work in Cornwall's Metalliferous Mining Industry' in P. Payton (ed.), *Cornish Studies Eight* (University of Exeter Press, 2000), pp. 69-96; L. Mayers, *Balmaidens* (The Hypatia Trust, Penzance, 2004).
22 G. Magee & A. Thompson, 'Remittances Revisited: A Case Study of South Africa and the Cornish Migrant, c.1870-1914' in P. Payton (ed.), *Cornish Studies Thirteen* (University of Exeter Press, 2005), pp. 256-287; G.B. Magee & A.S. Thompson, "Lines of Credit, Debts of Obligation': Migrant remittances to Britain, c. 1875–1913', *The Economic History Review*, 59 (2006), pp. 539-577.
23 L. Bryant, 'The Cornish Family' in P. Payton (ed.), *Cornwall Since the War* (Institute of Cornish Studies & Dyllansow Truran, 1993) pp. 181-197; B. Deacon, S. Schwartz & D.

Notes and References

Holman, *The Cornish Family* (Cornwall Editions, 2004); B. Deacon, *A Concise History of Cornwall* (University of Wales Press, 2007), pp. 167-168; B. Deacon, 'Communities, families and migration: some evidence from Cornwall', *Family & Community History*, 10 (2007), pp. 49-60.

24 Cornish Mining World Heritage Site website. http://www.cornish-mining.org.uk/delving-deeper/home-life. [accessed: 17 November 2014].

25 R.R. Blewett, 'The Village of St Day in the Parish of Gwennap', *Board of Education Short Course for Teachers in Public Elementary Schools on 'The Citizen in the Modern World'*, (1935).

26 B. Deacon & P. Payton, 'Re-inventing Cornwall: Culture Change on the European Periphery' in P. Payton (ed.), *Cornish Studies One* (University of Exeter Press, 1993), p. 67.

27 Payton, *Cornish Overseas*, p. 28.

28 Payton, *Cornish Overseas*. pp. 9 & 26-27.

29 Todd, *Cornish Miner in America*, frontispiece.

30 Schwartz, 'In Defence of Customary Rights' and 'No Place for a Woman'; S.P. Schwartz, 'Cornish Migration Studies: an Epistemological and Paradigmatic Critique' in P. Payton (ed.), *Cornish Studies Ten* (University of Exeter Press, 2002), pp. 136-165; S.P. Schwartz, 'Cornish Migration to Latin America: A global and transnational perspective', unpublished PhD thesis, University of Exeter (2003); S.P. Schwartz, 'Migration Networks and the Transnationalization of Social Capital: Cornish Migration to Latin America, A Case Study' in P. Payton (ed.), *Cornish Studies Thirteen* (University of Exeter Press, 2005), pp. 256-287.

31 Bryant, 'The Cornish Family'.

32 Mayers, *Balmaidens*.

33 G. Burke, 'The Impact of Industrial Change on Working Class Family Life in the Mining Districts of Nineteenth-Century Cornwall', *Bulletin of the Society for the Study of Labour History*, 48 (1984), pp. 13-14; 'The Cornish Diaspora of the Nineteenth Century' in S. Marks & P. Richardson (eds.), *International Labour Migration: Historical Perspectives* (Institute of Commonwealth Studies, London, 1984), pp. 57-75; 'The Decline of the Independent Bal Maiden; The Impact of Change in the Cornish Mining Industry' in A.V. John (ed.), *Unequal Opportunities: Women's Employment in England 1800-1918* (Blackwell, 1986), pp. 179-204.

34 Payton, *Cornish Overseas*, pp. 26-27.

35 M. Harper, *Emigrant Homecomings: The return movement of emigrants 1600-2000* (Manchester University Press, 2005).

36 E. Richards, *Britannia's Children: Emigration from England, Scotland, Wales and Ireland since 1600* (Hambledon and London, 2004), p. 164.

37 W.D. Jones, *Wales in America - Scranton and the Welsh 1860-1920* (University of Wales Press, 1993), p. 215.

38 K.A. Miller, *Emigrants and Exiles - Ireland and the Irish Exodus to North America* (Oxford University, 1985), p. 292.

39 T.M. Devine, *To the Ends of the Earth: Scotland's Global Diaspora 1750-2010* (Penguin Books, 2011), p. 205.

40 M. Harper, *Adventurers & Exiles - The Great Scottish Exodus* (Profile Books, 2004). pp. 283-324.

41 Abrams, *Myth and Materiality*.

42 No diary of a wife 'left behind' describing her experience of managing on her own in Cornwall has been located at the time of going to press.

43 D.A. Gerber, *Authors of Their Lives: The personal correspondence of British Immigrants to North America in the Nineteenth Century* (New York University, 2006), p. 7.

44 D. Fitzpatrick, *Oceans of Consolation: Personal accounts of Irish Migration to Australia* (Cork University Press, 1995) contains some brief correspondence by Irishwoman Mary Anne Dooley to her family after her husband emigrated to Australia - the only published letters from a wife 'left behind' found to date. See also: Gerber, *Authors of Their Lives*, P. O'Farrell, *The Irish in Australia* (New South Wales University Press, 1987); C. Erickson, *Invisible Immigrants: The adaptation of English and Scottish immigrants in nineteenth century America* (Cornell University Press, reprint, 1990).

45 R. Arnold, *The Farthest Promised Land - English Villages, New Zealand Immigrants of the 1870s* (Wellington, New Zealand, 1981), p. 10.

46 J. Rowe, *Cornwall in the Age of Industrial Revolution* (Cornish Hillside Publications, 1993), pp. 320-321.
47 H. Thomas, *Cornish Mining Interviews* (The Camborne Printing & Stationery Co Ltd, 1896), p. 244.
48 *Report of the Royal Commission on Divorce and Matrimonial causes*; Evidence, Vol II (Marriages, etc: Divorce), British Parliamentary Papers, 1912-13 (Cd. 6480), p. 26 (12,838).
49 L.L. Price, '"West Barbary:" or, Notes on the System of Work and Wages in the Cornish Mines', *Journal of the Royal Statistical Society*, 51 (1888), p. 507.
50 *Royal Cornwall Gazette*, 15 July 1876.
51 Blewett, 'The Village of St Day', pp. 3-4.
52 Schwartz, 'Cornish Migration Studies', p. 148.
53 L. Reeder, *Widows in White: Migration and Transformation of Rural Italian Women, Sicily, 1880-1920* (University of Toronto Press, 2003); C.B. Brettell, *Men who Migrate, Women who Wait: Population and history in a Portuguese parish* (Princeton University Press, 1986)
54 Harzig & Hoerder, *What is Migration History?*, p. 3.
55 Deacon, *Concise History of Cornwall*, pp. 164-165, citing G. Burke, 'The Cornish Miner and the Cornish Mining Industry: 1870-1921', unpublished PhD thesis, University of London (1981), p. 451.
56 Schwartz, 'Cornish Migration Studies', p. 159.
57 Individual male/female duality means that culturally assigned masculine or feminine traits do not necessarily correspond with biologically determined sex.
58 Reeder, *Widows in White*, p. 102.
59 Brayshay, 'Demography of Three West Cornwall Mining Communities' (1977) and 'Depopulation and changing household structure', p. 39.
60 C. Archambault, 'Women Left Behind? Migration, Spousal Separation, and the Autonomy of Rural Women in Ugweno, Tanzania', *Signs*, 35 (2010), p. 923.
61 Schwartz, 'Cornish Migration Studies', p. 148.
62 Reeder, *Widows in White*; D. Gabaccia, 'When the migrants are men: Italy's women and transnationalism as a working-class way of life' in P. Sharpe (ed.), *Women, Gender and Labour Migration: Historical and global perspectives* (Routledge, 2001), p. 190-208; Brettell, *Men who Migrate, Women who Wait*; See also: R. Duroux, 'The Temporary Migration of Males and the Power of Females in a Stem-family Society: The case of 19th-century Auvergne', *The History of the Family*, 6 (2001), pp. 33-49; C. Sarasúa, 'Leaving Home to Help the Family? Male and female temporary migrants in eighteenth- and nineteenth-century Spain' in P. Sharpe (ed.), *Women, Gender and Labour Migration*, pp. 29-59; B.A. Engel, 'The Woman's Side: Male Out-Migration and the Family Economy in Kostroma Province', *Slavic Review*, 45 (1986), pp. 257-271. B.A. Engel, *Between the Fields and the City. Women, Work and the Family in Russia, 1861-1914* (Cambridge University Press, 1994).
63 L. Peavy & U. Smith, *Women in Waiting in the Western Movement* (University of Oklahoma, 1994); C. Twomey, *Deserted and Destitute: Motherhood, Wife-Desertion and Colonial Welfare* (Australian Scholarly Publications, 2002). Spousal separation arising from gold fever is also touched upon by Elizabeth Jameson in 'Where Have All the Young Men Gone?' in K.N. Owens (ed.), *Riches for all - The California Gold Rush and the World* (University of Nebraska Press, 2002).
64 Reeder, *Widows in White*, p. 57.
65 Gabaccia, 'When the migrants are men', p. 204.
66 C. Brettell, *Men who migrate*, and 'Migration' in D.I. Kertzer & M. Barbagli (eds.), *Family Life in the Long Nineteenth Century 1789-1913* (Yale University Press, 2002), p. 235.
67 Schwartz, 'Cornish Migration Studies', p. 148.
68 Burke, 'The Cornish Miner', p. 448.
69 Deacon, Schwartz & Holman, *Cornish Family*, pp. 43-45.
70 This research combined quantitative analysis and qualitative evidence, balancing the potential opposing biases of the separate quantitative and qualitative approaches. The nature of the qualitative evidence, often arising out of the social problems encountered by the wives, has a natural tendency to emphasize the more dramatic and negative aspects of some

Notes and References

wives' experience, while quantitative analysis of the census returns encompassed a wider range of wives and the more mundane aspects of their lives. Notes on this methodology together with the maps, graphs and figures produced by this research can be found online at: www.humblehistory.com. For full details see: L. Trotter, '19th Century Emigration for Cornwall as Experienced by the Wives 'Left Behind', Unpublished PhD thesis, University of Exeter (2015). See also: L. Trotter, ''Husband Abroad': Quantifying spousal separation associated with emigration in nineteenth-century Cornwall' in P. Payton (ed.), *Cornish Studies Twenty* (University of Exeter Press, 2012), pp. 180-198; L. Trotter, 'Desperate? Destitute? Deserted? Questioning perceptions of miners' wives in Cornwall during the great emigration, 1851-1891' in P. Payton (ed.), *Cornish Studies Nineteen* (University of Exeter Press, 2011), pp. 195-224, (based on the author's MA dissertation, University of Exeter (2010).

71 For a discussion on deliberate male desertion through emigration, see: O. Anderson, 'Emigration and Marriage Break-Up in Mid-Victorian England', *The Economic History Review*, 50 (1997), pp. 104-109.

1. Considerable numbers?

1. Dickerson, *Cornish Immigrants to South Africa*, p. 7.
2. Payton, *Cornish Overseas*, pp. 17-18.
3. For Cornish emigration to Latin America see: Schwartz, *Cornish in Latin America*; Payton, *Cornish Overseas*, pp. 90-128.
4. A.K. Hamilton-Jenkin, *The Cornish Miner* (David & Charles, Newton Abbot, 1972), pp. 325-326.
5. *West Briton*, 2 February 1849.
6. Deacon, Schwartz & Holman, *Cornish Family*, p. 43.
7. Although it is an excellent source of demographic data for the 19th century, the census is far from infallible and the caveats for its interpretation are well known and documented. See: E. Higgs, *Making Sense of the Census Revisited – Census Records for England and Wales 1801-1901* (Institute of Historical Research, London, 2005).
8. Census of England and Wales, 1841, Census Enumerators Book. (HO107/137 ED16 viewed on microfilm, Cornish Studies Library)
9. Schwartz, *Cornish in Latin America*; Mills & Annear, *Book of St Day*, p. 125.
10. Schwartz and Parker cite Gray's Terrace in Lanner. Schwartz & Parker, *Lanner*, p. 146. However analysis of the census returns for 1871-91 does not support the accuracy of this memory.
11. Blewett, 'The Village of St Day'.
12. Deacon cites Sheila Johansson, 'The demographic transition in England: mortality and fertility change in Cornwall 1800-1900', unpublished PhD thesis, University of Indiana (1974), p.276. Deacon, *Concise History of Cornwall*, p. 162.
13. In Camborne, Redruth and St Just 23-30% of the heads of households between 1851 and 1871 were female. Brayshay, 'The Demography of Three West Cornwall Mining Communities, pp. 349-350. In Lanner in 1851 it was just under 25%. Schwartz & Parker, *Lanner*, p. 29.
14. Abrams, *Myth and Materiality*, p. 65 & 75.
15. Deacon, Schwartz & Holman, *Cornish Family*, p. 43.
16. Deacon, *Concise History of Cornwall*, p. 162.
17. L. Trotter, 'Desperate? Destitute? Deserted? (2011), pp. 198-201. Methodological differences might account for Brayshay's lower figure, which was based on a 10% sample that may have missed clusters of wives, compared with the complete parish population analysis of the Gwennap study.
18. Schwartz & Parker, *Lanner*, p. 29. It should be noted that there are inconsistencies in the calculation given in this work: in 1891, of the 500 households in Lanner, 105 or 32% are described as being headed by widows. However, 105 out of 500 equates to 21% rather than 32%.
19. Brayshay, 'Demography of Three West Cornwall Mining Communities', p. 350. Table 58.
20. Trotter, 'Desperate? Destitute? Deserted?' (2011), p. 200.
21. Deacon, *Concise History of Cornwall*, p. 162.
22. See Table 1 in Trotter, 'Desperate? Destitute? Deserted?' (2011), p. 201., citing

data from Brayshay, 'Demography of Three West Cornwall Mining Communities', p. 350 and Schwartz & Parker, *Lanner*, p. 163.
23 The contribution in Shetland was even greater with half of the female heads of household being widows and 20-30% single women. Abrams, *Myth and Materiality*, p. 75.
24 Brayshay, 'Demography of Three West Cornwall Mining Communities', p. 351.
25 These figures exclude any wives of men likely to be absent for reasons other than migration.
26 Payton, *Cornwall*, pp. 203-207.
27 B. Deacon, 'In Search of the Missing 'Turn': the Spatial Dimension and Cornish Studies' in P. Payton (ed.), *Cornish Studies Eight* (University of Exeter Press, 2000), pp. 213-230. See also R. Perry, '"The Breadwinners': Gender, Locality and Diversity in Late Victorian and Edwardian Cornwall' in P. Payton (ed.), *Cornish Studies Eight* (University of Exeter Press, 2000), pp. 115-126; K. Milden, "Are You Church or Chapel?' Perceptions of Spatial and Spiritual Identity within Cornish methodism' in P. Payton (ed.), *Cornish Studies Twelve* (University of Exeter Press, 2004), pp. 144-165; P. Tremewan, 'The Relief of Poverty in Cornwall, 1780-1881 - from collateral support to respectability' in P. Payton (ed.), *Cornish Studies Sixteen* (University of Exeter Press, 2008), pp .78-103.
28 B. Deacon, 'Communities, families and migration', p. 59.
29 Schwartz, *Cornish in Latin America*, pp. 361-380.
30 These distribution maps can be found online at www.humblehistory.com and in L. Trotter, '19th Century Emigration for Cornwall as Experienced by the Wives 'Left Behind', Unpublished PhD thesis, University of Exeter (2015).
31 These distribution maps can be found online at www.humblehistory.com and in Trotter (2015).
32 Payton, *Cornish Overseas*, p. 257.
33 Christopher Candy Ellis left Cornwall in 1854 and served in the Union Army. Ellis family history (http://trees.ancestry.co.uk/tree/31099258/person/12365905801) [accessed 11 December 2013].
34 *Royal Cornwall Gazette*, 25 July 1867.
35 *Royal Cornwall Gazette*, 18 July 1867.
36 *Royal Cornwall Gazette*, 18 July 1867.
37 *Royal Cornwall Gazette*, 25 July 1867.
38 *Royal Cornwall Gazette*, 25 July 1867.
39 The other parishes in the Redruth Poor Law Union were Gwinear, Gwithian, Illogan, Redruth, Phillack and Stithians.
40 *Royal Cornwall Gazette*, 25 July 1867.
41 *Royal Cornwall Gazette*, 15 August 1867.
42 *A Directory of Redruth and its Neighbourhood*, (John S. Doidge, 1866)
43 *Royal Cornwall Gazette*, 15 July 1876.

2. Money from abroad

1 G. Magee & A. Thompson, *Empire and Globalisation: Networks of people goods and capital in the British World, c.1850-1914*. (Cambridge University Press, 2010), pp. 64 & 97-105.
2 M.L. Shandley, *Feminism, Marriage and the Law in Victorian England, 1850-1895* (Princeton University Press, 1989), p. 190.
3 Brayshay, 'The Demography of Three West Cornwall Mining Communities, pp. 349-351. Schwartz & Parker, *Lanner*, p. 37; Carharrack Old Cornwall Society, *The Book of Carharrack* (Halsgrove, 2003), p. 26 & 49.
4 Higgs, *Making Sense of the Census*, p. 111.
5 In 1896 it was estimated that remittances to Redruth alone were £1000-£1300 a week. Payton, *Cornish Overseas*, p. 352. By the early 1900s every mail arriving in Cornwall was thought to be bringing in £20,000 to £30,000. Magee & Thompson, *Empire and Globalisation*, p. 103.
6 R. Perry, 'The Making of Modern Cornwall, 1800-2000' in P. Payton (ed.), *Cornish Studies Ten* (University of Exeter Press, 2002), p. 175; Schwartz, 'Cornish Migration Studies, pp. 149-152.
7 Magee & Thompson, *Empire and Globalisation*, p. 98.
8 Gerber, *Authors of Their Lives*, p. 157.
9 Mary Hodge, Letter, 15 February 1851, Moira Tangye ion.
10 Joel Eade, Letter, 11 March 1864, Moira Tangye Collection.
11 Gerber, *Authors of Their Lives*, p. 151.
12 Henry Richards, Letters, 6 June 1854, 22 September 1856, Moira Tangye Collection.
13 Henry Richards, Letter, 15 September 1867, Moira Tangye Collection.
14 F. Michell, *Annals of an Ancient Cornish*

Notes and References

Town - Redruth (Frank Michell, Redruth, 1979), p. 176.
15 *West Briton*, 21 March 1862.
16 *Royal Cornwall Gazette*, 15 August 1867.
17 John Gundry, Letter, 1864, Moira Tangye Collection.
18 Joel Eade, Letter, 1 February 1864, Moira Tangye Collection..
19 J. Bogle, *Caroline Chisholm - The Emigrant's Friend* (Gracewing Books, Leominster, 1993)
20 Magee & Thompson, 'Lines of Credit, Debts of Obligation', p. 542.
21 Magee & Thompson, 'Lines of Credit, Debts of Obligation', p. 543; *Royal Cornwall Gazette*, 20 May 1858.
22 J. Tyacke, *Cornwall Family History Society Journal*, March 1997, p. 15.
23 *Colorado Genealogical Chronicles, Vol. XXVIII – Register of British International Money Orders Issued 1871-1875 at Central City, Colorado*, Foothills Genealogical Society, 1997, copy at Royal Institute of Cornwall.
24 Joel Eade, Letter, 1 February 1864, Moira Tangye Collection.
25 In 1856 there were 23 banks in Cornwall, including branches. *West Briton*, 29 August 1856.
26 William Dawe, Letter, 21 February 1885, Moira Tangye Collection.
27 Mary Trescowthick, Letter, 12 December 1876, Moira Tangye Collection.
28 John J. King, Letter, 23 November 1900, Moira Tangye Collection.
29 *Cornishman*, 24 January 1884.
30 51% (280 out of a total of 539). This was higher than the figure of 39% for Cornwall as a whole. *House of Commons Parliamentary Paper 3562. Twenty-sixth annual report of the Registrar-General of Births, Deaths, and Marriages in England, 1865.* p.vii & 15.
31 D.J. Steel, *National Index of Parish Registers. Vol 1: Sources of birth, marriages and deaths before 1837* (London, 1968), p. 57.
32 Elizabeth Datson, Letter, 9 November 1886, Moira Tangye Collection.
33 *Royal Cornwall Gazette*, 3 June 1869.
34 *Royal Cornwall Gazette*, 22 September 1854.
35 *West Briton*, 11 September 1857.
36 *Royal Cornwall Gazette*, 15 August 1867.
37 Alfred Jenkin letter books, Courtney Library, Royal Institution of Cornwall (HJ/1/17-18)
38 *Carlisle Journal*, 2 January 1852.
39 Henry Richards, Letter, 23 October 1857 Moira Tangye Collection.
40 Michell, *Annals of an Ancient Cornish Town*, p. 175.
41 Dawe, *Cornish Pioneers in South Africa*, p. 228.
42 Blewett, 'The Village of St Day', p. 3.
43 Michell, *Annals of an Ancient Cornish Town*, p. 202.
44 *Royal Cornwall Gazette*, 15 December 1898.
45 Dawe, *Cornish Pioneers in South Africa*, p. 228.
46 Hamilton-Jenkin, *Cornish Miner*, pp. 325-326.
47 *Cornwall Family History Society Journal*, October 1976, p. 11.
48 'The Cornish in Latin America' website. http://projects.exeter.ac.uk/cornishlatin/contractwilliamnicholls.htm. [accessed 19 September 2013].
49 Some attempts at quantification have been made using data on money orders found in the Post Office Archives, but this also excludes remittances arriving as cash. See Magee & Thompson, *Empire and Globalisation*.
50 Todd, *Search for Silver*, pp. 144-146.
51 Schwartz, *Cornish in Latin America*, pp. 387-391.
52 *Cornishman*, 19 January 1893.
53 John Stanton Jr letter book, Courtney Library, Royal Institution of Cornwall (LL/STA/1).
54 The historical currency converter on the Measuring Worth website calculated $20 as equal to £3.69 decimal. http://www.measuringworth.com/calculators/exchange/index.php [accessed: 23 Feb 2013]
55 William Arundel Paynter, Letters, 7 February 1859, 24 February 1859 and 15 January 1860, Cornwall Record Office, FS.3/1033/102, 104 & 111.
56 John Dower, Letters, 1865-1868, John Tregenza Papers, series 14, MSS0049, Barr Smith Library, The University of Adelaide.
57 Alfred Jenkin letter books, (HJ/1/17 & 18). Letters 17 June and 8 October 1836, and 17 January 1837.
58 Deacon, Schwartz & Holman, *Cornish Family*, p. 158.

3. Making Ends Meet

1. L. Davidoff, *Worlds Between: Historical Perspectives on Gender and Class* (Polity Press, 1995). pp. 151-154; R.B. Shoemaker, *Gender in English Society, 1650-1850 - the emergence of separate spheres?* (Routledge, 2013), pp. 203-207.
2. J. Bailey, *Unquiet Lives: Marriage and Marriage Breakdown in England 1660-1800* (Cambridge University Press, 2003), pp. 70-72.
3. Schwartz, *Cornish in Latin America*, pp. 79, 430-432.
4. Higgs, *Making Sense of the Census*. pp. 102-103.
5. Mayers, *Balmaidens*, p. 30.
6. N. Phillips, *Women in Business, 1700-1850* (The Boydell Press, 2006), p. 6.
7. J. Perkin, *Women and Marriage in Nineteenth Century England* (Routledge, 1989), p. 295.
8. *Cornishman*, 31 May 1883.
9. Additional information courtesy of descendant Courtenay V. Smale, March 2018.
10. Interview with Lillian Harry broadcast in 'Destination America: Episode 8: Made in Britain' by Thames Television, 1976. Copy archived by The Pennsylvania Public Libraries Film Centre of the State Library of Pennsylvania. https://archive.org/details/destinationamerica3madeinbritainreel2
11. Mayers, *Balmaidens*, pp. 151-164.
12. *Cornishman*, 12 December 1878.
13. *Cornishman*, 2 February 1897.
14. *Cornishman*, 3 November 1898.
15. Michell, *Annals of an Ancient Cornish Town*, p. 166.
16. *Cornishman*, 4 September 1879.
17. *Cornishman*, 4 September 1879.
18. Twomey, *Deserted and Destitute*, pp. 19-35.
19. Brayshay, 'Demography of Three West Cornwall Mining Communities', p. 81.
20. *Cornishman*, 6 May 1886.
21. Passenger list, *SS City of Rome*, arrived New York 21 May 1886; 1900 US Federal census. [accessed via www.ancestry.co.uk]
22. *Cornishman*, 31 May 1888.
23. Phillips, *Women in Business*; H. Doe, *Enterprising Women and Shipping in the Nineteenth Century* (The Boydell Press, 2009).
24. Bailey, *Unquiet Lives*, pp. 69-76.
25. Phillips, *Women in Business*.
26. Doe, *Enterprising Women*, p. 17.
27. J. Maltby, *The Wife's Administration of the Earnings? Working-Class Women and Savings in the Mid-Nineteenth Century*, 2009, retrieved 28/11/2014 http://eprints.whiterose.ac.uk/8795/.
28. *Cornishman*, 19 January 1882.
29. *Cornishman*, 10 May 1894.
30. N.E. Hannan, *Letters of a South African Miner 1898-1904; Joseph Tucker to his son Joseph Wherry Tucker* (Norman E. Hannan, 1981).
31. *Cornishman*, 5 June 1879.
32. *Cornishman*, 18 February 1892.
33. *Cornishman*, 7 December 1893.
34. Power of Attorney, William Thomas Tregonning, private collection of Lorna Leadbetter.
35. Schwartz, 'Cornish Migration Studies', p. 148.
36. Burke, 'The Decline of the Independent Bal Maiden', p. 199; Perkin, *Women and Marriage*, p. 146; G.S. Frost, *Living in Sin: Cohabiting as husband and wife in nineteenth century England* (Manchester University Press), pp. 78-79; Deacon, Schwartz & Holman, *Cornish Family*, p. 53.
37. K. Gleadle, *British Women in the Nineteenth Century* (Palgrave, 2001), p. 125.
38. Deacon, Schwartz & Holman, *Cornish Family*, p. 53.
39. Deacon estimates that a quarter of miners in Redruth, and as many as a half in St Agnes, had access to such plots. Deacon, *Concise History of Cornwall*, p. 126.
40. Bryant, 'The Cornish Family', p. 186. For an explanation of the importance of smallholding to Cornish mining families, see D. Rose, 'Home Ownership, 'Subsistence and Historical Change: The mining district of West Cornwall in the late nineteenth century' in N. Thrift & P. Williams (eds.) *Class and space - the making of urban society* (Routledge & Kegan Paul, 1987).
41. John Dower, Letter, 20 October 1865, John Tregenza Papers.
42. Rose, 'Home Ownership,' p. 119.
43. Brettell, *Men who Migrate*, p. 95; Brettell, 'Migration', p. 235.
44. Duroux, 'The Temporary Migration of Males, p. 37.
45. Reeder, *Widows in White*, p. 156.

Notes and References

46 Jameson, 'Where Have All the Young Men Gone?', p. 221.
47 John Dower, Letter, 18 June 1866, John Tregenza Papers.
48 Schwartz & Parker, *Lanner*, p. 165.
49 The Cahill Partnership & Cornwall Archaeological Unit, 'Cornwall Industrial Settlements Initiative Redruth and Plain-an-Gwarry (Camborne/Redruth Area)', (2002).
50 *Cornishman*, 5 March 1891.
51 *Cornishman*, 15 September 1892.
52 *Royal Cornwall Gazette*, 18 July 1867. In 1865 it was reported that unprecedented emigration had left many traders affected by bad debts, *West Briton*, 22 September 1865, R.M. Barton, *Life in Cornwall in the Late Nineteenth Century (D. Bradford Barton, Truro, 1972)*, p. 136.
53 *Cornishman*, 22 July 1897.
54 *Cornishman*, 19 March 1884.
55 *Royal Cornwall Gazette*, 17 August 1855.
56 *West Briton*, 14 & 21 March 1862.
57 *Cornishman*, 24 January 1895.
58 Bailey, *Unquiet Lives*, pp. 56-59.
59 Such notices appeared regularly in the pages of the *West Briton*.
60 *West Briton*, 9 May 1862.
61 *West Briton*, 26 March 1858.
62 *West Briton*, 28 Apr 1870. A husband was technically only liable for debts incurred by his wife as his agent in purchasing necessary goods and services such as food, clothing, accommodation and medical care. Bailey, *Unquiet Lives*, p. 57.
63 *Cornishman*, 24 January 1895.
64 *Royal Cornwall Gazette*, 24 January 1895.
65 *Royal Cornwall Gazette*, 25 April 1895.
66 *Royal Cornwall Gazette*, 25 April 1895.
67 *Cornishman*, 24 January 1895.
68 Blewett, 'The Village of St Day', p. 3.
69 Schwartz, *Cornish in Latin America*, p. 408-411.
70 *Royal Cornwall Gazette*, 25 April 1895.
71 *Cornishman*, 24 January 1895.
72 *Royal Cornwall Gazette*, 24 January 1895.
73 For a discussion on the legal interpretation of coverture see Phillips, *Women in Business*. pp. 23-47.
74 *Cornishman*, 30 June 1892.
75 Tremewan, 'The Relief of Poverty in Cornwall', pp. 78-103.

4. 'If you can accord'

1 Bryant, 'The Cornish Family', pp. 181-197; Deacon, Schwartz & Holman, *Cornish Family*.
2 Bryant, 'The Cornish Family', p. 186 & 192.
3 Deacon, Schwartz & Holman, *Cornish Family*. pp. 44-45.
4 A. Burton, *Richard Trevithick, Giant of Steam* (Aurum Press, 2000), pp. 208-209; P.M. Hosken, *The Oblivion of Richard Trevithick* (The Trevithick Society, Camborne, 2011), pp. 169 & 263.
5 *Cornishman*, 23 February 1899. More of Mary Ann's story is told in Chapter 11.
6 *Cornishman*, 29 August 1895.
7 *Cornishman*, 15 September 1892.
8 Brayshay, 'The Demography of Three West Cornwall Mining Communities. See also M. Anderson, *Family Structure in Nineteenth Century Lancashire* (Cambridge University Press, 1971).
9 *Royal Cornwall Gazette*, 18 July 1867.
10 For Camborne, Redruth and St Just see Brayshay, 'Demography of Three West Cornwall Mining Communities', p. 360, and Brayshay, 'Depopulation and Changing Household Structure, p. 37-39. Tywardreath and West Cornwall figures from Deacon, Schwartz & Holman, *Cornish Family*. pp. 43-44.
11 For research methodology see Trotter (2015).
12 J.R. Gillis, *For Better or Worse: British Marriages, 1600 to the Present* (Oxford University Press, 1985), p. 234; Schwartz & Parker, *Lanner*, p. 163. *Report of the Royal Commission on Divorce and Matrimonial Causes* (Cd. 6480), p. 26 (12,838).
13 See detailed graphs on the author's website: www.humblehistory.com
14 Bryant, 'The Cornish Family', p. 192.
15 Brayshay, 'Depopulation and changing household structure', p. 39.
16 Joel Eade, Letter, February 1864, Moira Tangye collection.
17 Additional information courtesy of descendant Teresa Farris, April 2012.
18 'Memories of Sarah Glasson', *Cornwall Family History Society Journal*, No. 93, September 1999, p. 30-31.
19 Additional information courtesy of descendant Margaret Stevens, February 2013.

20 *Cornishman*, 24 May 1917.
21 See, for example, the letters from John Dower to his wife that make many references to married colleagues in Australia whose wives in Cornwall who are known to her. The University of Adelaide, Barr Smith Library, John Tregenza Papers, series 14, MSS0049.
22 Howlett, 'Family and Household', pp. 298-300.
23 Howlett, 'Family and Household', p. 302.
24 Additional information courtesy of descendant Linda Lowrey, July 2012.
25 Bryant, 'The Cornish Family,' p. 183.
26 Additional information courtesy of descendant Allan Lance, July 2012.
27 A 'row' is the name given in Cornwall to a terrace of small cottages that were not built as a unified architectural unit but constructed independently.
28 Additional information courtesy of descendant Patricia Woolcock, August 2012).
29 Additional information courtesy of descendant Kitty Quayle, May 2012.
30 Schwartz & Parker, *Lanner*, p. 89.
31 Duroux, 'The Temporary Migration of Males, p. 37.
32 *Cornishman*, 24 January 1889.
33 Ann Goldsworthy, Letter, 18 February 1861, private collection of descendant Amanda Drake.
34 M.K. Nelson, 'How Men Matter:' Housework and self-provisioning among rural single-mothers and married-couple families in Vermont, US', *Feminist Economics*, 10(2004), p. 13.
35 Nelson, 'How Men Matter', p. 16.
36 Nelson, 'How Men Matter', pp. 20-26.
37 Nelson, 'How Men Matter', p. 24.
38 *Cornishman*, 19 January 1888.

5. Deserted, Desperate & Destitute?

1 Deacon, *Concise History of Cornwall*, pp. 126-127.
2 For the background to the Poor Law see G.R. Boyer, *An Economic History of the English Poor Law, 1750-1850* (Cambridge University Press, 1990); F. Driver, *Power and Pauperism - The Workhouse System 1843-1884* (Cambridge University Press, 1993); D. Englander, *Poverty and Poor Law Reform in Britain: From Chadwick to Booth, 1834-1914* (Longman, 1998); L.H. Lees, *The Solidarities of Strangers: the English poor laws and the people, 1700-1948* (Cambridge University Press, 1998); A. Brundage, *The English Poor Laws, 1700-1930* (Palgrave, 2002). For the treatment of women, see M. Levine-Clark, 'Engendering Relief: Women, Ablebodiedness, and the New Poor Law in Early Victorian England', *Journal of Women's History*, 11.4 (2000), 107-130.
3 S. King & A. Tomkins, *The Poor in England 1700-1850 - An economy of makeshifts* (Manchester University Press, 2003). pp. 39-75.
4 Tremewan, 'The Relief of Poverty in Cornwall'.
5 *Royal Cornwall Gazette*, 14 January 1853.
6 Philippa was still a pauper in the 1881 census when she was lodging elsewhere.
7 Higgs, *Making Sense of the Census*, p. 83.
8 Additional information courtesy of descendant Courtenay V. Smale, March 2018.
9 Minutes of the Redruth Board of Guardians, 1857, Cornwall Record Office, PURED/1.
10 Payton, *Cornish Overseas*, pp. 262-264.
11 *West Briton*, 23 August 1867.
12 Although populated by many of the same people involved with the various Cornish boards of guardians, the 1867 committee and its Distress Fund operated as a charity outside the Poor Law, and used its funds in ways that the guardians could not under Poor Law rulings, eg. providing clothing and bedding, and helping 'deserted' wives to join their husbands abroad.
13 Rowe, *Cornwall in the Age of Industrial Revolution*, p. 321.
14 *Royal Cornwall Gazette*, 25 July 1867.
15 *Royal Cornwall Gazette*, 18 July 1867; 25 July 1867.
16 *Royal Cornwall Gazette*, 18 July 1867.
17 *Royal Cornwall Gazette*, 25 July 1867.
18 *West Briton*, 2 June 1870.
19 *Royal Cornwall Gazette*, 25 July 1867.
20 *Cornishman*, 31 October 1878.
21 Michell, *Annals of an Ancient Cornish Town*, p. 166.
22 *West Briton*, 26 May 1870; *Cornishman*, 20 February 1879.
23 *Royal Cornwall Gazette*, 23 November 1877.

Notes and References

24. *Royal Cornwall Gazette*, 21 February 1879.
25. *Royal Cornwall Gazette*, 30 November 1877.
26. *Cornish Telegraph*, 25 December 1877.
27. Royal Cornwall Gazette, 21 December 1877.
28. *Royal Cornwall Gazette*, 7 March 1879.
29. *Royal Cornwall Gazette*, 21 February 1879.
30. *Royal Cornwall Gazette*, 30 November 1877; 21 December 1877; *Cornishman*, 12 December 1878.
31. *Royal Cornwall Gazette*, 21 February 1879.
32. Rowe, *Cornwall in the Age of Industrial Revolution*, p. 321.
33. *Cornishman*, 6 January 1887.
34. *Cornishman*, 23 February 1888.
35. *Cornishman*, 21 December 1893.
36. *Cornishman*, 17 June 1897.
37. *Cornishman*, 30 June 1898.
38. *Royal Cornwall Gazette*, 15 December 1898.
39. *Cornishman*, 30 June 1898.
40. Three were in St Agnes, two in St Mary's parish and one each in Kenwyn, Perranzabuloe and Kea, *Royal Cornwall Gazette*, 15 December 1898.
41. *Royal Cornwall Gazette*, 9 February 1899.
42. *Cornishman*, 18 May 1899.
43. *Cornishman*, 1 September 1898; *Royal Cornwall Gazette*, 18 May 1899.
44. *Cornishman*, 26 August 1897.
45. *Cornishman*, 20 July 1893, October 1893; 1 March 1894; 30 August 1894; 8 November 1894.
46. *Cornishman*, 10 May 1894.
47. *Cornishman*, 22 December 1892.
48. *New York Sun*, 19 October 1899; *Cornishman*, 14 March 1901; 4 April 1901; 21 November 1901.
49. *Cornishman*, 13 February 1902.
50. Michell, *Annals of an Ancient Cornish Town*, p. 206.
51. *Cornishman*, 12 December 1878.
52. Price, 'West Barbary', p. 507.
53. Thomas, *Cornish Mining Interviews*, p. 244.
54. S. Webb & B. Webb, *English Poor Law Policy* (Frank Cass, London, 1910), p. 6.
55. M. Levine-Clark, 'From 'Relief' to 'Justice and Protection': The Maintenance of Deserted Wives, British Masculinity and Imperial Citizenship, 1870–1920', *Gender & History*, 22 (2010), p. 304.
56. A. Kidd, *State, Society and the Poor in Nineteenth-Century England* (Macmillan Press, 1999). pp. 141-143. Anna Clark traces the evolution, as viewed by the poor laws, of the male breadwinner wage and the dependent working-class wife through three stages: from a privilege and responsibility, through a reward for respectability by the 1870s, to a right by the early 20th century. A. Clark, 'The New Poor Law and the Breadwinner Wage: Contrasting Assumptions', *Journal of Social History*, 34 (2000), 261-281.
57. The Poor Law Commission was replaced by the Poor Law Board in 1847, which in turn was replaced by the Local Government Board in 1871. See P. Carter & N. Whistance, *Living the Poor Life; a Guide to the Poor Law Union Correspondence, c.1834 to 1871*, held at The National Archives (British Association for Local History, 2011), p. 6.
58. The workhouse test derived its name because it 'tested' the level of destitution. Conditions inside were deliberately made so harsh that only those who were truly desperate would contemplate applying.
59. Webb & Webb, *English Poor Law Policy*, p. 15.
60. Webb & Webb, *English Poor Law Policy*, pp. 40-41.
61. Webb & Webb, *English Poor Law Policy*, pp. 36 & 42.
62. S. Webb & B. Webb, *English Poor Law History: Part II: the last hundred years, Vol 1* (Frank Cass, London, 1929). pp. 438-439.
63. Webb & Webb, *English Poor Law History*, pp. 444-447.
64. Webb & Webb, *English Poor Law Policy*, p. 321; Webb & Webb, *English Poor Law History*. pp. 444-448.
65. *West Briton*, 22 December 1870.
66. *Cornishman*, 11 May 1893.
67. *Cornishman*, 10 May 1894.
68. *Cornishman*, 31 January 1895.
69. *Royal Cornwall Gazette*, 15 July 1864.
70. *Cornishman*, 15 March 1895.
71. Webb & Webb, *English Poor Law History*, p. 10 & 143.
72. *Cornishman*, 5 March 1891.
73. *Cornishman*, 20 April 1899.
74. Little has been published on poor law loans, with exception of Chapters 2 and 3 in C. Grover, *The Social Fund 20 Years On: Historical and Policy Aspects of Loaning Social Security* (Ashgate Publishing, Farnham, 2013).

75　Webb & Webb, *English Poor Law History*, pp. 449-453.
76　*Cornishman*, 7 December 1893.
77　*Cornishman*, 12 April 1894.
78　*Cornishman*, 14 November 1889.
79　*Cornishman*, 18 February 1892.
80　*Cornishman*, 26 September 1895.
81　Webb & Webb, *English Poor Law Policy*, pp. 40-41.
82　*Selections from the Correspondence of the Local Government Board*, Vol. 2, Making of the Modern Law Print Edition: Legal Treatises 1800-1926, p. 71.
83　*Cornishman*, 29 October 1891.
84　*Cornishman*, 1 March 1894.
85　*Cornishman*, 15 September 1881.
86　*Cornishman*, 22 December 1881.
87　*Cornishman*, 8 November 1883.
88　*West Briton*, 2 June 1870.
89　*Royal Cornwall Gazette*, 5 July 1871; 12 August 1871.
90　*Royal Cornwall Gazette*, 2 September 1871; 21 October 1871.
91　*Royal Cornwall Gazette*, 2 September 1871.
92　*Royal Cornwall Gazette*, 14 December 1877.
93　*Cornishman*, 8 August 1878.
94　Webb & Webb, *English Poor Law Policy*, pp. 176-178.
95　*Cornishman*, 23 February 1888.
96　*Royal Cornwall Gazette*, 10 June 1876; *Cornishman*, 25 March 1886; 15 December 1887.
97　*Cornishman*, 22 December 1881.
98　*Cornishman*, 8 April 1886.
99　*Cornishman*, 18 November 1886.
100　*Cornishman*, 13 October 1892.
101　*Cornishman*, 23 February 1888.
102　*Cornishman*, 11 April 1895.
103　Tremewan's study that shows lower expenditure on poor relief in the mining districts only covered the period up to 1881. Tremewan, 'The Relief of Poverty'.
104　*Cornishman*, 8 June 1893.
105　*Cornishman*, 12 September 1895.
106　*Cornishman*, 15 September 1892.
107　*Cornishman*, 18 February 1892.
108　H. Harris Collection, Cornwall Record Office AD 1207/6.
109　Report of Thomas Cornish, Hon. Sec. of The Distress Fund, published in *Royal Cornwall Gazette*, 20 February 1868.
110　*Royal Cornwall Gazette*, 30 November 1877; 21 December 1877.
111　The poor law unions in Cornwall were: Bodmin, Camelford, Falmouth, Helston, Launceston, Liskeard, Penzance, Redruth, St Austell, St Columb Major, St Germans, Stratton and Truro.
112　Webb & Webb, *English Poor Law Policy*, p. 321; Webb & Webb, *English Poor Law History*, pp. 444-448.

6. 'Unworthy' Wives and 'Forgetful' Husbands

1　The same arguments would be re-iterated at many meetings. For just a few examples see: *Cornishman*, 8 April 1886; 18 November 1886; 23 February 1888; 15 September 1892.
2　*Cornishman*, 1 September 1881.
3　*Cornishman*, 8 August 1878.
4　*Cornishman*, 22 December 1881.
5　*Cornishman*, 18 November 1886.
6　*Royal Cornwall Gazette*, 10 June 1876.
7　*Royal Cornwall Gazette*, 14 December 1877.
8　*Cornishman*, 28 April 1881. See also *Royal Cornwall Gazette*, 30 November 1877.
9　*Royal Cornwall Gazette*, 9 December 1881.
10　*Cornishman*, 16 October 1879.
11　*Cornishman*, 13 October 1892.
12　*Cornishman*, 15 March 1894.
13　*Cornishman*, 13 October 1892.
14　*West Briton*, 7 March 1907.
15　*Cornishman*, 30 June 1898.
16　*Cornishman*, 31 December 1885.
17　*Cornishman*, 22 December 1881.
18　*Cornishman*, 18 November 1886.
19　*Cornishman*, 23 February 1888.
20　*Cornishman*, 20 February 1890.
21　*Cornishman*, 15 September 1892.
22　*Royal Cornwall Gazette*, 6 April 1899.
23　*West Briton*, 20 November 1873; 4 December 1873; *Royal Cornwall Gazette*, 6 December 1873.
24　*West Briton*, 22 January 1874.
25　*West Briton*, 29 January 1874.
26　*Cornishman*, 2 February 1882.
27　*Cornishman*, 24 May 1883.
28　*West Briton*, 31 July 1875.
29　Reports of sentences regularly appeared in the newspapers. Examples can be found in the *West Briton*, 8 May 1840, 5 November 1841, 1 March 1844, 26 September 1845, 12 September 1851, 6 May 1856, 13 January 1870; *Royal Cornwall Gazette*, 6 March 1875.
30　*West Briton*, 1 August 1862.

Notes and References

31 *West Briton*, 22 May 1840.
32 *Cornishman*, 24 August 1893.
33 *West Briton*, 15 March 1844.
34 *Royal Cornwall Gazette*, 25 March 1871.
35 *Cornishman*, 22 June 1893.
36 *Cornishman*, 7 December 1893.
37 *Cornishman*, 18 February 1892.
38 *Cornishman*, 3 November 1898.
39 *Cornishman*, 15 March 1894.
40 *Cornishman*, 23 May 1895.
41 Levine-Clark, 'From 'Relief' to 'Justice and Protection'', p. 309. Levine-Clark references the work of Olive Anderson on 19th century emigration and marriage break-up, which equates the wife being 'left behind' as the end of the marriage and therefore desertion.
42 *Cornishman*, 8 October 1885.
43 *Cornishman*, 15 September 1892.
44 *Royal Cornwall Gazette*, 18 July 1867.
45 *Cornishman*, 22 August 1889.
46 *Cornishman*, 14 September 1893.
47 *Cornishman*, 19 January 1893.
48 *Cornishman*, 14 September 1893.
49 *Cornishman*, 9 May 1895.
50 *Cornishman*, 21 December 1893.
51 *Cornishman*, 17 November 1898.
52 *Cornishman*, 15 August 1895.
53 *Cornishman*, 18 February 1892.
54 *Cornishman*, 22 September 1898.
55 *Cornishman*, 11 April 1895.
56 *Cornishman*, 15 September 1892.
57 *West Briton*, 26 May 1870.
58 *Cornishman*, 12 September.
59 Michell, *Annals of an Ancient Cornish Town*, p. 204.
60 *Cornishman*, 24 November 1892.
61 *Cornishman*, 15 September 1898.
62 *Cornishman*, 15 December 1898.
63 *Cornishman*, 3 November 1898.
64 *Cornishman*, 26 September 1895.
65 *Cornishman*, 8 June 1893.
66 *Cornishman*, 26 January 1899.
67 *Cornishman*, 22 November 1894.
68 Deacon, *Concise History of Cornwall*, p. 142.
69 Schwartz, *Cornish in Latin America* p. 473
70 Alfred Jenkin, Letter to J. Poingdestre, Swansea, 16 Jan 1837, RIC, AJ/1/17-18.
71 *Cornishman*, 8 November 1894.
72 *Cornishman*, 23 May 1895.
73 *Cornishman*, 26 September 1895.
74 *Cornishman*, 12 September 1895.
75 *Cornishman*, 30 June 1898.
76 *Cornishman*, 21 November 1895.
77 *Cornishman*, 22 September 1898.
78 *Cornishman*, 31 October 1878.
79 Redruth Select Vestry Book 1838-1852 quoted in Michell, *Annals of an Ancient Cornish Town*, p. 78.
80 *Cornishman*, 30 June 1898.
81 *Cornishman*, 15 June 1899.
82 *Cornishman*, 21 December 1893.
83 *Cornishman*, 30 June 1898.
84 *Cornishman*, 11 May 1893. Such notices were placed in *Poor Law Union Gazette*.
85 *Cornishman*, 4 August 1892.
86 *Cornishman*, 22 June 1893.
87 *Cornishman*, 7 December 1893.
88 *Cornishman*, 17 January 1895. Mrs Bessie Sowden continued to live in Rosewarne Road Camborne with her two children. She still described herself as married in the 1911 census but whether her husband was heard from again isn't known.
89 *Cornishman*, 14 October 1897.
90 *Cornishman*, 17 June 1897.
91 *Cornishman*, 4 August 1892; 21 December 1893; 30 June 1898.
92 *Royal Cornwall Gazette*, 1 December 1898.
93 *Cornishman*, 30 June 1898.
94 *Royal Cornwall Gazette*, 1 December 1898; 15 December 1898.
95 *Cornishman*, 1 December 1898.
96 *Cornishman*, 15 December 1898; *Royal Cornwall Gazette*, 15 December 1898; 9 February 1899.
97 Michell, *Annals of an Ancient Cornish Town*, p. 195.
98 *Cornishman*, 24 December 1891.
99 *Cornishman*, 18 February 1892.
100 *Cornishman*, 22 December 1892.
101 *Cornishman*, 19 January 1893.
102 *Cornishman*, 14 September 1893.
103 *Cornishman*, 7 December 1893.
104 *Cornishman*, 12 April 1894.
105 *Cornishman*, 12 April 1894.
106 *Cornishman*, 14 February 1895.
107 *Cornishman*, 9 May 1895.
108 *Cornishman*, 4 July 1895.
109 *Cornishman*, 11 February 1897.
110 *Cornishman*, 15 December 1898.
111 *Cornishman*, 12 January 1899.
112 *Cornishman*, 15 December 1898.
113 *Cornishman*, 12 January 1899.
114 *Royal Cornwall Gazette*, 9 February 1899.
115 *Royal Cornwall Gazette*, 6 April 1899.
116 *Cornishman*, 26 January 1899.

117 *Cornishman*, 6 April 1899.
118 *Cornishman*, 26 January 1899.
119 *Cornishman*, 29 December 1898.
120 *Cornishman*, 9 February 1899.
121 *Cornishman*, 23 February 1899.
122 *Cornishman*, 6 April 1899.
123 *Royal Cornwall Gazette*, 27 November 1902.
124 *West Briton*, 1 August 1907; 25 March 1907; 14 March 1911; 11 February 1911; 28 February 1911; 14 March 1911. See also Levine-Clark, 'From 'Relief' to 'Justice and Protection".
125 *Cornishman*, 30 May 1907.
126 *Cornishman*, 24 August 1911; *West Briton*, 9 May 1912.
127 *West Britain*, 5 February 1912.
128 *West Briton*, 18 January 1912.
129 *Cornishman*, 26 September 1923.
130 *Cornishman*, 17 October 1923. For a discussion of the introduction of reciprocal legislation for the maintenance of wives within the British Empire in the early 20th century see Levine-Clark, 'From 'Relief' to 'Justice and Protection".
131 *Royal Cornwall Gazette*, 16 February 1883; 6 July 1883; 20 July 1883.
132 Twomey, *Deserted and Destitute*.
133 Tremewan, 'The Relief of Poverty in Cornwall'.
134 Burke, 'The Decline of the Independent Bal Maiden', p. 200.
135 *Cornishman*, 30 May 1907.

7. Lodgers and Lovers

1 *Report of the Royal Commission on Divorce and Matrimonial Causes*, (Cd. 6480), p. 26 (12,838).
2 Schwartz & Parker, *Lanner*, p. 163.
3 Davidoff, *Worlds Between*; P. Sharpe, *Women's Work - The English experience 1650-1914* (Arnold, London, 1998), p. 269.
4 *Report of the Royal Commission on Divorce and Matrimonial Causes* (Cd. 6480), p. 25 (12,826).
5 *Report of the Royal Commission on Divorce and Matrimonial Causes* (Cd. 6480), p. 25 (12,824).
6 Blewett, 'The Village of St Day', p. 3.
7 *Royal Cornwall Gazette*, 9 October 1880; *Cornishman*, 14 October 1880.
8 In a similar report a young wife from Camborne, whose husband had only recently left the country, eloped with a married man who was said to have had a wife and children in the north of England. *Cornishman*, 8 February 1883.
9 *Cornishman*, 24 July 1879.
10 *Cornishman*, 3 April 1890.
11 *Cornishman*, 19 February 1880.
12 *Cornishman*, 18 November 1880; 3 February 1881; *Royal Cornwall Gazette*, 4 February 1881.
13 Gillis, *For Better or Worse*, p. 234.
14 *Cornishman*, 1 March 1894.
15 *Cornishman*, 14 September 1893.
16 Co-dependency as a motivation for relationship formation is discussed in more detail later in the next chapter.
17 *Cornishman*, 14 April 1892.
18 *Cornishman*, 18 December 1884.
19 *Cornishman* 11 April 1895; 25 March 1897.
20 *Cornishman*, 6 March 1879.
21 *Cornishman*, 25 March 1897.
22 *Cornishman*, 12 September 1895.
23 *Cornishman*, 29 October 1891.
24 *Cornishman*, 17 September 1891.
25 At the time Esther was described as having been in the workhouse for "some years", so she may have gone in for, or just after, the birth of the baby. The illegitimate daughter grew up in the workhouse, remaining there until she was 15 when the guardians helped her to join one of her older half-brothers in Australia. *Royal Cornwall Gazette*, 13 January 1872; 9 March 1872; *Cornishman*, 19 June 1884, with supplementary details from the census returns.
26 Deacon, Schwartz & Holman, *Cornish Family*, pp. 24 & 44.
27 *Cornishman*, 8 August 1878.
28 For similar cases see: *Cornishman*, 31 January 1884; 12 October 1893.
29 In 1881 defence lawyers in an affiliation case successfully argued that "no married woman with her husband alive, and unable to prove non-access, could claim an order". *Cornishman*, 5 May 1881.
30 *Cornishman*, 29 April 1886.
31 *Cornishman*, 7 September 1882.
32 *Cornishman*, 25 August 1881.
33 *Cornishman*, 31 May 1883.
34 *Cornishman*, 11 April 1895.
35 *Cornishman*, 25 March 1897.
36 A.-M. Kilday, *A History of Infanticide in Britain c.1600 to the Present* (Palgrave Macmillan, 2013).

Notes and References

37 Kilday, *History of Infanticide*. Chapter 4; P. Knight, 'Women and Abortion in Victorian and Edwardian England', *History Workshop*, No. 4 (1977), pp.57-68.
38 *Cornishman*, 2 October 1879; 6 November 1879.
39 *Cornishman*, 3 March 1881.
40 Kilday, *History of Infanticide*, pp. 82-83.
41 Knight, 'Women and Abortion', pp. 58-61; Kilday, *History of Infanticide*, pp. 82-83.
42 Knight, 'Women and Abortion', pp. 63-64.
43 Kilday, *History of Infanticide*, p. 52.
44 Kilday, *History of Infanticide*, pp. 83, 109 & 140.
45 For examples see: *Royal Cornwall Gazette*, 10 July 1875; *Cornishman*, 18 December 1884.
46 Kilday, *History of Infanticide*, pp. 85 & 159.
47 *West Briton*, 9 February 1880, quoted in P. Payton, *Cornish Overseas*, p. 351.
48 Kilday, *History of Infanticide*, pp. 58-64.
49 *Royal Cornwall Gazette*, 14 January 1871.
50 *Royal Cornwall Gazette*, 11 February 1858.
51 *Royal Cornwall Gazette*, 17 March 1898.
52 Barton, *Life in Cornwall in the Late Nineteenth Century*, p. 43.
53 *West Briton*, 8 April 1859, quoted in Barton, *Life in Cornwall*, p. 54.
54 *Royal Cornwall Gazette*, 28 November 1867.
55 Kilday, *History of Infanticide*, p. 141.
56 *Royal Cornwall Gazette*, 28 November 1867.
57 Michell, *Annals of an Ancient Cornish Town*, p. 172.
58 For a detailed discussion of public attitudes to infanticide see Kilday, *A History of Infanticide*. Chapter 5.
59 Gillis, *For Better or Worse*, pp. 120-127.
60 Kilday, *History of Infanticide*, p. 137 & 145.
61 Kilday, *History of Infanticide*, p. 82; Knight, 'Women and Abortion'.
62 Kilday, *History of Infanticide*, p. 146.
63 *Cornishman*, 15 March 1894.
64 *Cornishman*, 7 December 1893.
65 Kilday, *History of Infanticide*. pp. 161-164.
66 *Royal Cornwall Gazette*, 26 September 1856.
67 Examples include Mary Lark, Elizabeth Ann Allen and Mary Jane Richards as mentioned, as well as Catherine Tyacke of Perranuthnoe, whose husband had been in America for 6 or 7 years (*West Briton*, 8 December 1854), and Mary Ann Roberts of Calstock, whose baby son died under suspicious circumstances just after her husband returned from 3 years abroad (*West Briton*, 1 August 1856).
68 *Royal Cornwall Gazette*, 12 September 1856.
69 *Royal Cornwall Gazette*, 28 June 1873.
70 There are many press reports of this case, the most detailed being in the *Royal Cornwall Gazette*, 27 March 1875.
71 Kilday, *History of Infanticide*, p. 123.
72 Brayshay, 'The Demography of Three West Cornwall Mining Communities', p. 354.
73 Kilday, *History of Infanticide*. pp. 52-53.
74 Reeder, *Widows in White*, pp. 64-67.
75 The lives of women in general in rural and Catholic Sicily would have been very different from those in Cornwall, where Methodism and industrial employment allowed them more independence. See Schwartz, 'In Defence of Customary Rights'; L. Mayers, *Balmaidens*.
76 Twomey, *Deserted and Destitute,* pp. 139-142.
77 *West Briton*, 30 January 1873; *Cornishman*, 19 January 1888.
78 *Cornishman*, 31 July 1879.
79 *Cornishman*, 31 May 1883.
80 *Cornishman*, 12 November 1891; *Royal Cornwall Gazette*, 21 November 1891.
81 Blewett, 'The Village of St Day', pp. 3-4.
82 *Cornishman*, 28 August 1878.
83 Thomas Hockin, Letter, 1856, Moira Tangye collection.
84 *Cornishman*, 10 August 1893.
85 *Report of the Royal Commission on Divorce and Matrimonial Causes* (Cd. 6480), p. 25 (12,834).
86 *Cornishman*, 24 January 1884.
87 *Cornishman*, 28 September 1882.
88 John Dower, Letter, 22 March 1866, John Tregenza Papers.
89 Gillis, *For Better or Worse*, p. 234.

8. Double Standards and Five-Dollar Divorces

1 J. Tosh, *Manliness and Masculinities in Nineteenth-Century Britain* (Pearson Education Ltd, Harlow, 2005), p. 174.
2 Anderson, 'Emigration and Marriage Break-Up. See also O. Anderson, 'Civil Society and Separation in Victorian Marriage', *Past & Present*, 163 (1999), pp.

161-201.
3. Most temporary migration was motivated by a desire to improve family finances but at least one husband left to work abroad in order to raise the money to pay for a divorce. *Report of the Royal Commission on Divorce and Matrimonial Causes* (Cd. 6480), p. 25 (12,817).
4. A.L. Rowse, *A Cornish Childhood* (Jonathan Cape, 1942; Truan edition 1998), p. 36.
5. Schwartz, *Cornish in Latin America*, pp. 521-522.
6. *Report of the Royal Commission on Divorce and Matrimonial Causes* (Cd. 6480), p. 28 (12,890).
7. Knight, 'Women and Abortion', pp. 57-60. S.J. Davies, 'An Investigation into Attitudes towards Illegitimate Birth as Evidenced in the Folklore of South West England', unpublished PhD thesis, University of Plymouth (1999). pp. 126-129.
8. Schwartz, *Cornish in Latin America*, p. 440.
9. Shandley, *Feminism, Marriage and the Law*, p. 45.
10. For the description of 19th century divorce, see: Roderick Phillips, *Putting Asunder: A history of divorce in Western society* (Cambridge University Press, 1988); R. Probert, *Divorced, Bigamist, Bereaved?: the family historian's guide to marital breakdown, separation, widowhood, and remarriage from 1600 to the 1970s* (Takeaway Publishing, Kenilworth, 2015). pp. 23-73.
11. Datson v. Datson & Medlin, Divorce and Matrimonial Causes File, 1893. The National Archives (TNA), J 77/15591; *Royal Cornwall Gazette*, 25 May 1893.
12. Jackson v. Jackson & Harris, Divorce and Matrimonial Causes File, 1870. TNA, J 77/1610; *Royal Cornwall Gazette*, 11 February 1871.
13. The birth certificates of the illegitimate children were sometimes produced in evidence at the divorce hearing and are preserved amongst the divorce files.
14. *Royal Cornwall Gazette*, 11 February 1871.
15. In some cases examined in the Divorce and Matrimonial Causes Files (TNA, J 77) where fathers were given custody, children were found to be living with their mothers.
16. Hodge v. Hodge & Wickett, Divorce and Matrimonial Causes File, 1895. TNA, J 77/16835; *Cornishman*, 2 May 1895.
17. Biddick v. Biddick & Cawse, Divorce and Matrimonial Causes File, 1898. TNA, J 77/19391; *Cornishman*, 26 January 1899.
18. Quick v. Quick & Heather, Divorce and Matrimonial Causes File, 1899. TNA, J 77/260; *Cornishman*, 2 November 1899.
19. Wearne v. Wearne & Noakes, Divorce and Matrimonial Causes File, 1869. TNA, J 77/1324; *West Briton*, 12 May 1870.
20. Traditional Cornish attitudes to betrothal sanctioned pre-marital sex. See Deacon, Schwartz & Holman, *Cornish Family*, p. 24.
21. Tonkin v. Tonkin, Divorce and Matrimonial Causes File, 1895. TNA, J 77/17469; *Cornishman*, 11 June 1896.
22. Jackson v. Jackson & Harris, Divorce and Matrimonial Causes File, 1870. TNA, J 77/1610.
23. 1860 US Federal Census, original image accessed via Ancestry.co.uk.
24. *West Briton*, 7 November 1887.
25. Abstract will, Thomas Jenkyns, 1893. National Probate Calendar (Index of Wills and Admons).
26. *Report of the Royal Commission on Divorce and Matrimonial Causes* (Cd. 6480), p. 25 (12,817).
27. *Report of the Royal Commission on Divorce and Matrimonial Causes* (Cd. 6480), p. 26 (12,828); Tonkin v. Tonkin, Divorce and Matrimonial Causes File, 1895. TNA, J 77/17469; *Cornishman*, 11 June 1896.
28. See Biddick v. Biddick & Cawse, Divorce and Matrimonial Causes File, 1898. TNA, J 77/19391.
29. *Report of the Royal Commission on Divorce and Matrimonial Causes* (Cd. 6480), p. 26 (12,831).
30. However, Granger claimed in 1910 that American courts did not grant a divorce without proper proof. *Report of the Royal Commission on Divorce and Matrimonial Causes* (Cd. 6480), p. 26 (12832).
31. *Royal Cornwall Gazette*, 19 September 1867.
32. *West Briton*, 16 June 1870.
33. *Royal Cornwall Gazette*, 20 July 1856; 23 January 1875.
34. *Royal Cornwall Gazette*, 23 January 1875.
35. *Royal Cornwall Gazette*, 11 October 1894.
36. *Cornishman*, 24 September 1896.
37. Probert, *Divorced, Bigamist, Bereaved?*, pp. 115-119.
38. Frost, *Living in Sin*, pp. 82-84.

Notes and References

39 The idea of wife sales arose from a misinterpretation of the doctrine of coverture, that a wife was her husband's property and so could be sold, thereby freeing the husband of any further responsibility for her. See S.P. Menefee, *Wives for Sale: an ethnographic study of British Popular Divorce* (Blackwell, 1981); E.P. Thompson, *Customs in Common* (Penguin Books, 1993). pp. 404-443.
40 Frost, *Living in Sin*, pp. 73 & 85-86.
41 Menefee, *Wives for Sale*. It was claimed in 1949 that the last attempted wife sale in Cornwall was in 1846. *Cornishman*, 21 April 1949.
42 *West Briton*, 16 October 1857.
43 Frost, *Living in Sin*, pp. 110-111. See also Joanne Bailey's discussion of marital co-dependency in Bailey, *Unquiet Lives*.
44 Frost, *Living in Sin*, pp. 78-79 & 109-111.
45 Frost, *Living in Sin*, p. 108.
46 Frost, *Living in Sin*, pp. 113-114 & 226-227.
47 Frost, *Living in Sin*, p. 231.
48 Phillips v. Phillips and Medlyn, Divorce and Matrimonial Causes File, 1865. TNA, J 77/408.
49 R. Probert, *Marriage Law for Genealogists* (Takeaway Publishing, Kenilworth, 2012), p.64.
50 Probert, *Marriage Law for Genealogists*, pp. 73-83 & 115.
51 For explanation of the laws concerning bigamy, see Probert, *Divorced, Bigamist, Bereaved?* pp. 97-148.
52 *Cornishman*, 22 September 1892.
53 *Cornishman*, 15 September 1892.
54 *Cornishman*, 20 February 1879; 16 March 1882; 27 October 1892.
55 *Cornishman*, 3 November 1892.
56 *West Briton*, 6 August 1874.
57 Schwartz & Parker, *Lanner*, p. 161; K. Skues, *Cornish Heritage* (Werner Shaw Ltd, London, 1983), pp. 488-489.
58 Schwartz, *Cornish in Latin America*, p. 433.
59 David Coppin, pers. comm. (30 October 2012).
60 Francis Dunstan, pers. comm. (28 April 2012).
61 Liz Coole, pers. comm. (19 February 2013).
62 Skues, *Cornish Heritage*, pp. 488-489.
63 Carolyn Haines, pers. comm. (3 May 2012).
64 Frost, *Living in Sin*, p. 72.
65 Frost, *Living in Sin*, p. 111.

9. Meeting Again on Earth or in Heaven

1 The number of wives 'left behind' in St Cleer found in the census was very small in comparison with the other parishes making it difficult to detect any trends.
2 Graphs showing the outcomes after ten years, along with more details of the methods used in the research, can be found at www.humblehistory.com.
3 Digitised images of the US Federal Census were accessed via the Ancestry website, www.Ancestry.co.uk.
4 Harper, *Emigrant Homecomings*, pp. 2-6; M. Wyman, 'Emigrants Returning: The evolution of a tradition' in M. Harper (ed.), *Emigrant Homecomings: The return movement of emigrants 1600-2000* (Manchester University Press, 2005), pp. 16-31.
5 J. Lucassen & L. Lucassen, *Migration, Migration History, History: Old Paradigms and New Perspectives*, 2nd revised edition (Peter Lang, Bern, 1999), p. 29; Wyman, 'Emigrants Returning'.
6 The culture of labour mobility in Cornwall was not restricted to the mining industry as Cornish fishing boats and their crews undertook regular seasonal relocations to both Irish and Scottish fishing grounds. See J. Rule, *Cornish Cases – Essays in Eighteenth and Nineteenth Century Social History* (Clio Publishing, Southampton, 2006), pp. 249-250.
7 Payton, *Cornish Overseas*, p. 93.
8 D. Baines, *Emigration from Europe 1815-1930* (Cambridge University Press, 1991). pp. 34-37.
9 L.P. Moch, 'The European Perspective; Changing conditions and multiple migrations, 1750-1914' in D. Hoerder & L.P. Moch (eds.), *European Migrants: Global and Local Perspectives* (Northeastern University Press, Boston, 1996), p. 129.
10 H. Rossler, 'Constantine Stonemasons in Search of Work Abroad, 1870-1900' in P. Payton (ed.), *Cornish Studies Two* (University of Exeter Press, 1994), 48-82.
11 Wyman, 'Emigrants Returning'.
12 E. Richards, 'Running Home from Australia: Intercontinental mobility and migrant expectation in the nineteenth century' in M. Harper (ed.), *Emigrant*

Homecomings: The return movement of emigrants 1600-2000 (Manchester University Press, 2005), p. 125.
13. B.S. Elliot, "Settling Down': Masculinity, class and the rite of return in a transnational community' in M. Harper (ed.), *Emigrant Homecomings*, p. 154.
14. Henwood quoted in Payton, *Cornish Overseas*, p. 95.
15. Rossler, 'Constantine Stonemasons'.
16. Additional information courtesy of family, William and Patricia Woolcock, 2013.
17. 'Daffodils Never Hear', Williams family history website, http://at.orpheusweb.co.uk/Daffodil/index.htm (accessed 9 September 2011)
18. Harper, *Emigrant Homecomings* (2005), p. 1. The money earned abroad not only supported families in Cornwall, it created inward investment enabling business creation and diversification. See Schwartz, 'Cornish Migration Studies', pp. 151-152.
19. Henwood quoted in Payton, *Cornish Overseas*, p. 95.
20. Examples from the *West Briton* include the arrival in Penzance of a ship carrying 2-3 tons of gold dust reported on 25 April 1856, and the discovery of a 185 lb nugget by men from Illogan reported on 27 August 1858. Barton, *Life in Cornwall*, p. 20 & 49.
21. *West Briton*, 2 January 1852.
22. *West Briton*, 30 March 1866; Barton, *Life in Cornwall*, p. 141.
23. *Royal Cornwall Gazette*, 18 July 1867.
24. Priscilla Parkin, Letter, 28 October 1888, Moira Tangye Collection.
25. Schwartz, *Cornish in Latin America*, p. 126. Payton, *Cornish Overseas*, p. 115.
26. Alfred Jenkin letter book, RIC, AJ/1/17-18; *A Cornishman in Cuba*. The diary of James Whitburn, Cornwall Record Office, AD/1341.
27. *Royal Cornwall Gazette*, 21 December 1872.
28. *Cornishman*, 10 May 1883.
29. Payton, *Cornish Overseas*, p. 373.
30. *Royal Cornwall Gazette*, 18 July 1867.
31. *Cornishman*, 26 October 1893.
32. *Cornishman*, 12 April 1894.
33. Schwartz, *Cornish in Latin America*, pp. 122-125 & 534-536.
34. Harper makes the same point regarding the temporary emigration of artisans from Scotland. M. Harper, *Adventurers & Exiles*, p. 282.
35. Harper, *Emigrant Homecomings* (2005), p. 4.
36. Extracts, Diary, Capt John James, Cornwall Record Office, FS/3/1148. See also C. Pooley & J. Turnbull, *Migration and Mobility in Britain since the 18th Century* (Routledge, 2003), pp. 295-297 & 328.
37. R. Woods, *The Population of Britain in the Nineteenth Century* (Macmillan, 1992), p. 25.
38. *Royal Cornwall Gazette*, 25 July 1867.
39. *Royal Cornwall Gazette*, 10 October 1867.
40. *West Briton*, 27 November 1873.
41. Michell, *Annals of an Ancient Cornish Town*, p. 209.
42. *West Briton*, 8 August 1862; Payton, *Cornish Overseas*, p. 257.
43. Payton, *Cornish Overseas*, pp. 364-367; *Cornishman*, 23 November 1899.
44. Alfred Jenkin letter books, quoted in Schwartz, *Cornish in Latin America*, p. 391.
45. *Royal Cornwall Gazette*, 10 October 1867.
46. *West Briton*, 16 January 1873.
47. Wyman, 'Emigrants Returning,' pp. 21-22.
48. Elaine Hamby, pers. comm. (3-10 May 2012).
49. *Report of the Royal Commission on Divorce and Matrimonial Causes* (Cd. 6480), p. 28.
50. *Cornishman*, 14 March 1901.
51. Richards, 'Running Home,' p. 96.
52. Schwartz, 'Cornish Migration to Latin America', p. 237; *Cornishman*, 14 March 1901.
53. Reeder, *Widows in White*, pp. 153-154; Wyman, 'Emigrants Returning,' p. 25.
54. Schwartz, *Cornish in Latin America*, pp. 368-9.
55. Richards, 'Running Home,' p. 81.
56. Michell, *Annals of an Ancient Cornish Town*, p. 201.
57. Richards, 'Running Home', pp. 86-90.
58. Charlotte Hearle, pers. comm. (23 July, 3 August 2012).
59. The only notable variation is that in both St Agnes and St Just only 10% of husbands of the 1851 cohort were absent at the time of the 1861 census. In St Just this mirrors the higher percentage of husbands from that cohort who were found back with their wives, indicating a greater proportion of reunions there in the 1850s despite the fact that the numbers of absent husbands increased both numerically and as a percentage of the total number of married

Notes and References

couples between 1851 and 1861. However, something different appears to have happened in St Agnes where the number who had returned was also at its lowest in 1851 so the husbands who were no longer absent in 1861 were not with their wives in Cornwall. Two possible explanations might be suggested: the 1851 St Agnes cohort in 1861 shows both the highest level of wives described as widows and the highest number untraced, so it is possible that these St Agnes men had died or were assumed dead, or that their wives had joined them in a part of the world for which emigration records are less accessible. Further research may identify a particular migration stream from St Agnes in the 1850s that might account for this.
60 Schwartz & Parker, *Lanner*, p. 163.
61 See Anderson, 'Emigration and Marriage Break-Up'.
62 *Royal Cornwall Gazette*, 18 July 1867.
63 Phillips, *Putting Asunder*, p. 286.
64 Phillips, *Putting Asunder*. pp. 298-370. Many mistakenly thought that after seven years they were free to remarry, confusing the fact that they could not be prosecuted for bigamy in those circumstances, with the idea that this made a second marriage legal. Frost, *Living in Sin*, p. 84.
65 *Cornishman*, 26 March 1885.
66 For the legal aspects of establishing the death of a spouse with regards remarriage, see Probert, *Divorced, Bigamist, Bereaved?*, pp. 149-155.
67 *Cornishman*, 17 March 1881.
68 *Cornishman*, 2 January 1896; 16 January 1896; 16 March 1899.
69 *Cornishman*, 20 April 1905.
70 *Cornishman*, 15 December 1881.
71 Mine captain Josiah Gilbert went to great expense in 1895 to bring the body of his wife back from Montana for burial in Helston, Cornwall. *Royal Cornwall Gazette*, 10 October 1895.
72 Schwartz, *Cornish in Latin America*, p. 460.
73 Alfred Jenkin, an agent for the Cobre Mines in Cuba is recorded in 1838 as being engaged in seeing that the possessions of men killed there were returned to their families. Michell, *Annals of an Ancient Cornish Town*, p. 109. Alfred Jenkin letter books, RIC, 2 & 10 Nov 1836; 14 July 1838; 28 July 1838.

74 *Cornishman*, 9 September 1897. For an example of Poor Law support see *Cornishman*, 23 November 1882, and other charitable assistance: *Cornishman*, 9 January 1879, *Royal Cornwall Gazette*, 24 June 1887.
75 Correspondence of Mary Ann Scoble, Cornwall Record Office, AD 833/1-10.

10. Under sailing orders

1 Deacon, *Concise History of Cornwall*, p. 163.
2 Schwartz & Parker, *Lanner*, p. 155.
3 *Cornwall Family History Journal*, Number 96, June 2000, p. 5.
4 *Cornwall Family History Journal*, Number 35, December 1985, p. 27-28.
5 Elliot, 'Settling Down', p. 155; Gerber, *Authors of Their Lives*, p. 155. For a detailed discussion on transnationalism and migration, see Harzig & Hoerder, *What is Migration History?*
6 W.E. Van Vugt, *Britain to America: Mid-nineteenth-century immigrants to the United States* (University of Illinois Press, 1999), p. 123.
7 Additional information courtesy of descendant Kitty Quayle, May 2012.
8 Van Vugt, *Britain to America*, p. 123.
9 Elliot, 'Settling Down', p. 155.
10 Van Vugt, *Britain to America*, p. 122.
11 Schwartz, *Cornish in Latin America*, p. 347-350.
12 Trotter, 'Desperate? Destitute? Deserted?' (2010), p. 46; Trotter, 'Desperate? Destitute? Deserted?' (2011), pp. 208-209.
13 Peavy & Smith, *Women in Waiting in the Western Movement*; Jameson, 'Where Have All the Young Men Gone?', pp. 217-221.
14 Van Vugt, *Britain to America*, p. 93.
15 *Cornwall Family History Journal*, Number 3, January 1877, p. 15.
16 Twomey, *Deserted and Destitute*.
17 *Cornwall Family History Journal*, Number 45, September 1987, p. 18.
18 Shirley Westaway, pers. comm. (4 May 2012).
19 For a description see Chapter 2 of E.J. Errington, *Emigrant Worlds and Transatlantic Communities: Migration to Upper Canada in the First Half of the Nineteenth Century* (McGill-Queen's University Press, Montreal, 2007).

20. William Paynter, Letter, 15 April 1860, Cornwall Record Office, FS.3/1033/112.
21. William Paynter, Letter, 15 January 1860 Cornwall Record Office, FS.3/1033/111.
22. 1881 St Blazey census, TNA, RG11/2300 ED16.
23. For example, see *Cornishman*, 3 December 1896.
24. *Cornishman*, 3 October 1895.
25. *Cornishman*, 6 May 1897.
26. *Cornishman*, 15 July 1897.
27. *Cornishman*, 6 May 1897.
28. Todd, *Search for Silver*, p. 144.
29. *Cornwall Family History Journal*, Number 76, June 1995, p. 35.
30. For a description see Chapter 3 of Errington, *Emigrant Worlds*.
31. Daffodils Never Hear', Williams family history website.
32. In 1895 the Helston poor law guardians were granting relief to children whose mother had gone to Africa leaving them with their grandmother. *Cornishman*, 20 June 1895.
33. For example, when Mary Jane Mitchell followed her husband to Western Australia in 1875 the couple's daughters stayed at school in England. *Cornwall Family History Journal*, Number 90, December 1998, p. 6.
34. William Paynter, Letter, 15 April 1860, Cornwall Record Office, FS.3/1033/112.
35. Notes from diary kept by Rachel Carmen, 1864-5, courtesy of descendant Jane Hollow.
36. *Cornwall Family History Journal*, Number 90, Dec 1998, p. 2.
37. Family history submitted by Harriet Sturk to http://www.mariposaresearch.net/COLLINS-NORTHEY.html (accessed: 9 September 2011)
38. William Payter, Letter, 15 April 1860, Cornwall Record Office, FS.3/1033/112.
39. Teresa Farris, pers. comm. (30 April 2012).
40. John Dower, Letter, 25 September 1867, John Tregenza Papers.
41. E. Richards, 'How did Poor People Emigrate from the British Isles to Australia in the Nineteenth Century?', *The Journal of British Studies*, 32 (1993), 250-279.
42. Michell, *Annals of an Ancient Cornish Town*, p. 120.
43. Webb & Webb, *English Poor Law Policy*, p. 141. The Poor Law Commissioners issued a circular in 1851 refusing to sanction this type of grant after unions in parts of Ireland had started making them. They felt that "the giving of aid under such circumstances would operate as a direct premium to desertion of families, and tend to foster a general expectation that the emigration of the husband would lead to the transmission of his children at the public expense". *Royal Cornwall Gazette*, 24 October 1851.
44. The National Archives (TNA), MH 12/9362/107, MH 12/490/44-45; MH 12/15161/327-327; MH 12/9231/205. A very limited amount of MH 12 Poor Law Union correspondence has been catalogued in detail and digitised by the Living the Poor Life Project. The Truro Poor Law Union (1834-1849) is the only Cornish union to be included. Carter & Whistance, *Living the Poor Life*.
45. TNA, MH 12/1528/238, 239, 245, 246, 255, 256. For similar correspondence see: TNA, MH 12/16246/255.
46. *Royal Cornwall Gazette*, 12 December 1867; *Cornishman*, 19 January 1882, 8 March 1888, 15 July 1897.
47. A man in Mansfield was granted parish help for his family to emigrate to America but his wife refused to go, so he went alone. Within the year he had written to say that he was in 'prosperous circumstances', the wife had changed her mind and the guardians were willing to help. The Poor Law Commissioners however refused to sanction the expenditure not only on the grounds that she had been deserted but also that the Poor Law could only assist emigration to British colonies. The guardians tried to counter the first objection by pleading that this wasn't the usual case of desertion. Their solution to the Commissioners second objection was inspired. The clerk explained that he had erroneously stated that the husband was in New York; he was actually in Canada, at Vespra, Lake Simcoe. One can't help wondering if the Poor Law Commissioners' grasp of geography was good enough to realise that Lake Simcoe was conveniently just over the US/Canadian border from New York state. Either way they refused to sanction the payment. TNA, MH 12/9361/30; MH/12/9361/31; MH 12/9361/36; MH 12/9361/37.
48. In 1871 the Liskeard Union appealed the

Notes and References

auditors decision to disallow the £5 they had given to a wife receiving relief to enable her to join her husband in America. *Royal Cornwall Gazette*, 8 April 1871.
49 *Royal Cornwall Gazette*, 25 July 1867.
50 *Royal Cornwall Gazette*, 25 July 1867.
51 *Royal Cornwall Gazette*, 25 July 1867.
52 *Royal Cornwall Gazette*, 14 August 1867.
53 *Royal Cornwall Gazette*, 10 October 1867. The Fund was soon also used for broader purposes, especially providing clothing and bedding, but was always cautious that it should not interfere with the workings of the poor law unions.
54 Payton, *Cornish Overseas*, p. 264.
55 *Royal Cornwall Gazette*, 31 October 1867.
56 *Royal Cornwall Gazette*, 31 October 1867.
57 *Royal Cornwall Gazette*, 14 November 1867.
58 *Royal Cornwall Gazette*, 31 October 1867.
59 *Royal Cornwall Gazette*, 20 February 1868.
60 *Royal Cornwall Gazette*, 2 April 1868.
61 *Royal Cornwall Gazette*, 2 April 1868.
62 *Royal Cornwall Gazette*, 12 November 1868.
63 *Royal Cornwall Gazette*, 16 May 1879.
64 *Royal Cornwall Gazette*, 30 November 1877; 21 December 1877.
65 *Royal Cornwall Gazette*, 21 February 1879; 16 May 1879.
66 *Cornishman*, 30 July 1896.
67 *Cornishman*, 26 June 1879.
68 *West Briton*, 7 May 1868, in Barton, *Life in Cornwall*, p. 170. 'The Queen and the Cornish Miners', *Manchester Times*, 2 May 1868.
69 *Cornishman*, 4 December 1884.
70 *Royal Cornwall Gazette*, 28 Nov 1867.
71 *Cornishman*, 2 February 1882; 27 August 1896.
72 *West Briton*, 30 March 1855.
73 *West Briton*, 8 October 1868, in Barton, *Life in Cornwall*, p. 175.
74 *Cornishman*, 13 October 1892.
75 New South Wales, Australia, Immigration Deposit Journals, digital images of originals accessed on line at Ancestry.co.uk.
76 *Cornishman*, 23 November 1882.
77 *Cornishman*, 9 May 1895.
78 *Cornishman*, 4 August 1892; 19 January 1893.
79 See also *Cornishman*, 21 June 1894.
80 Van Vugt, *Britain to America*, pp. 80 & 126.
81 *Royal Cornwall Gazette*, 1 November 1900.
82 C. Barker, 'The miner's wife', in *Women of West Cornwall* (Penwith Local History Group, 2016), pp.1-7.
83 *Cornishman*, 13 October 1881.
84 Todd, *Search for Silver*, pp. 161-162.
85 Carlene Harry, 'St Just to Bald Mountain: the story of Mary Wall', CALH Journal, No 63, Spring 2012, p.31-32; Interview with Lillian Harry broadcast in 'Destination America: Episode 8: Made in Britain' by Thames Television, 1976.
86 *Cornishman*, 19 May 1892.
87 *Cornishman*, 8 March 1894.

11. Two Lives Compared

1 There are 14 letters by William Paynter to his wife Sophia from January 1859 to April 1860 (copies at Cornwall Record Office: FS.3/1033/98-112). Material from William Paynters letters is reproduced by kind permission of his descendant Marleen Carver. There are 23 surviving letters by John Dower to his wife Mary Ann from October 1865 to November 1868 (letter dated 18 December 1865, Royal Institution of Cornwall, Courtney Library; the remaining letters are in the private archive of descendant Emily Jane Oldenburg, by whose kind permission they are quoted here; copies at The University of Adelaide, Barr Smith Library, John Tregenza Papers, series 14, MSS0049)
2 Gerber, *Authors of Their Lives*, pp. 6 & 81-82; B.S. Elliott, D.A. Gerber & S.M. Sinke, *Letters across Borders: The epistolary practices of international migrants* (Palgrave, 2006).
3 It is very rare to find references to sex in migrant letters, although an unusually explicit exchange between a husband and wife in America is noted by Peavy and Smith. Many more such letters may have been written, but would perhaps have been less likely to survive or be made available for study due to censorship within the families concerned. Peavy & Smith, *Women in Waiting*, pp. 33-34.
4 Gerber, *Authors of Their Lives*, pp. 107-112.
5 Another possible explanation for this variation is that some of the surviving letters are in fact later copies of the originals. See John Tregenza, Letter, 17 March 1976. The University of Adelaide,

271

6. Barr Smith Library, John Tregenza Papers. John Dower, Letter, 20 or 28 March 1867.
7. Engel, 'The Woman's Side' p. 266; Reeder, *Widows in White*, p. 195. See also Chapter 2 of Gerber, *Authors of Their Lives*.
8. William Paynter, Letter, 13 January 1859.
9. William Paynter, Letters, 7 February; 2 April 1859.
10. John Dower, Letter, 20 October 1865.
11. John Dower, Letter, 20 October 1865.
12. John Dower, Letter, 19 November 1865.
13. John Dower, Letter, 18 December 1865.
14. John Dower, Letter, 22 March 1866.
15. John Dower, Letter, 18 June 1866.
16. John Dower, Letter, 22 November 1866.
17. John Dower, Letter, 20 or 28 March 1867.
18. John Dower, Letter, 1 March 1868.
19. William Paynter, Letter, 13 September 1859.
20. William Paynter, Letter, 13 January 1859.
21. William Paynter, Letters, 7 and 13 January 1859.
22. Twomey, *Deserted and Destitute*, pp. 116 & 124-125.
23. James Bonwick's *The Australian Gold Digger's Monthly Magazine*, Vol. 1, No. 1, October 1852, p. 14.
24. Parreñas, 'Transnational Fathering'.
25. William Paynter, Letter, 13 January 1859.
26. Mat Hore, Letter, 26 November 1876, Moira Tangye Collection.
27. Richard Colliver, Letters, 26 April and 13 December 1914, Moira Tangye Collection.
28. William Trewin, whose father abandoned the family when they could not join him in America, carried with him all his life a letter containing the words "Kiss the dear boy for me" written just after his birth by the father he never knew. Information courtesy of Elizabeth Cameron, (22 June 2012).
29. John Dower, Letters, 18 June 1866; 24 June 1867.
30. John Dower, Letter, 20 or 28 March 1867.
31. William Paynter, Letter, 13 September 1859.
32. For examples see: *Cornishman*, 27 May 1880; 15 March 1883; 12 December 1895.
33. For examples see: *Cornishman*, 26 October 1882; 11 October 1888.
34. For an example see: *Royal Cornwall Gazette*, 23 December 1887.
35. For example see: *Cornishman*, 16 January 1896.
36. *Cornishman*, 15 September 1881; 22 December 1881; 2 February 1882; 8 November 1883.
37. *Cornishman*, 16 July 1881.
38. In 1871 female matchworkers led the successful opposition to a tax on matches proposed by the then Chancellor of the Exchequer, Robert Lowe. See: Jonathan Parry, 'Lowe, Robert, Viscount Sherbrooke (1811–1892)', *Oxford Dictionary of National Biography*, Oxford University Press, 2004; online edn, May 2011 [http://www.oxforddnb.com.lib.exeter.ac.uk/view/article/17088, accessed 15 January 2015].
39. *Cornishman*, 14 May 1896.
40. John Dower, Letter, 25 December [1867?].
41. Ann Goldsworthy, Letter, 18 February 1861, private collection of descendant Amanda Drake.
42. Elaine Hamby, pers. comm. (May 2012).
43. *West Briton*, 23 January 1857 and 30 January 1857.
44. Joel Eade, Letter, 1 February 1864, Moira Tangye Collection.
45. William Paynter, Letter, 1 February 1859.
46. Erickson, *Leaving England*, p. 261.
47. Gerber, *Authors of Their Lives*, pp. 88-89.
48. Tosh, *Manliness and Masculinities*, p. 251.
49. Both John and William use near identical phrases; John: "My dear I hope you are minding the one thing needfull." [sic]; William: "...my dear let me urge you once more before I close this to mind the one thing needful".
50. William Paynter, Letters, 7 February and 15 November 1859.
51. John Dower, Letter, 2 February 1868.
52. John Dower, Letter, 6 November 1868.

12. Choice and Power

1. Schwartz, 'In Defence of Customary Rights', p. 18.
2. Magee & Thompson, 'Remittances Revisited', p. 299.
3. Deacon, Schwartz & Holman, *Cornish Family*, p. 158.
4. Burke, 'Decline of the Independent Bal Maiden', p. 200.
5. Burke, 'The Cornish Miner', p. 331 & 448; Schwartz, 'Cornish Migration Studies', p. 148. Deacon, Schwartz & Holman, *Cornish Family*, p. 53.
6. Biddick v. Biddick & Cawse, Divorce and

Notes and References

    Matrimonial Causes File, 1898. TNA, J 77/19391.
7 William Cobbett, *Emigrants' Guide in 10 letters Addressed to the Taxpayers of England* (London 1829), pp. 34-35, quoted in C. Erickson, L*eaving England – Essays on British Emigration in the Nineteenth Century* (Ithaca & London, 1994), p. 241. Much recent scholarship has reconciled ideas of more polarised models of marriage recognising that despite legal patriarchy most marriages were compassionate in practice with a less gendered power balance. See R.B. Shoemaker, G*ender in English Society*, pp. 101-113.
8 Alfred Jenkin letter books, in Schwartz, *Cornish in Latin America*, pp. 431-2. See also Deacon, Schwartz & Holman, *Cornish Family*, p. 152.
9 *Royal Cornwall Gazette*, 28 January 1853.
10 William Toll, Letter, 13 September 1849, in Payton, *Cornish Overseas*, pp. 116-117.
11 Richard Hore, Letter, 6 January 1874, Moira Tangye Collection.
12 Payton, *Making Moonta*, p. 132.
13 Van Vugt, *Britain to America*, p. 123; Richards, *Britannia's Children*, p. 164.
14 *Royal Cornwall Gazette*, 25 July 1867.
15 *Cornishman*, 11 October 1879; R.E. Lingenfelter, T*he Hardrock Miners - a history of the Mining Labour Movement in the American West 1863-1893* (University of California Press, 1974). pp. 9-10.
16 Matthew Hore, Letter, 26 November 1866, Moira Tangye Collection.
17 Francis E. Dunstan, pers. comm. (28 April 2012).
18 Biddick v. Biddick & Cawse, Divorce and Matrimonial Causes File, 1898. TNA, J 77/19391.
19 *West Briton*, 13 June 1912.
20 Schwartz, *Cornish in Latin America*, pp. 495-500.
21 *West Briton*, 14 March 1862.
22 Schwartz, *Cornish in Latin America*, p. 497.
23 Schwartz, *Cornish in Latin America*, pp.161, 318 & 499-505.
24 Alfred Jenkin, 13 Feb 1838. Alfred Jenkin letter Books, RIC, H/1/17-18.
25 Lingenfelter, *Hardrock Miners*, pp. 9-10. Harper notes that Scottish artisans left their families behind for the same reason. Harper, *Adventurers & Exiles*, p. 262.
26 D. Hoerder, 'Segmented Macrosystems and Networking Individuals: The balancing functions of migration processes' in J. Lucassen & L. Lucassen (eds.), *Migration, Migration History, History: Old Paradigms and New Perspectives*, 2nd revised edition (Peter Lang, Bern, 1999), p. 80; D. Hoerder, *Cultures in Contact: World Migrations in the Second Millennium* (Duke University Press, 2002), p. 343.
27 Hoerder describes this as a 'holistic-material-emotional approach' where the individual skills and resources of family members are allocated towards maximum mutual benefit. See Hoerder, *Cultures in Contact*, p. 20.
28 Census Returns of England and Wales, 1871, TNA, RG10/2261, folio 5.
29 *Cornishman*, 19 July 1894.
30 Elaine Hamby, pers. comm. (4 May 2012).
31 Elizabeth Cameron, pers. comm. (22 June 2012).
32 Erickson, *Leaving England*, p. 25.
33 *Cornishman*, 22 November 1883.
34 Schwartz & Parker, *Lanner*, p. 166.
35 Baines, *Emigration from Europe*, p. 9.
36 Erickson, *Leaving England*, p. 25.
37 Brettell, 'Migration', p. 245; Harzig & Hoerder, *What is Migration History?*, p. 75.
38 Hoerder, *Cultures in Contact*, p. 20.
39 See Brettell, *Men who Migrate*; D. Gabaccia, 'Women of the Mass Migrations: From minority to majority, 1820-1930' in D. Hoerder & L.P. Moch (eds.), *European Migrants: Global and Local Perspectives* (Northeastern University Press, Boston, 1996), 90-111; Reeder, *Widows in White*.
40 Ann Goldsworthy, Letter, 18 February 1861, private collection of descendant Amanda Drake.
41 Burton, *Richard Trevithick*, pp. 181-182; Hosken, *Oblivion of Richard Trevithick*, pp. 252-253.
42 Census Returns of England and Wales, 1871, TNA, RG10/2345, folio 6.
43 For emigrant family decisions on who should go and who should stay see Chapter 1 of Errington, *Emigrant Worlds*.
44 *Cornishman*, 12 September 1895.
45 For examples, see *West Briton*, 7 February 1871 in Barton, *Life in Cornwall*, p. 200; *Cornishman*, 28 January 1897.
46 *Cornishman*, 8 November 1894.
47 Schwartz, *Cornish in Latin America*, pp. 198 & 248.

48 William Paynter, Letter, 15 October 1859. Cornwall Record Office: FS.3/1033/108.
49 *Cornishman*, 22 August 1889.
50 *Cornishman*, 23 November 1899.
51 The *Index of Cornish People Overseas* held at the Courtney Library, Royal Institute of Cornwall includes the names of married men who enlisted in the Mine Guard of the Rand Rifles in 1901 extracted from The National Archives, WO126/112.
52 The term of the lease was dictated by the lifespan of the longest living of three named individuals. Schwartz & Parker, *Lanner*, p. 161.
53 *Royal Cornwall Gazette*, 1 February 1853.
54 *West Briton*, 22 January 1864, in Barton, *Life in Cornwall*, p. 117.
55 Deacon, Schwartz & Holman, *Cornish Family*, p. 188; Payton, *Cornish Overseas*, p. 350.
56 *Cornishman*, 3 December 1896.
57 *Cornishman*, 9 March 1899.
58 *Cornishman*, 7 December 1893. For more on planned desertions see Anderson, 'Emigration and Marriage Break-Up'.
59 *Cornishman*, 22 October 1896.
60 *Cornishman*, 27 November 1902.
61 *Royal Cornwall Gazette*, 18 March 1842; *West Briton*, 18 March 1842.
62 *Royal Cornwall Gazette*, 11 February 1858.
63 *Royal Cornwall Gazette*, 12 Apr 1861.
64 *Cornishman*, 7 February 1889.
65 *West Briton*, 19 December 1862.
66 Moonta *People's Weekly*, 24 May 1924 quoted in Payton, *Cornish Overseas*, p. 350.
67 Christian burial was widely denied in cases of suicide prior to the 1882 Interments (*Felo de Se*) Act, unless the individual was suffering from a mental illness.
68 *West Briton*, 21 March 1862.
69 *Royal Cornwall Gazette*, 29 July 1887.
70 St Lawrences Register of Admissions 'Pauper' Jan 1 1870 - Dec 31 1875, Cornwall Record Office, HC1/4/2/1.
71 Reeder, *Widows in White*, pp. 65-67.
72 Twomey, *Deserted and Destitute*.

13. The Worst Kind of Widowhood?

1 Brayshay, 'The Demography of Three West Cornwall Mining Communities'.
2 Mills & Annear, *Book of St Day*, pp. 155-156.
3 Reeder, *Widows in White*.
4 Duroux, 'The Temporary Migration of Males'.
5 Brettell, *Men who Migrate*.
6 Duroux, 'The Temporary Migration of Males', pp. 35-36 & 42-43.
7 Rose, 'Home Ownership, Subsistence and Historical Change'; see also Deacon, Schwartz & Holman, *Cornish Family*, pp. 38-40.
8 Abrams, *Myth and Materiality*.
9 Bryant, 'The Cornish Family', p. 186.
10 Schwartz & Parker, *Lanner*, p. 89. For a detailed description and discussion of women's work in Cornish mining see: Burke, 'Decline of the Independent Bal Maiden'; Schwartz, 'In Defence of Customary Rights'; Schwartz, 'No Place for a Woman'; Mayers, *Balmaidens*.
11 Schwartz, 'Cornish Migration to Latin America', p. 252.
12 Burke, 'The Cornish Miner', p. 444; Bryant, 'The Cornish Family', p. 186; Deacon, Schwartz & Holman, *Cornish Family*. pp. 46-53.
13 Burke, 'The Cornish Miner', p. 444. Schwartz, 'Cornish Migration Studies', p. 148.
14 *Cornishman*, 2 February 1893.
15 See J. Humphries, "Because they are too menny." Children, Mothers, and Fertility Decline: The evidence from working-class autobiographies of the eighteenth and nineteenth centuries', *Discussion Papers in Economic and Social History*, No. 64 (2006).
16 Brettell, *Men who migrate*. pp. 182-194.
17 Reeder, *Widows in White*, p. 106.
18 Engel, 'The Woman's Side', p. 264.
19 Deacon, Schwartz & Holman, *Cornish Family*, p. 53.
20 Schwartz, 'Cornish Migration to Latin America', p. 252.
21 Schwartz, 'Cornish Migration Studies', p. 149.
22 Deacon, Schwartz & Holman, *Cornish Family*, p. 148.
23 Duroux, 'The Temporary Migration of Males', p. 48.
24 Additional information courtesy of descendant Elizabeth Cameron, June 2012.
25 Van Vugt, *Britain to America*, p. 126.

Index

A

abandonment, families 248; wives 12, 14, 94, 110, 119, 152, 244 *see also* desertion

'able-bodied' 96, 103-104, 106

abortion 150-151, 154, 156, 163

Abrams, Lynn 7

accidents 104, 182, 187, 205, 228-229 *see also* injury

accommodation 74-91, 94, 107, 222

accountants 19

adoption 151-152

adultery 7, 123, 141-150, 154, 157, 159-161, 163-169, 172-175

advance of wages 50

affiliation orders 148-149, 151

Africa 46, 48, 63, 67, 79, 101-2, 120-124, 129, 131-134, 166, 178, 196, 214, 228-230 *see also* South Africa

agency 2, 221-222, 225-226, 242 *see also* independence

agents 45, 47, 50, 182-3, 190-191, 221, 223 (emigration) 118; (recruiting) 24, 45 *see also* mine agents

agriculture 3-4, 72, 95

agricultural work (female) 54, 65, 242; (male) 95, 239 *see also* farming

Alaska 174, 230

Allen family 152

America 1, 6, 12, 18, 29, 35-39, 43, 57, 60-63, 67-69, 73, 82-86, 88-91, 95-96, 100-101, 106, 108-110, 115-116, 121-122, 126-128, 130-134, 137, 144-147, 149, 152, 156, 159, 160, 164-165, 168-169, 174, 178-181, 183-186, 192-196, 199, 203-205, 214, 225, 227-229, 231, 233, 237, 239, 248; Central 1; Latin 15-16, 18, 24, 47-48, 163, 175, 180, 182, 187, 190, 194, 222, 229; North 1, 19, 30, 87, 98, 102, 178, 185, 197; South 1, 16, 19, 23, 47, 58-59, 60, 87, 99, 102, 134, 140, 164, 173, 178, 197, 218, 228 *see also* USA and individual countries, states and places

American Civil War 29, 185, 229

'American house' 186

Anderson, Olive 162, 175

Andrew family 67-68, 133

Andrewartha family 50

Angove family 55, 83-84, 118

Angwin family 41

Annear family 82

annuities 35-38

Appledore, Devon 87, 88

Arabic (ship) 204

Archambault, C. 11

Argentina 179; Rosario 134

Arizona 170

Australia 1, 12, 19, 29, 36, 40, 45, 49, 58, 60, 64, 67, 69, 82, 84, 89, 95, 98, 101, 120-121, 127, 130, 139, 156-158, 167, 174-175, 178, 182-183, 187, 193, 195-196, 198, 203, 207-208, 210-212, 214-215, 218, 221, 224, 227, 229, 231-233; Pentworth Gold Mine 67 *see also* individual states and places

Auvergne, France 65, 91, 238, 239, 246

Axford family 82

B

baby abandonment 150-152; farming 150

Bailey family 59

Bailey, Joanne 61

Baines, Dudley 225

bakers 59-60

Baldhu 90

bal maidens 5, 53, 240

Ball family 133, 150

Banfield family 225

banker's drafts 39-46, 70, 102, 116, 182, 237; forgery 44-45; fraud 43-45

Bank failures 45-46

banking 38-42, 44-46, 48, 50, 62, 63, 70, 102, 116, 237, 243-244

Bank notes 38-39, 45

The Married Widows of Cornwall

Bank of California 46
bankruptcy 59, 67
Baripper 126, 132
Barnett family 83
Barrow-in-Furness, Lancashire 27, 192
Barry family 44
Bartle family 37, 53
Barton, Rita 152
Bate family 36
Bawden family 48, 67-69, 190
Beacon 130, 132, 206
Beckerleg family 85
beer houses 61, 180, 216
behaviour 92-93, 110, 112, 116, 121, 140, 142, 145, 158-160, 162, 164-165, 168-169, 171-173, 210, 212-213, 245-246 see also scrutiny
Benbow family 208
Bennett(s) family 53, 68, 73, 204, 229
Benny family. 54
Berdiner family 173
Berryman family 37, 59, 96
'beyond the seas' 104-105
Biddick family 166-167, 220, 222
bigamy 7, 147, 164, 168, 170-171, 174-175
bills of exchange 43
Birmingham 119
birth rate 241-242
birth records 15
births 16, 81, 107-108, 145, 147-148, 151-156, 164, 173, 215, 233; concealing 139, 151-152, 153, 154, 156
Bishop family 93
Black Country 120
blacksmiths 3, 39, 82, 85, 194
Blackwater 89, 173, 205, 227
Blamey family 18, 36-37, 73
Blewett, Richard 46, 70, 143
Blight family 150
boarders 76, 79, 84, 143 see also lodgers
boarding houses 59, 197
boarding schools 166, 197

Bodinar family 83
Bodmin iv, 30, 119, 126, 156, 158, 233, 262; St Lawrence's Hospital 233
Boer War 185, 204
Bolitho family 82
Bolitho Consolidated Bank 63
Bolitho, William 122
Bolivia 68, 175, 181, 229-230; Tocopilla Mines 68
Bonwick, James 212
boot makers 19
boots (as poor law relief) 109, 111, 130, 213
Boswarthan 58
Boyns family 188
Brampton, Derbyshire 27, 192
Bray family 35-36, 146
Brayshay, Mark 4, 10, 11, 35, 74, 80, 236
Brazil 19, 24, 67, 102, 179, 182, 193-195, 223, 239; Morro Velho 223
Brea 130
Brea family 197
Breage 35, 53, 79, 81, 84-86, 90, 102, 149
Brettell, Caroline 12-13, 239, 241
British colonies 41, 120, 169, 199, 202 see also individual countries and places
British Empire 41, 139, 228
Brotton, Yorkshire 27, 192
Bryant, Lyn 5-6, 240
Buckingham family 101
building workers 179
Buller Downs 108, 129
Bullock family 57, 96
Bunt family 119
burials 104, 136, 178, 132; abroad 190, 205
Burke, Gill 4, 6, 13, 140, 220, 241
Burrows family 67
businesses (run by wives) 57-61, 86, 226, 243, 245
butchers 19, 69, 166
Butte City 170, 196

Index

C

cabinet makers 19

California 19, 29-30, 36, 46, 54, 81, 88-89, 98-99, 121, 131, 136, 144, 152, 181, 186, 190, 194-195, 197-198, 202, 212, 215, 221-222, 224, 229; Californian gold rush 88; Grass Valley 124, 195; San Francisco 197

Callington 100, 152

Calstock 153, 265

Camborne iv, 10, 17, 20-21, 23-28, 30, 39, 41, 44, 48, 53, 57, 60, 63, 67-68, 71, 74-78, 82-84, 96, 99-101, 107-108, 118, 121-123, 128, 130-132, 134, 141, 144-145, 152, 156, 159, 167, 173, 177-178, 189, 193, 203, 205, 214-215, 228-230

Camelford 30, 262

Canada 19, 41, 120, 159, 187, 193, 198-199, 203, 207; Lake Superior 102, 201 see individual provinces and places

Cardew family 35, 84

Cardiff 174

Carharrack 18, 35, 89, 133, 230

Carlyon family 73, 86, 136-137

Carmen family 197

Carn Brea 42, 133, 215

Carnbell 130, 134

Carnkie 133

Carnmenellis 173

Carnyorth 205

carpenters 3, 81, 84, 124

Carpenter family 215

carriers 19, 59

Carter family 43, 48

Carvolth family 55

cattle dealers 19

census enumerators 17-18, 36-37, 53, 65, 79, 173, 189, 227

Central Mining District 24-25, 33

Chacewater 30, 88, 99-100, 156, 175, 180, 232

Champion family 81, 198

Chapman family 150

Chappell family 55

charity 76, 81, 98, 112, 191, 260

charwomen 54-57, 77, 83-84, 95, 119

Chenhall family 88

Cheshire 27, 192

childbirth 84, 88, 147, 151-152, 154, 240, 242

child care 42, 56-58, 78, 80-84, 88, 171, 211, 236, 244, 246

children born abroad 59-60, 84, 87, 194-195, 204, 248

Chile 19, 67-68, 84-85, 87, 89, 124, 174, 203, 205, 225, 230, 232, 243; Checo Mines 68

Ching family 47

Chipman family 19

Chisholm, Caroline 40, 95

Christmas 187, 217

Chynoweth family 16, 47, 65

Clark family 55,

clay mining 25

Clemence family 79, 196

Clemmow family 85

Clift family 143, 158

Coad family 195

Coakes family 55

coal mining 19, 27, 59, 192

Cobbett, William 220

co-dependency 171-176, 245

cohabitation 143, 146, 160, 170-174

Collett family 91

Collins family 16, 59, 68, 197

Colliver family 213

Colonial Office 138

Colorado 41-42, 66, 68, 106, 134-136, 149, 204-205; Bald Mountain 68, 205; Bear Creek 134; Central City 41; Cripple Creek 135; Denver 205; Nevadaville 205

Columbia 19, 230

Combellack family 222

commercial travellers 19

Congdon family 54

contraception 150, 154, 163

contracts for work abroad 15, 47-49, 61, 67, 68, 69, 70, 117, 162, 171, 180-183, 188, 197, 221, 239, 241 cooks 56, 57, 163, 165

Copperhouse, Hayle 131, 134

copper mining 8, 19, 23-24, 48, 53, 83-84, 86, 96, 181

copper miners 81, 84, 86, 96, 181

copper ore dressers 53, 83

Cornish families 72; dispersed 5; transnational nuclear 5, 226, 239, 249

Cornish Mining World Heritage Site 5

correspondence 7-9, 38-39, 41, 44-46, 49-50, 62, 64, 80, 86, 91, 115-116, 121, 123, 126, 144, 149, 159, 166-168, 177, 180, 189, 201, 203, 207-214, 216-217, 219, 230, 246

count house women 57

court cases 39, 43, 44, 61, 66, 69, 73, 93, 128, 142, 144, 146, 148, 149, 153, 156, 158, 168-169, 174, 177, 238, 243

courting 154, 167

Cousin Jennies 6

Coutts and Co Bank 40

coverture 61, 66, 71, 103-104, 238-239, 267

credit 3, 46, 52, 66-67, 69-71, 94, 98-99, 112, 124, 167, 238 see also debts

crime 118, 144, 212, 229 see also theft, fraud, banker's draft forgery

Crimean War 41

Crowan 17, 30, 35-36, 55, 100

Cuba 16, 19, 24, 35, 45, 47, 50, 54, 67-68, 124, 146, 182-183, 185, 191, 215, 221, 223; Cobre Mines 67, 68, 182, 190, 221, 223; Cobre Mining Association / Company 45, 50, 185; Havana 146

culture of mobility 4, 187

Cumberland 27, 192

currency exchange 39, 40, 43, 45, 48

Curnow family 61

D

Daddow family 132-133

Dadds family 202

Daniel family 155

Darlington family 84

Datson family 44, 164-165

Davey family 54, 96, 133

Dawe family 42

Deacon, Bernard 1, 5, 10, 13, 51, 72, 192, 198, 219, 242

Dead Letter Office 45

Deadwood Dick 57, 96

deaths 21, 42, 72, 88, 177, 186, 188, 193, 205, 210, 215, 225, 243, 248; children 91, 145-146, 152-156, 183, 186, 215, 227, 233, 265; husbands 45, 85, 89, 101, 133, 169, 171, 173, 182, 187-191, 204-206, 218-219, 228-229; wives 152, 171, 178, 189, 205, 223; see also infanticide, suicide

debts 43, 59, 61, 66-71, 73, 136-137, 181, 238, 243; adverts denying liability for 67-70; see also bankrupcy, insolvency

demographic gender imbalance 7, 20-21, 101, 240

Derbyshire 15, 27

disappearances 21, 229, 230

desertion 1, 7, 11-12, 14, 21, 32, 37, 63, 74, 76, 81, 94-99, 101-114, 117-121, 125-140, 142, 155, 158, 160, 162, 164, 169-170, 172, 174, 177, 188, 198-200, 203, 212-214, 218-219, 227, 238, 244

desire for 'home' 186

destitution 11, 94-95, 97-98, 103, 112, 122, 147, 149, 181, 185, 218, 235-236 see Chapter 5

distress (economic) 8-9, 29-30, 32, 50, 55-56, 97-102, 109, 112, 130, 147, 200-203, 222, 236

distress committees and funds 97-100, 109, 200-202, 222

Devon 15, 24, 87, 192

Devoran 41, 68

diamond mining 19

Dingle family 54, 84

Divine, T.M. 7

divorce 133, 141-142, 164-174, 176, 186, 188, 238; self-divorce 170

Dobb family 35

'Doctor Dick' 150, 151

Doe, Helen 61

Doidge, John S. 31

278

Index

domestic labour 5, 52, 54-55, 65, 77, 81, 83-84, 91-93, 167, 171, 194, 196, 211-212, 222, 224, 245-246
domestic economy 70, 244
domestic service 56-57, 78, 165
domestic violence 172
Dower family 3, 49, 64-65, 82, 89, 91-92, 160, 207-209, 212-214, 216-218, 230, 246-247
drapers 59- 60, 181
dressmakers 54, 59, 83-84
Drew family 66
drunkenness 40, 61, 108, 123-125, 137, 139, 151, 216, 223, 230, 233
Duloe 233
Dunn family 83
Dunstan family 54, 87, 90, 137, 221, 224
Durham 27, 192
Duroux, R. 91, 238-239, 246
dyers 54

E

Eade family 38, 40, 42, 80-81, 88, 215
East Indies 19
economic cycles 184; depression 6, 29, 57, 66, 97-100, 112, 184-185, 192, 200, 202, 228, 235; abroad 98, 185, 192; volatily 23-24
economy of makeshifts 94
Ecuador 48
Eddy family 27, 59
Eden family 50
education 46, 54, 58, 69, 84, 97, 109, 143, 166, 204, 213-214, 225, 238, 243-244
Edwards family 54
Egloshayle 203
elderly relatives 224, 245
Elliot, B.S. 194
Ellis family 29, 68
employees 48, 76, 183
employers, husband's 47, 49, 50, 107, 126-128, 136, 140, 172, 183, 203, 217, 223, 244; wives as 60, 65
employment 5, 29, 30, 36, 48-49, 100-101, 120, 124, 182, 184-185, 199, 201, 221, 223-224,

243-244; wives 52-59, 64, 66, 72, 77, 96, 105, 150, 165, 168, 172, 236; advert 56,
engineers 17, 24, 31, 84, 180; fitters 32; mine 16, 69, 72, 85, 165, 182, 227; smiths 86, 167
Ennor family 45
Erickson, Charlotte 216, 225
Eustice family 145, 149
Eva family 36, 134
'explicitly' abroad 19-20, 24, 28, 31, 36, 78
extradition 120

F

factories 53
Falmouth iv, 25, 30, 46, 133, 146, 165, 262
Falmouth Chamber of Commerce 46
Family Colonisation Loan Society 40
family history 9, 16, 175, 178, 184, 187, 193
fancy goods sellers 59
farmers 3, 4, 19, 81, 85, 158, 181, 187; farmers and farm labourers (wives as) 65
Farndale, Yorkshire 27, 192
fathering 212; absence 248
Faul family 35, 59
Feock 55
fishing 3, 72
Fitzpatrick, David 8
Ford family 82
Foss family 214
Four Lanes 120, 173
Fox family 41, 89
France 12, 65, 91, 238; Paris 69, 156, 166
Francis family 48, 54-55, 57
fraud 43-45, 115-116
friendly societies & clubs 112
frivolity 8, 69-70, 159, 217
Frost, Ginger 170-172, 176
fundholders 59-60

G

Gabaccia, Donna 12-13
Gay family 132, 133

Gerber, David 8, 207

Germoe 73

Gerrans 90, 181

Gibson family 55

Gidley family 89

Gilbert, Davis 73

Gilbert family 135, 269

Gill family 59

Gillis, John 145, 161

Glamorgan, Wales 27, 192

Glasson family 81

Gleadle, Kathryn 63

gold mining 12, 19, 38-39, 42, 45, 58, 64, 67, 70, 85-86, 88-89, 95, 157-158, 181-182, 190, 195, 212, 229, 239

gold nuggets 39, 181

Goldsithney 196

Goldsworthy family 54, 91, 131, 134, 203, 215, 227

Gorran Haven 193

gossip 142, 159 *see also* rumour

Grampound Road 158

Granger, Thomas (judge) 69-71, 141-143, 159, 163, 169, 186

Gray family 60, 133, 155, 225

greengrocers 59

Grenfell family 57, 82, 133, 205

Gribble family 50, 54, 207

grocers 53, 59-60, 67, 86, 181

Gulval 65

Gundry family 39

Gwennap iv, 18, 20-21, 23-26, 28, 30, 36-37, 41, 49, 53-55, 59-60, 64, 67, 73, 76-78, 82-84, 87, 89, 96, 101-102, 112, 133, 147, 177-178, 180, 183-184, 189, 192, 194-195, 203, 208, 227, 241

Gwinear 35, 54, 131, 134, 231, 256

Gwithian 59, 100, 256

H

Hall family 82, 87

Ham family 40, 126

Hamley family 203

Hancock family 59, 159, 232

Hardy, John 183

Harper, Marjory 7, 181, 184

Harris family 54, 56, 68, 231

Harry family 53, 57, 90, 205

Harvey family 67, 73, 85, 222

Harzig, Christiane 1, 2, 9

Havis family 159

Hawke family 89

Hayle 24, 73, 133, 185

health 64, 151, 154, 155, 163, 164, 182, 183, 204, 214, 217, 222, 225, 233, 246, 248 *see also* illness

Helston 8, 25, 30-31, 44, 79, 98, 106, 110-111, 115, 118, 120, 135-138, 143, 168, 185, 230, 232, 241, 262, 269-270

Henwood family 43

Henwood, George 180

Hick(s) family 36, 48, 84, 95, 175, 231

Hill family 83

Hixes Mill 198

Hockin(g) family 55, 63, 82, 123, 159, 190

Hodge family 38, 60, 69, 165

Hoerder, Dirk 1, 2, 9, 226

Hollow family 90, 158

Holman Brothers 24

Holman, David 13

home-pay 3, 34, 47, 48, 50, 140, 182, 196, 217, 236-237, 239, 244

Honey family 73

Hooper family 59, 85

Hore family 212, 222

Hosea family 106

Hoskin(g) family 39, 196

household collapse / huddling 74, 77-78, 80-81, 87-88, 93, 236

household composition 74-88

household repairs 91-92, 167

Howlett, Neil 87

Hulf family 95

Husband family 48, 86

Index

I
Idaho 204
illegitimate children 105, 107, 121, 146-156, 158, 164-165, 167
Illinois, Chicago 169
illiteracy 38, 43-44, 209
illness 27, 42, 64, 96, 99, 104, 107, 118, 136, 155, 160, 182, 183, 203, 204, 214, 215, 218, 224, 225, 227, 232-233, 244, 248; mental 104, 135, 163, 226, 232-233 *see also* health
Illogan 17, 24, 47, 54-55, 59, 73, 82, 85, 101, 109, 111, 132-133, 145, 147, 202, 256
Inch family 175
independence 5, 35, 60-64, 72-73, 77, 80, 85, 88, 94, 104, 164, 181, 211, 234, 236, 239-240, 242, 244-248 *see also* agency
India 19, 214
infanticide 150-156
injury 58, 64 *see also* accidents, health
innkeepers 59, 63, 181
imprisonment 34, 119, 124, 146, 150
insolvency 61 *see also* bankrupcy, debt
internal migration 15, 27, 29-31, 192
International Exhibition (London 1862) 187
international labour market 179-180, 184
investments 36, 59-60, 66, 72
Ireland 7-8, 45, 184-185, 198
Irish Emigrant Society 40
iron mining 19, 27, 85, 134, 192
Italy 12, 13, 179, 238
Ivey family 156

J
Jackson family 55, 165, 168
Jacobstow 95
James family 50, 63, 65, 184
jealousy 219
Jeffery family 48
Jenkin(g)(s)/Jenkyn family 27, 37, 86, 169, 194
Jenkin, Alfred 45, 50, 124, 183, 185, 190, 221, 223
Jennings family 149, 158

Job family 36, 54
Johns family 50
Jones family 81, 133, 158
Jones, William 7

K
Kea 231, 261
Keast family 84
Keen family 144
Kemp family 86
Kent family 203, 230
Kenwyn 25, 54-55, 203, 261
Kernick family 54
Kilday, Anne-Marie 150-151, 154-156
King family 43
Kinsman family 36
Kneebone family 55
Knight, Pamela 151
Knuckey family 133

L
Lakeman family 55
Lancashire 27, 119, 162, 192
Lance family 36, 89
Lang family 36
Langdon family 84
Lanner 4, 20-21, 35, 39, 60, 108, 133, 141, 193, 225, 240, 242
Lark family 152
Launceston iv, 30, 262
laundresses 53, 55-56, 58, 77, 148, 224
Lavers family 158
Lawrence family 196
lead mining 19, 24, 168
Leah family 196
Lean family 60, 159, 225, 242
Leckie, William 50
Lelant 30, 67, 98, 185, 225
Lemon family 60
letters *see* correspondence
Levine-Clark, Marjorie 120

libel 128-129, 135
Lind, Jenny 187
Lingenfelter, Richard 223
Liscard, Cheshire 27, 192
Liskeard iv, 1, 14, 25, 30, 32, 41, 54-55, 59, 96, 110, 262, 270
Liverpool 143, 196, 209
loaves (as poor relief) 106, 109, 129-131, 133
lodgers 3, 23, 26-27, 59, 66, 69, 75-76, 79, 84, 91, 96, 107, 141-143, 145, 147, 149, 151, 153, 155, 157, 159-161, 175, 185
London 42, 44-45, 47, 50, 104, 118, 162, 164, 179, 187, 199-200
loneliness 81-82, 84, 163, 165, 167, 215-216, 220, 230, 247
Long family 36
Louisiana, New Orleans 194
Lucassen, J & L. 179
Ludgvan 29, 54-55, 59, 84

M

Mackinny family 191
Maddern family 58
Madron 55, 58, 63, 82, 122
Magee, Gary 5, 34, 219
Magor family 59, 67, 96, 97
maiden name (use of) 79-80, 173
Mallet family 232
Maltby, Josephine 62
Manchester and County Bank 48
mangle keeper 55
Marazion 30, 36, 48, 54-55, 59-60, 98
mariners 3, 17, 19, 25, 27, 87, 145, 243
Marks family 196
marriage breakdown 69, 123, 142, 162, 177 *see also* divorce
Married Women's Property Act 62-63
Martin family 37, 41, 59, 67, 163, 198
masons 85, 118, 179-180
match-sellers 214
matriarchy 90, 240-241
Mat(t)hews family 53-54, 84, 167

May family 54, 69, 73, 86, 221, 233
Mayers, Lynne 4, 6
Medlyn family 173
Victoria, Melbourne 44, 58, 197-198, 229; Melbourne Ladies Benevolent Society 58
memorials 190
Menetee, S.P. 171
Menheniot 27
Merritt family 84
Methodism 52, 70, 94, 124, 216
Mexico 19, 24, 47, 68, 102, 156, 167, 174-175, 193-196, 205, 223-224, 229-230; Pachuca 67, 68, 175; Real del Monte Mining Company 47; Santa Maria Mine 229
Michell family 36, 54, 89
Michigan 39, 45, 48, 80, 85-86, 109, 129, 134, 169; Central Mines 86; Houghton 39; Iron Mountain 134
Midling fanily 55
Miles family 35
military 19, 27, 96, 229
milliners 54
Millom, Cumberland 27, 192
Mills family 36, 53
mine agents 27, 31, 82, 127, 173, 175
mine captains 39, 85, 184
mine work (for wives) 53, 57, 83
Minnesota 130; Lake Superior 102, 201
miscarriage 150-151
missionary wives 7
Mitchell family 158, 193
money orders 41-43, 46, 102, 237
Montana 66, 130, 134, 189, 229, 269
Moore family 93
Morcom family 36, 44, 83, 229
Morvah 187
Mounts Bay 46
Mousehole 174
Mullion 37-38

N

name duplication 44

Index

naming and shaming 127, 129, 135
Nankivell family 195
necessaries 69
Nelson, Margaret K. 91-93
Nevada 134
Newfoundland 184
New Grenada, South America 59
New South Wales 134, 203; Newcastle 134; Sydney 40, 187
New York 40, 45, 179, 183, 205, 225
New Zealand 19, 47, 59, 84, 175, 183, 193, 218
Newlyn 30, 63, 99, 233
Newquay 116
Nicholls family 37, 47, 59, 65, 68
Ninnis family 36
Noakes family 167
Noall family 59
non-access (paternity) 148-149
non-consummation of marriage 160
Norman family 134
North Carolina 168
Northey family 96
Northill 181
Northumberland 192
Norway 60, 184
Nova Scotia 28, 182-183
nurses 54

O
Oat(e)s family 53, 197
Odgers family 134, 195
Offences Against the Person Act (1861) 151
Ontario 41; Bruce Mines 41; Coburg 203
Orchard family 60
Oruba (ship) 196
Osborne family 149
ostrich farming 19
outdoor relief 97, 98, 101, 103-112, 114-117, 120, 122, 125, 150, 155, 237, 238; crusade against 105, 110, 238; Outdoor Relief Prohibitory Order 104 *see also* Poor Law

Oxland, Rev Harry 73

P
Panama 197
paper money 42
parenting 212-214
Parker, R. 4, 240
Parkyn family 55
Parliament 104, 118, 164
Pascoe family 87, 96
Pascoe, Richard 150-151
Paul 193
paupers 37, 94-96, 98, 101, 106, 108-109, 111, 116, 118, 233
Payne family 54
Paynter family 3, 49, 196-198, 207-209, 211-217, 229, 246-247
Payton, Philip 4-6, 179, 201
Pearce family 35, 50, 59
Peavy, Linda 12
Pedraza, Silvia 3
Penaluna family 57, 83, 89, 173
Pendeen 46
Pengelly family 59
paternalism 140, 183, 244
patriarchal control 63, 158
Penglaze family 55
Penkridge, Staffordshire 27, 192
Pennington, Cumbria 192
Penponds 131, 133
Penrose family 54, 82
Penryn 37
pensioners 19
Penzance iv, 8, 25, 29, 31, 37, 46, 57, 59, 96-98, 101, 105-106, 109-111, 114, 116-119, 122-123, 126, 129, 143, 146, 148, 150, 155-156, 160, 174, 183, 190, 196, 205, 214, 221, 262
Perranarworthal 24, 232
Perranuthnoe 17, 175, 265
Perranzabuloe 150, 186, 215, 261
Perry family 44
Peru 16, 19, 35, 73, 230; Cerro de Pasco 16

Peters family 54, 191
Phillack 59, 100, 132-134, 256
Phillips family 73, 86, 173
Phillips, Nicola 61
Phillips, Roderick 188-189
Phillipson family 19
phthisis 183
piecework 57
Piper (emigration agent) 118
plasterers 19
Plymouth 46, 86, 126, 143
Polgear family 131
police 30-31, 99
Polkinghorne family 54, 83
Pollard family 54, 82, 85
Pomery family 193
Pool 42, 48, 135
Pooley, C. 53
poor law 3, 8, 29, 32, 66, 71, 94-95, 98, 102-104, 106-107, 109-115, 120, 127, 138-139, 142, 148-150, 155, 170-172, 177, 198-200, 202-203, 207, 220, 224, 229, 235-238, 244, 246; guardians 8, 30, 46, 57, 66, 73, 94, 97-98, 101-103, 105-112, 114-139, 143, 145-146, 148, 150, 155, 160, 170, 174, 189, 198, 199-200, 202, 213, 224, 229, 230, 237; loans 34, 40, 50, 66, 106-107, 129, 237-238; local bye-laws 104-105, 107, 109, 111, 113; Local Government Board (LGB) 105, 108, 111, 118, 135, 138, 261; Poor Law Amendment Act (1844) 104; Poor Law Board 105, 203, 261; Poor Law Commission 104, 113, 199, 261; poor relief 5, 94-95, 102, 111-112, 139, 147, 218, 237-238; relief repayment 106 *see also* outdoor relief
Pope family 79
Popham family 132, 134
Portreath 183, 215
Portugal 9, 12-13, 65, 239-240, 242
postal services 39, 41, 46, 49, 105, 125, 189, 237, 231, 244 *see also* Dead Letter Office
Post Office 41, 42, 44, 46, 49, 71, 115-116
Powell family 54, 84

power of attorney 63
Praed family 35, 48
Praze 119
preachers 19
pregnancy 21, 82, 84, 88, 90, 109, 145, 150-154, 156, 160, 164-165, 167, 176, 215, 220, 232, 241-242, 247
press agencies 40
Price, L.L. 102
Probus 199
property 60-63, 172, 191, 196, 225, 229, 242, 245, 247
prostitution 5, 66, 148, 157, 158, 172
Prowse family 106
publicans 19

Q

quarrymen 19, 179
Quebec 199
Queen Victoria 202
Quick family 167
Quiller family 55

R

Rab(e)y family 54, 182, 194
Randall family 199
rape 166
Rapson family 35, 81
receiving community 10, 15
recruitment 15, 18, 23-24, 47-48, 99, 124, 182 221, 223
Redford family 63
Redruth iv, 10, 16-17, 21, 24-25, 30-36, 39, 43-44, 46, 53-56, 59-60, 63, 66-67, 73-75, 82-84, 89, 97-98, 101-102, 108-111, 115, 117-123, 125-135, 138, 140, 145, 154-155, 165, 170, 173-175, 183, 185, 189-190, 198, 200-201, 204, 215, 230-231, 256, 258, 262
Reed family 37, 73, 81, 96
Reeder, Linda 10, 12, 157, 233, 238-239, 242, 246
refusal to allow husband's emigration 221; to emigrate 162, 175, 220-222, 244, 270; to

Index

stay behind 220-222
Register of British International Money Orders 41
religious faith 216 *see also* Methodism
remarriage 45, 79, 81, 84, 157-158, 167, 170-172, 174, 178, 189, 205, 247
remittances 3, 5, 8, 10, 13, 34, 37-51, 57, 66-67, 69, 72, 80, 83, 94, 98, 100-106, 112, 115, 122-123, 139, 146-147, 154, 159, 173, 183, 219, 226, 231, 236-237, 244; cash 38; concealing 115-116, 128, 139; costs of 39-40; delays. 44, 95; 'envelope' 38; irregular 8, 49-52, 57, 98, 103, 112, 123, 217, 238; lost 44-45; networks 39; 'pocket' 38, 74; 'second' orders 45, 49 *see also* banker's drafts, money orders
repatriation 183
repeat migration 180
reputation 107, 142, 144-145, 147 160, 245
respectability 44, 55-56, 94, 103, 107-108, 129, 156-160, 217, 223
retail business 57, 59
retirement 19, 64, 175
return migration 4, 7, 29, 60, 62-63, 67, 69-70, 79, 86-87, 89, 102, 117, 120, 129, 138, 146, 153, 160, 164-165, 167, 169, 173, 175, 178-188, 191, 194, 197, 202-205, 218-219, 221, 224, 227, 233, 241-242, 244, 247-249
Reynolds family 54, 221
Richards family 39, 45, 55, 57, 67, 73, 85, 132, 134, 149, 152, 156, 189
Richards, Eric 7, 186-187, 198
Rickard family 59
Ripper family 36
Robarts family 54
Roberts family 50, 82, 153, 187, 193, 265
Rodda family 59, 159
Rogers family 54, 66, 84, 107, 130, 223
Rose, Damaris 64
Rouse family 194, 196
Rowe family 37, 168, 215, 231
Rowe, John 6, 8, 100
Rowse family 36, 194
Rowse, A.L. 6, 163

Royal Commission on Divorce and Matrimonial Causes 141, 186
Royal Commission on the Poor Law 138
Royal Institute of Cornwall 48
Rule family 67, 68, 83, 107, 119, 134
rumour 107, 115, 155, 159, 160, 175, 232 *see also* gossip
Rundle family 39
Russia 12, 19, 242
Rutter family 84

S

safety fuse workers 53
sailors 3, 17, 19, 25, 27, 87, 145, 243
Salter family 159
Sa(u)nders family 193, 206
savings 46, 62-63, 72, 80, 84, 107, 186, 230
school *see* education
schoolteachers 45, 54, 96, 97
Schwartz, Sharron 4, 6, 9-11, 13, 24, 35, 47, 90, 124, 141, 163, 193-194, 219, 221, 229, 240-241, 245
Scotland 7-8, 28-29, 185 *see also* Shetland
Scown family 132, 134
scrutiny 156-158, 160, 245-246
Seaham, Co. Durham 192
seamstresses 54, 165
second families 175, 213
seduction 142, 157-158, 168
self-improvement 52, 216
Semmens family 55
sending community 2, 8, 10-12, 34, 38, 225-226, 233, 240, 243, 248-250
separate spheres 52, 245
Serpell family 144
servants 56, 60, 75-76, 147, 165, 173, 194
sewing 57, 59, 196
sextons 152-153
sex 93, 142-143, 157, 161, 163-164, 167, 171, 216-217, 233; pre-marital 154
Shears / Sheers family 39, 45, 82
shepherds / stockmen 40

Shetland 7, 20, 240, 243; Lerwick 20
Shincliffe, Co. Durham 192
shipping firms 40
shipwreck 39, 197
Short family 48, 86, 204
Sicily 9-10, 12, 65, 157, 233, 238-239, 242
silver mining 19, 136, 168, 181
Silver City, USA 136
silversmiths 39
Simon familys 36
Sims family 68
Sincock family 48, 132, 134
Sithney 149, 184
Skewes family 175
Skinner family 36
Skinners Bottom 215
Sluggett family 95
smallholdings 3, 13, 64-65, 72, 107, 236, 240
Smith family 53, 89
Smith, Ursula 12
Smitheram family 198
Snow family 175
social problems 14, 109, 248
social status 52, 65, 70, 94
soldiers 19, 27, 96, 229
South Africa 1, 19, 39, 46, 48, 62-63, 70, 101-102, 107-108, 117, 125, 129, 137-145, 160, 165-166, 175, 179, 183, 185, 187, 190-191, 196, 204, 219-220, 222, 229, 243; Algoa Bay 196; Cape 37, 46, 68, 96, 102, 118; Cape Colony 87; Cape Copper Company 48; Cape Town 165, 229; Fordsburg 134; Free State 120; Johannesburg 126-128, 134, 138, 190, 222; Kimberley 129, 229; Port Nolloth 68; Simmer and Jack Mine 123, 126-127; South African Cornish Association 229; Transvaal 122, 131, 134-135, 138-139, 185; Transvaal Cornish Association 138
Southampton 46
South Australia, Moonta 229; Port Adelaide 198; Wallaroo Mines 221; Yorke Peninsula 221
Sowden family 128, 134

Spain 12, 19, 179; Rio Tinto 118
Spargo family 195
Sparnon family 27
spendaholics 70
spinsters 21-22
St Agnes iv, 16, 20, 23, 25-26, 28, 30, 47, 53, 65, 76- 78, 89-99, 102, 152, 173, 177-178, 189, 193, 195, 215, 227, 258, 261, 268-269
St Allen 54
St Austell iv, 8, 17, 25, 30-31, 36, 45, 59, 98, 106, 110, 115, 166, 200, 262
St Blazey 17, 30, 37, 39, 45, 79, 86, 196
St Buryan 55, 106
St Cleer iv, 23, 48, 83-84, 86, 177, 189, 192-193, 267
St Clement 36, 60, 96
St Columb 30, 98
St Columb Major 57, 262
St Columb Minor 55
St Day 4, 16, 20, 41, 46, 68, 70, 106, 126, 133, 135, 143, 183
St Dennis 59
St Erth 30, 37, 59, 166
St Eval 182
St Ewe 69
St Germans 30, 262
St Gluvias 37
St Hilary 17, 190, 204
St Ives 25, 30, 59, 63, 98, 115, 119
St Just in Penwith iv, 10, 16, 20-21, 23-26, 28-29, 37, 41, 46, 53, 57, 59, 65-66, 74-78, 82, 98-99, 102, 106, 122, 147, 149-150, 177-178, 180, 184, 188-189, 192-193, 196, 201, 205-206, 221, 227, 229, 268
St Keverne 106
St Lawrence's Hospital, Bodmin 233
St Neot 41
St Tudy 159
Staffordshire 27
Stapleton family 81
steamships 179
Stephens family 54-55, 60, 126, 223
Stevens family 54, 59

Index

stillbirths 152-153, 155-156
Stithians 129, 132-133, 155, 256
Stratton 30, 95, 262
straw bonnet makers 54
strikes 101
suicide 231-233
Sullivan family 144
suspicion 62, 70, 116, 123, 142, 152, 153, 155, 157, 160. see also rumour, gossip
Swansea, Wales 124, 183
Sweet family 82

T
Tabb family 60
taileresses 54
Taylor family 68
Temby family 54
temperance 124, 139, 216-217
temporary migration 2, 3, 7, 13, 18, 65, 87, 90, 162, 179-188, 191-200, 220, 224, 239, 241-243
Tennessee 184
Terrill family 54, 133, 135
The Cornish Bank 102
theft 38, 43-45, 137, 158, 197
Thomas family 50, 55, 130, 149, 170, 181, 198, 218
Thomas, H. Preston 135, 138
Thomas, W. Herbert 124-125, 132, 174, 230, 231, 237
Thompson, Andrew 5, 34, 219
Tiddy family 65, 126
tin mining 17, 19, 24, 31, 53, 82, 85, 147, 181, 198
tin dressers 17, 31
Tinney family 55
Tippett family 55
Tipton, Staffordshire 192
Titanic (ship) 196
Todd, A.C. 1, 6, 205
Toll family 221
Tonkin(g) family 55, 73, 133, 167, 227, 231

Tosh, John 162, 216
Towednack 59, 149
Toy family 82
Trebilcock family 18, 36, 232
Tregajorran 133
Tregellas family 60
Tregembo family 85
Tregeseal 106
Treglown family 59, 71
Tregon(n)ing family 36, 43, 59, 63, 160, 206
Treloar family 41, 82
Tremewan, Peter 140
Tremewen family 202
Trenbath family 54
Trenberth family 82
Trengove family 36
Tresawna family 131
Trescowthick family 42
Trestrail family 54, 84
Trethew(e)y family 59, 67, 133
Trevarton family 84
Trevithick, Jane and Richard 16, 72-73, 227
Treweek family 87
Trewen family 79
Trewin family 39, 82, 225, 248, 272
Trewithian Downs 134
Trezona family 133, 134
Truran family 89
Truro iv, 30-31, 36, 49, 98-99, 101, 110, 129, 135, 139, 143, 150, 170, 174, 197, 199, 205, 227, 262
trust deed 16
Tucker family 62-63, 108, 129, 243
Tuckingmill 67
Turkey 19, 233
Turner family 67
Twomey, Christina 12, 139, 157
Tyack(e) family 36, 79, 175, 265
Tywardreath 17, 30, 39, 74

U

uncertainty 14, 189, 228-229, 231, 247
unemployment 100-101, 244
United States 7, 19, 41, 112, 120-121, 130, 134, 136, 169, 179, 187, 193-194, 199, 201, 205, 230; US Federal census 168, 178, 195 *see also* America
Uren family 82, 133
Uruguay 197
Utah 136; Salt Lake City 134

V

Vanguard (ship) 197
Varker family 204
Veal family 59, 82, 205
venereal diseases 164
Ventonleague 130, 134
Victoria 89-90, 208, 210; Bendigo 193, 195
Vincent family 60
visitors 5, 17, 73, 79, 87, 96, 173, 187, 196
visits home 187, 204, 212, 236
Vivian family 60, 67
Vogue 133
Vught, W.E. Van 194
vulnerability 44, 92-93, 137, 157, 159, 166-167, 248

W

Wakefield expedition 47
Wales 7-8, 15-16, 27, 29, 119, 124, 134, 148, 167, 192, 195, 202-203, 209
Wall family 149
Wallis family 86
Walters family 182
wars 29, 41, 101-102, 179, 185, 204, 220, 229
Warren family 37
washerwomen 55, 95 *see also* laundresses
Waters family 83, 147
Watling family 133
Wearne family 167
Webb family 233
Webb, Beatrice and Sidney 103-105, 107-108
Webber family 55, 134

Week St Mary 95
Wellington family 53
Wendron 25, 67-68, 131, 153, 203
Werry family 86
Wesleyan relief fund 100, 202
West Cornwall Bank 44, 62
West Cornwall Convalescent Hospital 27
West Indies 18
Western Australia 196, 270; Coolgardie 128; Guliowa Mine 196; Kalgoorie 195; Murchison 196; Yalgoo 196
wet-nursing 150
Whachum 152-153
Wheal Ellen Mining Company 49, 208
Wheal Harriet 129
Wheal Owles 122
Whitburn family 182, 183, 215
White family 46, 82
Whitford family 134
widows in white 9-10, 12, 65, 233, 238
widows of the living 9, 12, 65
wife sales 171
Williams family 24, 36-37, 47, 54-55, 82, 84, 134, 143, 158, 175, 181, 186, 196-198, 205, 215, 224
Wills family 37, 62
Wilton, Morrish 203
wire workers 53
Wisconsin 194-195; Mineral Point 194-195, 204
wisdom (accumulated knowledge) 90, 93, 228, 239, 244
Witt, Dr George 187
Woods, Robert 184
Woolcock family 90, 181
workhouse 63, 96-97, 103-108, 110, 112, 116, 119-122, 125, 143, 147-148, 150, 165; workhouse test 110, 121

Y

Yorkshire 27, 192
Youren family 36, 59

Printed in Great Britain
by Amazon